AA

Book of Britain's
WALKS

Produced by AA Publishing
© AA Media Limited 2010

First published 1999
Reprinted 2000, 2001 and 2003
New edition with new walks 2010
Reprinted May 2011

Published by AA Publishing (a trading name of AA Media Limited, whose registered office is Fanum House, Basing View, Basingstoke, Hampshire RG21 4EA; registered number 06112600).

 This product includes mapping data licensed from the Ordnance Survey® with the permission of the Controller of Her Majesty's Stationery Office. © Crown Copyright 2011. All rights reserved. Licence number 100021153.

ISBNs: 978-0-7495-6609-8
and 978-0-7495-6610-4 (SS)

A CIP catalogue record for this book is available from the British Library.

The contents of this book are believed correct at the time of printing. Nevertheless, the publishers cannot be held responsible for any errors or omissions or for changes in the details given in this book or for the consequences of any reliance on the information it provides. This does not affect your statutory rights. We have tried to ensure accuracy in this book, but things do change and we would be grateful if readers would advise us of any inaccuracies they may encounter.

We have taken all reasonable steps to ensure that these walks are safe and achievable by walkers with a realistic level of fitness. However, all outdoor activities involve a degree of risk and the publishers accept no responsibility for any injuries caused to readers whilst following these walks. For more advice on using this book and walking safely see page 8.

Some of these routes may appear in other AA walks books.

Visit AA Publishing at theAA.com/shop

Walks written and compiled by:

Chris Bagshaw, Kate Barrett, Bill Birkett, Sheila Bowker, Nick Channer, Paddy Dillon, Rebecca Ford, David Foster, John Gillham, David Hancock, Des Hannigan, Tom Hutton, Tom Kelly, Dennis Kelsall, Deborah King, Andrew McCloy, Moira McCrossan, Terry Marsh, John Morrison, Andrew Noyce, Nick Reynolds, Beau Riffenburgh and Liz Cruwys, Julie Royle, Jon Sparks, Ann F Stonehouse, Hugh Taylor, Ronald Turnbull, Sue Viccars, David Winpenny.

Introduction by Roly Smith
Section introductions by Charles Phillips

Editor: David Popey
Project Editor: Charles Phillips
Design: Keith Miller
Picture Research: Vivien Little
Proofreader: Pam Stagg
Production: Stephanie Allen

Cartography provided by the Mapping Services Department of AA Publishing

Repro and colour separation by Keenes Repro

Printed and bound by Leo Paper Products, China

A04743

AA

Book of Britain's
WALKS

More than 100 walks exploring the best of Britain

Contents

Introduction

There can be no doubt that Britain is a nation of walkers. It is now the most popular outdoor leisure activity by a long way, with more than three quarters of the adult population (77 per cent, or about 38 million people) walking for pleasure at least once a month. That's many more than go angling, play golf or watch football, activities which were traditionally the most popular of outdoor pursuits.

To be more accurate, we are a nation of ramblers, and the use of that gentler, very British term is significant. In America, walkers are known as hikers or backpackers, and in continental Europe they are excursionists, all signifying a much more serious enterprise. Rambling, on the other hand, means to wander where you fancy or to generally rove about. This book is aimed at those ramblers who want to find out more, to seek out the relatively undiscovered corners, and delve behind the usual tourist board clichés.

By far the best way to see and really experience the fascinating landscapes which make up the British Isles is on foot. Car or coach-bound tourists can only expect to receive a packaged and sanitised view of Britain as seen through a window. It is only the walker who is really able explore the warp and weft of the land, to seek out its real character, and to experience the indefinable sense of history which lies deeply ingrained in every field, hedge, hill and dale.

Why Walk?

Apart from the physical pleasure of 'getting away from it all', there are many other reasons why walking is best. In these increasingly health-conscious days, walking is now recognised as the nearest thing you can get to perfect exercise. You can go as fast or as slow as you like, you are exercising just about every muscle, and you are getting plenty of fresh air. And perhaps most importantly, it is free. There's no need to go to the gym if there's a footpath outside your door.

The government's Chief Medical Officer, recently recommended that adults should take at least 30 minutes of moderate physical exercise, such as walking, five days a week. It is recognised that regular, brisk walking will improve the performance of your heart, lungs and circulation, lower your blood pressure and reduce the risk of heart disease and strokes.

It can also help manage your weight, reduce the risk of diabetes and colon, breast and lung cancer, and improve flexibility and strength in joints, muscles and bones, thus reducing the risk

by Roly Smith, President of the Outdoor Writers' and Photographers' Guild

of osteoporosis. There are mental benefits too, as it has been shown that walking can also improve your mood and reduce the harmful effects of that insidious modern killer – stress.

Where to Walk

Apart from its health-giving qualities, another important factor in walking in Britain is the wonderfully varied and outstandingly beautiful scenery with which our islands are blessed. There are few other countries in the world where, during the course of a day's walk, you can pass from airy coastal cliffs or sandy beaches, through lovely riverside meadows and woods to crag-bound lakes and towering mountains.

Humans have shaped the British landscape over 10,000 years of history, and it has accurately been described as a palimpsest – a living manuscript that has been written on over and over again. With a little help, such as that given by the expert authors within this volume, it can also be read like a book.

There are many walks to spectacular natural landscapes, from the views of the wild Torridon Hills from Loch Kernsary near Poolewe in the Scottish Highlands to the heathery staircase of the Roman Steps from Cwm Bychan in the rugged Rhiniog Mountains of Snowdonia. In between are the peaty wildernesses of Kinder Scout in the Dark Peak and the isolated moorland summit of High Willhays, the highest point of Dartmoor.

Britain is a land rich in history and folklore. You can re-trace the steps of the legendary outlaw Robin Hood through the ancient woodlands of Sherwood Forest, or see where the Devil himself was reputed to have dug his eponymous Dyke on the rolling South Downs to let in the sea and flood local churches.

Old Nick is also said to be responsible for the deep depression known as The Devil's Beef Tub, near Moffat in the Southern Uplands of Scotland, a place where the reiving clans hid their rustled cattle. The Merry Maidens stone circle on the Penwith peninsula in Cornwall is claimed to be a group of young girls caught dancing on the Sabbath and turned them to stone – a common fate commemorated in many of our prehistoric stone circles.

Other walks dip into the rich treasury of British history, such as the impressive ruins of Middleham Castle in Yorkshire, the favoured home of the future Richard III; the mountain-rimmed scene of the infamous Glencoe Massacre in Scotland, and the elegant cathedral spire and close at Salisbury in Wiltshire.

Many of the areas visited are renowned for their wildlife, such as the butterfly-haunted reed beds of Wicken Fen in Norfolk, and the wildfowl haven of the Martin Mere Wetland Centre in Lancashire. Other paths follow in the footsteps of the great writers, painters or poets who have been inspired by the ever-changing scenery and timeless sense of history.

Walkers' Rights

There are 140,000 miles (225,000km) of public rights of way in England and Wales, and following the passing of the Countryside and Rights of Way (CROW) Act in 2000, there is also now the right of free access to 6,250 square miles (16,200sq km) of open country, mainly mountains and moorlands. In Scotland, there is a de facto right of access above the enclosed foothills. The government has recently announced that it intends to introduce the same 'right to roam' along the 2,733 miles (4,400km) of the English and Welsh coastline, under the Coastal Access and Marine Act which received royal assent in November 2009.

Elsewhere, you should keep to those rights of way which have the same status in law as a highway like the M1 motorway. Therefore, if you find one that is blocked, you have the right to clear it to allow your free passage. However, we do not recommend you argue or try to force a way; it is better to report the blockage to the relevant local authority footpath officer. If you stray from a right of way, unless you are on access land, technically you will be trespassing, but unless you do damage you cannot be prosecuted, despite what some signs still say. All the routes in this book have been rigorously checked and are either on rights of way or on well-established, legal paths.

When out in the country, you should always respect the life of the people who live and work there, especially the farmers, who have to such a large extent created the landscapes we know and love today. The Countryside Code is a common sense set of principles which is probably best encapsulated by the maxim: 'Take only photographs, leave only footprints'.

Happy walking!

Using this Book

The *Book of Britain's Walks* divides the country into six regional sections with up to 18 walks per section. The route of each walk is shown on a map, and clear directions help you follow the walk. Each route is accompanied by background information about the walk and the area.

Route Information

A panel with each walk details the total distance, terrain, conditions underfoot, parking, public toilets and any special conditions that apply, such as restricted access or level of dog friendliness. The minimum time suggested for the walk is for reasonably fit walkers and doesn't allow for stops. An indication of the gradients you will encounter is shown by the rating ▲▲▲ (no steep slopes) to ▲▲▲ (several very steep slopes). Walks are also rated for their difficulty – those rated ●●● are usually shorter and easier with little total ascent. The hardest walks are marked ●●●.

Parking and Getting Started

Many of the car parks suggested are public, but occasionally you may find you have to park on the roadside or in a lay-by. Please be considerate when you leave your car, ensuring that access roads or gates are not blocked and that other vehicles can pass safely. The start of each walk is given as a six-figure grid reference prefixed by two letters indicating the 100-km square of the National Grid to which it refers. Each walk has a suggested Ordnance Survey Explorer map where you'll find more information on using grid references.

Dog Friendliness

Keep your dog under control at all times, especially around livestock, and obey local byelaws and other dog control notices. Remember, it is against the law to let your dog foul in many public areas, especially in villages and towns.

The route information often contains specific advice regarding the dog friendliness of the walk. Not all routes are appropriate for dog walkers so read the advice provided before setting out.

Walking in Safety

All these walks are suitable for any reasonably fit person, but less experienced walkers should try the easier walks first. Although each walk here has been researched with a view to minimising the risks to the walkers who follow its route, no walk in the countryside can be considered to be completely free from risk. Walking will always require a degree of common sense and judgement to ensure that it is as safe as possible.

❑ Be particularly careful on cliff paths and in upland terrain, where the consequences of a slip can be very serious.

❑ Remember always to check tidal conditions before walking along the seashore.

❑ Some sections of route are by, or cross, busy roads. Take care and remember traffic is a danger even on minor country lanes.

❑ Be careful around farmyard machinery and livestock, especially if you have children with you.

❑ Be aware of the consequences of changes in the weather and check the forecast before you set out. Carry spare clothing and a torch if you are walking in the winter months. Remember that the weather can change very quickly at any time of the year, and in moorland and heathland areas, mist and fog can make route finding much harder. Don't set out in these conditions unless you are confident of your navigation skills in poor visibility. In summer, remember to take account of the heat and sun; wear a hat and sunscreen, and carry spare water.

❑ On walks away from centres of population, you should carry a whistle and survival bag. If you do have an accident requiring the emergency services, make a note of your position as accurately as possible and dial 999.

Right: Winter beauty at lake Buttermere
Page 6: Cook Monument, North York Moors National Park

Southwest England

Southwest England

The Southwest of England tapers into a long and varied peninsula, stretching from the rural heart of England to the cliffs and coves of the Lizard and Land's End. Tiny fishing villages and smugglers' haunts contrast with bustling seaside resorts such as Newquay and Penzance, and the rolling farmland of central Devon.

Despite the extensive granite uplands rising inland, you're never far from the sea, with Atlantic breakers crashing against the north coast and the gentler waters of the English Channel washing the south coast. One effect of the ocean's proximity is that this corner of England gets its fair share of mist and rain – Dartmoor, in particular, has a reputation for being foggy – but the warming effects of the Gulf Stream make themselves felt, and the region has more hours of sunshine each year than almost anywhere else in England.

The Southwest boasts two national parks: the wild and extensive upland bogs of Dartmoor – with the giant granite blocks or tors such as High Willhays (see Walk 7) – and the cliffs and rolling heaths of Exmoor. Areas of Outstanding Natural Beauty encompass large stretches of the Cornish coast, Bodmin Moor and parts of Devon and Dorset, as well as the Quantock Hills and North Wessex Downs. There are lengths of designated Heritage Coast, with dramatic landscape and rich history, Sites of Special Scientific Interest such as the Teign Valley woodlands in Devon (see Walk 4) and a wealth of natural history to explore in the uncultivated land of the Cotswold escarpment, or the rugged, recessed gorges of the Mendips. It's worth seeking out these fine landscapes, although in some cases, where the need to protect is greatest, access may be limited. As the land diminishes westwards, vowels in local speech

become longer and the structure of the local dialect hints that this was once a place apart, with a rich tradition all its own. In the rolling downs of Devon and Dorset there are echoes of Alfred's Kingdom of Wessex in the late 9th century, although the latter is now a name more commonly associated with the poet and novelist Thomas Hardy. The literary tradition is strong in the Southwest, and Hardy's novels contain some of the best descriptions ever of the English countryside. Walk 1 offers the chance to visit Hardy's birthplace, a cottage built originally by his grandfather in the Dorset village of Higher Bockhampton, and the churchyard in nearby Stinsford where the author's heart is interred. (Stinsford is the village Hardy called 'Mellstock' in novels such as *Under the Greenwood Tree*.)

The Southwest is an area rich in legend and ancient history. The hills of the Dorset and the Wessex Downs are scored by ancient earthworks and decorated with chalk figures, including the celebrated and enigmatic Cerne Abbas Giant (see Walk 3). Untouched by the Romans, Cornwall was a last bastion of Celtic culture in England, when the rest of the country had become Anglo-Saxon. This is also the legendary homeland of King Arthur.

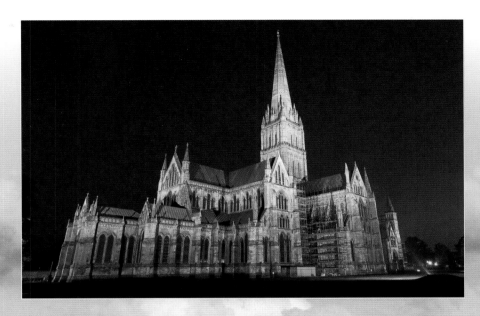

Above: Salisbury Cathedral's 404ft (123m) spire is the tallest in England

Main picture: Rocky Devon coastline, including Foreland Point

Far left above: The Westbury White Horse in Wiltshire

Far left below: Beautiful upland views in Southwest England

Previous pages: Sunrise from Crocken Tor on Dartmoor

Old Markets and Historic Churches

Our ancient forebears trod along the crest of the downs when Britain was a wild and wooded place, and so there is no shortage of footpaths and trackways to explore. Inland walks visit now quiet places that once had wider fame – such as the ancient Devon town of Bampton (see Walk 6), once known far and wide as a setting for wool and cattle markets, and home to the Bampton Notts breed of sheep, celebrated as the finest in Devon. Such settlements often contain beautiful historic churches. In Bampton, parts of the fine St George's Church, with its remarkable saddleback roof, date back as far as the 11th century. In Bridford, on the edge of Dartmoor (see Walk 4), the 15th-century church stands on the site of a 12th-century chapel, and contains a magnificent carved rood screen of 1508 that is worth travelling many miles to see.

For those whom only the most spectacular walks can satisfy, the Southwest is blessed with a continuous coastal path from Minehead in Somerset to Poole Harbour in Dorset. The South-West Coast Path is no mere seaside stroll but one of the most varied and interesting walks in Britain. Trodden by excisemen and smugglers over the centuries, this path takes in a succession of rugged cliffs and coves. On Cornwall's Atlantic coast these include the beautiful clifftop grasslands at Bude (see Walk 10) and tumbling sea cliffs at Portreath (see Walk 11), where the collapsed sea cave of Ralph's Cupboard was, according to some sources, named after a legendary giant, Wrath (or Ralph), said to lie in wait there and attack passing shipping by hurling boulders into the Atlantic waves.

At the opposite end of the scale, attractive historic towns offer the walker a rich urban landscape to discover. In Salisbury, for example (see Walk 15), attractions include the 13th-century Bishop's Palace and a series of elegant period buildings in Cathedral Close, as well as the cathedral itself with its breathtaking spire, at 404ft (123m), the tallest in England. The Cathedral is perhaps the country's finest example of the Early English Gothic architectural style.

Country Houses and Estates

The area is rich in historic country houses set in beautiful estates. These include the exquisite Elizabethan mansion of Longleat, the first English house in the Italianate (or Renaissance) style, visited by Queen Elizabeth I in 1575, and many years later the first stately home in Britain to open to members of the public (see Walk 16). In Cornwall the 16th-century Mount Edgcumbe House stands at the heart of a beautiful 865-acre (350ha) landscaped park (Walk 9), and in Wiltshire the Palladian mansion of Lydiard House (see Walk 17) is likewise situated in beautiful parkland that also includes an 18th-century walled garden.

Best of the Rest

Swanage

Locals George Burt and John Mowlem imported fine stonework, statues and arches to this Dorset town from London in the late 19th century, at a time when they were shipping local Purbeck marble to the capital. Don't miss the Town Hall's Portland stone façade (see Walk 2), designed by none other than Sir Christopher Wren, and originally the front of Mercers' Hall in Cheapside, London.

Coleton Fishacre

The country house of Coleton Fishacre in Kingswear, South Devon, was built in 1925–26 in the Arts and Crafts style by architect Oswald Milne for Rupert and Lady Dorothy D'Oyly Carte, proprietor of the Savoy Hotel and the D'Oyly Carte Opera Company. It stands in a beautiful 24-acre (9.7ha) garden renowned for its exotic plants (see Walk 5). House and garden were acquired by the National Trust in 1982 and the house has been open to members of the public since 1999.

Merry Maidens

This late neolithic/Bronze Age stone circle in a field beside the B3315 road (see Walk 8) contains 19 granite standing stones arranged in a perfect circle. The name derives from a later legend of 19 girls turned to stone for dancing on a Sunday. The circle is also known as 'Dawn's men', a corruption of Dans Maen (Cornish for the Dancing Stones), another reference to the same story. Two other standing stones, in a field on the other side of the B3315, are called 'the Pipers' and said to be the musicians who tempted the girls to dance. The stones were originally part of a ceremonial landscape and remains of neolithic and Bronze Age burials have been found near by.

Kingsand and Cawsand

These twin villages on the Rame Peninsula, Cornwall, beside Plymouth Sound were the haunts of smugglers in the 18th century. Until 1844 Kingsand was in Devon and the border with Cornwall ran in between the two villages – look out for a house named Devon Corn, with the old boundary marker outside it (see Walk 9).

Burrow Mump and the Somerset Levels

At one time the conical hill of Glastonbury Tor in Somerset was an island, for the surrounding flatlands were underwater, and the Tor is associated with the Isle of Avalon of Arthurian legend, where the king was taken after the final Battle of Camlann. Monks from Glastonbury Abbey drained the flats beneath the ancient earthwork of Burrow Mump (see Walk 13) to create highly fertile water meadows that may have given Somerset its name through the words 'Sumor Saete' ('Land of Summer'). Burrow Mump was a Celtic stronghold and then a fortified outpost of King Alfred's royal island at Athelney. Monks from Athelney Abbey built the now tumbledown church atop the Mump, dedicated to St Michael.

Lydiard House

The Palladian mansion of Lydiard House stands beside the beautiful St Mary's Church in 260 acres (105ha) of parkland on the edge of Swindon in Wiltshire (see Walk 17). The site was the home of the Viscounts Bolingbroke from the Elizabethan period onwards, but the present house was built in 1743. A £5 million programme of restoration began in 2005. The grounds contain a beautifully maintained 18th-century walled garden and the house has many original furnishings.

Above: Bard of Wessex – a 1931 statue of poet and novelist Thomas Hardy stands in Dorchester, Dorset

Left: The ruins of Botallack Tin Mine cling to a cliff above pounding waves near St Just, Cornwall

Far left: In the heart of the Cotswolds – a field of rape seed and a single tree near WInchcombe, Gloucestershire

1 By Hardy's Cottage and 'Egdon Heath'

From Thomas Hardy's birthplace, a walk across wooded heath and farmland leads to the place where the novelist, quite literally, left his heart

Below: Hardy memorial in Higher Bockhampton

Bottom: The cottage in which Hardy was born, in Higher Bockhampton

Bottom right: Kingston Maurward House, Stinsford

You can't go far in Dorset without coming across references to novelist and poet Thomas Hardy (1840–1928). Writing about a rural scene that was already vanishing at the end of the 19th century, he did more than anybody to establish an identity for the county, which he thinly disguised as a fictional Wessex. His complicated tales of thwarted desire and human failing, littered with memorable, realistic characters and evocative descriptions of recognisable places, have become literary classics.

Hardy was born at Higher Bockhampton in the cottage built by his great grandfather, set in a lovely garden. The cottage is now owned by the National Trust. However a much better collection of Hardy relics is held in Dorchester's museum, which includes a re-creation of his study. Hardy went to school locally and later in Dorchester. He joined his father playing fiddle in the lively Stinsford church band. Apprenticed as an architect, he befriended the dialect poet William Barnes.

Retreat to Dorset

Hardy moved to London, where he worked as draftsman in an architect's office, but in 1867 retired to Dorset for health reasons and began writing seriously. His first published novel was *Desperate Remedies* (1871), swiftly followed by *Under the Greenwood Tree* (1872), *A Pair of Blue Eyes* (1873) and *Far From the Madding Crowd* (1874). After the success of this book he married Emma Gifford; they lived for a time at Sturminster Newton. Success continued, and the highlights include *The Return of the Native* (1878), *The Mayor of Casterbridge* (1886), *The Woodlanders* (1887, Hardy's own declared favourite), *Tess of the D'Urbervilles* (1891) and *Jude the Obscure* (1895).

National Treasure

In 1885 Hardy and his wife moved to the home he had designed at Max Gate, on the outskirts of Dorchester (his Casterbridge), and he remained there for the rest of his life. Emma died, estranged and childless, in 1912, and two years later Thomas married Florence Dugdale. In 1928, when he died, Hardy was a celebrated grand old man of letters, in fact, a national treasure. He was buried in Westminster Abbey. He had requested that his heart, however, be buried in Stinsford (his Mellstock) churchyard, and so, he has two graves, the latter lying between the tombs of his two wives.

The Hardy influence is still strong in Dorset. Fact and fiction become blurred in 'Tess's Cottage', and many pubs proudly identify themselves as their fictional counterpart. A long distance footpath, the Hardy Way, links many of his favourite sites.

1 By Hardy's Cottage and 'Egdon Heath'

Explore the countryside that Thomas Hardy loved – and immortalised in his celebrated novels

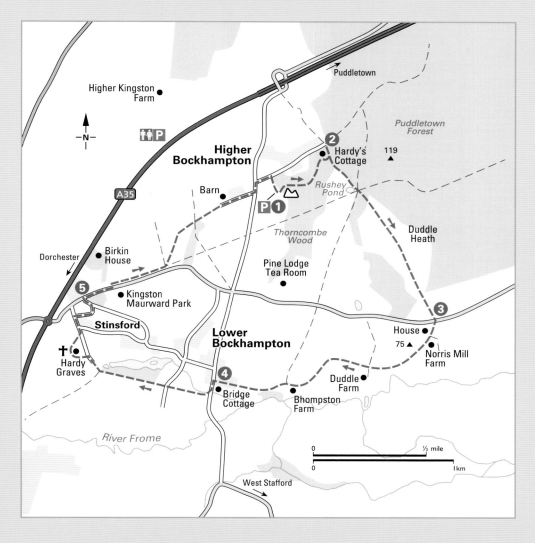

Distance 5 miles (8km)

Minimum Time 2hrs

Ascent/Gradient 328ft (100m) ▲▲▲

Level of Difficulty ●●●

Paths Woodland and heathland tracks, muddy field paths and bridleways, firm paths, road, 13 stiles

Landscape Woodland, tree-clad heath, open meadows, waterway, rolling farmland

Suggested Map OS Explorer 117 Cerne Abbas & Bere Regis or OL15 Purbeck & South Dorset

Start/Finish Grid reference: SY 725921

Dog Friendliness Not allowed in Hardy's garden or cottage; deer shooting year-round in woods – keep dogs close

Parking Thorncombe Wood (donations) below Hardy's Cottage

Public Toilets None en route; nearest north-west on A35

1 Take the steep woodland path to the right of the display boards, signposted 'Hardy's Cottage'. Turn left at the fingerpost and follow the winding route down to a crossroads of tracks, marked by a monument. Turn left for Hardy's Cottage.

2 Retrace your route up behind the cottage and bear left, signed 'Rushy Pond' on a path that bears right. At a crossroads by the pond take the path ahead signed 'Norris Mill'. Immediately fork right; the path heads down between fences, soon passing through heathland then between rhododendrons. Cross a stile and bear right. Enter a field by a stile and turn left up the field, towards a house.

3 Cross the road on to a farm track which keeps to the right of some barns. Where the track ends, bear right over a field. Cross

a pair of stiles in the hedge, then go straight ahead across the fields and a drive, passing Duddle Farm (left). Cross a bridge and stile down into a field. Go straight on and bear left, following the track round the hill. Cross a stile by a converted barn and walk up the drive. At the fingerpost keep straight on through a gate. Bear left to a stile and walk along the field-edge to a gate, then walk down the field to a gate at the far corner. Go through and straight on, with the river away to your left. Go through the farmyard and along a road.

4 Turn left by Bridge Cottage. Cross the river and immediately turn right, on to a causeway. After 0.5 mile (800m) turn right, signed 'Stinsford'. Walk up and turn left into the churchyard, just below the church. Pass the church to your left, and the Hardy graves to your right. Leave by the top gate and walk up

the road. Pass Casterbridge training centre and turn right along the road. Take the next turn left to the main road by a lodge.

5 Turn right, up the road. After the entrance to Birkin House, bear left through a gate and immediately turn right on to a path through woodland, parallel with the road. Descend, cross a stile and bear left, signposted 'Higher Bockhampton', and inside the field bear diagonally right uphill. At the top corner keep straight on through a gate and follow the fence up towards a barn. Pass this and take a gate on the left and bear right on a track to the road. Turn left, then right by the postbox, and right again to return to the car park.

2 The Swanage Eccentric

A walk through Swanage and out to Durlston Head reveals the legacy of an unusual local contractor who not only exported stone but imported it, too

Above: Signpost to the stone globe Burt set up on Durlston Head

Below: Punch and Judy shows are performed on Swanage beach

Bottom: A jetty in Swanage

In the early 19th century Swanage was a small, bustling industrial port that shipped stone from the 60 or so quarries in the area. A growing fashion for seabathing would, in time, change the focus of the town for ever. The real changes to the face of Swanage came, however, with the extraordinary collecting habit of one George Burt, a contractor with an eye for fancy architecture.

Instant Architecture

With his uncle, John Mowlem, a local stonemason and philanthropist, Burt shipped marble from the quarries of Purbeck to London, where old buildings were being knocked down to make way for a wave of new construction. Reluctant to see such splendid stonework discarded, Burt salvaged whole pieces, transported them back in the company ships, and re-erected them in Swanage, giving it an instant architectural heritage.

The first influence you see of this man is as you walk past the Town Hall. Burt had donated a reasonably plain and simple building to the town in 1872, but in 1883 he added a façade by Sir Christopher Wren, appropriately in Portland stone, which he had rescued from the front of the Mercers' Hall in London's Cheapside. Architectural commentator Sir Nikolaus Pevsner described its florid carvings of stone fruit and wreaths as 'overwhelmingly undisciplined'. Next, in the park near the pier, are a grand archway removed from

Hyde Park Corner, three statues and some columns rescued from Billingsgate Market. There's also an absurd but rather elegant clock tower, designed by Arthur Ashpital; this was removed from the south end of London Bridge in 1867, where it had been set as a memorial to the Duke of Wellington.

Burt's Folly

Durlston Castle is an original folly by Burt dating from 1887, designed from the start as a clifftop restaurant on Durlston Head. It has an unexpected educational element, as useful facts and figures from around the world are carved into great stone slabs set into the walls below – for example, in terms of sunshine, the 'longest day' in London is 16.5 hours, while in Spitzbergen it is three and a half months. Burt added a large stone globe of the world set among stones bearing biblical and Shakespearean quotations.

Railway Revival

George Burt was also influential in bringing the railway to Swanage in 1885 – this gave major impetus to the development of the town as a seaside resort. The railway closed in the early 1960s, but was revived by enthusiasts who, early in 2002, achieved their ambition of linking back up to the main line station at Wareham. Today it transports visitors on a nostalgic trip between Swanage and Corfe Castle.

2 The Swanage Eccentric

See London architecture in a rural setting – and admire George Burt's clifftop 'folly'

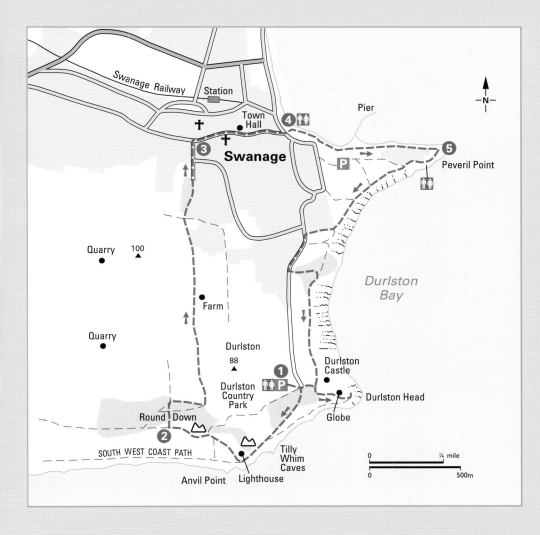

Distance 4.25 miles (6.8km)

Minimum Time 2hrs 30min

Ascent/Gradient 509ft (155m) ▲▲▲

Level of Difficulty ●●●

Paths Grassy paths, rocky tracks, pavements, 4 stiles

Landscape Spectacular cliff scenery, undulating hills, Swanage town

Suggested Map OS Explorer OL15 Purbeck & South Dorset

Start/Finish Grid reference: SZ 031773

Dog Friendliness Some town walking

Parking Durlston Country Park (fee)

Public Toilets Durlston Country Park; behind Heritage Centre on harbour (small charge); Peveril Point

1 Take the footpath directly below the visitor centre car park, signed to Tilly Whim and coast path. Steps lead down through some trees. With the sea ahead, follow the path round to the right, joining the coastal path. Keep right, towards the lighthouse, down the steep path. As you climb up the other side, look back and down to see the spectacular Tilly Whim Caves cut into the ledges of the cliff. Pass the lighthouse and turn right, then go through a kissing gate to follow the path with butterfly markers up the steep side of Round Down, with views to St Adhelm's Head.

2 At the top bear right, heading inland and parallel with a wall. Go down a slope, through a gate and across a footbridge, then turn up to the right. At a wooden gate turn left over a stone stile, following the butterfly marker. After another stile you can see the roll of the Purbeck Hills ahead and the roofs of

Swanage to the right. Cross a stile and go down a broad, grassy track. Beyond a stile by a farm this track narrows and begins to climb steeply. Continue straight ahead on to the road and follow this into the town, with the prominent church in front of you.

3 Turn right on to the main road. It's worth pausing to admire the little square with its butter cross and old stone houses tumbling down to the church. Continue along the street, but look out for: the modest metal plaque above the front door of No 82A, home of Taffy Evans; the elaborate Wesley memorial; and the extraordinary Town Hall with its Wren frontage.

4 At the square bear left beside the Heritage Centre, towards the harbour. Turn right and pass the entrance to the pier. Follow the fingerpost to the coastal path, then bear right, up the hill, past a modern apartment block and

a bizarre stone tower, to reach the tip of Peveril Point, with its coastguard station.

5 Turn right and walk up the grassy slope along the top of the cliffs. Take the path in the top corner and follow the Victoria's head markers to a road. Turn left through an area of pleasant Victorian villas. Erosion of the coastal path means a well-signed detour here, along the street, down to the left and left through a gate into woodland, signposted to the visitor centre and lighthouse. Follow the path for about 0.5 mile (800m) along the cliff top to Durlston Head. Pass Durlston Castle on your left and turn down to examine Burt's great stone globe. Stagger back up the steep hill to return to the car park.

3 Giant Steps to Cerne Abbas

A valley walk from Minterne Magna leads to views of a familiar but mysterious hill-cut giant, a fertility symbol who may represent a Roman or Celtic god

Top: Ivy shrouds the Royal Oak pub, Cerne Abbas

Above: The giant on the hill

Right: Landscape near Minterne Magna

The chalk outline of the Cerne Abbas Giant is so familiar that the reality, seen from the hillside opposite rather than above from the air, is a surprise. His proportions change at this shallower angle, and this of course is how he was designed to be seen – all 180ft (55m) of him. Quite when he was made, and by whom, is part of his mystery.

Was he drawn by the Romans, a portrait of the demi-god Hercules? Could he be a post-medieval caricature of Oliver Cromwell? On the other hand he might be of Celtic origin, for the giant has been linked to a pan handle discovered 12 miles (19km) away on Hod Hill. Made of bronze, it depicts a naked man clutching a club in one hand and a limp hare in the other. The man has wings and is surrounded by other symbols that identify him as Nodens, a Celtic god of healing and fertility. His features and the angle of his legs suggest close resemblance to the Giant, and place him in the 1st century AD. Whatever the truth of it, the Giant has been seen as a symbol of fertility for centuries. The fencing now around the Giant is to prevent him from being eroded.

A Holy Visitor

St Augustine visited Cerne and preached to the locals on the spot now marked by St Augustine's Well. A verse on the wall there records how he offered two shepherds the choice of beer or water to drink. When they primly asked for water, the saint rewarded them with a brewery.

An abbey was founded here in AD 987. Its most famous inhabitant, Aelfric, produced a number of schoolbooks in Anglo-Saxon. A Latin primer, in which pupils adopt the characters of working people, is a fascinating record of daily life. The abbey was dissolved in 1539, along with Dorset's other monastic houses, but an imposing gatehouse remains, along with other buildings, including an ancient hospital, set around a flowered courtyard.

The village of Cerne Abbas is a lovely mixture of old houses, some half-timbered, some stone, with flint, thatch and brick in evidence. The Red Lion Hotel claims to be one of 13 original public houses and if that seems excessive in a place this size, it should be explained that Cerne was once a major staging post on the coaching routes.

3 Giant Steps to Cerne Abbas

Take a look at the remains of an ancient abbey before climbing to admire the famous chalk hill carving

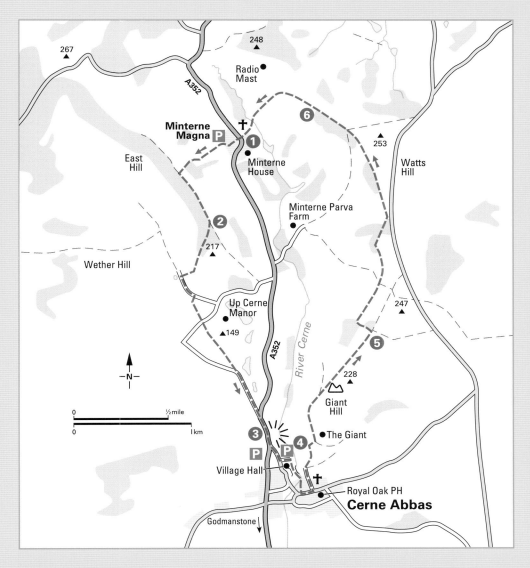

Distance 5.5 miles (8.8km)

Minimum Time 2hrs 30min

Ascent/Gradient 591ft (180m) ▲▲▲

Level of Difficulty ●●●

Paths Country paths and tracks, minor road, main road, 5 stiles

Landscape Head of Cerne Valley, scattered with old settlements

Suggested Map OS Explorer 117 Cerne Abbas & Bere Regis

Start/Finish Grid reference: ST 659043

Dog Friendliness Lead essential on road stretches

Parking Car park (free) opposite church in Minterne Magna

Public Toilets Cerne Abbas

1 With the road behind you, take the bridleway on the left side of the car park, which soon bends right and then left round some trees, and left again on the other side. Follow the track, keeping right at a fork, uphill, and where the hedge begins pass round to the right side of it. At the top, turn left on a track inside the woods.

2 Fork right down through the woods. At the bottom turn left along the road. After a bend take the footpath right, across the field. After a line of trees veer diagonally left, towards the right-hand of two white gates. Cross a road, pass to the right of this gate, and go straight on down the field, with Up Cerne Manor in view to the left. Pass another white gate to the right of a pond then turn left on the road. At the end bear right on to the A352.

3 Soon cross to the car park for the best view of the Giant. Fork left on the road down to the village and turn left, signposted 'Village Hall'. Turn right by the stream, signposted 'Village Centre'. Continue to the high street. Turn left, and left again in front of the New Inn, and left by the Royal Oak, to the church. Walk past the Old Pitchmarket to the Abbey. Turn right into the churchyard and bear left. Go through a gate and head left.

4 Cross a stile, then turn right up some steps. Now follow the path to the left, round the contour of the hill and past a National Trust sign for the Cerne Giant, below a fence. After 0.25 mile (400m), as the path divides, keep right, up the hill, to the top. Bear left along the ridge, cross a stile by a fingerpost and head diagonally right, to another fingerpost.

5 At the fingerpost turn left, signed 'Wessex Ridgeway', and go down through a gate. Soon turn right and follow the bridleway along the hillside. Keep straight ahead at a junction of tracks (signed 'Barne's Lane'), then dip down through a gateway and go straight on inside the top edge of some woods. Keep straight on to go through a gate near the road. Turn left away from the road (signed 'Minterne Magna') along the left edge of the large field. At a gateway turn left on to a gravel lane.

6 Directly above Minterne House, turn left through a small gate and signed 'Minterne Magna', towards the mast and follow fingerposts to the village, down through several gates and then along a broad track past the church to return to the car park.

4 A Dartmoor Outlier Above the Teign Valley

This exploration of the ancient woodlands of the Teign Valley includes a climb to an outlying Dartmoor tor and a visit to a fine 15th-century church in Bridford

In early springtime many people travel out to Steps Bridge (built in 1816) to stroll along the River Teign, enjoying the sight of thousands of tiny wild daffodils crowding the river banks. But there's a better way to explore this valley, which includes a close look at an example of that most characteristic Dartmoor feature, a tor, and a pint at a Teign Valley pub as an added bonus!

Left: River Teign in Bridford Wood

Below: The granite mass of Blackingstone Rock – steps (upper right) lead to the top

The Teign Valley Woodlands

Much of the ancient semi-natural woodland and valley meadows around Steps Bridge is a Site of Special Scientific Interest (SSSI), and many acres are owned by the National Trust. Dunsford Wood (on the opposite bank of the Teign from the car park) is a Devon Wildlife Trust nature reserve.

These woodlands are glorious all year round: there are snowdrops in February, daffodils in early spring, wood anemones and ramsoms; then foxgloves, woodrush and cow-wheat in summer. Look out for the nest of the wood ant by the side of the path, which can be as much as a metre high. If you place your cheek or hand near to a nest you'll get a shock – the ants squirt formic acid from their abdomens in a defensive move, and it stings!

On the Edge of Dartmoor

Blackingstone Rock is another outlying tor, 1 mile (1.6km) south-west of Heltor Rock. Turn right rather than left at Point 4 and you will soon be aware of its huge, granite mass rising above the lane on the left. You can get to the top by climbing up an almost vertical flight of steps which were added in the 19th century for that purpose. The views of the surrounding countryside are worth the effort.

While you're in Bridford, part way round the walk, it's worth going inside the church. The original chapel on this site was dedicated by Bishop Bronescombe in 1259, to the murdered Archbishop Thomas à Becket, who had died at Canterbury Cathedral in 1170. The present building dates from the 15th century, and its most famous feature is the eight-bay rood screen, thought to date from 1508. The faces of the carved and coloured figures were mutilated by Puritan soldiers during the Civil War. The doors are also unusual in that they are made in one piece rather than being divided in the middle.

4 A Dartmoor Outlier Above the Teign Valley

Enjoy wild daffodils at Steps Bridge, a magnificent view from Heltor Rock and the rood screen in Bridford church

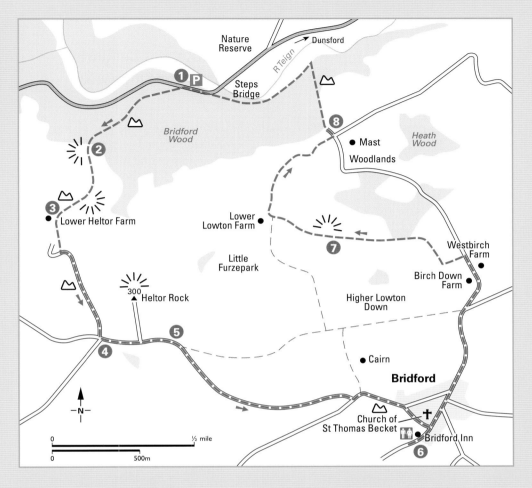

Distance 5 miles (8km)

Minimum Time 2hrs 45min

Ascent/Gradient 393ft (120m) ▲▲▲

Level of Difficulty ●●○

Paths Woodland paths, open fields and country lanes, 3 stiles

Landscape Steeply wooded valleys and undulating farmland

Suggested Map OS Explorer 110 Torquay & Dawlish

Start/Finish Grid reference: SX 803884

Dog Friendliness Keep under control at all times

Parking Free car park (and tourist information board) at Steps Bridge

Public Toilets None en route

1 From the car park cross the road, following the signs to the former youth hostel. Turn right up the concrete track, then left as signed towards the building; the path bears right, and is signed for Heltor Farm. The path leads uphill through oak then beech woodland. At the top of the wood cross a ladder stile as signed.

2 Follow wooden footpath posts straight up the field and through a small gate. Keep up the left edge of the next field; pass through a gateway and look left to see Heltor Rock.

3 At the end of the field turn left as signed through a wooden gate into a plantation; follow the path to meet a gate on to a lane. Turn left and walk uphill to meet a tarmac lane.

4 Turn left (signs for Bridford). After 200yds (183m) turn left over a stile up the narrow fenced permissive path to Heltor, from where you can enjoy an amazing panorama. Retrace your steps to the road and turn left.

5 After about 1 mile (1.6km) the lane bears left, then right, to reach the edge of Bridford. Turn right down a small steep lane signed 'Parish Hall & Church'. Follow the church wall path, down steps and right to find the Bridford Inn.

6 Turn left from the pub and follow the lane through the centre of the village. Take the fourth turning (Neadon Lane) on the right, by a telephone box. Just past where a bridleway joins (from the left) the lane dips to the right, downhill; take the left fork and carry on straight ahead to pass Birch Down Farm on the right. Keep straight on again at Westbirch Farm; turn left as signed to Lowton Farm on a fenced path, which bears right to a kissing gate; pass through the gate and continue up the right edge of the next field to a stile in the top corner. Then cross over a tumbledown granite wall and carry straight on through an area of gorse bushes. Cross a stile by some beech trees.

7 Follow the fenced path along the top of two fields, and down a green lane to reach Lower Lowton Farm. Turn right as signed before the farm on a permissive bridlepath, which descends (with a stream, right) then rises to the next signpost; turn right for Steps Bridge down the narrow green lane, passing through a small gate. Continue down the deeply banked green lane until you reach a surfaced lane though a gate.

8 Turn left through the middle gate, signed 'Byway to Steps Bridge'. At the edge of Bridford Wood (by the National Trust sign) turn right following the footpath signposts. The path is fairly narrow and quite steep. Go left, then right, to cross a track, keeping downhill. The path drops down steps then runs to the left, now high above the river to Steps Bridge where it meets the road opposite the former café. Turn left here to return to your car.

5 Wartime Secrets at Inner Froward Point

After skirting the gardens at Coleton Fishacre country house, this delightful coastal ramble leads to an intriguing surprise on the cliffs near Kingswear

Below: Pudcombe Cove, from the coast path

Below right: Garden at Coleton Fishacre

Bottom: Kingswear Castle

This is a walk that's full of surprises. Starting near the lovely National Trust house and gardens at Coleton Fishacre, it runs along a particularly beautiful piece of the South West Coast Path (much of which was purchased by the National Trust in 1982), dropping down into Pudcombe Cove, and along the lower edge of the Coleton Fishacre gardens, before climbing steeply up the other side of the valley and back on to the open cliff. Shetland ponies have been allowed to graze freely here in the past to encourage regeneration of the indigenous vegetation. Further on along the path you will find all sorts of strange concrete structures scattered about the cliffs, causing you to wonder what on earth it is you've stumbled across.

The scenery changes again as the walk takes you inland along the eastern side of the Dart estuary, with fine views of the 15th-century Dartmouth and Kingswear castles. For sheer variety and constantly changing themes, this walk is very hard to beat!

An Arts and Crafts House

Given to the National Trust in 1982 by Roland Smith, Coleton Fishacre enjoys a spectacular setting in this very quiet corner of South Devon – it's very much off the beaten track. The house, reflecting the Arts and Crafts tradition, was designed and built in 1925–26 for Rupert and Lady Dorothy D'Oyly Carte, of Gilbert and Sullivan fame. It is sited at the head of a deep, sheltered combe, providing the perfect environment for its 15-acre (6ha) sub-tropical garden, based around a succession of streams and water features that fall gently down the narrow combe towards the sea at Pudcombe Cove.

Coastal Defences

The remains of Kingswear Castle (1491–1502) are passed after Point 6. Similar in shape to the square tower at Dartmouth Castle on the opposite shore, it was abandoned soon after 1643, outclassed by the range of guns available at its counterpart, and today belongs to the Landmark Trust and is available as holiday accommodation.

The official title of the group of buildings on the coast path south of Kingswear is the Inner Froward Point Coast Defence Battery, dating from the Second World War and almost complete, apart from the guns. There are the remains of all kinds of wartime constructions here, apart from the lookout just above the sea. The site includes the foundations of several Nissen huts, two shell magazines, two gun positions and a shell incline, and two searchlight emplacements near sea level. It's all a trifle unexpected after the peaceful approach along the coast path but reflects the importance of the river mouth to successive military generations.

5 Wartime Secrets at Inner Froward Point

Take in superb views of the sea and the offshore Mew Stone and discover the remains of military defences

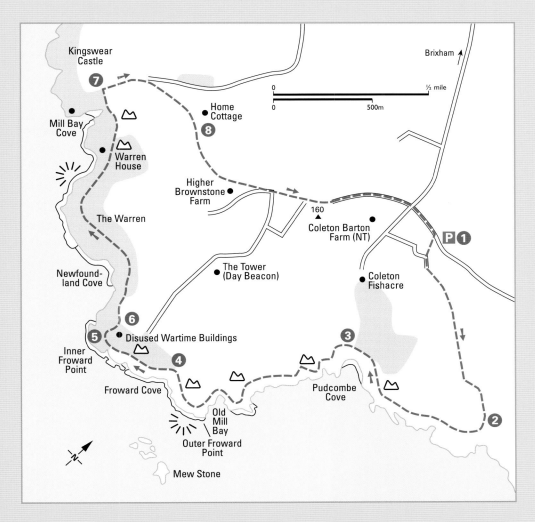

Distance 4.75 miles (7.7km)

Minimum Time 3hrs

Ascent/Gradient 525ft (160m) ▲▲▲

Level of Difficulty ●●●

Paths Varying coast path, tracks and lanes, steep steps, 7 stiles

Landscape Coastal cliff top and deep combes

Suggested Map OS Explorer OL20 South Devon

Start/Finish Grid reference: SX 910512

Dog Friendliness Dogs should be kept under control at all times

Parking National Trust car park at Coleton Camp

Public Toilets None en route

1 Walk through the kissing gate in the top right corner of the car park to take the National Trust's permissive path towards a metal gate and stile ('link path to Ivy Cove'). Keeping the hedge right, walk downhill to cross another stile, then another, and then another at the bottom of the field. Bear left to another stile. Continue uphill to reach the coast path (signs to Pudcombe Cove, right).

2 Turn right and follow the path along the cliff. Eventually go through a gate and descend steeply and over a footbridge to reach the gate at the bottom of Coleton Fishacre gardens. (There is no public right of way into the gardens here.)

3 Turn left, following coast path signs, to pass steps to the cove and go very steeply up wooden steps to leave the estate via a gate and on to Coleton Cliffs. The path drops

steeply, then climbs again above Old Mill Bay – with great views of the Mew Stone – followed by a steep climb up to Outer Froward Point, with views towards Start Point. The path undulates, then climbs steeply to reach the back of Froward Cove. Follow coast path signs left for Kingswear.

4 Pass through a gate, then follow coast path signs left, going very steeply downhill through a wooded section. The path then undulates towards Inner Froward Point.

5 The lookout (once housing a searchlight) is the next landmark, followed by 104 concrete steps climbing up the cliff. Follow the miniature railway line uphill and keep to the concrete walkway and steps as you pass through a collection of disused wartime buildings. At the top there is a junction of paths and a wooden footpath sign.

6 Turn left for Kingswear to walk through woodland behind Newfoundland Cove, through a gate and eventually a V-stile, and down a broad woodland track (estuary on the left). Plod down 84 steps to Mill Bay Cove and turn right down a tarmac way. Turn left over a stile and climb the 89 steps up to a lane, then 63 more steps to another lane.

7 Turn right (signed 'Brownstone'). After 250yds (229m) the lane forks; gratefully take the right fork downhill to Home Cottage.

8 Follow the footpath signs, right, up a steep, rocky path to a concrete lane, and on to pass Higher Brownstone Farm. Walk on up the lane to pass the National Trust car park, then the gates to Coleton Fishacre, and back to Coleton Camp car park.

6 The Bampton Notts

This walk strays off the beaten track in a little-known corner of Northeast Devon to explore two villages with fine churches and a fascinating agricultural history

Above: Ruby red beef herd on the hills above the village

Below: Beautiful Bampton

Bampton is one of those places that isn't really on the way to anywhere. As you drive north towards Exmoor from Tiverton you might sweep past the turning to Bampton, making for Dulverton up the Barle Valley. But it would be a mistake not to go and have a look at this quiet, ancient town, situated at a natural crossing place on the River Batherm, and whose Saxon origins are still evident in the layout of its building plots, streets and almost circular churchyard. In 1258 a royal charter established St Luke's Fair, which survives today as a funfair and street market.

An Agricultural Community

Bampton held important cattle and wool sheep markets from the 14th century, and the various fine buildings to be seen in the town today are evidence of wealthier times in the 17th and 18th centuries, when the cloth industry was at its most prosperous. In those days the town was famous for the Bampton Notts, said to be the finest breed of sheep in Devon, but which died out in the late 19th century. Before the coming of the railway in 1884 the sheep were herded on foot to Bristol, 60 miles (97km) away, for sale.

Concern for Grazing Sheep

It's worth deviating from your route a little to have a look at the church of St Michael and All Angels in Bampton, dating in part from the 12th century, though an earlier one occupied the site. A late Saxon or early Norman window arch can be seen high in the south wall. An interesting feature here is the stone casing around two enormous yew trees in the churchyard, to prevent the sheep that used to graze here from being poisoned. The roots of these huge trees may be responsible for the cracks that have appeared in the south wall.

As the walk penetrates deeper into the Devon countryside, it reaches the tiny village of Morebath, essentially a farming community, as it has been since Saxon times. There are warm springs of chalybeate water here in a marshy basin, from which the name Morebath derives. The simple tower of St George's Church probably dates from the 11th century; don't miss the saddleback roof, part of the 19th-century restoration, which is unlike anything seen elsewhere in the county.

6 The Bampton Notts

Follow part of the Exe Valley Way, with views of Exmoor, and explore Bampton and Morebath

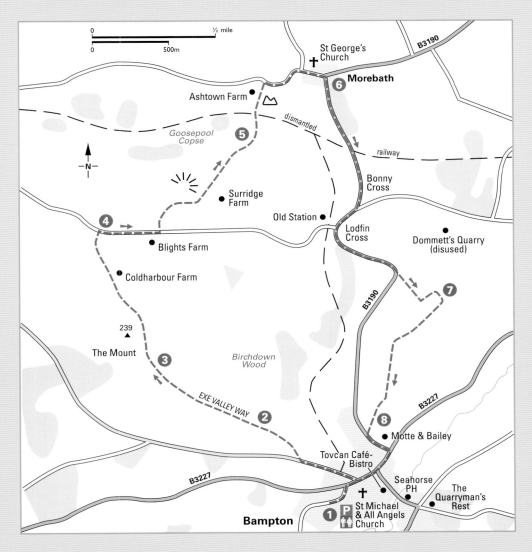

Distance 5.25 miles (8.4km)

Minimum Time 2hrs 30min

Ascent/Gradient 425ft (130m) ▲▲▲

Level of Difficulty ●●●

Paths Fields, tracks and lanes, 7 stiles

Landscape Rolling hills and wooded combes

Suggested Map OS Explorer 114 Exeter & the Exe Valley

Start/Finish Grid reference: SX 956223

Dog Friendliness Several difficult stiles; dogs to be kept under control

Parking Station Road car park by church in centre of Bampton

Public Toilets By car park

1 Leave the car park by the toilets, cross the road and turn left up the steep, narrow lane signposted 'Dulverton'. After a few minutes follow Exe Valley Way (EVW) signs right up a drive, left through a gate and up the field keeping right. Cross over the stile and go left on the track to reach a double stile in the top corner of the field. Over that, turn immediately right over another then turn left through a bank of trees and right, uphill (keeping the trees right).

2 Follow EVW signs over the next stile, carry on straight across the field to another stile (top left) and then cross the next field to an open gateway. Turn left, then immediately right, keeping the hedge on your left to reach a metal gate at the hilltop, with fine views towards Exmoor.

3 Continue downhill through open fields, with the hedge right, to reach Coldharbour Farm. Bear left before the farmhouse then straight on a grassy track, through a gate and downhill to reach the lane.

4 The EVW goes left here but the route turns right up the lane to reach Blights Farm. Turn left up the drive towards Surridge Farm. Just before reaching the farmhouse turn left through big metal gates, then another at the hilltop, continuing down through another gate on to a lane with views of Morebath ahead.

5 The lane joins a track; go downhill and over the dismantled railway towards Ashtown Farm, then right down the drive. Turn right and follow the deep lane uphill past The Old Vicarage to the centre of Morebath village.

6 Turn right down the B3190. At Bonny Cross keep right (signed 'Bampton'), past Lodfin Cross and the old station. When the road bends right take the track ahead, uphill.

7 At the hilltop a footpath sign leads right through a kissing gate. Go down the field, through a gate and over a stile, then straight on through a gate, over another stile, then through a gate at the top of the next field. Turn left through a gate. Cross the field diagonally towards the left-hand gate at the top. Pass through the next field to a stile at the top, then down a fenced path towards Bampton. Cross over the next stile and field to gain the road.

8 Cross over, turn left, then bear right down the old road into the town. Turn right towards the church and your car.

7 Dartmoor's Highest Tors

A relatively undemanding walk provides a taste of the wild and rugged beauty of Dartmoor, and leads through a beautiful area of ancient oak woodland

Above: Dartmoor ponies – a mare and her foal

Below: High Willhays, here distant and shrouded in mist

If you want to get a 'quick fix' and to experience examples of almost everything that Dartmoor has to offer, but fairly easily and in a relatively short time – then this is the walk for you. Within 10 minutes of the A30 as it races past Okehampton you can get the lot: a tranquil reservoir, a sparkling river and waterfall tumbling though a beautiful tree-lined valley, wide expanses of open moorland, an area of ancient lichen-encrusted oak woodland and a great view of the highest tors on the moor – and all without expending too much effort.

You don't have to tramp for miles over unhospitable moorland or get to grips with a compass to get a real feel of the moor. Note: Do not attempt this walk in mist.

Blackator Copse

Owned by the Duchy of Cornwall, this is one of the best areas of ancient high-altitude oak woodland in Britain, and was established as a National Nature Reserve in 1996. There is a huge variety of mosses and lichens covering the granite boulders from which the stunted oaks emerge. It makes a wonderful focus for the walk.

There are two other areas of upland woodland on the moor – at Piles Copse in the Erme Valley and at Wistman's Wood by the side of the West Dart River just north of Two Bridges. In all three places the oaks have remained ungrazed because the clutter of granite boulders beneath has protected them from the local sheep.

Blackator Copse feels little visited and remote. The atmosphere here is quite magical.

Dartmoor's Highest Tors

Dartmoor is basically a huge granite intrusion, pushed up through surrounding sedimentary rocks, formed in the same way as Bodmin Moor in Cornwall and the Isles of Scilly. Where it is exposed to the elements this raised granite plateau has been weathered into giant blocks, creating the tors so characteristic of the area.

The highest part of the moor lies in the north-east corner just south of the A30, where it rises to 2,037ft (621m) at High Willhays, seen from this walk. The average height of the moor, however, is around 1,200ft (366m).

Railway Stone

Sold by British Rail after privatisation, Meldon Quarry is around 200 years old, and was originally mined for a range of minerals. Tin, copper, limestone, roadstone and aplite, arsenic, copper, granite and churt have all come from here.

The Black Down copper mine was in operation in the 19th century, as was the Hornfeld Quarry, which produced ballast for the new railways being laid in the area. The quarry today produces ballast, roadstone, concrete aggregates and building stone, and covers 235 acres (95ha).

7 Dartmoor's Highest Tors

Enjoy superb views of Yes Tor and High Willhays on Dartmoor – without having to climb either of them

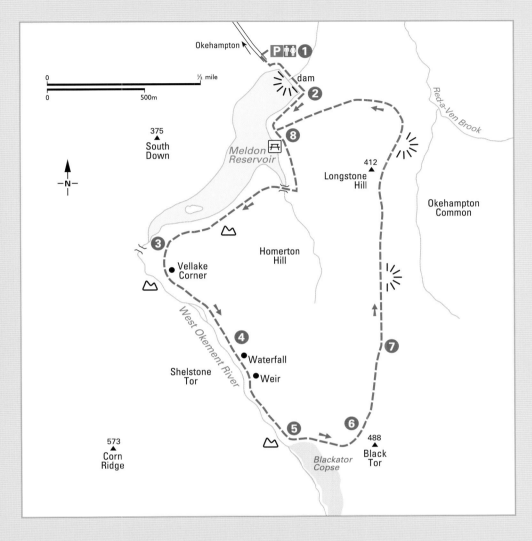

Distance 4.5 miles (7.2km)

Minimum Time 2hrs

Ascent/gradient 722ft (220m) ▲▲▲

Level of Difficulty ●●●

Paths Grassy tracks and open moorland, some boggy patches

Landscape Reservoir, ancient oak woodland and open moorland

Suggested Map OS Outdoor Leisure 28 Dartmoor

Start/Finish Grid Reference: SX 562918

Dog Friendliness Keep dogs under control, watch for sheep

Parking Car park at Meldon Reservoir (voluntary contributions)

Public Toilets At car park

1 Walk up the stone steps by the toilets, through the gate and go left on a tarmac way towards the dam, signposted 'Bridleway to Moor'. Cross over the dam.

2 Turn right along a stony track. You will soon see a gate (right) leading to a waterside picnic area. Don't go over the stile, but leave the track here to go straight on, following the edge of the reservoir through a side valley and over a small footbridge. The narrow path undulates to a steepish descent at the end of the reservoir to meet the broad marshy valley of the West Okement River; the swell of Corn Ridge, 1,762ft (537m), lies ahead.

3 Pass the small wooden footbridge and take the narrow path along the left edge of the valley, keeping to the bottom of the steep slope that rises on your left. The path broadens uphill and becomes grassy as it rounds Vellake Corner above the tumbling river below to the right.

4 At the top of the hill the track levels and Blackator Copse can be glimpsed ahead. Follow the river upstream past a waterfall and weir, go left of a granite enclosure, and along the left bank through open moorland to enter Blackator Copse – a wonderful picnic spot.

5 Retrace your steps out of the trees and bear right around the copse edge, aiming for the left outcrop of Black Tor on the ridge above. Pick your way through the bracken to gain the left edge of the left outcrop. The right outcrop rises to 1,647ft (502m).

6 Climb to the top of the tor if you wish; if not keep ahead in the same direction, away from Blackator Copse, aiming for a fairly obvious track visible ahead over Longstone Hill. To find it go slightly downhill from the tor to cross two small streams, then pass between granite blocks marking the track.

7 The intermittent track runs straight across open moor. Where the Red-a-Ven Brook Valley appears below to the right, enjoy the view of (left to right) Row Tor, West Mill Tor and Yes Tor. High Willhays, Dartmoor's highest point, lies just out of sight to the right. The track bears left around the end of the hill, with good views towards the quarry and viaduct, and drops back to the reservoir.

8 Bear right on the track, then left over the dam and back to the car park.

8 Merry Maidens and the Way Down to Lamorna

On an invigorating coastal walk magnificent sea views give way to a close encounter with two Bronze Age monuments

Top: The Merry Maidens stone circle

Above: Seashore at Lamorna Cove

Above right: Tater-du Lighthouse above greenstone cliffs near Lamorna

The coast at Lamorna, to the south-west of Penzance, is one of the loveliest in Cornwall. This is a south-facing coast, protected from prevailing westerly winds although storms from the south and east can be merciless here, as witnessed by a bitter record of terrible shipwrecks over the years. The bare granite cliffs are enhanced by swathes of lush vegetation that turn the coast into something of a wild garden in spring and summer.

Granite Quarrying

The walk starts from the hugely popular Lamorna Cove, once the scene of granite quarrying. The sturdy quay at Lamorna was built so that ships could load up with the quarried stone, but because the swell and the tidal regimen made berthing difficult much of the stone was in fact carried laboriously overland by horse and wagon to Newlyn Harbour and to Penzance.

The coast path west from Lamorna winds its sinuous way through tumbled granite boulders, then climbs steeply to the cliff tops. It passes above Tater-du Lighthouse, by jet black, greenstone cliffs, a startling accent among all these miles of golden granite, although the upper parts of the greenstone are dusted with ochre-coloured lichen.

Soon the path descends steeply to the delightful St Loy's Cove, a secluded boulder beach where a brisk little stream pours out of a wooded valley. Spring comes early at St Loy; the subtropical vegetation through which the walk leads reflects the area's mild and moist microclimate.

Back to the Bronze Age

From St Loy's woods you climb inland to reach two enthralling ancient monuments. The first is the Tregiffian burial chamber, a late Bronze Age entrance grave that was fortuitously uncovered during road widening in the 1960s. The cup-marked stone is a reproduction, the valuable original is in the County Museum at Truro.

Just along the road from Tregiffian stands one of Cornwall's most famous monuments, the Merry Maidens stone circle. This late Neolithic/Bronze Age structure represents an ancient ceremonial and ritual site of major importance. Its popular name, appended by a much later superstitious society, refers to a myth of young girls being turned to stone for dancing on a Sunday. In a field on the other side of the B3315 are two tall standing stones, the mythical 'Pipers' who supplied the sacrilegious music. The true spirit of the stones reflects a far more intriguing ancient culture. The final part of the walk leads from the Merry Maidens to a wonderful old trackway that leads over water-worn stones into the Lamorna Valley.

8 Merry Maidens and the Way Down to Lamorna

Step back into Cornwall's ancient past at the Tregiffian burial chamber and Merry Maidens stone circle

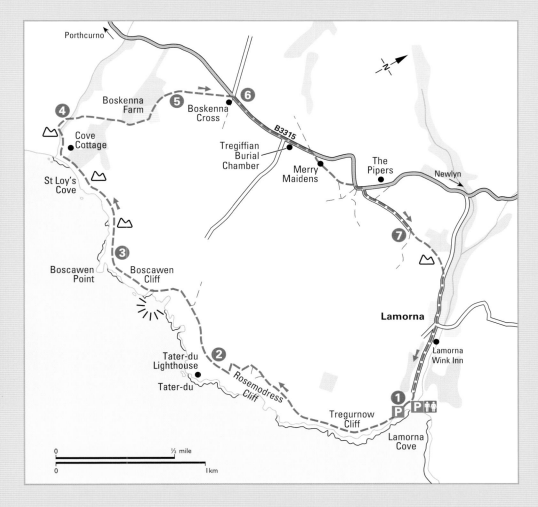

Distance 6 miles (9.7km)

Minimum Time 3hrs 30min

Ascent/Gradient 558ft (170m) ▲▲▲

Level of Difficulty ●●●

Paths Good coastal footpaths, field paths and rocky tracks

Landscape Picturesque coastline, fields and wooded valleys, 7 stiles

Suggested Map OS Explorer 102 Land's End

Start/Finish Grid reference: SW 450241

Dog Friendliness Dogs on leads through grazed areas

Parking Lamorna Cove or Boskena Cross

Public Toilets Lamorna Cove

1 From the far end of the seaward car park in the cove, above Lamorna Harbour, follow the coast path along through some awkward rocky sections. Continue on the coast path past the tops of Tregurnow Cliff and Rosemodress Cliff.

2 Pass above the entrance ramp and steps of Tater-du Lighthouse. Pass a large residence on the right and then, where the track bends right, keep left along the narrow coast path, at a signpost.

3 Descend steeply (taking great care when the ground is muddy) from Boscawen Cliff to St Loy's Cove. Cross over a section of sea-smoothed boulders that may be slippery when wet. About halfway along the beach, follow a path inland through trees and alongside the stream. Cross a private drive – Cove Cottage is just to the right – and then draw breath and climb steeply uphill. Go over a stile on to

a track, turn right over a stile and follow the path through trees.

4 By a wooden signpost and an old tree, go sharply down right and cross the stream on large boulders, then go left along a hedged-in path. In about 100yds (90m), go sharp right and up to a surfaced lane. Follow the lane uphill. At a junction with another track, keep going ahead and uphill. At Boskenna Farm buildings, follow the surfaced lane round left and keep ahead.

5 From the lane, at the entrance drive to a bungalow on the right, the right of way goes through a field gate, then slants diagonally right across the field to a wooden stile in a wire fence. Beyond this, the way (there's no path) leads diagonally across the field to its top right-hand corner, where a stile leads into a large roadside lay-by with a granite cross at its edge. An alternative to

the field route is to continue from the bungalow entrance along the farm lane, and then to turn right along the public road, with care, to reach the lay-by.

6 Follow the road to the Tregiffian burial chamber on the right and then to the Merry Maidens stone circle. From the stone circle, follow a grassy path towards a gate in the field corner. Go over a steep stile on the left, turn right along the field-edge for about 55yds (50m) and go left across the field past a telegraph pole. Go over a stile on to a road, then go down the left-hand of two lanes, a surfaced lane with a 'No Through Road' sign.

7 Where the lane ends keep ahead on to a public bridleway. Follow a shady and very rocky track, that can be slippery in wet weather, downhill to the public road. Turn right and walk down the road, with care, passing the Lamorna Wink Inn, to the car park.

9 The Cornish Shores of Plymouth Sound

A pleasant ramble offers the chance to enjoy a fine country park walk and visit the spot, once familiar to smugglers, where the old Devon/Cornwall border ran

Below: The beach at Cawsand

Below right: A riot of colour in the gardens of Mount Edgcumbe Country Park

Bottom: Waves break over rocks at Cawsand, where at one time smugglers hauled boats ashore

The Mount Edgcumbe Country Park is a green oasis that flies in the face of Plymouth's crowded waterfront opposite. The two are separated by The Narrows, a stretch just a few hundred yards in length of the Hamoaze, the estuary formed by the rivers Tavy, Lynher and Tamar by the entrance to Plymouth Sound. Mount Edgcumbe stands on the Cornish side of the river, although it was not always 'Cornish'. In Anglo-Saxon times, Devon extended across the estuary as far as Kingsand, the half-way point in this walk. Today, however, Mount Edgcumbe and its waterfront settlement of Cremyll are emphatically Cornish. They stand on the most easterly extension of the Rame Peninsula, known with ironic pride by local people as the 'Forgotten Corner'.

In truth Rame is one of the loveliest parts of the Southwest, let alone of Cornwall, and this walk takes you round the shores of the inner estuary, and then over the spine of the eastern peninsula to Kingsand, before returning to Cremyll along the open shores of Plymouth Sound.

Empacombe

The first section of the route takes you to peaceful Empacombe, where there is a tiny harbour contained within a crescent-shaped quay. It was here, during 1706–9, that workshops servicing the building of the famous Eddystone Lighthouse were located. Behind the harbour is the Gothic façade of Empacombe House.

The path follows the wooded shoreline of the tidal basin known as Millbrook Lake, then climbs steeply inland to reach Maker Church on the highest point of the peninsula. From here you wander through tiny fields to reach a track that leads in a long descent to the village of Kingsand.

Anglo-Saxon Defences

Kingsand is a charming village, linked seamlessly by the long and narrow Garrett Street to the equally charming Cawsand. These were very successful smugglers' havens during the 18th and early 19th centuries. In Garrett Street, opposite the Halfway House Inn, look for a sign on the wall indicating the old Cornwall–Devon border. The Cornish side of Plymouth Sound was incorporated into Anglo-Saxon territory in AD 705 in order to secure both banks of the estuary against raids mainly conducted by Vikings. Kingsand remained as part of Devon until 1844.

From Kingsand the route follows the coastal footpath along the more bracing sea shore of Plymouth Sound. Finally you reach the delightful park environment that surrounds Mount Edgcumbe House. Here it is well worth taking a few minutes to visit the house, which was built in 1547–53, and explore the lovely gardens.

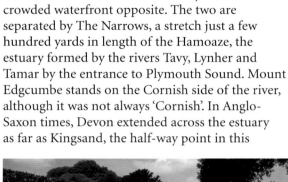

9 The Cornish Shores of Plymouth Sound

Take in beautiful river and sea views on this gentle circuit of the Rame Peninsula's eastern end

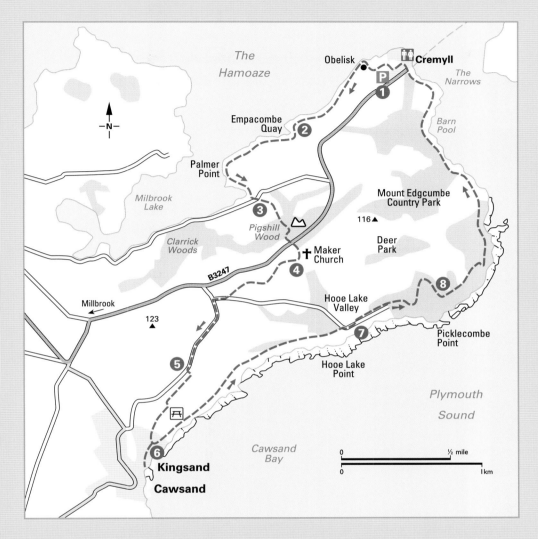

Distance 8 miles (12.9km)

Minimum Time 4hrs

Ascent/Gradient 328ft (100m) ▲▲▲

Level of Difficulty ●●●

Paths Good throughout. muddy in places in wet weather, 7 stiles

Landscape Wooded shoreline of tidal creek, fields, woods and coast

Suggested Map OS Explorer 108 Lower Tamar Valley & Plymouth

Start/Finish Grid reference: SX 453534

Dog Friendliness Dogs on leads through grazed areas

Parking Cremyll car park. Alternatively reach Cremyll by ferry from the Plymouth side. Daily service between Admiral's Hard, Stonehouse, Plymouth and Cremyll

Public Toilets Cremyll and Kingsand

1 Go left along the footway opposite the car park entrance. Where the footway ends at an old fountain and horse trough, cross back left and go through a gap by a telephone kiosk, signposted 'Empacombe'. Keep left past the Old School Rooms. Turn right at a junction then pass an obelisk and follow the path alongside the tree-hidden creek to Empacombe.

2 At a surfaced lane, by a house, keep ahead and go down to Empacombe Quay. Turn left beyond the low wall (dogs under control please) and skirt the edge of the small harbour to reach a stone stile on to a wooded path. Continue round Palmer Point and on to a public road.

3 Go through the kissing gate opposite, signposted 'Maker Church, Kingsand'. Follow the track ahead for 55yds (50m), then bear right, up the open field (no obvious path) heading between telegraph poles, and through a kissing gate into Pigshill Wood. Climb uphill following footpath signs. Cross a track, then go up some stone steps to reach more steps on to a public road. Cross, with care, and follow a path to Maker Church.

4 Turn sharp right in front of the church, follow the field-edge, then go over a stile on the left. Follow the next field-edge and cross a stile on the left, then follow the path past a house and across a lane into a field. Cross two fields to reach a lane. Turn up right, then go left at a junction.

5 Where the road levels off, bear off left down a track at a public footpath signpost. Keep ahead at a junction and, after a long level stretch, go left at a junction to reach Kingsand via Devonport Hill and Kingsway. To explore Kingsand and Cawsand, bear left down the narrow Heavitree Road.

6 To return to Cremyll, at Kingsway go through a gate into Mount Edgcumbe Country Park. Follow a good track to a public lane at Hooe Lake Valley.

7 Rejoin the coast path, signposted a little way along the lane. Keep to the upper path at a junction, then merge with a track from the left and continue through the woods.

8 Go left up some wooden steps, then zig-zag uphill to an arched ruin. Descend another set of wooden steps, cross a broad path by a gate, and zig-zag down through woods to the coast. Follow the coast path back to Mount Edgcumbe and Cremyll.

10 A Wild Flower Fiesta on the Cliffs at Bude

An invigorating walk that takes in varied settings such as clifftop grasslands and inland woods finishes with a stretch past an area of protected wetland

Above: Walkers happily share Bude's beaches with dogs, boating enthusiasts and surfers

Below: Dunes on the way to Maer Cliff

The windswept coastal grasslands of North Cornwall seem unlikely havens for plant life, but around the seaside resort of Bude the cliff edges in particular provide a unique refuge for a fascinating range of wild flowers. This walk follows the flat cliff land north of Bude with an inland section on the return. Along the way you'll find numerous wild flowers that turn the cliff top into a riot of colour in spring and early summer.

Grasslands

The walk starts from the northern outskirts of Bude at Crooklets Beach and within minutes takes you out on to the cropped grasslands of the National Trust's Maer Cliff and Maer Down. In spring the dominant flower here is the spring squill, whose distinctive powder-blue flowers are dotted across the grass. Other early plants which flourish here are the lilac-coloured early scurvy grass, the pink thrift and white sea-campion. At Northcott Mouth the cliffs give way to a wide stony beach.

Here the route of the walk turns inland and climbs steadily uphill to follow the line of an old bridleway, often choked with a tangle of grass and brambles, but with typical hedgrow plants such as foxglove and red valerian poking through.

Yellow Heads

Soon you reach the road to Sandy Mouth Beach and the cliff path back to Crooklets. Once more there are many wild flowers here. The grass is laced with the yellow and orange flowers of kidney vetch and the yellow heads of hawkweed and, by July, is scattered with the pink and white florets of the aromatic wild carrot.

From Crooklets the walk angles inland to a final stroll through an area of woodland, a dramatic contrast in habitat to the open cliff top. Here primroses and daffodils appear, brightening up the early spring. A mixture of trees such as sycamore, beech, alder, cypress, Scots pine and Corsican pine create a sheltered and moist environment within which plants like the tall yellow flag iris and the lilac-coloured water mint thrive.

The last section of the walk leads you past the Maer Lake Nature Reserve, a large area of wetland, flooded in winter, that is in the care of the Cornwall Wildlife Trust and the Cornwall Birdwatching and Preservation Society. There is no public access to the area from the roadside but you can get a good view of the birds through binoculars.

10 A Wild Flower Fiesta on the Cliffs at Bude

Marvel at the wild flowers that defy the battering of sea winds on Cornish cliffs

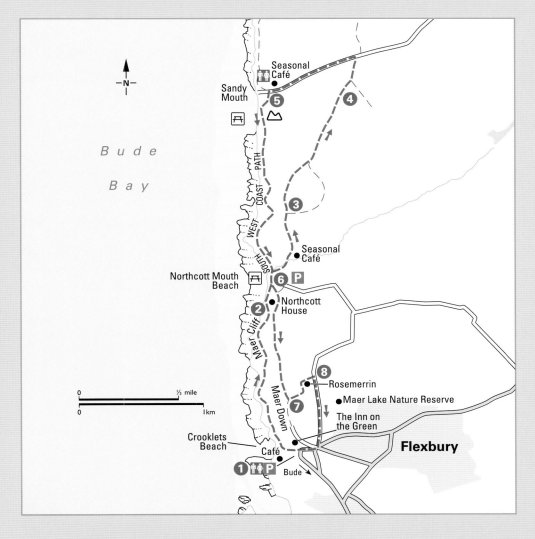

Distance 5 miles (8km)

Minimum Time 2hrs 30min

Ascent/Gradient 262ft (80m) ▲▲▲

Level of Difficulty ●●●

Paths Excellent throughout. The National Trust is carrying out regeneration of some eroded sections; please heed notices

Landscape Coastal cliffs. Keep well back from the cliff edges

Suggested Map OS Explorer 111 Bude, Boscastle & Tintagel and 126 Clovelly & Hartland

Start/Finish Grid reference: SS 204071

Dog Friendliness Dogs on leads through grazed areas

Parking Crooklets Beach car park. Follow signs for Crooklets. Large pay-and-display car park, can be very busy in summer

Public Toilets Crooklets Beach and Sandy Mouth

1 From Crooklets Beach car park, go towards the beach, turn right to cross a bridge and head for some steps. Pass behind some beach huts, then turn left along a stony track between walls. Go up some steps and on to the coast path, signposted 'Maer Cliff'. Follow the coast path.

2 Go through a gate and then walk along a track behind a white building called Northcott House. Bear off to the left, by a signpost, down a path to reach the sea at Northcott Mouth beach. From here, bear right along a track that will take you back inland, past a group of houses on the left, and continue uphill to pass some more houses.

3 Where the track bends right, leave it and keep straight ahead to an open gateway. Keep going along a banked bridle path ahead.

4 Reach a field gate and follow a track through the fields. At a junction with another track, keep straight ahead and continue to a T-junction with a public road. Turn left and walk down the road, proceeding with care on account of possible traffic, to Sandy Mouth.

5 Pass the National Trust information kiosk and descend towards the beach, then go left and uphill and follow the coast path back to Northcott Mouth beach, and a lifeguard hut passed earlier on your route.

6 Follow the roadside path just past the lifeguard hut and then retrace your steps towards Northcott House, which you passed earlier. Go along the track behind the building and then keep ahead along a broad track with a field hedge on your left.

7 As buildings come into view ahead, turn left over a stile with a footpath sign in a wall corner. Follow the field-edge ahead into a hedged-in path. Continue walking between trees to a lane by a house at Rosemerrin. Continue until you reach the road.

8 Turn right along the road, with Maer Lake Nature Reserve down to your left. Follow the road to a crossroads and turn right to return to the car park.

11 Cliffs and Deep Woods at Portreath and Tehidy

Before taking refuge at last in the calm of Tehidy Woods, this dramatic coastal walk offers spectacular views of cliffs, beaches, rocky islands and pounding waves

Below: A young fern in Tehidy Woods

Bottom left: At 'Hell's Mouth', on the Tehidy estate, 200ft (61m) cliffs plunge into the waves

Bottom right (upper): The Portreath tramroad cycle path starts at Portreath Beach car park

Bottom right (lower): One of the many wild residents of Tehidy Woods

The sea cliffs near Portreath in Mid Cornwall are made up of unstable shale and sandstone. Yet their very friability lends itself to the formation of fantastic offshore islands and ridges of marginally harder rock. From the edge of the cliffs a flat platform of land, Carvannel Downs, once submerged beneath the sea, runs inland. It is a featureless landscape except where the dark curtain of Tehidy Woods breaks the profile. There can be no greater contrast hereabouts than that between the bare, windswept cliffs and the enfolding trees, and this walk samples both environments.

Awesome Cliffs

The walk starts from Portreath's popular beach and harbour and soon leads on to the awesome cliffs to the west of Portreath. You stroll along the edge of the flat, heath-covered Carvannel Downs aware always of the 260ft (80m) cliffs only a few steps away. Below lie vast rock islands dotting the inaccessible sands of Western Cove. The Horse is a breathtaking ridge of rock and grass that projects from the cliff face and makes up the east wall of Ralph's Cupboard, a vast dizzying gulf that belies the quaintness of its name and that is said to be the remains of a huge cavern whose roof collapsed. Do not be tempted to go too near the edge of the cliffs, however, especially in windy weather. Far ahead you can see Godrevy Lighthouse on its rocky island.

Smugglers' Cove, Mine Owners' Woods

Beyond Ralph's Cupboard the path leads steeply down into Porth-cadjack Cove. Here a thin stream of water pours over the lower cliff edge and 19th-century smugglers used to hoist their contraband from the beach using elaborate pulley-systems.

Beyond, above Basset's Cove, the route turns inland and draws you into the enfolding trees of Tehidy Woods, once the estate of the Basset family who were famous mine owners. The Bassets planted extensive woodlands around their Georgian house and these now mature woods still offer shelter and security after the exhilarating exposure of the cliffs.

11 Cliffs and Deep Woods at Portreath and Tehidy

Combine steep climbs and clifftop vistas with a ramble inland past a farm and a golf course

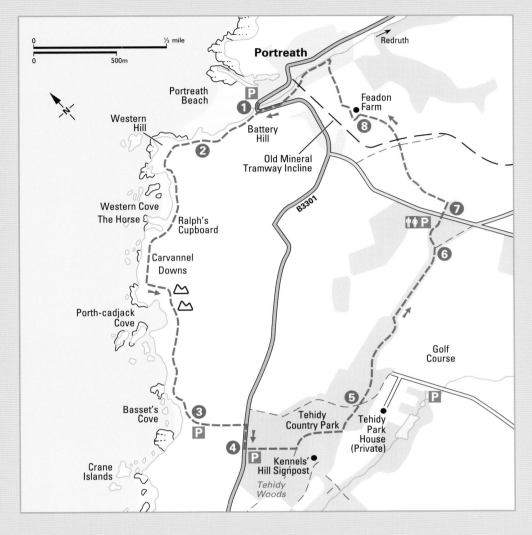

Distance 4 miles (6.4km)

Minimum Time 3hrs

Ascent/Gradient 459ft (140m) ▲▲▲

Level of Difficulty ●●●

Paths Good coastal path, woodland path, farm tracks

Landscape Precipitous sea cliffs and deep woodland

Suggested Map OS Explorer 104 Redruth & St Agnes

Start/Finish Grid reference: SW 654453

Dog Friendliness dogs on leads through grazed areas

Parking Portreath Beach, Basset's Cove, North Cliffs, Tehidy Country Park, East Lodge

Public Toilets Portreath and East Lodge car park

1 Cross the bridge opposite Portreath Beach car park and turn right up Battery Hill, following signs for 'Coast Path'. Take the lane uphill and carry on to where it ends at a section of houses situated above the beach. Then go left in front of garages, signposted 'Coast Path Gwithian'.

2 Follow the path through a gate and then keep straight uphill to the cliff top. Don't go too close to the cliff edge. Turn left and follow the path round the cliff edge above Ralph's Cupboard. Continue by steep paths into and out of Porth-cadjack Cove.

3 Keep going until you reach a car parking area above Basset's Cove. From there follow the broad track inland, then when you reach the public road, cross over and turn right for a short distance.

4 Turn left into a car park. Go through the car park and down a tree-lined track. Turn left at a T-junction and follow a track to another T-junction. Turn left along another broad track.

5 Reach a junction and four-way signpost beside two seats. (A café can be reached in 0.25 mile [400m] down the right-hand signposted track.) On the main route, keep straight on, signposted 'East Lodge'. Reach a junction by a seat. Keep right and go through a wooden kissing gate. Eyes left here before crossing to check for keen golfers about to tee-off. Go through a kissing gate and continue to follow the track alongside the golf course.

6 About 40yds (37m) beyond the end of the golf course section, at a junction, bear off left into woods. Stay on the main path,

ignoring side paths, then bear round right to East Lodge car park and to a public road.

7 Cross the road diagonally right and then go left between wooden posts with red marks. Keep to the track ahead, pass chalets and reach a T-junction above farm buildings at Feadon Farm and the Duchy College.

8 Turn left, then in a few paces turn right down a concrete track. At a farmyard go sharp left by a public footpath sign and follow a path down through woods keeping to the main path, to reach a surfaced road. Just past 'Glenfeadon Castle' turn left along Glenfeadon Terrace, pass beneath a bridge, then at a junction keep ahead along Tregea Terrace and back to Portreath Beach car park.

12 Kilve and East Quantoxhead

With two Tudor villages, industrial remnants and an instructive display of geology underfoot, this is a walk to stimulate the brain as well as the lungs

The chantry chapel in the East Somerset village of Kilve is built in the local grey shale, but with the arches picked out in orange Quantock sandstone. The sandstone is easier to work into shaped blocks, but has been eroded by the sea winds. This chantry housed five priests whose sole function was the saying of prayers and Masses for the deceased Simon de Furneaux and his family.

The doctrine was that the rich could pay their way out of purgatory by setting up such chapels. This created employment for priests, but contributed to the general loss of credibility of the Catholic faith. In fact Kilve Chantry closed even before the Reformation, when a Lollard dissenter married into the family in the late 14th century. Later the chapel was used by smugglers for storing brandy and burned down around 1850 in an alcohol fire. Behind the ruins, the Chantry House has a pigeon loft still in use.

The old (possibly Saxon) preaching cross in Quantoxhead churchyard is a viewpoint for the Manor House. It also looks on to the back of Quantoxhead Farm, where the semi-circular wing is a horse-gang. This once housed a capstan where horses walked in circles to power, via an endless belt, farm machinery in the main building. The church itself has fossils incorporated into the walls, and Tudor-carved pew ends.

The Spies who Wrote Sonnets

When Samuel Taylor Coleridge and William Wordsworth walked here, their particular interest was in the Holford stream. Coleridge planned a poem in his deceptively simple 'conversational' style, tracing the stream from its birth high in Hodder Combe. However, the two poets had already aroused local suspicions by their comings and goings, and both had been enthusiastic supporters of the French Revolution in its early days. This was 1797: England was in the grip of invasion fever; and Kilve has a small but usable harbour. Accordingly, a government agent called James Walsh was sent to investigate.

Walsh quizzed a footman about the poets' dinner-time conversation: it was reported as being quite impossible to understand – which was, of course, most suspicious. The agent followed Wordsworth and Coleridge to Kilve. Lurking behind a gorse bush, he heard them discussing 'Spy Nosy' and thought he'd been found out. They had actually been talking about the German philosopher Spinoza. Coleridge did not write his poem 'The Brook' – but Wordsworth did. Twenty years later, he adopted his friend's plan into a sequence of sonnets on Lakeland's River Duddon.

Below: Evidence of the geological past piles up on the beach near Kilve

Bottom left: A thatched cottage overlooks the village pond in East Quantoxhead

12 Kilve and East Quantoxhead

With the risk of French invasion now passed, feel free to investigate these Tudor villages without fear of arrest

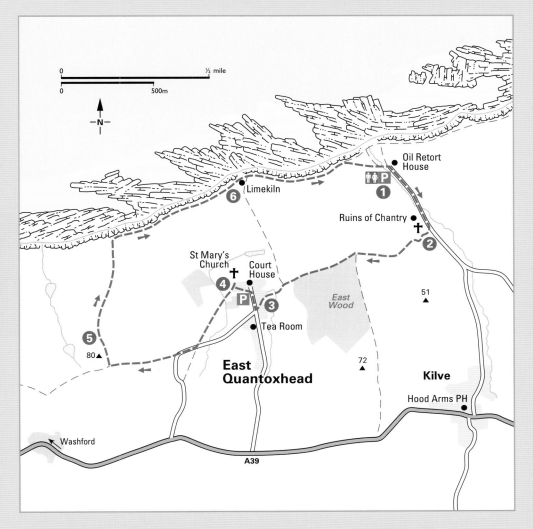

Distance 3 miles (4.8km)

Minimum Time 1hr 30min

Ascent/Gradient 250ft (76m) ▲▲▲

Level of Difficulty ●●●

Paths Tracks, field paths, and grassy cliff top, 4 stiles

Landscape Tudor villages, farmland and coastline

Suggested Map OS Explorer 140 Quantock Hills & Bridgwater

Start/Finish Grid reference: ST 144442

Dog Friendliness Extra care along cliff top, unstable near edge

Parking Pay-and-display at sea end of Sea Lane

Public Toilets At car park (closed October to February)

1 From the car park head back along the lane to the ruined chantry. Turn into the churchyard through a lychgate. Such gates were built to shelter coffins and their bearers: this one is too small for its purpose, so must be a modern reconstruction. Pass to the left of the church, to reach a kissing gate.

2 A signposted track crosses a field to a gate; bear right to another gate and pass along the foot of East Wood. (At its far end, a stile allows wandering into the wood, from April to August only.) Ignoring the stile on the left, keep ahead to a field gate with a stile and a track crossing a stream.

3 The track bends left past the gardens and ponds of East Quantoxhead to reach a tarred lane. Turn right, towards the Tudor Court House, but before its gateway bear left into a car park. Pass through to a tarred path and a kissing gate. In an open field this path bears right, to St Mary's Church.

4 Return to the kissing gate but don't go through, instead bear right to a field gate, and cross the field beyond to a distant gate and lane. Turn right and, where the lane bends left, keep ahead on to a green track. At its top, turn right at a 'Permissive path' noticeboard.

5 Follow field-edges, with hedges on your right, down to the cliff top, and turn right. A clifftop path leads to a kissing gate before a sharp dip, with a ruined lime kiln opposite. This was built around 1770 to process limestone, which was shipped from Wales, into lime for the fields and for mortar. The foreshore below the kiln is limestone, but it was still easier to bring it by sea across the Bristol Channel.

6 Turn around the head of the dip, and back left to the cliff top. Here an iron ladder descends to the foreshore: you can see alternating layers of blue-grey lias (a type of limestone) and grey shale. Fossils can be found here, but be aware that the cliffs are unstable – hard hats are now standard wear for geologists. Alternatively, given a suitably trained dog and the right sort of spear, you could pursue the traditional sport of 'glatting' – hunting conger eels in the rock pools. Continue along the wide clifftop path until a tarred path bears off to the right, crossing the stream studied by Coleridge. As you come into the car park, on your left is the brick chimney of a short-lived Oil Retort House (for oil distillation from the grey shale) from 1924.

13 Catching the Burrow Mump on the Levels

The Burrow Mump is only 100ft (30m) tall, but it commands wide-ranging views across the Somerset Levels, and was the site of a succession of fortresses

Above: The ruined Chapel of St Michael perches on the top of Burrow Mump

Above right: The King's Sedgemoor Drain near Westonzoyland on the Somerset Levels

After the last ice age, around 10–18,000 years ago, the area now known as the Somerset Levels was under the sea. Drainage started in Roman times, but gathered pace in the early Middle Ages. The three centuries following the Norman Conquest of 1066 (until the Black Death of around 1350) brought increasing prosperity and security locally – shown by, among other things, the windmills that sprung up along the Polden Hills. The growing population required more land to be drained for the plough and the cow.

Summer Pasture

The water-meadows around Burrow Mump were first drained by the monks of Glastonbury Abbey in about 1255. The monks raised walls to keep out the pervasive waters of the River Parrett and formed fertile water-meadows. In winter the meadows were allowed to flood, and their soils were enriched by silt from the river; in summer the drained grasslands formed highly fertile grazing land for their cattle, with convenient and effective wet fencing and plenty of fresh drinking water. This agricultural process may give us the origin of 'Sumor Saete' or Somerset, the 'land of summer'.

Drainage continued through the ages: the King's Sedgemoor Drain, with its arrangement of sluices and pumps, was constructed in the 19th century; and managed drainage came to the Huntspill River area during World War Two. Wind pumps were replaced by steam-powered engines and then by the diesel one that may be heard thumping in

the distance at the start of the walk. Our route is around the drove tracks and the river barriers, with a final ascent of Burrow Mump for an overall view.

A Stronghold for King Alfred

In the days when the surrounding ground was swamp, Burrow Mump was occupied by the local Celtic people against the Romans. In the Anglo-Saxon era, it was a strongpoint of King Alfred's; he fortified it against Danish raiders coming up the River Parrett. Later it held a Norman castle.

Once the surroundings were drained, the Mump's tactical value decreased, and the present Chapel of St Michael was built by the monks of Athelney Abbey. Even so it remained an obvious strongpoint, and the chapel was held by the Royalists in 1645 after their crushing defeat by Cromwell's New Model Army at the Battle of Langport. It was partially destroyed on that occasion, restored in the 18th century, and has fallen back down again since then.

View from a Hill

Half a dozen parish churches can be seen in various directions from the Burrow Mump. The closest of these, looking due north, is St Mary's in Westonzoyland, with its square tower. Here captured rebels were imprisoned by government troops after their defeat at the Battle of Sedgemoor in 1685. Closer at hand, the pattern of droves (tracks) and walls – river barriers, originally 12ft (4m) high and 30ft (9m) wide – can be seen.

13 Catching the Burrow Mump on the Levels

Taste the contrasts of the Somerset Levels before climbing the Burrow Mump

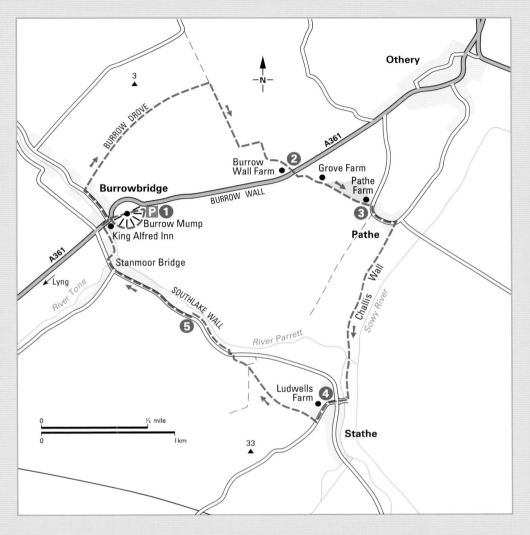

Distance 5.25 miles (8.4km)

Minimum Time 2hrs 15min

Ascent/Gradient 150ft (46m) ▲▲▲

Level of Difficulty ●●●

Paths Tracks, paths, unfrequented field-edges, 2 stiles

Landscape Flat pasture with ditches and one surprising, small hill

Suggested Map OS Explorer 140 Quantock Hills & Bridgwater

Start/Finish Grid reference: ST 360305

Dog Friendliness Good on drove tracks, where dogs are separated from livestock by deep ditches

Parking National Trust car park (free) at Burrow Mump

Public Toilets None en route

1 A gate leads on to the base of the Mump. Circle the hill's base to the left to a small gate and steps down to the Burrow Bridge. Just before the bridge turn right into Riverside. After 350yds (320m) turn right into Burrow Drove, which becomes a tractor track. On either side and between the fields are deep ditches, coated in bright green pondweed. At a T-junction there's a culvert of 19th-century brick on the left. Turn right here on a new track: it passes round to left of Burrow Wall Farm, to the busy A361.

2 A 'public footpath' sign points to a track opposite. After just 30yds (27m), turn left over a stile. With the bushy Burrow Wall on your right, cross a field to the usually muddy Grove Farm. Go through two gates below a wooded bank rising to continue along fields, to the right of buildings, on the left. At the corner of the second field a rusty gate leads up between brambles to a green track: turn right here to reach a lane near Pathe, a farm.

3 Turn right along the lane, ignoring a track on the right, to reach a side-lane on the right. Cross a bridge here to a hedge-gap on the right and a very narrow footbridge. Continue through several fields, with a wide ditch on the right. Near by, on the left, is the low banking of Challis Wall, concealing the Sowy River. The ditch on the right gradually gets smaller. When it finally ends bear right to the River Parrett and follow it to a latticework road bridge. Cross this into Stathe.

4 Keep ahead through the village past Ludwells Farm, to reach a kissing gate on the right waymarked 'Macmillan Way'. Follow the right edge of one field to a gatepost; cross to the hedge opposite and follow it round to the left, to a stile. Continue ahead with a hedge on your right, to where a hedged track leads to a road. Turn left, scrambling up the banking, to walk on the Southlake Wall between a road and river.

5 As the road turns away from the river, rejoin it. Once across Stanmoor Bridge you can bear right (if not too nettly) for a river bank path to Burrowbridge. Turn right across the bridge and, this time, climb to the top of Burrow Mump for fine views of Somerset.

14 The Villages of Hunstrete and Compton Dando

Although it takes in both Two Rivers Way and Three Peaks Walk, this is a gentle ramble through a quiet corner of the ancient kingdom of Somerset

Above: The walk leads though gentle hills, with villages hidden in the occasional small valley

Below: Sunrise over the trees and green fields of Somerset

Somerset as an entity is older than England itself; it came into existence as a kingdom of the Saxons in the 6th century. This book conforms to the boundaries established, perhaps by King Alfred the Great, in the 9th century. Local government reorganisation in 1974 split off a section and called it 'Avon' – the people of Somerset were not pleased. 'Destruction of Somerset Day' happened to be 1st April, and to mark this particular All Fools' Day a muffled quarter-peal of Somerset Surprise Major was rung from Yatton church.

The Name Game

Local government re-organisation in 1996 largely restored the ancient county. However, this corner remains separate as a unitary authority called Bath and North East Somerset, resulting in the unfortunate acronym, 'BANES', while the other end of Avon has become another unitary authority,

North Somerset. The very names of them are an admission that they may be convenient units of government but aren't actually proper places.

Although it has no striking natural features, 'BANES' does have a character of its own. It can be seen as the final petering-out of the Cotswolds, even if it does lack the Cotswolds' sudden edges. It's rich farming country, with small woods on the slopes and stream banks too steep for the plough.

Influence of Bath

A remnant of that farming wealth is at Hunstrete, where there's an attractive angling lake that makes a good picnic spot. It was one of six dug into the grounds of Hunstrete House – a magnificent country mansion of 17 bays with statues to match that was planned in the 1780s under the influence of Bath's new streets and squares, incomplete in 1797 and already falling down in 1822.

The authorities charged with making up reasons for footpaths have had to use some imagination. At the start of this walk you'll use the Two Rivers Way: the rivers are Yeo and Chew. From Lord's Wood to Hunstrete you're on the Three Peaks Walk: these are not Ben Nevis, Snowdon and Scafell Pike; they aren't even Yorkshire's Whernside, Pen-y-ghent and Ingleborough. They are, in fact, Maes Knoll, Knowle Hill and Blackberry Hill, but none of this detracts from the pleasure of this walk.

14 The Villages of Hunstrete and Compton Dando

Enjoy a few hours' serenity in a rich landscape nestling between the busy cities of Bristol and Bath

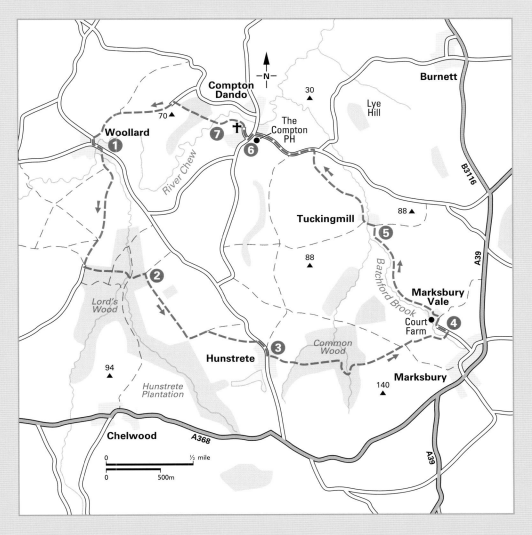

Distance 6.25 miles (10km)

Minimum Time 3hrs 30min

Ascent/Gradient 700ft (213m) ▲▲▲

Level of Difficulty ●●●

Paths Tracks, field paths, woodland paths and byways, 11 stiles

Landscape Rolling farmland with plantations and small streams

Suggested Map OS Explorer 155 Bristol & Bath

Start/Finish Grid reference: ST 632644

Dog Friendliness Freedom in some woods and on tracks fenced off from farmland

Parking Street parking near bridge in Woollard; also opposite pub in Compton Dando (Point 6)

Public Toilets None en route

1 From Woolard's crossroads take the road signposted 'Hunstrete' across the River Chew, then bear right at a 'Circular Walk' sign. The byway is underwater at first, but a path parallels it on the right. At the high point of the byway, where it becomes fully tarred, turn left through a gate into Lord's Wood. A wide path runs downhill, crossing a track, to a pool. Pass around to the left of this, to a waymarker and a track junction. The track opposite leads up to the edge of the wood.

2 Turn right, and drop to a hidden footbridge under trees. Head uphill, passing the right-hand edge of a plantation, to Pete's Gate beside a corner of Hunstrete Plantation. Turn left to a field gate. Turn right, around the field corner, to go through a gate. Continue along the same hedge, bending right at the field end, to reach a lane at the edge of Hunstrete.

3 Turn left beside Cottage No 5. Go down the right-hand side of a field to a stile into Common Wood. The track ahead passes through a paintball sports area. After it crosses a stream and bends left, take a signposted green path that rises to the top of the wood. Pass through a small col with a lone ash tree, and keep straight on, down across a field to a short hedged path. Go straight down the left edge of the field to a signpost, and turn right to join a lane at Marksbury Vale.

4 Turn left towards Court Farm; just before you reach the buildings turn right over a stile, and then follow the right-hand track for 100yds (91m) to a stile on the left. Pass to the right of the farm buildings as far as a rough track following Batchford Brook. After that head downstream until you reach a track at Tuckingmill.

5 Follow the track past a handsome 18th-century manor house to a ford. Cross the footbridge and turn right, alongside the stream, which is again the line of an underwater byway – rejoin it as it emerges. It leads to a road, with Compton Dando 700yds (640m) away on the left.

6 Turn right into Church Lane, and then go through the lychgate. A stile leads down steps, one of which is a 17th-century gravestone. Turn left behind the mill house and pass to the left of the mill pond, to reach a footbridge over the River Chew.

7 Bear left into Park Copse. At its top follow the right-hand edge of a field round to a stile. In the lane beyond turn left; it becomes a hedged track and runs past a tiny gorge as it descends to Woollard.

15 Salisbury's Historic Trail

A delightful urban walk, this leads into the 13th-century Cathedral Close, with views of Salisbury's breathtaking spire, and includes a stroll along the River Avon

Above: Detail of the carving that adorns the cathedral

Below: A house in the gracious Cathedral Close

Below right: The tower and spire are illuminated at night

Salisbury, or New Sarum, founded in 1220 following the abandonment of Old Sarum and built at the confluence of four rivers, is one of the most beautiful cathedral cities in Britain. Relatively free from sprawling suburbs and high-rise development, the surrounding countryside comes in to meet the city streets along the river valleys. Throughout the city centre, buildings of all styles blend harmoniously, from the 13th-century Bishop's Palace in The Close, through the medieval gabled houses and historic inns and market places to the stately pedimented Georgian houses and even the modern shopping centre.

Majestic Cathedral and Close

Salisbury's skyline is dominated by the magnificent spire of the cathedral, a graceful centrepiece to the unified city. An architectural masterpiece, built in just 38 years during the 13th century, the cathedral is celebrated for its uniformity of style. The tower and spire, with a combined height of 404ft (123m) – the tallest in England – were added in 1334, and the west front of the building is decorated with row upon row of beautifully carved statues in niches.

The rich and spacious interior contains huge graceful columns of Purbeck stone, and many windows add to the airy, dignified interior. Of particular interest are the impressive tombs and effigies in the nave, the cloisters and the library, home to a copy of the Magna Carta.

Originally built to house the clerics, the Cathedral Close is the one of the largest and finest in Britain. It is entered by a series of medieval gateways and contains several grand structures in a rich variety of architectural styles, dating from the 13th century to the present day.

Four of these fine buildings are open to the public as museums. The highlights are probably Malmesbury House, originally a 13th-century canonry, with its magnificent roccoco plasterwork and an Orangery that once sheltered Charles II, and Mompesson House (owned by the National Trust), an exquisite Queen Anne building with period furnishings, china and paintings.

From Silver Street to Ox Row

Beyond The Close, Salisbury is a delight to explore. You can wander through a fascinating network of medieval streets and alleys, with names like Fish Row, Silver Street and Ox Row, lined with half-timbered and jettied houses. On this walk you will see the 15th-century St Thomas's Church, noted for its Doom painting (c1475), believed to be the largest painting of the Last Judgement in existence, the hexagonally buttressed 15th-century Poultry Cross, the last of four market crosses in the city, the timbered medieval house of John A'Port (Crew Clothing Co) in Queen Street, and the Joiners' Hall with its superb Jacobean façade in St Ann Street.

Away from the hustle and bustle, your riverside stroll through Queen Elizabeth Gardens and along the Town Path to Harnham Mill will reveal the famous view across the water-meadows to the cathedral, admired by many an artist – not least the great Romantic painter John Constable.

15 Salisbury's Historic Trail

Admire a wealth of architectural treasures dating back to the 13th century

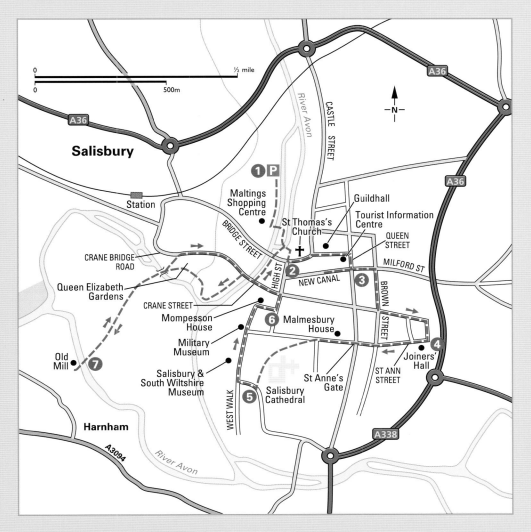

Distance 3 miles (4.8km)

Minimum Time 2hrs (longer if visiting attractions)

Ascent/Gradient Negligible ▲▲▲

Level of Difficulty ●●●

Paths Pavements and metalled footpaths

Landscape City streets and water-meadows

Suggested Map OS Explorer 130 Salisbury & Stonehenge; AA Street by Street Salisbury

Start/Finish Grid reference: SU 141303

Dog Friendliness Not suitable for dogs

Parking Central car park (signed off A36 ring road)

Public Toilets Central car park, Market Place, Crane Bridge Road

1 Join the Riverside Walk and follow the signposted path through the Maltings Shopping Centre towards St Thomas's church. On reaching St Thomas's Square, close to the Polly Tearooms, bear right to the junction of Bridge Street, Silver Street and the High Street.

2 Turn left along Silver Street and cross the road to the Poultry Cross. Keep ahead along Butcher Row and Fish Row to pass the Guildhall and tourist information centre. Turn right along Queen Street and turn right along New Canal to view the cinema foyer.

3 Return to the crossroads and go along Milford Street past the Red Lion. Turn right along Brown Street, then left along Trinity Street to pass Trinity Hospital. Pass Love Lane into Barnard Street and follow the road right to reach St Ann Street, opposite the Joiners' Hall.

4 Walk down St Ann Street and keep ahead on merging with Brown Street to reach the T-junction with St John's Street. Cross straight over and go through St Ann's Gate into the Cathedral Close. Pass Malmesbury House and Bishops Walk and take the path diagonally left across the green to reach the main entrance to the cathedral.

5 Pass the entrance, walk beside the barrier ahead and turn right. Shortly, turn right again along West Walk, passing Salisbury and South Wiltshire Museum and the Military Museum. Keep ahead around Chorister Green to pass Mompesson House.

6 Bear left through the gates into the High Street and turn left at the crossroads along Crane Street. Cross the River Avon and turn left along the metalled path beside the river

through Queen Elizabeth Gardens. Keep left by the play area and soon cross the footbridge to follow the Town Path across the water-meadows to the Old Mill (hotel) in Harnham.

7 Return along Town Path, cross the footbridge and keep straight ahead as far as Crane Bridge Road. Bear right, recross the Avon and turn immediately left along the riverside path to Bridge Street. Cross straight over and follow the path ahead towards The Mill. Walk back through the Maltings Shopping Centre to the car park.

16 The Longleat Estate

Glorious walking through woods and landscaped parkland can be combined with a visit to the opulent Elizabethan mansion of Longleat House

Above: King of the parkland

Above right: Longleat House is largely unchanged since the 1580s, save for a few baroque alterations made in the 1690s

Below: A resident of the Longleat safari park. The giraffes at Longleat share their enclosure with Grant's zebra

Your first view of Longleat is an unforgettable one. As you stroll down the azalea-and-rhododendron-lined path to Heaven's Gate, nothing prepares you for the superb panorama that stretches to the distant Mendip Hills. Central to this composition is Longleat House, an exquisite Elizabethan stone manor in a glorious, wooded, lakeside setting that looks more like a fairy-tale palace from a distance.

Longleat's Lions

Longleat was the first stately home in Britain to open its doors to the public as a commercial proposition, first doing so in 1949. It set a trend that many would follow. Lions made Longleat famous in 1966 and since then the Marquess of Bath's home has amassed an ever-expanding roll-call of family attractions to keep it viable, including a safari park, hedged mazes, safari boats and a narrow gauge railway.

Thankfully, there are also thousands of acres of landscaped parkland and estate woodland to explore. You can escape the summer crowds in enjoying the wonderful setting.

Majestic Mansion

Architect and builder Sir John Thynne, an ancestor of the Marquess of Bath, completed the Elizabethan mansion in 1580 on a site chosen for its beauty. The house was revolutionary in its design as it showed no thought for defence, its great bayed walls of stone and mullioned glass windows setting a new trend in Elizabethan architecture.

The magnificent exterior is more than matched by the splendours found inside. Longleat contains a mixture of furnishings and artefacts reflecting the tastes and interests of the Thynne family throughout the centuries. Notable artefacts include a 16th-century oak shuffle-board (33ft (10m) long), a 17th-century gilt steeplechase cup and a library table commissioned from John Makepeace.

Rich 17th-century Flemish tapestries, Genoese velvet and ancient Spanish leather clothe the walls, while the state rooms are ornamented with marble fireplaces and painted ceilings inspired by Italian palace interiors. A tour will also reveal a fine collection of paintings, from 16th-century portraits and 18th-century Dutch paintings to early Italian pictures and notable hunting scenes. The fully restored Victorian kitchens give an interesting picture of life below stairs.

'Artist' Lord Bath

The colourful current Lord Bath began painting in the early 1960s and covered his private rooms in the West Wing with an amazing cycle of paintings. Expressing what he calls 'keyhole glimpses of the psyche' are vast murals with satirical and erotic love scenes, while on the staircase hang portraits of his numerous 'wifelets', or mistresses, arranged in chronological order. Born in 1932, this bearded Bohemian is a sound businessman who has used his gifts to turn Longleat into a thriving, multi-million pound tourist attraction.

16 The Longleat Estate

Drink in beautiful views from Heaven's Gate then wander the wooded arcadia of the Longleat Estate

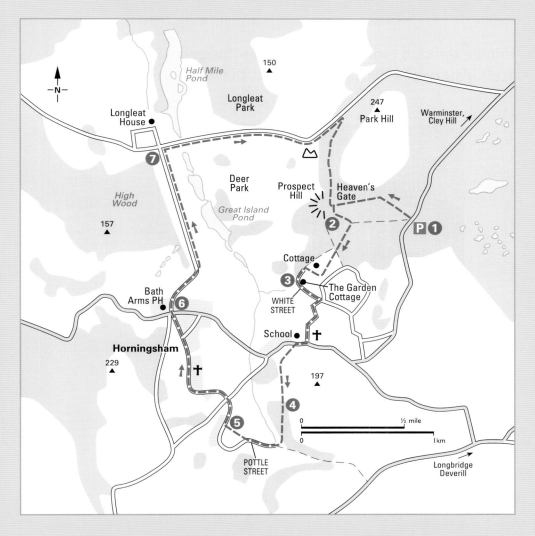

Distance 5.25 Miles (8.4km)

Minimum Time 2hrs 30min (longer if visiting Longleat attractions)

Ascent/Gradient 508ft (155m) ▲▲▲

Level of Difficulty ●●●

Paths Field, woodland and parkland paths, roads, 4 stiles

Landscape Wooded hillside, village streets, parkland

Suggested Map OS Explorer 143 Warminster & Trowbridge

Start/Finish Grid reference: ST 827422

Dog Friendliness On lead through grounds

Parking Heaven's Gate car park, Longleat Estate

Public Toilets Longleat attractions complex

1 Cross the road and follow the path into the trees. Disregard the straight track left, bear right and then left along a gravelled path through mixed woodland to double gates and reach the viewpoint at Heaven's Gate.

2 Facing Longleat, go through the gate in the left-hand corner. After 180yds (165m) at a crossing of paths, turn right, then keep right at a fork and head downhill through woodland to a metalled drive by a thatched cottage. Turn right on to the waymarked bridleway and pass the cottage gate. Now follow the path left, heading downhill close to the edge of the woodland to reach a lane running beside The Garden Cottage.

3 Turn left along White Street to a crossroads and turn right downhill. Ascend past the church to a T-junction and turn right.

Turn left opposite the school, following the bridle path up a track and between sheds to a gate. Bear left with the grassy track, pass through two gates and bear slightly right to a gate and stile on the edge of woodland.

4 Follow the path through the copse and soon bear off right diagonally downhill to a gate. Turn left along the field-edge to reach a track. Turn right, go through a gate beside a thatched cottage and follow the metalled lane (Pottle Street). In 200yds (183m), cross the stile on your right and cross the field to a stile and rejoin the lane.

5 Turn right and follow this quiet lane to a crossroads. Proceed straight across and follow the road through Horningsham village, passing the thatched chapel, and continuing as far as the crossroads opposite the Bath Arms.

6 Go straight across the crossroads, walk down the estate drive and through the gatehouse arch into Longleat Park. With the magnificent house ahead of you, walk beside the metalled drive with the lakes and weirs to your right. At a T-junction in front of the house, keep ahead to visit the house and follow the path left to reach the other tourist attractions.

7 For the main route, turn right and walk beside the drive, heading uphill through the Deer Park. Bear left with the drive and climb steeply, then turn sharp right through a wooden gate on to a metalled drive. With beautiful views across the parkland, gently ascend Prospect Hill and reach Heaven's Gate viewpoint. Retrace your steps to the car park.

17 Lydiard Park – Swindon's Surprising Secret

This charming ramble through Lydiard Park provides intriguing insights into the sometimes difficult history of a house and grounds that have known hard times

Right on the edge of the modern town of Swindon lies the 244-acre (99ha) Lydiard Park, an easily accessible and delightful buffer against any further westward urban spread. Within the wooded and eminently explorable park is one of Wiltshire's smaller and lesser known stately homes, a Palladian mansion, the ancestral home of the Viscounts Bolingbroke, and their church, St Mary's, in the village of Lydiard Tregoze. This walk takes you through the park to the edge of the sleepy hamlet of Hook Street, following signposted paths.

Lydiard House and Park

The present house, built in 1743, was saved from dereliction by the Swindon Corporation in 1943. Part of the property now serves as a hostel but the ground floor has been restored to its former glory, complete with ornate plasterwork, original family furnishings, a rare painted glass window, portraits of the St John family (the Bolingbrokes) who lived here from Elizabethan times, and lifelike waxworks.

As one of Wiltshire's smaller stately homes, Lydiard House has an intimate atmosphere rarely found in larger houses that have opened their doors to the public. Here you have the impression of stepping back in time to pay a social call on wealthy relations, members of a family that like many has had its share of ups and downs. Even the park has had its misfortunes; it was used as a prisoner of war camp at the end of the Second World War and later lost all the fine elm trees, which lined the driveway from 1911, to Dutch elm disease.

The Bolingbroke Family

During the Civil War the Bolingbrokes sided with the losing Royalists. Although rewarded at the Restoration, they were disappointed when Henry St John (1652–1742) was bestowed with the title of a 'mere' Viscount in 1712 rather than becoming an Earl. Rather too close a friendship with France in the early 18th century led to a period of exile for Henry before he received a royal pardon. In 1768 the Second Viscount, Frederick St John, sensationally for the time, divorced his wife, Lady Diana Spencer, daughter of the Duke of Marlborough. Further periods of 'absenteeism', this time to Germany and heavy mortgage liabilities

Above left: Late sunlight through trees in Lydiard Park

Left: The elegant Palladian mansion of Lydiard House

Below left: The lake in Lydiard Park was restored, with fountain, in a £5 million landscape scheme that began in 2005

finally saw the break up of the estate in the 1920s and 30s. The church contains a further history of the family in the form of memorials. Family trees, paintings, stained-glass windows and tomb effigies are all in evidence. The most impressive of the latter is The Golden Cavalier, a magnificent, lifesize, fully gilded statue of Sir John St John (1585–1648). He emerges from his tent fully clad for one of the Civil War battles. As imposing as he looks one cannot but think of the inner sadness of a man who in that conflict lost his king and three of his sons.

17 Lydiard Park – Swindon's Surprising Secret

Take a wander around a Palladian mansion and country park on Swindon's urban fringe

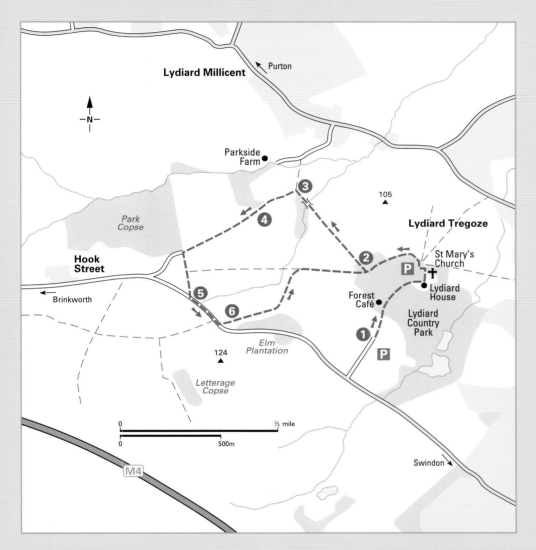

Distance 2.5 miles (4km)

Minimum Time 1hr

Ascent/Gradient 65ft (20m) ▲▲▲

Level of Difficulty ●●●

Paths Well-defined parkland paths and tracks, one stretch of quiet road

Landscape Farmland, parkland, woodland

Suggested Map OS Explorer 169 Cirencester & Swindon

Start/Finish Grid reference: SU 101844

Dog Friendliness Can be off lead in country park

Parking Free parking at Lydiard Country Park

Public Toilets Lydiard Country Park

---

1 Turn left out of the car park, pass the Forest Café and continue along the track to Lydiard House and the church. With the church on your right, bear left through the car park, ignoring the gate on your right, and go through another gate. Walk beside a walled garden and follow the path left into woodland.

2 Just before reaching a small clearing, turn right signposted 'Lydiard Millicent and Purton' to reach a gate on the woodland edge. Proceed straight ahead across the field on a defined path to a bridge spanning a stream.

3 Pass beneath electricity cables and turn left at a junction signposted 'West Park Circuit'. Follow the straight path with plantations to the right and at the next junction, with a path to Lydiard Millicent

on the right, turn left on the path marked West Park Circuit.

4 Keep woodland on the right and follow a broad track. Go through gates and continue ahead, avoiding a left-hand path back to Lydiard House. Keep ahead with hedgerow and trees to your right and at the first field corner bear right to the road at Hook Street.

5 Turn left, follow the narrow lane between fields and trees, pass under cables again and avoid a stile and footpath on the right. Turn left a few paces beyond it, through a galvanised kissing gate.

6 Bear right, following the field-edge, and make for a copse. Pass alongside it to reach a gate. Just beyond it turn left on to

a grassy path running alongside wire fencing. Follow it across a long rectangular pasture and swing right with the field boundary. Merge with a clearly defined track, with Lydiard House seen ahead framed by trees. Head for the clearing and retrace your steps back to the country park and car park.

Southeast England

Southeast England

There is an air of industriousness in the Southeast of England. Road and rail routes hum with ceaseless activity, and even the sky is seldom free from aircraft.

All the conurbations in the Southeast, especially London, are in a constant state of motion. Yet amid the hustle and bustle there are green oases of peace and calm to discover, an immensely long and complex history to unravel, ancient ways to travel, mysteries to ponder – and the best way to see it all is on foot. This region boasts a gentle, rolling landscape with no towering heights, essentially agricultural but well wooded in places, threaded by a fine assortment of paths and tracks. Substantial areas of rolling downs and coast have been designated Areas of Outstanding Natural Beauty, and there is a network of long-distance walks.

If one geographical feature has shaped Britain's history more than any other, it is the English Channel. The Channel was formed at the end of the last ice age and made Britain into an island, a place apart from the rest of Europe, but the journey towards becoming an island nation was long and bloody. Wave upon wave of invaders had to be accommodated and assimilated – in their turn came Celts, Romans, Saxons, Vikings and Normans; some were invaders and mercenaries, others missionaries or refugees. All left their mark on the landscape, language and national character. As you tread in the footsteps of packmen

and pilgrims, warriors and wayfarers, you see a landscape that has altered little, despite the passing of the centuries. The white cliffs of Dover, the Seven Sisters and other chalk cliffs form England's southern bulwark. The eastern coast is altogether gentler and lower-lying, often crumbling into the sea – sand and shingle are constantly on the move. The Southeast's long coastline is rich in maritime history.

Royal Patronage

King's Lynn in Norfolk (see Walk 33) was first a small settlement called Lynn (from the Celtic word for lake). It became a major centre of trade in the Middle Ages, first under control of the Bishop of Norwich when the town was known as Bishop's Lynn, then – after its riches caught the eye of King Henry VIII – under royal patronage, and renamed King's Lynn. St Margaret's Church in the heart of the town was founded by Herbert de Losinga, first Bishop of Norwich, in 1101.

Sandwich in Kent (see Walk 24) has a proud history dating back to Saxon times as a major fishing and trading town, and became one of the 'Cinque Ports' in south-eastern England whose ships and men guarded the country against attack in the days before there was an English navy.

Dickens and Other Literary Greats

Heading inland from the eastern coast, you can visit scenes from Charles Dickens' youth and old age in Rochester on the River Medway in Kent (see Walk 23). Dickens lived in Rochester as a boy, before moving with his family to London, and many years later returned to the area, now a rich and successful novelist, to live at Gad's Hill Place in nearby Higham (where he died in 1870). He set many scenes from his novels in Rochester: Restoration House in the town, renamed Satis House in *Great Expectations* (1861) was Miss Havisham's refuge from the world, while Eastgate House features as Westgate House in *The Pickwick Papers* (1836–7).

Other areas of literary and artistic interest in the Southeast include Hampstead Heath in London (see Walk 27): John Keats lived on the edge of the

Heath after 1817, fell in love with his neighbour Fanny Brawne and wrote major works including 'The Eve of St Agnes' and the ode 'To Autumn'. Walks on the heath offer fine views of many of the main sights of London laid out below; if you wish you can make a small detour from the planned walk to visit Kenwood House, a 17th-century house remodelled in 1764–79 by renowned neoclassical architect Robert Adam. Kenwood House contains a superb art collection bequeathed by Cecil Guinness, 1st Earl of Iveagh, which includes celebrated works by Rembrandt and Vermeer, while film fans may like to know that parts of the 1999 hit *Notting Hill* were filmed here. To the west of London, Pangbourne in Berkshire (see Walk 26) was a resort beside the River Thames in the early 20th century, when writers such as D. H. Lawrence visited. The town was also the home of Kenneth Grahame, author of the children's classic *The Wind in the Willows*.

Between the River Thames and the English Channel the landscape rises and falls according to the underlying geology, forming ridges such as the

Above: Freshwater Bay, on the Isle of Wight

Above left: Goodwood House in West Sussex

Left: Poppies add colour to a field of wheat at Alfriston, East Sussex

Previous pages: Horsey Mill, Norfolk Broads

Best of the Rest

Devil's Dyke

Legend has it that the Devil himself made this steep-sided valley on the South Downs Way in Sussex (see Walk 21). He wanted to dig a channel for the sea to flow in and sweep away the local churches, but – according to the story – was disturbed by a woman whose lighting of a candle made him flee in the belief that dawn was approaching. In reality the formation, half a mile (800m) in length and 300ft (91m) deep, was created by water flowing off the South Downs at the end of the last ice age.

Great Dixter

The country house of Great Dixter in East Sussex (see Walk 22) contains a magnificent timber-framed Great Hall measuring 40 by 25ft (12 by 8m) and 31ft (9.5m) in height, and built in c.1440–54. The house, which was restored by English architect Edwin Lutyens for Nathaniel Lloyd in 1910-11, also has a splendid half-timbered front and porch, and beautiful gardens cared for by Nathaniel Lloyd's son, Christopher, until his death in 2006.

Stowe

One of England's most beautiful mansions set in an idyllic landscaped garden, Stowe House in Berkshire (see Walk 28) showcases the work of many of the country's leading 18th-century architects and gardeners including Sir John Vanbrugh, William Kent, James Gibbs, Charles Bridgeman and Lancelot 'Capability' Brown. The house was built in 1676–83 by Sir Richard Temple, 3rd baronet, but reworked in the 18th century. The surrounding park contains more than 30 picturesque classical temples and 'ruins' including the Temple of Venus and Temple of Ancient Virtue, both built by Kent, and the Temple of Bacchus and the Egyptian Pyramid designed by Vanbrugh.

Southwold

The north Suffolk town of Southwold (see Walk 31) was a bustling holiday resort in the late Victorian era. Its pier, built in 1899, was damaged in a storm in 1934, then put out of action in the Second World War due to fears that invading forces might target the town, but was restored in 2001. Today Southwold is an attractive seaside town, with a working lighthouse, and a colourful beach huts along the beach. Not least among its attractions is the locally brewed Adnams beer. Many film and TV celebrities own second homes in the town.

Blakeney Eye

The National Trust Blakeney Eye nature reserve in north Norfolk (see Walk 34) is the perfect place for a relaxing and invigorating walk, whether or not you are a birdwatcher, with a wealth of views across vegetation, beach, waves and Blakeney Point's sand and shingle peninsula. The spot was favoured by Victorian gentlemen dedicated to shooting and collecting waterfowl and rare birds, but since National Trust's arrival in 1912 the many species have been protected. Blakeney village was a significant medieval port before the creeks connecting it to the sea silted up: it has attractive streets of cottages, as well as a 15th-century church and 14th-century Guildhall.

Stockbridge

This Hampshire market town stands on the River Test and is a premier centre for trout fishing (see Walk 19). As you walk along the river you can see thatched fishing huts and iron traps once used for eel fishing. In the 19th century the town was associated with horse racing, and had no fewer than nine racing stables. The track – which stood above town on Stockbridge Down – held races that rivalled those at Ascot and Goodwood in importance. You can still visit the grandstand.

North Downs, Weald and South Downs. The North Downs Way footpath runs from Farnham all the way to Dover (see Walk 25). Parts of it follow the medieval Pilgrims' Way that ran from Winchester to Canterbury and was followed by Geoffrey Chaucer's pilgrims in his masterpiece of the 1300s, *The Canterbury Tales*. As you pass from Sussex to Kent there are apple orchards and hop gardens to delight the eye.

If you continue around the coast to Beachy Head, the South Downs Way offers a fine route inland. On the South Downs you will encounter one of Britain's most celebrated and attractive racecourses – the home of the prestigious summer flat horse-racing festival of 'Glorious Goodwood' (see Walk 20). The course lies north of the Trundle Iron Age hill-fort, which can be used as a vantage point by spectators, and on the estate of Goodwood House, home of the Duke of Richmond.

A Great Poet on the Isle of Wight

Off England's southern coast, the Isle of Wight offers a splendid network of well-marked paths and trails, which – though of limited compass – provide spectacular views of cliffs, gentle downs and lush woodlands. The island holds further delights for those interested in literature (see Walk 18). West Wight was home to English poet Alfred, Lord Tennyson from 1853 and at Farringford House or on the nearby down that today bears his name he wrote celebrated poems including 'The Charge of the Light Brigade' and the 'Idylls of the King'. You can pay your respects at the Tennyson Monument, a large granite cross erected on Tennyson Down, or visit All Saints' Church to see the grave of the poet's wife, Lady Emily.

North of the River Thames and London the only high ground is formed by the chalk escarpment of the Chilterns, famous for their well-established beech woods. You can traverse a stretch of the ancient Icknield Way along their foot or climb to Ivinghoe Beacon, Combe Hill or other notable heights to enjoy the view. While the landscape may look monotonously agricultural, and flatter than the uplands to the north and west, it repays careful exploration, especially in terms of its hidden secrets and historic interest.

Constable Country and into Norfolk

It's possible to drive across Suffolk and Norfolk and be aware only of the vast prairie-like fields, but take a walk through the landscape and you will be astounded by its variety and complexity. In Suffolk don't miss the idyllic Constable Country in Dedham Vale (see Walk 30), where you can stand in the very spot once occupied by English landscape artist John Constable when he created such masterpieces as *The Hay Wain*, *The White Horse* or *Boat Building at Flatford Mill*. In Norfolk,

Thetford Forest (see Walk 32) was one of the first areas planted by the Forestry Commission after its foundation in 1919 and it now covers more than 50,000 acres (20,250ha). In Cambridgeshire you can visit one of the country's oldest nature reserves at Wicken Fen (see Walk 29), founded by the National Trust in 1899 but since expanded to 1,600 acres (648ha) and a haven for beetles and spiders, as well as many exotic plants including rare orchids.

Top: The Guildhall, King's Lynn, Norfolk, was built in around 1410

Above: Curious thatched boat houses at Hickling Broad, Norfolk

Far left: Blakeney, Norfolk

18 Tennyson's Freshwater

From lofty downland with magnificent coastal views to tranquil estuary scenes, this exhilarating walk explores the landscape the Victorian poet loved so well

West Wight is a quiet area of great natural beauty, offering open countryside, rugged cliffs, wonderful views and a fascinating wildlife. This walk encapsulates the contrasting landscapes of the area, from the wildlife-rich tidal estuary of the River Yar to magnificent chalk headlands and hills with their breathtaking views.

The 'Most Beautiful View in England'

Of the many literary greats who sought seclusion and inspiration on the island during the 19th century, the poet Alfred, Lord Tennyson was probably the foremost. He chose to reside in West Wight, where he and his wife Emily came to Farringford House, a castellated late-Georgian house (now a hotel) set in parkland beneath Tennyson Down, in 1853. From the drawing room he could look out across Freshwater Bay and the slopes of Afton Down, a view he believed to be the most beautiful in England – 'Mediterranean in its richness and charm'.

Almost daily he would take long solitary walks across the chalk downland, enjoying the bracing air, which he declared to be 'worth sixpence a pint'. The island inspired some of his greatest poems. 'The Charge of the Light Brigade' was written on the Down that now bears his name, and 'Maud', 'Enoch Arden' and the 'Idylls of the King' at Farringford.

A Cultural Centre

Tennyson's poetry was so popular that he soon became one of the richest poets in the country. He soon changed the face of West Wight, as tiny Freshwater became the cultural centre of England, attracting the most eminent Victorians of his age – Charles Kingsley, Garibaldi, Lewis Carroll, Charles Darwin, Prince Albert, to name but a few.

Farringford was the perfect place to entertain friends and celebrities, despite or perhaps because of its remoteness, but it was the time spent alone wandering the Downs or with his wife Emily in their fine garden that made Farringford so special to Tennyson. Eventually he and Emily bought a house on the mainland and returned to Farringford only for the winter, when they would be undisturbed.

Memories and Memorials

Alfred died in 1892 and Emily in 1896. Memories of the poet and his family are dotted along this walk. On Tennyson Down, you will find the granite monument erected in his honour in 1897. You can take lunch or afternoon tea at Farringford Hotel. In Freshwater, step inside All Saints Church to view the memorials to the family, while in the peaceful churchyard you will find Emily's grave and a lovely view across the serene estuary of the River Yar.

Below: Cliffs and beach at Freshwater Bay

Bottom left: Looking along the coast from the Freshwater Bay viewpoint, with Tennyson Down in the distance

Bottom right: The Tennyson Monument on Tennyson Down

18 Tennyson's Freshwater

Tread in the poet's footsteps as you cross Tennyson Down and enjoy wonderful sea views

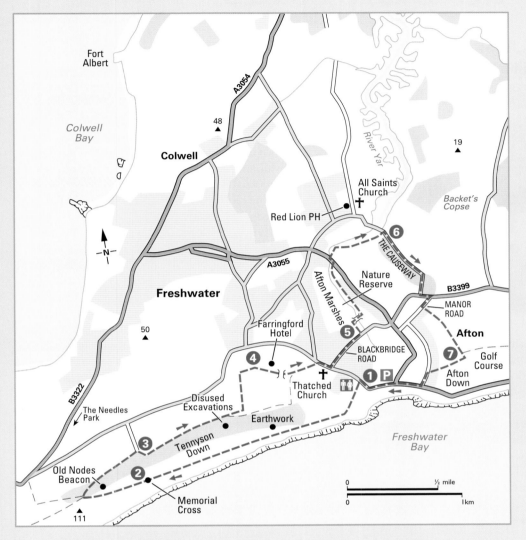

Distance 5.75 miles (9.2km)

Minimum Time 3hrs

Ascent/Gradient 623ft (190m) ▲▲▲

Level of Difficulty ●●●

Paths Downland, field and woodland paths, some road walking and stretch of disused railway, 4 stiles

Landscape Downland, farmland, freshwater marsh and salt marsh

Suggested Map OS Explorer OL29 Isle of Wight

Start/Finish Grid reference: SZ 346857

Dog Friendliness Let off lead on Tennyson Down and along old railway

Parking Pay-and-display car park at Freshwater Bay

Public Toilets Freshwater Bay and Yarmouth

1 From the car park, turn right along the road, then left before the bus shelter along a metalled track, signed 'Coastal Path'. After 50yds (46m) bear right through a gate and follow the well-walked path through a gateway and up to the memorial cross at the summit of Tennyson Down.

2 Continue down the wide grassy swathe, which narrows between gorse bushes, to reach the replica of the Old Nodes Beacon. Here, turn very sharp right down a chalk track. At a junction (car park right) keep straight on up the narrow path.

3 The path widens, then descends to a gate into woodland. Proceed close to the woodland fringe before emerging into more open countryside. Just beyond a disused pit on

your right, fork left at a waymark post down a narrower path. Cross a stile, then follow the enclosed path as it turns sharp left to a stile. Cross the next field to a stile and turn right along the field-edge to a stile.

4 Cross a farm track, go through a gate and walk along the track beside Farringford Hotel. Pass beneath a wooden footbridge and continue downhill to a gate and the road. Turn left if you wish to visit the hotel, otherwise turn right then, opposite the thatched church, turn left down Blackbridge Road. Just before Black Bridge, turn left into Afton Marshes Nature Reserve.

5 Join the nature trail, following it across a footbridge and beside the stream to the A3055 – this can be very wet in winter. Turn

left and almost immediately cross over to join the bridleway along the course of the old railway. In 0.5 mile (800m) you reach the Causeway. Turn left here to visit Freshwater church and the Red Lion.

6 Turn right and continue to the B3399, then left and shortly cross on to unmetalled Manor Road. In a few paces, bear left, signed 'Freshwater Way', and from this point ascend across grassland towards Afton Down.

7 Keep ahead at a junction of paths beside the golf course, soon to follow the gravel track right to the clubhouse. Go through a gate, pass in front of the building to reach the access track, keeping left to the A3055. Turn right downhill into Freshwater Bay.

19 A 'Testing' Trail From Stockbridge

Tales of fish, fillies and forts accompany you on this downland walk to the Danebury Hill Iron Age hill-fort from England's trout-fishing capital, Stockbridge

Above: The walk's return leg leads through the village of Longstock

Right: The charming High Street at Stockbridge

Below: A thatched fishing hut in the middle of the River Test, where eels were caught in traps made from hazel – and later iron

Stockbridge has developed from a frontier stronghold, built across the Test Valley by the Saxons to defend Wessex from marauding Danes, and a prosperous market town attracting Welsh sheep drovers en route to the markets in Surrey and Kent, to become Hampshire's 'fishing capital'. The clean waters of the River Test – one of England's finest chalk streams – are renowned for their trout fishing. On your journey down the long main street you will cross at least six branches of the Test and a short diversion on to Common Marsh will give you rare access to the river bank.

Most Select Fishing

Much of the river bank in this area is reserved exclusively for wealthy fishing syndicates. The imposing 17th-century Grosvenor Hotel is the headquarters of the oldest and most select fishing club in the world, the Houghton Club, founded in 1822. Membership is limited to 24 and the club rigorously controls the fishing of the Test.

Towards the end of your walk, as you cross the valley at Longstock, you will see one of the distinctive thatched fishing huts that are dotted along the river bank. Behind the hut and hidden in the reeds are the remains of a 'Danish Dock', built to harbour flat-bottomed longboats. These may have belonged to King Canute, who in the 11th century sailed up the Test and destroyed Romsey.

Horse Racing – and an Ancient Fort

Before fishing for sport dominated village life, Stockbridge was a famous horse-racing centre. In 1753–1898 a racecourse existed high on the downs above the village and was a venue for important meetings in the racing calendar, on a par with Ascot and Goodwood. At its peak the area had nine racing stables. You can still see the old, ivy-covered stadium across the field below Chattis Hill as you make your way towards Danebury Hill.

Your long climb out of the Test Valley culminates at an Iron Age hill-fort on top of Danebury Hill. The ancient earthwork covers an area of 13 acres (5.3ha) and is a magnificent sight, with a double bank and ditch and an inner rampart up to 16ft (5m) high. It was occupied by the Atrebates, a Celtic people, from about 550 to 100 BC and excavations have revealed a detailed picture of Iron Age society. Discoveries include a pattern of streets, circular houses, shrines and storage pits, and over 100,000 pieces of pottery. You can see many of the best finds in the Iron Age Museum in Andover.

19 A 'Testing' Trail From Stockbridge

Climb from a former Saxon stronghold to view an even older fortress – the Iron Age Danebury hill-fort

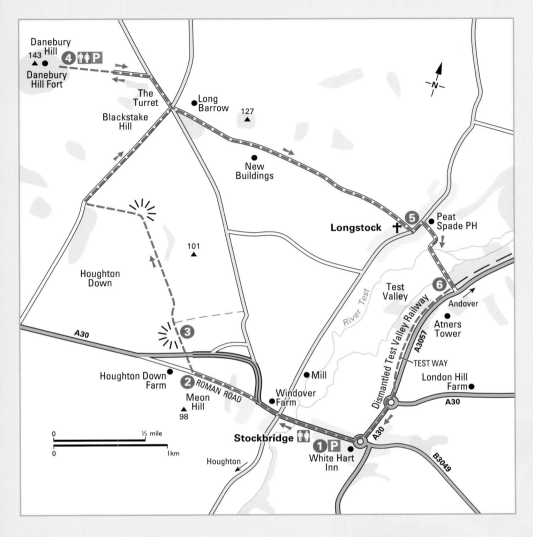

Distance 7 miles (11.3km)

Minimum Time 3hrs 30min

Ascent/Gradient 492ft (150m) ▲▲▲

Level of Difficulty ●●●

Paths Wide byways, field paths and railway track, 3 stiles

Landscape Open downland and river valley

Suggested Map OS Explorer 131 Romsey, Andover & Test Valley

Start/Finish Grid reference: SU 355351

Dog Friendliness Can run free on Danebury Hill (prohibited in hill-fort area)

Parking Along Stockbridge High Street

Public Toilets Danebury Hill (April to October) and Stockbridge

1 Walk west along the main street (A30), crossing the numerous braided streams of the River Test. Begin the climb out of the village and, just after the start of the dual carriageway, bear off to the left along Roman Road. Keep ahead at the end of the road, walking along the narrow defined path that climbs Meon Hill.

2 Just before Houghton Down Farm on your left, look out for a stile in the hedge on your right. Cross this and walk along the right-hand edge of a small orchard to a stile. Cross the A30, taking care, then walk through the gap opposite and along the right-hand edge of a large field.

3 Ignore the footpath turning on the right and keep to the main path, eventually bearing left with the field-edge to a grassy

track leading to a gate and stile. Turn immediately right along a wide, hedged track and follow this for 0.75 mile (1.2km) to a junction. To visit Danebury Hill Fort, turn left towards The Wallops for 400yds (366m), then left again along the drive to the car park and access to Danebury Hill.

4 Retrace your steps back to the road junction you passed before Danebury Hill and take the byway to the left beneath a height barrier. Remain on this track as it descends back into the Test Valley. It becomes metalled as it enters the village of Longstock.

5 At the T-junction by the church turn left, then right beside the Peat Spade pub, along 'The Bunny'. Cross numerous streams that make up the River Test, notably one with a fishing hut and replica metal eel traps.

6 Just before crossing a bridge over the disused Test Valley railway, and the A3057, take the narrow footpath on the right. Drop down and turn right along the old railway trackbed (here forming a part of the Test Way) for about a mile (1.6km) to the A3057. Taking great care, turn right, walking along the roadside for 100yds (91m) to the roundabout, then follow the grassy verge to the next roundabout by the White Hart Inn. Turn right here to return to Stockbridge and your car.

20 Good Going at 'Glorious Goodwood' Racecourse

From a country park, this well-planned walk takes you past the scene of a famous 18th-century hunt and up to see the Goodwood racecourse on the South Downs

Think of horse racing on the South Downs and you immediately think of Goodwood, without doubt one of Britain's loveliest and most famous racecourses. The course rises and falls around a natural amphitheatre, with the horses dashing along the ridge to create one of the greatest spectacles in the racing world.

Its superb position, high on the Downs, amid magnificent beechwoods, draws crowds from far and wide, and for one week every summer it becomes 'Glorious Goodwood' when thousands of racegoers travel to Sussex to attend one of the most prestigious events of the sporting and social calendar. According to The Times, Goodwood is 'the place to be and to be seen'.

The course opened in 1801 after the Duke of Richmond gave part of his estate, Goodwood Park, to establish a track where members of

the Goodwood Hunt Club and officers of the Sussex Militia could attend meetings. However, Goodwood's track record has not always been unblemished. Towards the end of the 19th century the racecourse acquired a rather unfortunate reputation in the area when the rector of nearby Singleton protested to the Chief Constable in the strongest terms over the rowdy behaviour of racegoers. As a result, the crowds were restrained.

The Charlton Hunt

The walk begins at Goodwood Country Park, a popular amenity area characterised by woodland and downland grass, and initially follows part of the Monarch's Way through extensive woodland, down to the village of East Dean. Along the road is neighbouring Charlton, famous for the Charlton Hunt. Established in the 18th century, the hunt's most memorable chase took place on 28th January 1738, beginning before eight that morning and not finishing until nearly six that evening. Many of those taking part were from the upper ranks of society; for ten hours that day a fox led the pack a merry dance in the surrounding fields and woods. Eventually, the hounds cornered their prey, an elderly vixen, near the River Arun.

If time allows, you may want to extend the walk at this point and visit the Weald and Downland Museum. The main walk finishes by skirting Goodwood and on race days crowds line the bridleway alongside it, watching as television camera crews dash back and forth. The sound of the PA system floats across the course as you witness all the colourful activity.

Right: Making a horseshoe at a smithy in the open-air Weald and Downland Museum

Below: Goodwood House hosts an annual Festival of Speed for vintage cars such as this 1937 Bugatti 575 Corsica Drophead

Below right: The view from the grandstand at Goodwood race course takes in the beauties of the surrounding countryside

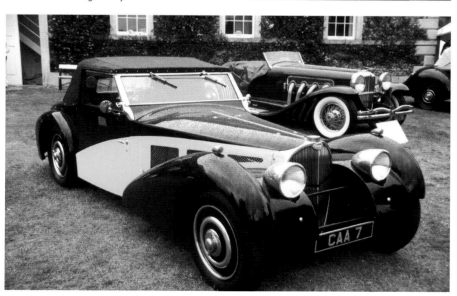

20 Good Going at 'Glorious Goodwood' Racecourse

Try a country pub or a visit to an open-air museum on the way to one of Britain's best known racecourses

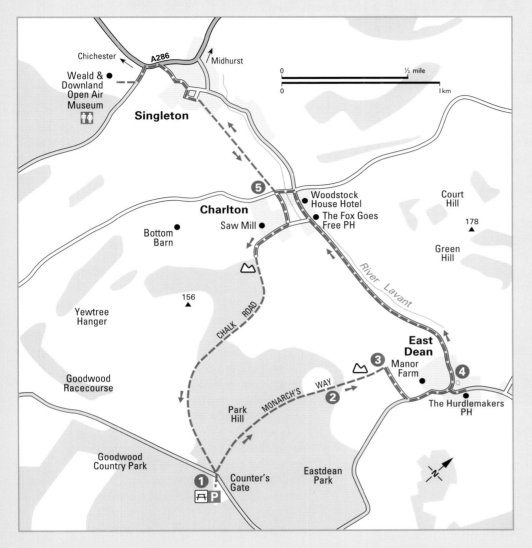

Distance 3.5 miles (5.7km)

Minimum Time 1hr 30min

Ascent/Gradient 328ft (100m) ▲▲▲

Level of Difficulty ●●●

Paths Woodland tracks and field paths, section of Monarch's Way and one lengthy stretch of quiet road, 4 stiles

Landscape Mixture of dense woodland and scenic downland

Suggested Map OS Explorer 120 Chichester, South Harting & Selsey or 121 Arundel & Pulborough

Start/Finish Grid Reference: SU 897113 (on Explorer 120)

Dog Friendliness Can run free on woodland tracks

Parking Counter's Gate free car park and picnic area at Goodwood Country Park or large free car park opposite racecourse

Public Toilets Weald and Downland Open Air Museum

1 Make for the western end of Counter's Gate car park and look for a footpath sign by an opening leading out to the road. Cross over to a junction of two clear tracks, with a path on the right. Follow the right-hand track, which is signposted 'public footpath' and part of the Monarch's Way, to a gate and stile. Continue to the next gate and stile and then cross a clearing in the woods.

2 Follow the gently curving path over the grassy, plant-strewn ground and down between trees to reach a gateway. Head diagonally right down the steep field slope to reach a stile in the corner.

3 Cross into the adjacent field and follow the boundary to a second stile leading out to the road. Bear left and walk down into East Dean, passing Manor Farm. Keep right at the junction in the village centre and, if it is opening time, why not follow the road for a short distance towards Petworth in order to visit The Hurdlemakers pub?

4 Leave East Dean by keeping the pond on your right-hand side and follow the road towards Midhurst and Singleton. On reaching Charlton village, pass The Fox Goes Free pub and the Woodstock House Hotel and take the next left turning. Follow the lane to a stile on the right and a turning on the left. If you are interested in investigating traditional village life at the Weald and Downland Open Air Museum at Singleton, cross over into the fields and follow the straight path. After your visit, return to this stile by the same route and take the road opposite.

5 Walk along to the junction and turn right by the war memorial, dedicated to fallen comrades of the Sussex Yeomanry in both world wars. Follow Chalk Road, which dwindles to a track on the outskirts of Charlton. Once clear of the village, the track climbs steadily between the trees. On the left are glimpses of a glorious, rolling landscape, while to the right Goodwood's superb downland racecourse edges into view between the trees. Follow the track all the way to the road and cross over to return to the Counter's Gate car park.

21 Devil's Dyke and 'the World's Grandest View'

There is steep climbing en route, but the spectacular and justly praised views from the beauty spot of Devil's Dyke make up for any amount of exertion

Above: Purple common spotted orchid

Below: Views stretch for miles in all directions

Sussex is rich in legend and folklore and the Devil and his fiendish works crop up all over the county. The local landmark of Devil's Dyke is a prime example – perfectly blending the natural beauty of the South Downs with the mystery and originality of ancient mythology. Few other fables in this part of the country seem to have caught the public imagination in quite the same way.

Devil's Dyke is a geological quirk, a spectacular, steep-sided downland combe or cleft 300ft (91m) deep and half a mile (800m) long. According to legend, it was dug by the Devil as part of a trench extending to the sea. The idea was to try to flood the area with sea water and, in so doing, destroy the churches of the Weald. However, it seems the Devil might have been disturbed by a woman carrying a candle. Mistaking this for the dawn, he quickly disappeared, leaving his work unfinished.

It's a charming tale but the reality of how Devil's Dyke came to be is probably a good deal less interesting. No one knows for sure how it originated, but it was most likely to have been cut by glacial meltwaters when the ground was permanently frozen in the ice age.

Rising to over 600ft (183m), this most famous of beauty spots is also a magnificent viewpoint.

The Clayton Windmills are visible on a clear day, as is Chanctonbury Ring; the artist John Constable described this view as the grandest in the world.

Victorian Crowds

Devil's Dyke has long been a tourist honeypot. During the Victorian era and in the early part of the 20th century, the place was akin to a bustling theme park with a cable car crossing the valley and a steam railway coming up from Brighton.

On Whit Monday 1893, a staggering 30,000 people visited Devil's Dyke. In 1928 HRH the Duke of York dedicated the Dyke Estate for the use of the public forever and in fine weather it can seem just as crowded as it was in Queen Victoria's day. With the car park full and the surrounding downland slopes busy with people simply taking a relaxing stroll in the sunshine, Devil's Dyke assumes the feel of a seaside resort at the height of the season.

Hang-gliders swoop silently over the grassy downland like pterodactyls and kite flyers spill from their cars in search of fun and excitement. But don't let the crowds put you off. The views more than make up for the invasion of visitors, and away from the chalk slopes and the car park the walk soon heads for more peaceful surroundings.

21 Devil's Dyke and 'the World's Grandest View'

See the views – as far as Haywards Heath and the Ashdown Forest – that Constable praised so highly

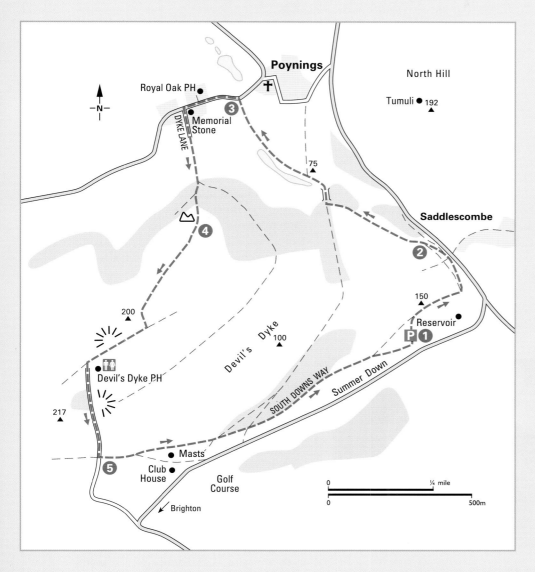

Distance 2.75 miles (4.4km)

Minimum Time 1hr 30min

Ascent/gradient 656ft (200m) ▲▲▲

Level of difficulty ●●●

Paths Field and woodland paths, 7 stiles

Landscape Chalk grassland, steep escarpment and woodland

Suggested Map OS Explorer 122 Brighton & Hove

Start/Finish Grid reference: TQ 269112

Dog Friendliness Mostly off lead. On lead on approach to Poynings

Parking Summer Down free car park

Public Toilets By Devil's Dyke pub

1 From the Summer Down car park go through the kissing gate and then veer right. Join the South Downs Way and follow it alongside lines of trees. Soon the path curves left and drops down to the road. Part company with the South Downs Way at this point, as it crosses over to join the private road to Saddlescombe Farm, and follow the verge for about 75yds (69m). Bear left at the footpath sign and drop down the bank to a stile.

2 Follow the line of the tarmac lane as it curves right to reach a waymark. Leave the lane and walk ahead alongside power lines, keeping the line of trees and bushes on the right. Look for a narrow path disappearing into the vegetation and make for a stile. Drop down some steps into the woods and turn right at a junction with a bridleway. Take the path running off half left and follow it between fields and a wooded dell. Pass over a stile and continue to a stile in the left boundary. Cross a footbridge to a further stile and now turn right towards Poynings.

3 Head for a gate and footpath sign and turn left at the road. Follow the parallel path along to the Royal Oak and then continue to Dyke Lane on the left. There is a memorial stone here, dedicated to the memory of George Stephen Cave Cuttress, a resident of Poynings for more than 50 years, and erected by his widow. Follow the tarmac bridleway; soon it narrows to a path. On reaching the fork, by a National Trust sign for Devil's Dyke, veer right and begin climbing the steps.

4 Follow the path up to a gate and continue up the stairs. From the higher ground there are breathtaking views to the north and west. Make for a kissing gate and head up the slope towards the inn. Keep the Devil's Dyke pub on your left and take the road round to the left, passing a bridleway on the left. Follow the path parallel to the road and look to the left for a definitive view of Devil's Dyke.

5 Head for the South Downs Way and turn left by a National Trust sign for Summer Down to a stile and gate. Follow the trail, keeping Devil's Dyke down to your left, and eventually you reach a stile leading into Summer Down car park.

22 Great Dixter and its Gorgeous Gardens

A delightful ramble on the Sussex/Kent border highlights the creativity of a great architect and a gifted gardener in restoring a 15th-century house and grounds

Below: Mauve and red flowers (*Verbena Bonariensis*) growing in the beautifully kept gardens at Great Dixter

Below right: Many shades of green in Great Dixter garden

Below: The gardens run all the way around the house, so a walk in the gardens allows you to see the house in all its aspects

Deep in the tranquil, rolling countryside of East Sussex, close to the Kent border, lies the wonderful Great Dixter, one of the county's smaller and more intimate historic houses. Built in the middle of the 15th century and later restored and enlarged by Sir Edwin Lutyens, Great Dixter is a popular tourist attraction as well as a family home.

These days this fine Wealden hall-house is owned and cared for by Olivia Eller. It was the home of her late uncle, the gardening writer Christopher Lloyd, who died in 2006. Christopher's father, Nathaniel, instructed Lutyens in 1910 to make major changes to Great Dixter, which at that time was in a poor state of repair. His main task was to clear the house of later alterations. Typically, the work was undertaken with great sensitivity.

But Lutyens didn't stop there. While restoration plans were beginning to take shape, he and Nathaniel Lloyd seized the opportunity to improve and enlarge the house. A complete timber-framed yeoman's hall at Benenden in Kent, scheduled for demolition, was dismantled and moved to Great Dixter, adding an entire wing to the house.

Medieval Splendour

They created one of Great Dixter's most striking features – the magnificent Great Hall, which is the largest surviving timber-framed hall in the country. Visitors never fail to be impressed by its medieval splendour – and in particular by its hammer-beam roof. The half-timbered and plastered front and the Tudor porch also catch the eye.

The contents of Great Dixter date mainly from the 17th and 18th centuries and were collected over the years by Nathaniel Lloyd. The house also contains many examples of delicately fashioned needlework, which were completed by his wife Daisy and their children.

However, a tour of Great Dixter doesn't end with the house. The gardens are equally impressive. Christopher Lloyd spent many years working on this project, incorporating many medieval buildings, establishing natural ponds and designing yew topiary. The result is one of the most exciting and colourful gardens of modern times.

Lutyens was just as inventive in the gardens as in the house. He often used tiles in a decorative though practical manner, to great effect. At Great Dixter he took a chicken house with crumbling walls and transformed it into an open-sided loggia, supported by laminated tile pillars.

Impressive in All Seasons

Beginning in Northiam, the walk heads round the edge of the village before reaching the house at Great Dixter. Even out of season, when the place is closed, you gain a vivid impression of the house and its Sussex Weald setting. Passing directly in front of Great Dixter, the route then crosses rolling countryside to join the Sussex Border Path, following it all the way back to Northiam.

22 Great Dixter and its Gorgeous Gardens

Admire Great Dixter in the full beauty of its rural setting

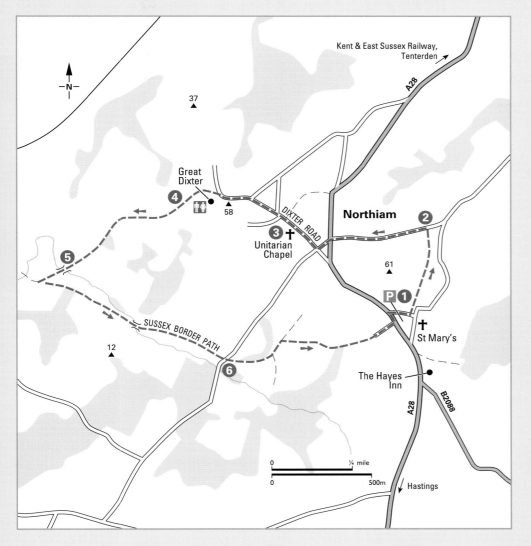

Distance 3 miles (4.8km)

Minimum Time 1hr 30min

Ascent/Gradient 98ft (30m) ▲▲▲

Level of Difficulty ●●●

Paths Field paths and quiet roads, 8 stiles

Landscape Undulating farmland and stretches of woodland

Suggested Map OS Explorer 125 Romney Marsh, Rye & Winchelsea

Start/Finish Grid Reference: TQ 828245

Dog Friendliness Dog stiles near Great Dixter and on Sussex Border Path

Parking Free car park on corner of Fullers Lane and A28, Northiam

Public Toilets Great Dixter, seasonal opening

1 Turn right out of the car park and walk along Fullers Lane towards St Mary's Church. Take the path on the left, signposted to Goddens Gill, and keep to the right edge of the field. Go through a gate in the corner and look for an oasthouse on the right. Make for a path on the far side of the field and follow it between fences towards a thatched cottage. Go through a gate to the road.

2 Turn left and head for the A28. Bear diagonally left across the A28 and follow Thyssel Lane signposted 'Great Dixter'. Turn right at the crossroads, following Dixter Road.

3 Pass the Unitarian Chapel and avoid the path on the right. Pass Higham Lane on the left and continue to follow the signs for Great Dixter. Disregard a turning on the right

(Dixter Lane) and go straight on, following a path between trees and hedges, parallel to the main drive to the house.

4 Pass the toilets and head towards a cattle grid. Cross the stile just to the left of it and follow the path signposted to Ewhurst. Follow the waymarks and keep the hedge on the left. Cross a stile in the field corner and then head diagonally down the field slope to the next stile. Follow the path down the field slope.

5 Make for a footbridge and then turn left to join the Sussex Border Path. The path skirts the field before disappearing left into some woodland. Emerging from the trees, cut straight across the next field to two stiles and a footbridge. Keep the woodland on the left and look for a gap in the trees. Cross a stream

to a stile and bear right. Follow the right edge of the field and keep on the Sussex Border Path until you reach the road.

6 Cross over the lane to a drive. Bear left and follow the path to a stile. Pass alongside woodland and then veer slightly away from the trees to a stile in the approaching boundary. Cross it and go straight ahead up the field slope. Take the first footpath on the right and follow it to a gap in the field corner. Cross a footbridge under the trees and continue along the right-hand edge of the next field to join a drive. Bear left and follow it to the A28. Cross over to return to the car park at Northiam.

23 A Dickens of a Walk at Rochester

THE BULL HOTEL
THIS "GOOD HOUSE" WITH "NICE BEDS" DESCRIBED BY
MR. JINGLE IN "PICKWICK PAPERS", IS ALSO "THE BLUE
BOAR" IN "GREAT EXPECTATIONS".

A walk through the Rochester streets Charles Dickens knew as a boy summons the spirit of celebrated characters and places from his novels

In *Our Mutual Friend* (1865), Charles Dickens wrote of 'a ship's hull, with its rusty iron links of cable run out of hawse-holes long discoloured with the iron's rusty tears'. You pass a decaying ship just like this as you walk along the Medway from Rochester to Upnor, and the spirit of Charles Dickens (1812–70) is with you throughout this walk. In the streets of Rochester you'll half expect to meet genial Mr Pickwick coming out of a pub, or see mad Miss Havisham peering from a window still wearing her ancient wedding dress.

Charles Dickens came to live near Rochester in 1816 as a 'queer small boy' of five, and the area held a fascination for him throughout his life, inspiring much of his work. Wherever you go you pass places that featured in his novels. For instance there is Eastgate House, which appears as Westgate House in *The Pickwick Papers* (1836–37), and Restoration House, which was Satis House in *Great*

Above right: The Bull Hotel is one of many Rochester buildings mentioned in Dickens' novels

Right: The walk also visits the quaint High Street of Upper Upnor before returning to Rochester

Below: Rochester's splendid Norman cathedral was the focal point of Dickens' last, unfinished novel *The Mystery of Edwin Drood*

Expectations (1861), the mysterious home of Miss Havisham. Travel a few miles from Rochester to Cooling churchyard and you can see the tiny 'stone lozenges', the children's gravestones that feature in the opening passage of *Great Expectations*.

Rochester to London

Dickens' life in Rochester was happy, although he was a delicate child and never enjoyed good health. However, when his family moved to London a few years later, his life changed. His father John, who always lived above his means, fell deeply into debt and was sent to the Marshalsea Debtor's Prison. Dickens had to work in a blacking factory to help support the family, an experience that shamed him and haunted him throughout his life. He went to work at an attorney's office at the age of 15, but was so keen to write that he taught himself shorthand and eventually found work as a journalist. In 1836 his first novel, *The Pickwick Papers*, was published.

The Writer Returns

His books made him wealthy and in 1856 Dickens bought Gad's Hill Place near Rochester, a house he had dreamed of owning since he was a child. Here he would write, entertain fellow authors like Hans Christian Andersen and Wilkie Collins, and go for long walks beside the desolate Medway marshes, just as he used to do with his father.

He loved to work in an ornate Swiss chalet, which he built in his garden. It had been sent to him as a gift by a friend and arrived, IKEA style, flat-packed in boxes. The chalet has now been moved and is in the centre of Rochester, by Eastgate House. Dickens died at Gad's Hill in 1870.

23 A Dickens of a Walk at Rochester

Summon memories of *The Pickwick Papers* and *Great Expectations* in a tour of Rochester's characterful streets

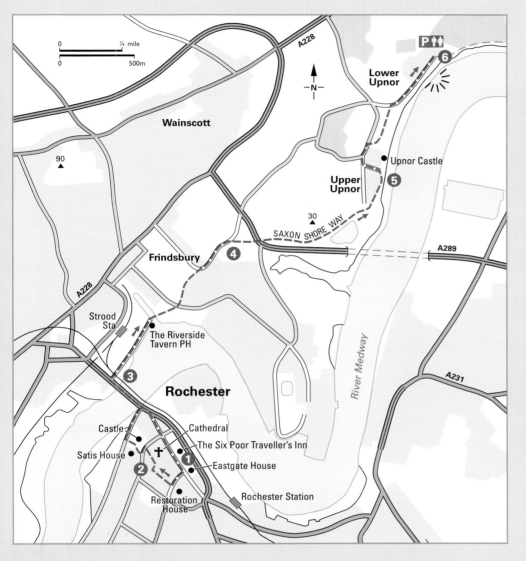

Distance 6 miles (9.7km)

Minimum Time 3hrs

Ascent/Gradient 98ft (30m) ▲▲▲

Level of Difficulty ●●●

Paths City streets and footpaths/cycleways

Landscape Historic townscapes and some rundown riverside sections

Suggested Map OS Explorer 163 Gravesend & Rochester

Start/Finish Grid reference: TQ 744685

Dog Friendliness Too busy for most dogs

Parking Blue Boar car park (fee)

Public Toilets At tourist information centre, also at Northgate

1 From the Blue Boar car park go left into the pedestrianised part of the High Street. Turn right up Crow Lane, then right by Restoration House into The Vines, a small park. Bear right half-way across the park, then turn right and walk down the hill to the cathedral.

2 Cross the road, turn left and walk round the castle. Pass Satis House, then turn right and walk by the River Medway until you reach Rochester Bridge. Cross the bridge and, at the traffic lights, go right along Canal Road, which runs under the railway bridge.

3 Walk along the river, pass The Riverside Tavern and follow the footpath sign. This brings you out to a new estate where you bear right along a footpath/cycle track, which is

part of the Saxon Shore Way. Keep walking in the same direction along this track, which is intersected by roads at several points. Watch out for the rusting hull of a ship.

4 At a bend in the road the Saxon Shore Way bears right, crosses industrial land and the A289, and then finally takes you close to the river bank again. At the river continue walking ahead as far as the entrance to Upnor Castle.

5 Turn left along Upnor's tiny, and extremely quaint, High Street, and then go to the right. Where a road joins from the left, keep walking ahead to join the footpath that runs to the right of the main road. Follow this to Lower Upnor, where you turn right to reach the quay and enjoy great views of the Medway. For even

better views, take a short detour up the hill to your left. Prehistoric wild animals once roamed these slopes, as archaeological evidence shows. One of the most interesting discoveries in the area was made in 1911, when a group of Royal Engineers working near Upnor dug up the remains of a mammoth dating back to the last ice age. It was taken to the Natural History Museum in London.

6 Retrace your steps back into Rochester. After crossing Rochester Bridge walk along the High Street, passing sights such as The Six Poor Travellers' Inn and Eastgate House, which is located beside the Blue Boar car park.

24 A Taste of Sandwich

From the medieval port of Sandwich a walk full of historic interest leads further back in time to Richborough Fort, dug in the Roman invasion of Britain in AD 43

Above: The inner defences of Richborough Fort – the fort was a supply base for the invading Roman army under Aulus Plautius

Below: Today the only waterborne vessels in the former port of Sandwich are pleasure boats on the River Stour

As you walk around Sandwich, you can't help but be struck by the town's picturesque appearance. With its half-timbered houses and historic churches, it has a quiet English charm. It's hard to imagine these narrow streets echoing with the footsteps of raiders, smugglers and pirates. Yet Sandwich was once the most important port in England – the Dover of its day – and was one of the original Cinque Ports.

The Cinque Ports (pronounced 'sink') was the name given to the confederation of five (later seven) important ports on the south-east coast that guarded England in the days before there was an official navy. Hastings, New Romney, Dover, Hythe and Sandwich, together with Rye and Winchelsea, were important fishing and trading centres. This meant they had plenty of men and ships that the king could press into service, whether his family wanted free transport to Europe or a force to repel invaders. It was convenient for the monarch – and in those days no one would argue.

By the 13th century, the towns had become so important to England that they were formally granted rights and privileges. These included freedom from taxes and customs duties, some trading concessions, and even their own courts. In return, each town had to supply a quota of men and ships whenever required. It was a pretty good deal and provided opportunities for merchants to make money. The Cinque Ports became some of the richest and most powerful centres in Europe.

Merchants, Smugglers and Pirates

The quay at Sandwich, now so quiet, would have bustled in those days as fighting men embarked for Europe, and ships laden with valuable cargoes of silks, spices and wine were unloaded. It would have been intimidating, too, for smugglers and pirates operated from here, attracted by the rich pickings on offer. All the ports had a violent reputation.

However, their power and influence was not to last. A terrible storm in 1287 permanently altered the coastline. The sea began to retreat and the harbour at Sandwich, and other ports, eventually became so choked with silt they could no longer be used. After a permanent navy was established the privileges of the Cinque Ports were revoked and Sandwich sank back into relative obscurity.

24 A Taste of Sandwich

Follow a gentle trail around this picturesque town

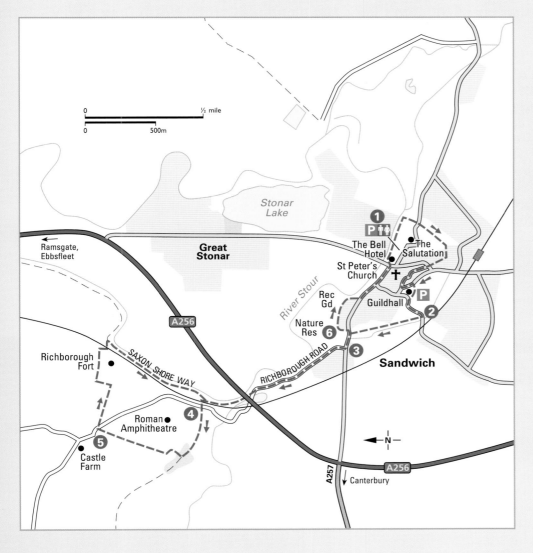

Distance 3 miles (4.8km)

Minimum Time 1hr 30min

Ascent/Gradient 98ft (30m) ▲▲▲

Level of Difficulty ●●●

Paths Easy town streets and field tracks, 9 stiles

Landscape Townscape, salt flats, golf course and beach

Suggested Map OS Explorer 150 Canterbury & The Isle of Thanet

Start/Finish Grid reference: TR 332582

Dog Friendliness Pretty good, can run free in some sections

Parking Car park (fee) at Sandwich Quay

Public Toilets New Street and the Quay, Sandwich and Sandwich Bay

1 Walk along the river bank away from the town, following the line of the old wall. At a bend in the river, turn right along a tarmac path to the road. Turn right, then left and continue along the path, passing the bowling green. Next turn right down steps into Mill Wall Place. When you reach the crossroads, go straight ahead along King Street, passing St Peter's Church, and then turn left along the intriguingly titled No Name Street. Afterwards cross New Street to the Guildhall, then walk though the car park and up to the Rope Walk, where rope makers used this long, straight area to lay out their ropes.

2 Turn right and when you reach the road, cross over and walk down The Butts. At the main road turn left, cross over and turn right up Richborough Road.

3 Walk ahead, past a scrapyard, and through a gate to join a footpath on the right. Follow the track round, under the main road and turn left to cross the railway line via stiles.

4 Cross the road, go through a kissing gate, then walk across the field to the trees, heading for the third telegraph pole. The path now goes into the trees: where it splits, fork right to a stile. Now follow the fence line and turn right at the marker beyond a ditch to reach a gate. Walk up the left-hand field-edge, cross a stile, go through a gate and cross a further stile to the road.

5 Cross over and walk up the track ahead. Richborough Fort is ahead. The track runs around the fort with expansive views over this seemingly endless landscape. At the

bottom of the track turn right along the end of a garden. Cross the stile and back over the railway, leaving it by another stile. The path now goes immediately right, over a bridge and back beside the river. You will eventually rejoin the road, and retrace your steps to the end of Richborough Road where you turn left.

6 Go left through a kissing gate, pass the Nature Reserve and go round the edge of a recreation ground. Bear right through trees and pass a car park to reach Strand Street and turn left. Go left in front of the Bell Hotel, and right past the Barbican and return to the car park.

25 The Puttenham Tales

Varied literary and historical associations add interest to a thoroughly engaging walk in the shadow of the Hog's Back and along part of the North Downs Way

The railway line no longer runs to Hayfield, high in the Peak District. With it have passed many of the 400 people who gathered at the little station for the mass trespass on Kinder Scout in 1932. But what has that to do with a gentle walk in the Surrey countryside? Have you stumbled into a different walk? Not at all. The 1930s saw an explosion of interest in walking, and the Kinder Scout trespass was a landmark along the way to the legislation which underpins the modern family of National Trails. First was the Pennine Way, opened in 1965; but other routes were soon to follow.

In September 1978 the North Downs Way was officially opened between Farnham and Dover, and you'll follow a section of it on your way through Puttenham. In many places, the route follows the old Pilgrims' Way that runs from Winchester, through Farnham and Guildford to Canterbury. The National Trail has a loop that allows modern-day pilgrims to visit Canterbury on their way to or from Dover, but you don't need to walk all the way to Archbishop Thomas à Becket's cathedral to enjoy a few stories of the road.

Sheridan's Mishap, Oglethorpe's Manor
About 400yds (366m) before you reach the North Downs Way, near the entrance to a Woodland Trust property on your right, you'll pass a bridleway which was part of the old carriage drive to Hampton Park. Legend has it that when poet and playwright Richard Brinsley Sheridan was visiting his friend Edward Long at Hampton in the early years of the 19th century, his coach turned over at this spot. Long subsequently planted seven trees to mark the route; one for each of his daughters.

A little further on, where a line of trees marks the path from Lascombe Farm out on to the common, you'll see the remains of an old wooden gate. This is Highfield Hatch, one of the 'hatches' or gates that were placed around the common to prevent grazing animals from straying on to the arable fields. General James Oglethorpe, who founded the American state of Georgia, bought the Puttenham estate in 1744. However, he actually lived in Godalming, and he sold the estate in 1761. The new owner demolished the little manor house, and built the Palladian mansion that you'll see from the footpath off Suffield Lane, just after leaving the North Downs Way. Although he renamed it The Priory (now called

Puttenham Priory), the building never had any religious connections. As you say goodbye to the North Downs Way, remember Hayfield – because, appropriately enough, the old railway trackbed has now been turned into a pleasant footpath.

25 The Puttenham Tales

Take a thought for pilgrims and others who have passed along what is now the North Downs Way

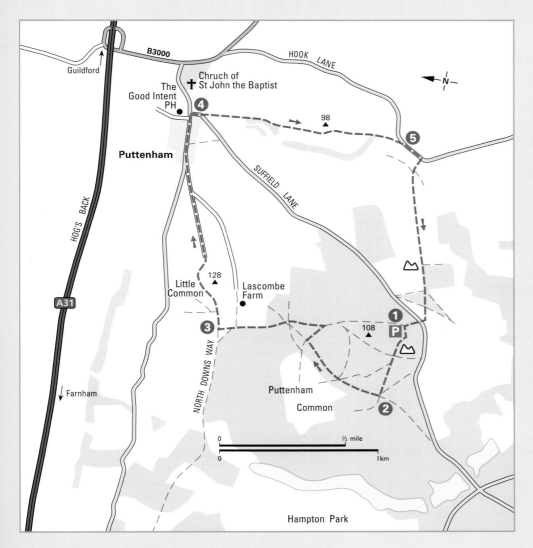

Distance 4 miles (6.4km)

Minimum Time 1hr 45min

Ascent/Gradient 295ft (90m) ▲▲▲

Level of Difficulty ●●●

Paths Woodland tracks and field-edge paths

Landscape Wooded heath and farmland

Suggested Map OS Explorer 145 Guildford & Farnham

Start/Finish Grid reference: SU 920461

Dog Friendliness Can run free on Puttenham Common, on lead in village

Parking Puttenham Common top car park

Public Toilets None en route

1 Head into the viewing area from the car park, dropping down into the trees with a wooden handrail running along on your right. Fork left through the woods, and bear right when the path forks again about 100yds (91m) further on. After 150yds (137m) cross another track at a clearing.

2 Turn right here opposite a green and mauve arrowed waymark post. Keep straight on until you reach another green and mauve banded waymark post 300yds (274m) further on. Fork right here, on to a narrow path that climbs gently through the bracken. Continue for 50yds (46m) beyond a line of electricity wires, then turn right, on to a broad sandy track. After 150yds (137m), turn sharp left on to a similar track. Pass a large red-brick house on your right, then, ignoring all turnings, follow the waymarked public bridleway all the way to the junction with the North Downs Way National Trail.

3 Turn sharp right here and follow the North Downs Way as it winds over Little Common and continues through Puttenham.

4 Turn right opposite The Good Intent, into Suffield Lane. As the lane swings to the right, nip over the stile by the public footpath signpost on your left, and follow the left-hand edge of an open field to the trees on the far side. Now take the waymarked route over a second stile to the left of the woods. Two more stiles now lead you away from the woods, keeping a post and wire fence on your right-hand side. Cross the stile beside a prominent oak tree and keep straight ahead, through the metal field gate. Bear right down a short, sharp slope towards the woods, and jump the stile leading out on to Hook Lane.

5 Turn right, and follow the road to the left-hand bend. Turn right again, over the stile by a public footpath sign. Two more stiles bring you to a right of way waymark; bear right here, and follow the post and wire fence on your right. Continue as far as a small wood, where you go through a kissing gate into an old sunken lane, and keep ahead for 150yds (137m) to a small waymark post. Continue straight on following public footpath signs to a T-junction with a public bridleway. Turn left and in 15yds (14m) turn right on a public footpath. Climb steeply here, for the short way back to Suffield Lane and the entrance to the car park where you started.

26 A Fashionable Riverside Resort at Pangbourne

Near an inland resort frequented by the elite of Edwardian England, this peaceful walk leads through countryside loved by the creator of *The Wind in the Willows*

During the Edwardian era the Thames-side settlement of Pangbourne became especially fashionable with artists, writers and anglers, yet apparently it did little to ignite the interest of one renowned literary figure. 'Pleasant house, hate Pangbourne, nothing happens', wrote D. H. Lawrence in 1919 when he and his wife rented a cottage in the village.

On the other hand, D. H. Evans, who founded the famous West End department store, clearly found Pangbourne to his liking. Towards the end of the 19th century he built seven very distinctive villas in the village. Known as the 'Seven Deadly Sins' and distinguished by domes, turrets, balconies and gables, the villas were not popular with everyone. There were those who claimed the seven villas had been built to house Evans' seven mistresses, while others believed he lived in a different one each day of the week. Lady Cunard, noted for her notorious parties, bought one of the houses. One local resident claimed the parties were riotous and wild, adding 'anything would have seemed wild compared to life in Pangbourne'.

Without the river, Pangbourne would hardly have gained its reputation as an inland resort. The spacious meadows, glorious hanging woods and varied assortment of pubs and hotels have made the village one of the most popular destinations on this stretch of the Thames.

Bedtime Stories of the Riverside

One man whose love for this river lasted a lifetime was Kenneth Grahame. He wrote *The Wind in the Willows* in 1908 and found the inspiration for his delightful story in this part of England. Grahame was born in 1859 and first came to live in Berkshire when he was five. His strength lay in his ability to create a magical world for children, providing a fascinating insight into a child's imagination and their view of the puzzling adult world.

Grahame and his wife became parents rather late in life and it was their son's bedtime stories, as well as letters sent to the boy by his father while away on holiday, that formed the basis for Grahame's classic *The Wind in the Willows*. Both father and son drew on their love of the Berkshire countryside and its wild creatures to complete the story. Having lived for much of his life in the Thames Valley, Grahame eventually moved to Pangbourne in 1924, buying Church Cottage in the centre of the village. His beloved Thames was only a short walk away and he died here in 1932.

Below: Church Cottage, the final home of Kenneth Grahame

Bottom: Artist E H Shepherd's illustrations to *The Wind in the Willows* were reputedly inspired by the landscape beside the Pang

Below right: The Church of St James the Less, Pangbourne

26 A Fashionable Riverside Resort at Pangbourne

Admire the gentle waters of the River Pang before heading for the Thames Path

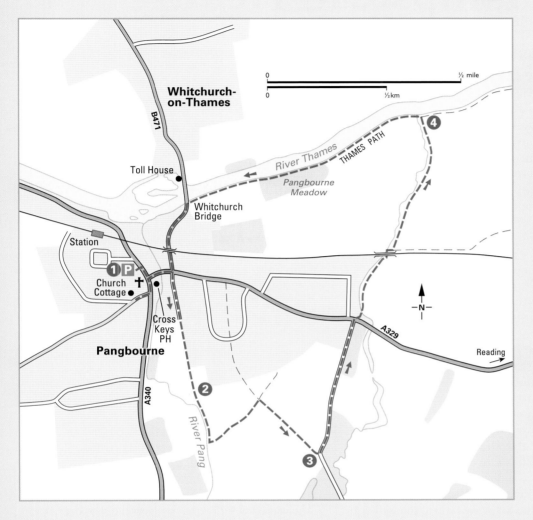

Distance 3 miles (4.8km)

Minimum Time 1hr 30min

Ascent/Gradient 220ft (67m) ▲▲▲

Level of Difficulty ●●●

Paths Field and riverside paths, stretches of road, section of thames path, 2 stiles

Landscape Gentle farmland on banks of Pang and Thames

Suggested Map OS Explorer 159 Reading, Wokingham & Pangbourne

Start/Finish Grid reference: SU 633765

Dog Friendliness On lead in Pangbourne, under control on farmland and by River Thames

Parking Car park off A329 in Pangbourne, near railway bridge

Public Toilets At car park

1 From the car park turn right to the mini-roundabout and walk along to the church and adjoining Church Cottage. Retrace your steps to the main road, keep the Cross Keys pub on the right and turn right at the mini-roundabout. Cross the Pang and bear right at the next major junction into The Moors. At the end of the drive continue ahead on a waymarked footpath. Pass alongside various houses and gardens and patches of scrub, then through a pretty tunnel of trees. Further on is a gate with a local map and information board. Beyond the gate the River Pang can be seen sweeping in from the right.

2 Follow the riverside path, with white willow trees seen on the bank. Make for a footbridge. Don't cross it, instead, turn sharp left and walk across the open meadow to a kissing gate in the far boundary. Once over it, keep alongside the hedge on the left and, as

you approach a Second World War pill box, turn right at a path intersection and cross a footbridge. Head for another footbridge on the far side of the field and then look for a third bridge with white railings, by the field boundary. Cross the bridge and the stile beyond it and then head across the field to the far boundary.

3 Exit to the road and bear left. Follow the lane between hedges and oak trees and walk along to the A329. Go diagonally right to the footpath by the sign for Purley Rise and follow the path north towards distant trees, a stream on your left. Through a kissing gate turn right at the next bridge and follow the concrete track as it bends left to run beneath the railway line. Once through it, bear right to a kissing gate and then follow the track along the left edge of the field, beside a rivulet. Ahead on the horizon are glorious hanging

woods on the north bank of the Thames. Pass double galvanised gates and a bridge on the left and continue on the footpath as it crosses this gentle lowland landscape. Go through a kissing gate and walk across the next field to reach the river bank.

4 On reaching the River Thames, turn left through a kissing gate and over a footbridge and head towards Pangbourne. Follow the Thames Path to Pangbourne Meadow and up ahead now is Whitchurch Bridge. As you approach it, begin to veer away from the river bank towards a car park. Keep left when you get to the road, pass beneath the railway line and turn right at the next junction. Bear right again at the mini-roundabout and return to the car park.

27 Spring has Sprung on Hampstead Heath

With a mixture of ancient woodland, bogs and grasslands, and with 25 ponds, the 800-acre (324ha) heath is an inspiring place for a country walk in the city

Hampstead first became fashionable in the 18th century, when the discovery of spring water transformed the village into a Georgian spa town. There was no stopping the writers, poets and painters who were attracted by the healthy aspect of these green, open spaces just 4 miles (6.4km) from central London. This remains the case today, although the only spring water you'll find now is that produced by manufacturers and sold by the bottle in shops and pubs.

Scene of a Murder

Hampstead has another claim to fame or, perhaps in this case, notoriety. The village was the scene of a murder that signalled the end of capital punishment in this country. The crime was committed by Ruth Ellis, who became the last woman to be hanged in Britain. Near the end of the walk, in a road called South Hill Park, is the Magdala Tavern. Ruth Ellis was a hostess at a nightclub in Soho. During this time she had a stormy relationship with a racing driver, David Blakely. When he ended the affair Ellis first caused a disturbance outside his Hampstead flat. Two days later, as he left the Magdala Tavern, she took a gun from her handbag and shot him – he was dead on arrival at hospital. The case aroused a great deal of public interest and although a newspaper paid for two defence barristers at her trial at the Old Bailey, Ellis remained adamant that she had intended to kill Blakely. With no doubts about her guilt, the jury took less than 30 minutes to agree on a verdict, and the rest is history.

Aside from that episode, Hampstead remains pretty much untainted by modern life. There are plenty of opportunities for you to wander off into the wilder side of the Heath should you wish. Indeed, one of the delights of this area is in exploring the many pathways that criss-cross the grasslands and delve into woodland. If you use the directions as a base and decide to veer off the beaten track, you shouldn't have many problems finding your way back to the main paths.

A Poet Inspired

Many writers seeking inspiration have discovered that the Heath is the perfect antidote to writers' block. English Romantic poet John Keats moved to the edge of the Heath in 1817, and it was there that he fell in love with his neighbour, Fanny Brawne, and wrote many of his celebrated works. No doubt he was inspired by the wonderful vistas and the variety of walks that make the area so special, both to locals and to its millions of visitors each year.

Above: Admiral's House in Hampstead was home to Victorian architect Sir George Gilbert Scott

Right: Wide-ranging views of London are one of the heath's attractions

27 Spring has Sprung on Hampstead Heath

Explore one of London's best-loved open spaces

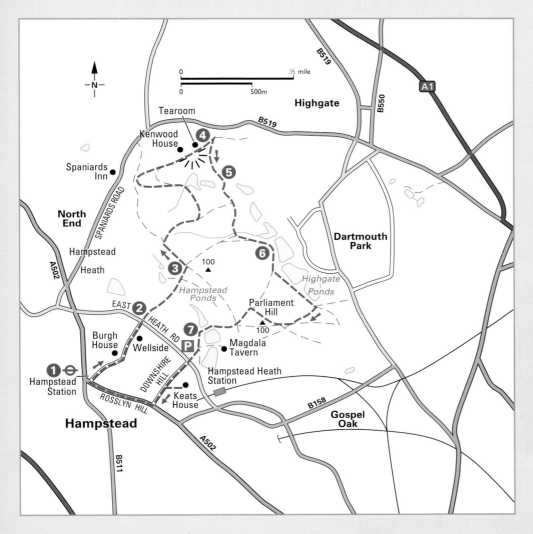

Distance 4.25 miles (6.8km)

Minimum Time 2hrs

Ascent/Gradient 344ft (105m) ▲▲▲

Level of Difficulty ●●●

Paths Mainly well-trodden heathland tracks

Landscape Heath and woodland scenery and some impressive views across London

Suggested Map OS Explorer 173 London North

Start/Finish Hampstead tube station

Dog Friendliness Keep dogs on leads near Kenwood House

Parking Car park off East Heath Road

Public Toilets Highgate

1 Turn left outside Hampstead tube along Hampstead High Street and left into Flask Walk. Continue down the hill past Burgh House and Hampstead Museum, along Well Walk and past Wellside on the right. Cross East Heath Road and continue along the Heath path.

2 Follow a tree-lined path past a fingerpost and a water tap and then after 100yds (91m) turn left at a crossing of paths by a bench. At a fork, bear left and soon afterwards turn right to go through a gate indicating the entrance to the 112 acres (45ha) maintained by English Heritage's Iveagh Bequest.

3 Turn left and bear left as the path descends gently through woodland. If you have a dog it should be on a lead now. Keep ahead to cross a bridge over a lake. Kenwood House can be seen over to the right. Turn left

and keep along a path that sweeps round, passing to the right of the house along a wide terrace that overlooks grassland. The Spaniards Inn is about 0.25 mile (400m) from here.

4 After passing the tearoom, take a left fork, signposted 'Kitchen Garden', to a pergola. Take a few moments here to enjoy the fine views over London, including the towers of Canary Wharf and the giant wheel of the London Eye. Next take a tarmac path to the right, which passes a metal gate.

5 Turn left, downhill, passing to the left of a lake and keep ahead through woodland. Look out for a metal gate on the right. Go through and then continue along the track ahead, taking the next left fork and heading uphill. At the next fork take the left-hand path, which then descends.

6 Pass three more ponds to turn sharp right after the last one, along a path to the right of a hedgerow that climbs uphill. At the next junction follow the right-hand path to the top of Parliament Hill where there are more views across London, including this time, St Paul's Cathedral. Continue ahead downhill along a path through the trees and between two ponds before heading uphill again.

7 Keep ahead as the path curves left and then bear right at a path junction, along a path to East Heath Road. Cross over into Devonshire Hill (turn first left into Keats Grove to visit Keats House), and continue ahead, turning right at the crossroads into Rosslyn Hill. Keep ahead uphill to reach Hampstead tube.

28 Stowe House and Gardens – 'A Work to Wonder at'

A beautiful park laid out around a colonnaded stately mansion, Stowe is a place where its creators set out to write liberty upon the English landscape

Stowe has been described as England's greatest work of art and possibly the world's most bewitching landscape garden – and was hailed by poet Alexander Pope as 'a work to wonder at'. But how did it all begin? It was Sir Richard Temple (1634–97), one of Marlborough's generals and described as 'the greatest Whig in the army', who first built a brick mansion here. Work continued thereafter for well over 100 years – and came to an end in 1839 only when Stowe's then owner, the 2nd Duke of Buckingham, a descendant of Lord Cobham, suffered financial problems and was declared bankrupt.

'Moral Gardening'

Temple's son (1669–1749, also Sir Richard) married a wealthy brewery heiress, became Lord and later Viscount Cobham, and began to extend the house and park. He prided himself on his reputation as a great radical – anti-Stuart and pro-liberty, greatly endorsing the ideals of the Glorious Revolution of 1688. Although work on the gardens at Stowe started in 1711, it wasn't until Lord Cobham fell out with the George II and Prime Minister Robert Walpole, that the idea of an experiment in 'moral gardening' really seized him.

Cobham threw himself wholeheartedly into the project. His aim was to create a garden of ideas: a place symbolising the notion of liberty. Historians maintain that Cobham was attempting to rewrite the history of Britain, using buildings and landscape. In 1713 Stowe had half a dozen garden staff, but five years later there were close to 30. Work at Stowe became a way of life, and so anxious was Cobham for the momentum not to be broken that, when his head gardener Edward Bissell broke his leg, he called for a specially adapted chair so that Bissell could continue to work.

A 'Fair, Majestic Paradise'

In total, Cobham designed eight lakes, constructed more than three dozen temples, and commissioned 50 statues and 40 busts. The country's finest artists and designers, including James Gibbs, William Kent and Sir John Vanbrugh, were employed to help create what James Thomson described as 'the fair majestic paradise of Stowe'. Lancelot 'Capability' Brown began his career here in 1741.

Lord Cobham's successors consolidated his work by improving and adding to the garden. However, by the mid-19th century, the family fortunes had ebbed away and the estate had to be sold. After a further sale in 1921, Cobham's vision of an earthly paradise was left virtually empty. The house became a school and the National Trust acquired the grand and beautiful gardens in 1989.

Above: The 'Elysian Fields' and the Temple of Ancient Virtue, both designed by William Kent

Above right: The ha-ha in Stowe grounds – a ha-ha was a ditch created to form a boundary between gardens and parkland

Right: Stowe's Palladian Bridge is one of three built in the era – the others are at Wilton House, near Salisbury, and Prior Park, Bath

28 Stowe House and Gardens – 'A Work to Wonder at'

Savour the delights of a famous 18th-century landscape garden and surrounding parkland

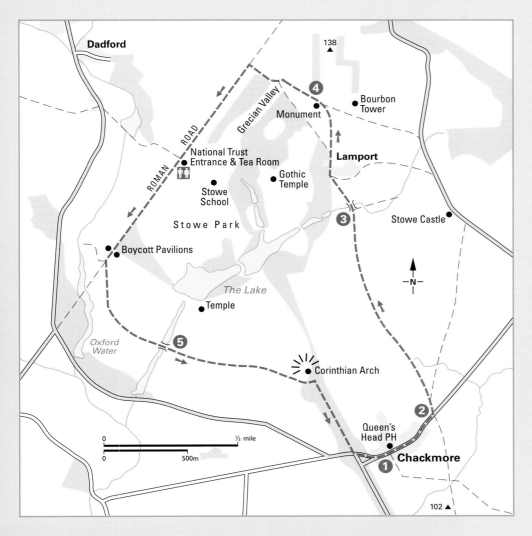

Distance 4.5 miles (7.2km)

Minimum Time 2hrs

Ascent/Gradient Negligible ▲▲▲

Level of Difficulty ●●●

Paths Field paths, estate drives, stretches of road, 3 stiles

Landscape Farmland and parkland

Suggested Map OS Explorer 192 Buckingham & Milton Keynes

Start/Finish Grid reference: SP 684357

Dog Friendliness Under control across farmland, on lead within Stowe Park

Parking On-street parking in Chackmore

Public Toilets Stowe Landscape Garden

1 Walk through Chackmore, pass the Queen's Head, and continue through the village. At the speed derestriction signs, keep ahead and look for a path on the left. Aim diagonally right in the field, passing under power lines. Make for a stile beneath the branches of an oak tree in the corner where waymarks indicate that the path forks.

2 Cross the field towards two stiles, making for the one on the left, beyond which is a plank bridge. Keep to the right boundary of an elongated field and when it widens, go diagonally right towards the far corner. Stowe Castle is over to the right, and to the left the outline of the Corinthian Arch is just visible among the trees. Through a gate join a path, pass under telegraph wires and look for a gap and waymark ahead. Walk ahead and then descend to the footbridge.

3 Go over the stream and through a gate into the field, then head up the slope, keeping to the left of two distant houses. Aim for a single-storey dwelling in the top corner and, as you climb the slope, the outline of the Gothic Temple looms into view. Go through a galvanised gate by a lodge at Lamport and continue ahead on the bridleway. The Bourbon Tower is clearly visible over to the right. Pass through a gate and keep ahead towards an obelisk monument commemorating the Duke of Buckingham. Merge with another path and keep a sports ground on your right.

4 Make for a gate leading out to the left of an avenue of trees running down towards the Grecian Valley. Cross over and follow the track on the right-hand side of the ha-ha up to a clump of trees. Bear left here and follow the wide avenue, part of a Roman road. Pass the

National Trust entrance building and shop and then the magnificent façade of Stowe School and keep along the main drive. On reaching the Boycott Pavilions, branch off half left along a track to a stile by the cattle grid and a sign for the Corinthian Arch. Down below lies the Oxford Water, crossed by a splendid 18th-century stone bridge.

5 Follow the drive through the parkland with glimpses of temples and classical designs. The drive eventually reaches the Corinthian Arch. Line up with the arch and pause here to absorb the breathtaking view of Stowe School, surely one of Britain's stateliest vistas. Walk down the avenue to the road junction, swing left and return to Chackmore.

29 Wicken – the Last Survivor

A pocket of authentic East Anglian fen, rich in wild flowers and virtually the last of its kind in England, is an atmospheric setting for this delightful nature walk

Wicken Fen is one of the oldest nature reserves in the country and, as the last surviving remnant of original fenland left in Britain, one of the most important, too. Over the last 400 years more than 99 per cent of East Anglia's ancient Great Fen has been drained and converted into farmland, richly productive for agriculture, but largely sterile for wildlife.

The National Trust's 1,600 acres (648ha) at Wicken have assumed a critical importance. Since they purchased their first tiny piece of land here in 1899, the Trust has made more than 60 separate acquisitions at Wicken, and the plan is to continue to add to their holdings by acquiring farmland to the south of the reserve and restoring it to its original wetland state. The ultimate aim is to create a nature reserve covering 10,000 acres (4,050ha) between Cambridge and Wicken Fen.

The nature reserve itself includes a boardwalk (0.75 miles/1.2km) and nature trail (2.25 miles/3.6km), while eight hides allow close-up views over ponds and ditches. Wicken Fen hosts more than 1,000 types of beetle, and visiting coleopterists (that's beetle-lovers to you and me) once included the young Charles Darwin, who came here to collect specimens while studying at Cambridge.

Plant Life

As well as 212 species of spider, Wicken Fen also supports nearly 300 different types of plant. In the summer the ponds and pools buzz with dragonflies and damselflies, and are full of yellow and white water lilies, water mint and water violets, plus the greater bladderwort, a carnivorous plant with small yellow flowers and virtually no roots that feasts on small aquatic life forms. The uncultivated grassland features early marsh and southern marsh orchids, usually flowering in June, while in the areas of sedge you can find milk parsley and the light purple flowers of the rare marsh pea. You should allow the bare minimum of an hour to explore the reserve.

For generations Wicken peat has been cut for burning, and sedge (a grass-like plant that grows on wet ground) has been harvested for thatching. The peat is now untouched, but sedge is still cut every three years in the summer – just as it has been at Wicken ever since 1419. Meanwhile konig ponies have been introduced to Verrall's Fen to stop cleared scrub from reinvading; and ditches are periodically dredged of choking vegetation by a process with the splendid name of 'slubbing'.

Far left: Butterflies are welcome, as the Wicken village sign implies

Left: Thin ice on a pond in Wicken Fen in winter

Below: Winds are often powerful across the fens. The boardwalk pathway on the nature reserve leads past a windmill

29 Wicken – the Last Survivor

Step back in time to a piece of the ancient Great Fen

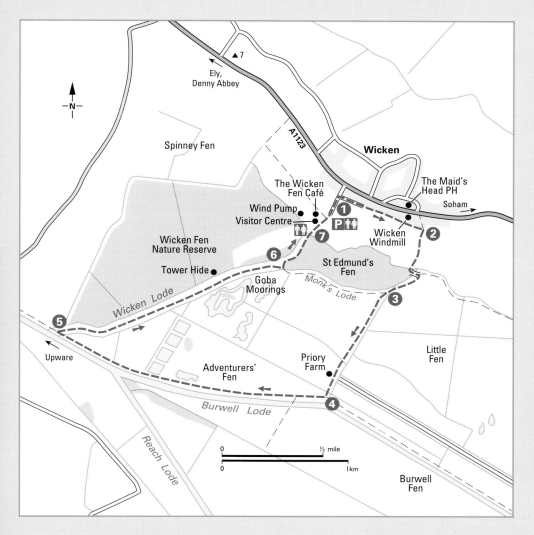

Distance 4.75 miles (7.7km)

Minimum Time 2hrs

Ascent/Gradient Negligible ▲▲▲

Level of Difficulty ●●●

Paths Mostly river banks and farm tracks, potentially slippery

Landscape Low-lying fenland of dykes, scrub and open fields

Suggested Map OS Explorer 226 Ely & Newmarket

Start/Finish Grid reference: TL 564706

Dog Friendliness Under close control due to livestock and nesting wildlife

Parking Wicken Fen nature reserve car park (pay-and-display) if visiting the reserve, otherwise off Wicken High Street

Public Toilets At nature reserve car park and visitor centre

1 From the nature reserve car park walk up Lode Lane towards the village of Wicken. Before you meet the main road turn right on to Back Lane and follow this route, which soon becomes a pleasant track running peacefully behind several houses. When you arrive at the far end of the lane, just after passing a windmill, turn right on to a wide track that runs across the fields. (If you have parked in the centre of the village you should take the signposted public footpath via Cross Green, just along from and opposite the pub, out to the fields.)

2 Follow this wide route down to two footbridges. Cross the second bridge and turn right along the bank of Monk's Lode, with St Edmund's Fen opposite. A lode, incidentally, is another name for an artificially cut waterway.

3 After about 550yds (503m), branch left before a fence and gate for a long straight track, known as a drove, and head out across the fields to Priory Farm. Join the surfaced lane and continue all the way to the end.

4 Turn right by the raised Cockup Bridge and walk along the bank of the Burwell Lode – don't be tempted by the footbridge. Continue for 1.5 miles (2.4km) past Adventurers' Fen, named after the 17th-century 'Gentlemen Adventurers' who first started draining the fens in earnest.

5 At a high-arched footbridge over Wicken Lode turn right and walk along this bank back towards Wicken Fen past a National Trust sign. If you continue across the footbridge and walk for another 0.25 mile (400m), you come to Upware, with a pub and picnic area.

Ignoring paths off into the open fen and fields on your right, continue along the bank until its junction with Monk's Lode. Across the water you pass the lofty thatched Tower Hide.

6 Cross the short bridge by Goba Moorings and continue alongside Wicken Lode, not along Monk's Lode (to the right). The lush vegetation of Wicken Fen is now either side.

7 When you get to the end turn left to the visitor centre (open daily from Easter to October, Tuesday to Sunday in winter). There is a small admission charge to the reserve itself, which is open daily from dawn to dusk. Nearby is the restored Fen Cottage, and a lovely thatched boathouse where the reserve's traditional working fen boat is kept. To return to the car park and village, simply walk back up the lane past the houses.

30 Constable Country at Flatford Mill

Offering a chance to follow in the footsteps of English artist John Constable, this charming walk leads through quintessential English countryside

John Constable (1776–1837), the greatest English landscape painter of all time, was born in East Bergholt and spent his childhood among the leafy lanes and pastoral landscapes of Dedham Vale. Even after he moved to London to join the Royal Academy, he returned to Suffolk each summer to draw fresh inspiration from the bucolic scenery of meadows, valleys, rivers, farmland and boats. He claimed to have seen pictures in these scenes long before he ever picked up a pencil and they remained his favourite subject throughout his life. 'I associate my careless boyhood with all that lies on the banks of the Stour. Those scenes made me a painter and I am grateful,' he wrote.

This walk takes you through the heart of Constable Country, which looks remarkably as it did when he painted it. Artists can still be seen with sketchbooks in hand, painting in the open air as Constable used to do. Several of his best-known works were painted in the vicinity of Flatford Mill, a watermill once owned by Golding Constable, the artist's father. The mill itself is now an environmental studies centre but you can stand outside and gaze across the mill pond at Willy Lott's House, familiar to art lovers around the world from its appearance in *The Hay Wain*. Willy Lott was a local farmer who lived in this house for 84 years and is said never to have travelled further than the churchyard of East Bergholt, where he is buried. Constable saw Lott as a symbol of the stability of the English countryside and this painting, more than any other, has come to represent the essence of rural England.

Childhood Home and Studio

The walk passes a number of sights associated with John Constable. His childhood home, East Bergholt House, is no longer there but a plaque on the railings marks the spot. His first studio is near by. On Fen Lane you walk along the route which Constable took on his way to school in Dedham each morning. Best of all, you get to stand in the places where Constable produced some of his finest paintings, such as *The Cornfield*, *The White Horse* and *Boat Building at Flatford Mill*.

If you want to know more, the National Trust organises one-hour guided walks from Bridge Cottage in summer, where you visit the scenes of the paintings in the company of an art expert. Constable Country has become a popular place to visit and it can get crowded on summer weekends. If you can, come during the week or out of season.

Above right: A place to rest at Flatford Mill

Above: Willy Lott's cottage, the house represented in Constable's *The Hay Wain*

Right: The pond at Flatford Mill

30 Constable Country at Flatford Mill

See Constable's studio and many of the scenes he painted

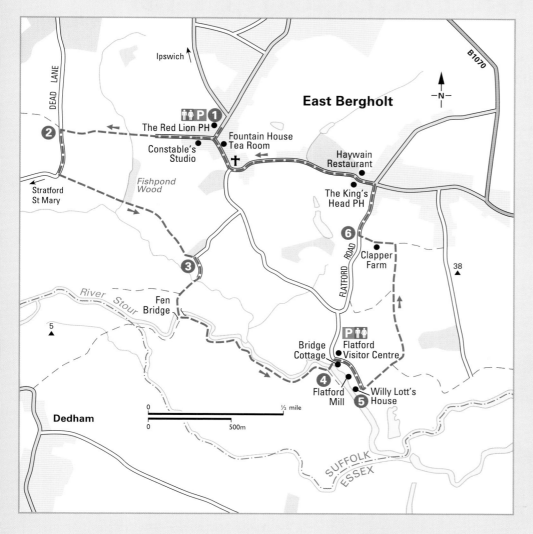

Distance 3.75 miles (6km)

Minimum Time 1hr 30min

Ascent/Gradient 246ft (75m) ▲▲▲

Level of Difficulty ●●●

Paths Roads, field paths and riverside meadows, 7 stiles

Landscape Pastoral landscapes of Stour Valley

Suggested Map OS Explorer 196 Sudbury, Hadleigh & Dedham Vale

Start/Finish Grid reference: TM 069346

Dog Friendliness Dogs should be kept mostly on leads

Parking Free car park next to Red Lion, East Bergholt

Public Toilets In car park and at Flatford visitor information centre

1 Turn right out of the car park, pass the Red Lion pub and the post office, then turn right along a lane, noting Constable's early studio on the left. Continue along this lane, past a chapel and a cemetery, through a gate and down the left side of a meadow to cross a footbridge. Climb the path for marvellous views of the Stour Valley and the church towers at Dedham and Stratford St Mary.

2 Turn left at a junction of paths to walk down Dead Lane, a sunken footpath. At the foot of the hill, turn left on to a field-edge path. The path goes right, then left to cross a stile on the edge of Fishpond Wood. Walk beside the wood for a few paces, then climb another stile into a field and walk beside the hedge to your right. The path switches to the other side of the hedge and back again before bending left around woodland to Fen Lane.

3 Turn right along the lane, crossing a cart bridge and ignoring footpaths to the left and to the right as you continue towards the wooden-arched Fen Bridge. Cross the bridge and turn left to walk beside the River Stour towards Flatford on the flood plain.

4 Cross a bridge to return to the north bank of the river beside Bridge Cottage. Turn right here, passing a restored dry dock on the way to Flatford Mill.

5 Walk past Willy Lott's House and turn left past the car park. An optional loop here, on a National Trust permissive path, leads right around the outside of Gibbonsgate Field beside a hedge. Otherwise, keep left on a wide track and go through the gate to join another National Trust path through Miller's Field. Stay on this path as it swings left and climbs

to the top of the field, then go straight ahead through a kissing gate. Keep ahead, ignore the stile on the left and follow a fenced path to a T-junction of paths. Turn left here along the track to the rear of barns and continue down the drive of Clapper Farm to Flatford Road.

6 Turn right along the road. At the crossroads, turn left passing the King's Head pub and Haywain Restaurant on the way back to East Bergholt. Stay on the pavement on the right side of the road to walk through the churchyard and back to the walk's start.

31 From Sunny Southwold and its Traditional Pier

This delightful ramble provides the perfect introduction to Southwold, a genteel town with none of the 'kiss-me-quick' brashness of some English resorts

In the summer of 2002, the arrival of the first steamboats for more than 70 years marked a return to the glory days for Southwold Pier. The pier was originally built in 1899, when Southwold was a flourishing Victorian holiday resort. Mixed bathing had just been introduced on the beach, on condition that men and women were kept at least 20yds (18m) apart and changed in separate 'bathing machines' into costumes which covered their bodies from neck to knees. In these days the *Belle* steamer brought holiday-makers on its daily voyage from London and the pier was a hive of activity as porters unloaded their cases and carried them to their lodgings.

Right: The day's last light falls on the River Blyth to the south of the town

Below: The character of Southwold seems to be summed up by the brightly coloured huts on the beach and promenade

Redeveloping the Pier

The T-end, where the boats docked, was swept away in a storm in 1934. During the Second World War, the pier was split in two as a precaution against a German invasion. By the time Chris and Helen Iredale bought the pier in 1987, storms and many years of neglect had reduced it to a rotting hulk. Years later, the couple have realised their dream of rebuilding and reopening the pier, so that visitors can once again stroll along the boardwalk with the sea spray in their faces and watch the boats unloading their passengers at a new landing stage.

An exhibition on the pier tells the history of the traditional British seaside holiday, complete with saucy postcards, kitsch teapots, palm readers, end-of-the-pier shows and old-style arcade machines – such as the 'kiss-meter' where you can find out whether you are flirtatious, amorous, frigid or sexy.

Old-fashioned Fun

A separate pavilion contains modern machines by local inventor Tim Hunkin, who also designed the ingenious water clock, with chimes and special effects every half hour. You can eat ice cream or fish and chips, drink a pint of the local beer, play pool in the amusement arcade or watch the fishermen. Especially in summer, the pier provides a focus for good old-fashioned fun.

In Southwold everything is done in good taste. In addition to its brightly coloured beach huts, it is known for its peaceful greens with their Georgian and Edwardian houses. Adnams brewery dominates the town and it is no surprise to discover that the beer is still delivered to pubs on horse-drawn drays. Southwold is that sort of place.

31 From Sunny Southwold and its Traditional Pier

Explore a charming holiday resort on an island surrounded by river, creek and sea

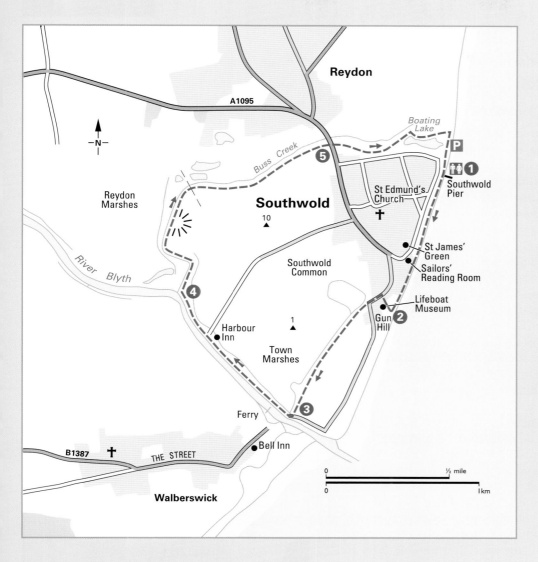

Distance 4 miles (6.4km)

Minimum Time 1hr 30min

Ascent/Gradient Negligible ▲▲▲

Level of Difficulty ●●●

Paths Riverside paths, seaside promenade, town streets, 2 stiles

Landscape Southwold and its surroundings – river, marshes, coast

Suggested Map OS Explorer 231 Southwold & Bungay

Start/Finish Grid reference: TM 511766

Dog Friendliness Most of walk suitable for dogs off leads

Parking Beach car park (pay-and-display) or free in nearby streets

Public Toilets Beside pier, near beach and car park at Southwold Harbour

1 Leave the pier and turn left along the seafront, either following the promenade past the beach huts and climbing some steps or walking along the clifftop path with views over the beach. After passing St James' Green, where a pair of cannon stand either side of a mast, continue along the clifftop path to Gun Hill, where six more cannon, captured at the Battle of Culloden near Inverness in 1746, can be seen facing out to sea.

2 From Gun Hill, head inland alongside the large South Green, then turn left along Queen's Road to the junction with Gardner Road. Cross this road, then look for the Ferry Path footpath, that follows a stream beside the marshes. Alternatively, stay on the clifftop path, and walk across the dunes until you reach the mouth of the River Blyth.

3 Turn right and walk beside the river, passing the Walberswick ferry, a group of fishing huts where fresh fish is sold, and the Harbour Inn. After about 0.75 mile (1.2km), you reach an iron bridge on the site of the old Southwold-to-Halesworth railway line.

4 Keep straight ahead at the bridge, crossing a stile and following the path round to the right alongside Buss Creek to make a complete circuit of the island. There are good views across the common to Southwold, dominated by the lighthouse and the tower of St Edmund's Church. Horses and cattle can often be seen grazing on the marshes. Keep straight ahead, going over a stile, through a gate to cross an embankment, then over another stile. Stay on the raised path to reach a white-painted bridge.

5 Climb up to the road and cross the bridge, then continue on the path beside Buss Creek with views of beach huts in the distance. The path skirts a boating lake on its way down to the sea. Turn right and walk across the car park to return to the pier.

32 Lynford's Stag and Arboretum

Across a landscape where society hunts were held, and where Ernest Hemingway shot, a peaceful walk leads through England's largest lowland pine forest

By 1916, with the horrors of the First World War in full swing, the British government realised that it could no longer rely on timber imports to supplement Britain's own wood production and sustain industrial output. The huge demands placed on woodland resources by the onset of trench warfare and the spiralling need for colliery pit props brought the realisation that it would have to establish a group responsible for planting strategic timber reserves, as well as chopping them down again. The solution was the Forestry Commission, established immediately after the war in 1919. It began by buying up large tracts of land that were suitable for growing trees. One of the first areas it obtained was the sandy heathland around the ancient priory town of Thetford, because this was an ideal habitat for many species of fast-growing conifers.

By 1935, the new Thetford Forest had reached the boundaries on today's maps, covering an area of approximately 50,000 acres (20,250ha). Originally, it was dominated by Scots pine, but this was changed to Corsican pine, which allows some 220,000 tons (224,000 tonnes) of timber to be cut every year. This is enough to build a 4ft (1.2m) high plank fence around the entire length of Britain's mainland coast. The amount taken is carefully controlled, so that the timber industry is sustainable – it never takes more than it plants.

Rare Species

The forest is more than just a giant timber-producing yard, however. It is home to numerous rare animals, birds and plants, including the native red squirrel, and people travel from miles around to enjoy the peace of the great forest trackways.

Lucky visitors who walk quietly may spot one of the park's four species of resident deer: fallow, roe, red and muntjac. It is also home to a large number of bats, including the pipistrelle and the barbastelle. A bat hibernaculum has been built, to give them somewhere to spend the daylight hours.

Lynford Stag is named for the life-sized metal deer that stands unobtrusively among the car parks and picnic benches. This was discovered by Forestry Commission workers when they were clearing the area for planting trees, and must have given them quite a surprise. It was made for Sir Richard Sutton, a keen hunter who owned nearby Lynford Hall. He used it for target practice and, if you approach it, you will see the scars of its previous existence.

Lynford Hall is a Grade II listed mock-Jacobean mansion standing amid imposing gardens overlooking a series of artificial lakes. The building began in 1857 on the site of an earlier hall dating to the 1720s. The estate was known for the splendid quality of its hunting, and birds and beasts continued to fall until 1924, when the hall was sold to the Forestry Commission. In the late 1940s, trainee foresters began to plant trees in its grounds. These now form the arboretum.

Top right: Sulphur Tufts mushrooms in Thetford Forest

Above right: A statue of two fighting bulls stands at the head of the long Sequoia Avenue

Right: Calming light beneath trees in Thetford Forest – keep your eyes peeled to see deer and red squirrel

32 Lynford's Stag and Arboretum

Tread the pine-carpeted paths of Thetford Forest

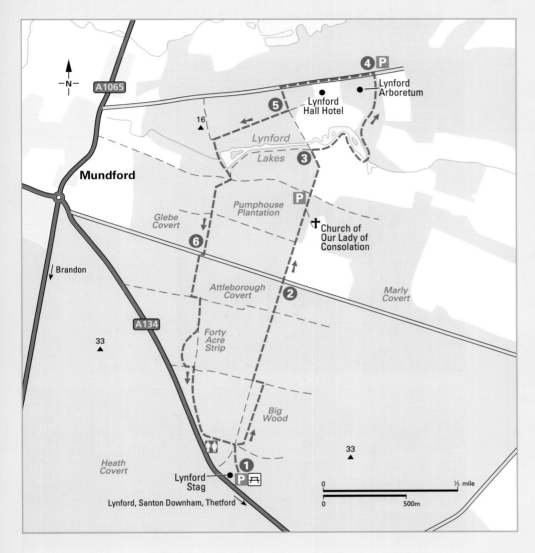

Distance 4.5 miles (7.2km)

Minimum Time 2hrs

Ascent/Gradient 66ft (20m) ▲▲▲

Level of Difficulty ●●●

Paths Wide grassy trackways and small paths

Landscape Coniferous and mixed deciduous forest

Suggested Map OS Explorer 229 Thetford Forest in The Brecks

Start/Finish Grid reference: TL 814917

Dog Friendliness On lead and keep away from children's play areas. No dogs (except guide dogs) in arboretum

Parking Lynford Stag picnic site off A134

Public Toilets Close to start

1 Leave the car park by the metal stag and follow the blue marker posts into the trees. Jig to the right and follow the markers north. The path then turns left; take the wide track to your right, next to a bench, leaving the blue trail to walk along the edge of the Christmas tree plantation until you reach a paved road.

2 Cross the road and continue on what was once part of the driveway leading to Lynford Hall. Pass a car park and a noticeboard with a map of forest trails. Continue along a gravel path, picking up the next set of blue and green trails. The Church of Our Lady of Consolation is behind the trees to your right. It was designed by Pugin in the 1870s for the Catholic owner of the hall, but the next owner, a Protestant, planted trees to shield it from view. Shortly, reach a stone bridge.

3 Turn right and follow the gravel path along the shore of Lynford Lakes with views across the water to Lynford Hall. Turn left across a bridge to enter Lynford Arboretum and follow the path through the arboretum until you reach a road.

4 Turn left along the road, passing Lynford Hall Hotel on your left. After you have walked past the building, turn left through the main entrance gates of the hotel and walk up the drive.

5 When you see a sculpture of two bulls fighting, turn right on to a wide grassy sward called Sequoia Avenue. Walk almost to the end of it, then follow the blue markers to the left into the wood. After a few paces you come to the lake. The blue trail bears to the left

at the end of the lake, but our walk continues straight ahead on the bridleway. The path jigs left, then right, but keep to the bridleway.

6 Cross a paved lane and continue straight on, towards the Christmas trees. Turn left at the end of the track, then almost immediately right, where you will pick up the blue trail markers again. Follow these until you reach the car park.

33 Fine Buildings in 'Lynn'

There is a feast of architectural delights to savour in King's Lynn, the once-wealthy Norfolk port that was a particular favourite of critic Nikolaus Pevsner

King's Lynn was originally just called Lynn, and was an unassuming little place. But in the early Middle Ages, things began to take off. Lynn was strategically placed on one of the most important waterways in medieval England and soon a huge amount of trade was passing through. It exported corn from Lincolnshire, lead from Derbyshire, salt from Norfolk and Lincolnshire and, most importantly, wool from the East Midlands. It imported dried cod from Iceland and timber, pitch and resin from the Baltic, as well as Flemish and Italian cloths.

With all these revenues, Lynn became a wealthy place, and Herbert de Losinga, the first Bishop of Norwich, decided he wanted it for himself. It became known as Bishop's Lynn, and so remained until the 1530s, when Henry VIII squashed its ecclesiastical association and named it King's Lynn, after himself. The change in name meant little to Lynn's merchants, who remained prosperous and continued to build their grand houses and churches, many of which can still be seen today.

Architectural Highlights

Almost every architectural period is represented, ranging from St Nicholas's Chapel, built between 1145 and 1420, to the picturesque Burkitt Court Almshouses, built in 1909 in memory of a Lynn corn merchant. One of the most visible landmarks is the Greyfriars Tower, which was part of a Franciscan Friary and was built in the 14th century. The beautifully proportioned Custom House, originally built in 1683 as a merchants' exchange, was hailed by archtectural critic Nikolaus Pevsner as 'one of the most perfect buildings ever built'.

St George's Guildhall is the largest surviving guildhall in England. It was built around 1410, and has been used as a warehouse, a store for guns during the Civil War and a court house. It is now the King's Lynn Arts and houses an art gallery, a theatre and a coffee shop.

Not all of Lynn's history has been a tale of prosperity. The town suffered during the Civil War, when Cromwell's Parliamentarians besieged the Royalist troops stationed here. In 1643 a cannon ball went through the west window of St Margaret's Church. The town also endured terrible floods, and the water levels are marked near the west door of St Margaret's. King's Lynn is a charming town, whether you are interested in walks, parks and gardens or in shopping and eating.

Left: King's Lynn Custom House designed by Henry Bell, and built in 1683

Below: The view from West Lynn, across the River Ouse

Bottom: The annual funfair lights up the main square

33 Fine Buildings in 'Lynn'

Wander cobbled lanes to visit King's Lynn's museums, see the river and take a ferry ride

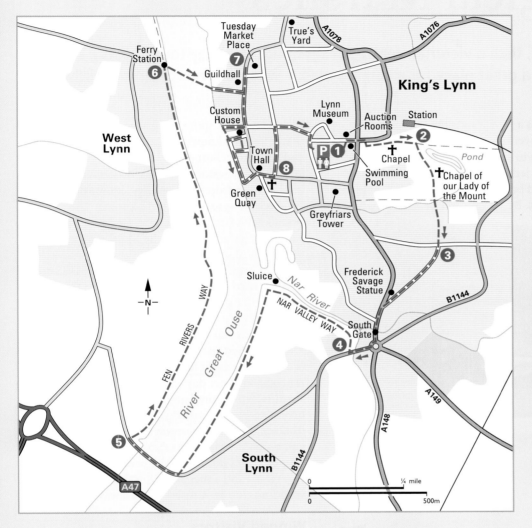

Distance 4 miles (6.4km)

Minimum Time 2hrs (allow longer for museums)

Ascent/Gradient Negligible ▲▲▲

Level of Difficulty ●●●

Paths Pavements, cobbled streets, grassy river path and steps to ferry (operates all year but not on Sundays)

Landscape Town buildings and open riverside

Suggested Map OS Explorer 250 Norfolk Coast West Ashdown

Start/Finish Grid reference: TF 620199

Dog Friendliness Dogs can roam free, but watch for traffic in town

Parking Blackfriar Street car park or St James multi-storey (pay-and-display)

Public Toilets At car park and various locations in town

1 From the car park, head for King's Lynn Auction Rooms, pass the fitness centre and swimming pool and cross the road to the park. Take the path towards the chapel of St John the Evangelist.

2 Turn right by the pond. On a little knoll to your left is the red-brick Chapel of Our Lady of the Mount, built in 1485 for pilgrims travelling to Walsingham. When you reach the ruinous walls of the town's defences, continue on the path straight ahead with the football ground to your left.

3 Keep straight ahead into Guanock Terrace, passing The Beeches guest house and Lord Napier pub to the statue of Mayor Frederick Savage. Bear left at London Road to 15th-century South Gate, then cross the road to the Honest Lawyer guest house. Walk past South Gate and turn right at the roundabout. Cross a bridge over the River Nar and take the unmarked path to the right immediately after the bridge.

4 Clamber up the bank and take the path to the left along the east river bank. After 0.75 mile (1.2km), turn right over the bridge.

5 Turn right on the far side of the bridge on to the Fen Rivers Way. Follow this path for just over a mile (1.6km), with views across the river to King's Lynn.

6 Take the ferry back to King's Lynn. (The ferry runs every 20 minutes from 7am to 6pm, not Sundays.) Walk up Ferry Lane as far as King Street, then turn left to see the Tuesday Market Place with its 750-seat Corn Exchange concert hall.

7 Retrace your steps past Ferry Lane and continue to Purfleet Quay, which houses the Custom House. At the end of the quay, cross the bridge and take a narrow lane opposite to reach cobbled King's Staithe Lane. Turn right to return to the river bank, then head left to Thorseby College, built in 1500 for 13 chantry priests. Turn left to walk along College Lane to reach the Saturday Market Place, with the Town House Museum to your left. Bear right and then left, passing the Town Hall and Old Gaol House, with St Margaret's Church dominating the square.

8 Turn left on to the pedestrian High Street for a flavour of the modern town. At the crossroads, turn right along New Conduit Street, then right on Tower Street. Take the alley to the left opposite Majestic Cinema to return to the car park.

Central England

Central England

Featuring many sites of national significance, the Midlands have a varied history as a centre of industry, 'the battlefield of England' and, in the twenty-first century, as one of the fastest-growing regions in Britain.

The area was first criss-crossed by a series of Roman roads – and the Roman-built Watling Street and Foss Way are still important cross-country thoroughfares. Canals converged on the big city of Birmingham. The town of Crewe grew at a fortuitous intersection of roads and railways. In modern times, several major motorways have interlinked in the region – home of the infamous Spaghetti Junction. Strangely enough, for all the through traffic the region sees, the Midlands are not high on the average explorer's itinerary.

People often think of the region in terms of simple images generated by names like 'the Potteries' and 'the Black Country' – as an area dominated by industry. For those interested in the country's industrial heritage there are certainly many sites to visit in the Midlands, including Coalbrookdale in Shropshire (see Walk 38), the place where the Industrial Revolution was born when, in 1709, Abraham Darby I developed a way of smelting iron with coke rather than laboriously produced charcoal. Within a century the locality was the world's leading industrial area.

Elsewhere in the region, Northamptonshire was known for its open-cast mining and Nottinghamshire for its coal fields. At Hartshill in Warwickshire (see Walk 40), at Hereford in Worcestershire (see Walk 35) and near Polesworth,

again in Warwickshire (see Walk 41), you can see sections of the canal network that supported such industrial expansion.

A Taste of the Wild in the Peak District

The region's real upland wilderness is the Dark Peak, the wilder northern part of the Peak District – more specifically, the grough-riven blanket bogs of the Kinder plateau. This can be reached from the village of Edale (see Walk 47) in a steep climb up Jacob's Ladder to meet a section of the Pennine Way footpath. The gentler White Peak, the southern part of the Peak District, is no less spectacular, but the landforms are altogether different and influenced to a large extent by the underlying carboniferous limestone.

Elsewhere, in the midst of urbanisation and extensive farming acreage, there are wonderful pockets of wilderness. In Cheshire, in an expanse of farmland, you can visit a fascinating section of lowland heath in the Little Budworth Country Park (see Walk 44). Here you can enjoy an expanse of grasses, bracken, heather and gorse.

Shropshire Hills

Further south the Malverns offer another taste of wildness in an essentially agricultural region, and the huddled Shropshire Hills also rise abruptly from fertile plains. You can climb Lyth Hill (see Walk 37) to see the magnificent and wide-ranging view that inspired novelist Mary Webb, the author of *Precious Bane* (1924), and *Gone to Earth* (1917),

Above: Goyt Valley reservoir

Left: On Kinder Scout

Main picture: Rape field in rural Northamptonshire

Previous pages: Historic Ironbridge in Shropshire

and near the town feature in his novels – including the former Moorgreen Colliery, which was Minton Pit in *Sons and Lovers* (1913), and Moorgreen Reservoir, which appeared under different names in both *Sons and Lovers* and the later novel *Women in Love* (1920). Like Coalbrookdale (see Walk 38), Moorgreen Colliery has been turned from a part of the industrial heartland into a scene of great natural beauty – just as the woods and meadows at Coalbrookdale are now managed by the Severn Gorge Countryside Trust, the area near Eastwood that once was home to Moorgreen Colliery has been landscaped, planted with trees and renamed Colliers Wood.

Robin Hood – and Centuries of War

To the northeast of Colliers Wood, still within Nottinghamshire, is an area of much older and more extensive woodland – Sherwood Forest, the onetime haunt of legendary outlaw Robin Hood (see Walk 49). This ancient woodland is today contained in the 450-acre (182ha) Sherwood Forest Country Park, and contains a collection of centuries-old oaks including one, the Major Oak, 52ft (15.8m) tall, that may be upwards of 1,000 years old. It has a hollow trunk 33ft (10m) in circumference that was reputedly used as a hiding place by Robin Hood and his Merrie Men during his battles against privilege and injustice.

This is a landscape well fought over through the centuries. At the close of the Wars of the Roses in 1485, one of the largest armies ever assembled descended on Bosworth Field in Leicestershire so that rival claims to the throne could be settled. The same thing happened at Naseby, Northamptonshire, in 1645 only this time it was full-blown civil war. In the Second World War the Midlands suffered mightily – and the complete levelling of Coventry in the Blitz of 1940–41 brought a new word into the German language or at least into the vocabulary of the German air force or Luftwaffe – *Coventrieren*, 'to Coventrate' or 'raze a city to the ground as Coventry was reduced to ruins'. If you're interested in military history

Above: Relaxing country walking near Church Stretton, Shropshire

Above right: Sherwood Forest's Major Oak is 52ft (15.8m) tall

Far right: High up in the Peak District

whose work enjoyed posthumous success after prime minister Stanley Baldwin called her a genius in 1928. *Gone to Earth* was made into a memorable film starring Jennifer Jones and David Farrar and was partly shot in location in Shropshire by Michael Powell and Emeric Pressberger in 1950.

Shakespeare and D. H. Lawrence

The Midlands hills and plains – and in some cases its industrial settlements – inspired several literary figures, not least of course the Stratford-born poet and playwright William Shakespeare, one of the world's literary giants whose influence straddles the centuries. You can walk in the footsteps of Shakespeare in rural Warwickshire, perhaps make a visit to Kingsbury (see Walk 39), which has associations with his mother Mary Arden, or stop at Hartshill (see Walk 40), which was home to his friend and fellow-poet Michael Drayton.

In Nottinghamshire the town of Eastwood was the birthplace of the major 20th-century novelist D. H. Lawrence (see Walk 48), and several sites in it's worth checking whether there are going to be any battle re-enactments at some of the more popular sites. Military stations are still found in the Midlands – there are airfields along the Lincolnshire coast, for example, and near Gedney you can watch RAF planes from RAF Holbeach at their bombing practice over the sea (see Walk 51).

Despite the hard edges brought by canal, rail and road links, industry and urbanisation, and the feeling that the countryside exists only in thin strips alongside the Midlands motorways, there is actually a good deal of charming countryside to explore. In the Midlands, more than any other part of Britain, millions of native trees are being planted in an effort to add green spaces to the predominantly grey urban environment, all part of the ongoing National Forest Campaign; give this time, and the countryside of the Midlands will look quite different within the next 50 years.

Next time you pass through the area, turn on to the quiet by-roads, enquire into the heritage of the region and explore its hidden features. A little guidance is all you need in places where nature or history are not readily apparent, and you will find it a surprising and interesting experience.

Best of the Rest

Bury Ditches
The early Iron Age hill-fort, dated to c600BC, is situated on top of Sunnyhill in Shropshire and commands magnificent views of the surrounding countryside (see Walk 36). At one time it was largely covered by conifers planted by the Forestry Commission but after a storm blew many of them down in 1978, the Commission removed the others to reveal the shape of the highly impressive oval fort. Bury Ditches is one of the best-preserved Iron Age sites in Britain.

Kingsbury Water Park
From the Church of St Peter and Paul in the village of Kingsbury, you can gaze out over more than 30 lakes and pools in the 620-acre (251-ha) Kingsbury Water Park (see Walk 39). The park was once an area of sand and gravel pits, and the region is rich in history, with particular associations with Sir Robert Peel – MP for Tamworth, founder of the Conservative party and prime minister 1834–5 and 1841–6 – who owned a great deal of land in the village in the mid-19th century. In the Water Park cycling, windsurfing, waterskiing, boating and fishing are on offer in addition to walking. The park is well known for its varied birdlife and is also a favourite with birdwatchers.

Rutland Water
Covering 3,100 acres (1,255ha), Rutland Water (see Walk 42) was originally known as Empingham reservoir and was formed in the 1970s by the flooding of the Gwash Valley to supply water to the East Midlands region. It is now a venue for varied water sports, including sailing and windsurfing as well as fishing, and at one end adjoins the beautiful Rutland Water Nature Reserve. In summer you can take a cruise on the water in the *Rutland Belle*.

Castle Ashby House
This beautiful house in the Northamptonshire countryside was begun in 1574 by William, Lord Compton and later improved by English classical architect Inigo Jones, but the main attraction is the magnificent 200 acres (81ha) of grounds landscaped by Lancelot 'Capability' Brown in 1760 (see Walk 43). The gardens also include a mile-long avenue planted in 1695 and a 16th-century walled area. The house has received three royal visits – from Queen Elizabeth I in 1600, King James I in 1605 and King William III in 1695.

The 'Rambler's Church'
On a hilltop above the village of Walesby in Lincolnshire, the 'Rambler's Church' (see Walk 50) is properly known as All Saints. Rebuilt in 1913 from a more ancient building, the church attracted local walkers, some of whom in the 1930s paid for a stained-glass window in the Lady Chapel depicting cyclists and walkers. Walkers gather for an annual service on Trinity Sunday (eight weeks after Easter). It stands on one of the highest spots in Lincolnshire, on the Viking Way footpath, and commands magnificent views as far as Lincoln.

Polesworth
This Warwickshire village (see Walk 41) contains the remains of an ancient nunnery founded in 827 by Egbert, king of Wessex in 802–839. The church, the 14th-century gatehouse and part of the cloister survive; after the abbey was closed during the Dissolution of the Monasteries (1536–41) some stones and the roof beams were used in building the manor house of Pooley Hall on the same site. At Pooley Hall, Sir Henry Goodere was a patron of the arts. However, the hall was demolished in the mid-19th century and the Polesworth vicarage was built on the site.

35 Hereford's Lost Canal

Many decades in the making, the Hereford and Gloucester Canal was only a going concern for a short period, but today is being restored for leisure use

Unless you know where to look, the only hint of the Hereford and Gloucester Canal in the city of Hereford today is in the street named Canal Road, which led to the canal's western terminus. In the east the canal joined the River Severn at Over, just west of Gloucester. The canal was opened in two phases, one from Gloucester to near Ledbury in 1798 and a second extending it to Hereford in 1845. But its success was short-lived and it was closed in 1881, after which parts of its southern section were used for the Ledbury and Gloucester railway. Since the 1980s the Hereford and Gloucester Canal Trust has striven to restore the canal to its former glory.

Monkhide Bridge

The Trust's greatest tangible achievements to date have been restoring the skew bridge at Monkhide, a section of canal at Yarkhill, and the Over Basin, across the border in Gloucestershire. But the Trust have also succeeded in partially winning over public opinion: gradually, people in authority have realised that this isn't just a matter of men playing with water and boats instead of railways and steam trains – and not just because some of the canal volunteers are women. Perhaps this is because the authorities have noticed the thriving canal leisure sector in Worcestershire, where almost as many people overnight on boats (13 per cent) as they do in bed and breakfast accommodation (14 per cent). A few years ago the planning authorities were successfully lobbied in Hereford city. The service road to a new retail park in the north of the city – connecting Newtown Road and Burcott Road – includes a bridge that spans the course of the old canal, instead of cutting through it or filling it with hardcore or concrete. The Canal Trust is working with Herefordshire Council to restore a stretch of derelict canal through the newly created Aylestone Park, just north of Hereford's centre.

If you choose visit the skew bridge at Monkhide, you may be disappointed because no provision has been made for access – you can't take a good look at engineer Stephen Ballard's mini-masterpiece, now a Grade II listed building. Ballard later worked as a railway engineer. His grandson, also called Stephen, unveiled a plaque on the bridge.

Records show that, typically, a lock keeper would be paid 14s per week but his employers would deduct 2s per week for rent. Lock cottages may have been rudimentary, but what could someone today earning, say, £350 per week rent for £50 per week? This brings to mind the old expression, 'the best place to put your money is in bricks and mortar' – house bricks, that is, not canal bricks.

Below: Beautiful skies over Herefordshire

Below left: The walk leads across arable fields with views of woodland

Below right: Gentle light on a lake at Canon Frome

35 Hereford's Lost Canal

Get a fascinating glimpse of Herefordshire history

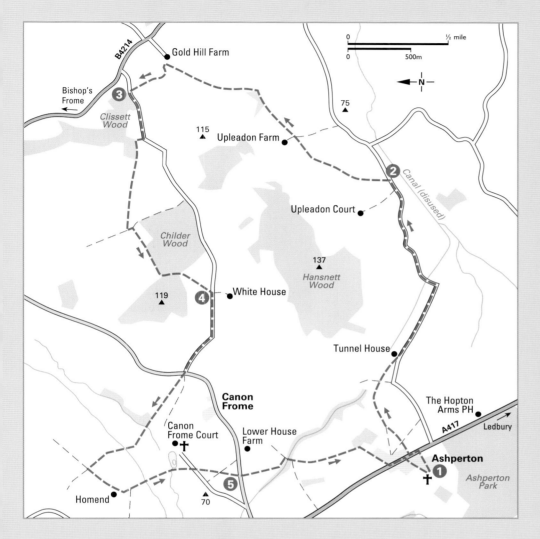

Distance 7.75 miles (12.5km)

Minimum Time 3hrs 30min

Ascent/Gradient 260ft (79m) ▲▲▲

Level of Difficulty ●●●

Paths Field and woodland paths, minor roads, at least 35 stiles

Landscape Gently undulating, mixed farming, woodland, derelict canal

Suggested Map OS Explorer 202 Leominster & Bromyard

Start/Finish Grid reference: SO 642415

Dog Friendliness Close control near livestock and on minor roads

Parking St Bartholomew's Church, Ashperton

Public Toilets None en route

1 From the church car park take the 'forty shillings' gate, behind houses, following waymarkers. Join a track to the A417. Turn left, then right, beside a high wooden fence. Follow a fingerpost across meadows for about 600yds (549m). Find a gate beside a cricket net. Cross the cricket field to a sightscreen, then a track, not joining Haywood Lane (to which the track leads) until some 250yds (229m) further, at the far corner. Turn left, passing Tunnel House. Continue for about 1 mile (1.6km). Find a stile on the left just beyond a gate about 100yds (91m) after the driveway to Upleadon Court.

2 Cross large arable fields and a ditch, then Upleadon Farm's driveway. Aim for the far left-hand corner, taking three gates, then skirt some woodland to your left, striking left (waymarked) at its corner, up a huge field. At Gold Hill Farm go right of a tall shed. Behind

this, turn left, over two stiles. Turn right, ascending beside a wooden fence, but from its first corner follow a hawthorn boundary remnant to a road.

3 Turn left for 0.25 mile (400m). Where the road turns left go ahead, initially beside a wood, entering a huge field. Veer slightly left to find a (hidden) handrailed bridge with a broken stile beyond it. Turn left but in 25yds (23m) turn right, before a gate. After 500yds (457m) enter trees. On leaving them strike half right for the large White House.

4 Turn right along the road. When you reach the junction, take the footpath opposite, across a long field. Beyond some trees, aim right of a solitary oak. Walk across fields, over three footbridges and under power lines, passing through a gap to another stile, but do

not cross this – note three waymarkers on its far side. Turn left. Just beyond Homend find a stile in a far left-hand corner of an old orchard, shielded by an ash and a larch. Turn left, soon moving right to double gates flanking a wide concrete bridge. After the leafy avenue keep ahead, veering right when a pond is behind trees to your left. Cross the driveway to Canon Frome Court, then another track, finally reaching a road by a spinney.

5 Cross over the road and walk straight to the canal. Turn left. In 140yds (128m) turn right, over the canal. Veer left and uphill, finding a large oak in the top left-hand corner. Keep this line despite the field boundary curving away. On reaching a copse turn right, later moving left into an indistinct lane. The village hall heralds the A417. Turn left, along the pavement, then right to the church.

36 Follow the Buzzard to the Heights of Bury Ditches

The Iron Age builders of Bury Ditches took advantage of Sunnyhill's steep southern slopes to create a formidable fortress in a commanding position

Above: Trees at Acton

Above right: Steep slopes deter approach from the south at Bury Ditches

It is impossible to spend much time in Shropshire without becoming aware of its hill forts. The south-west corner of the county is particularly rich in these impressive monuments, and the same is true of the neighbouring parts of Herefordshire and Montgomeryshire, so that there is hardly a hilltop in the area that doesn't provide a view of several forts. Some were built in the late Bronze Age, but most were constructed in the Iron Age – that is, after around 600 BC. They were built in stages, often over very long periods of time, possibly as much as 1,000 years in some cases.

Contour Fort

Bury Ditches, which crowns Sunnyhill (also called Tangley Hill), rises high above the valleys of the Clun and the Kemp. Elliptical in shape, it is an example of a contour fort, meaning that its Celtic builders took advantage of the topography, making the ramparts follow the natural contours of the landscape. Such construction wasn't always possible, but where the natural slope was steep, it enabled the builders to get away with fewer ramparts, or even none at all. On the relatively gentle northern slope of Sunnyhill summit, three substantial ramparts were considered necessary, but there are only two on the south side, below which the slope plunges down steeply.

Clearing the Land

The construction of the ramparts at Bury Ditches suggest that they were built in around the 6th century BC (in the early Iron Age). All the local community would have been involved, including young children. Trees would have to be cleared first, using axes made from flint, stone or bronze, and then the ramparts and ditches would be dug with deer-antler picks and shovels made from the shoulder blades of cattle. Earth, turf and stones would be carried away in hand baskets. It's a task of almost unimaginable proportions, especially when you consider that Bury Ditches covers a larger area than most hamlets and many villages in Shropshire.

It was once thought that hill-forts were used only for defence at times of danger, but excavation and other archaeological techniques have revealed that the larger ones were more like defended villages, where people lived and farmed. Did they also appreciate the view, in purely aesthetic terms? The immense panorama visible from the top of Bury Ditches is one of the finest in Shropshire, but it was lost for several years, after the Forestry Commission planted conifers there. A timely gale in 1978 flattened many of the alien trees and the Commission took the hint, removing the rest.

36 Follow the Buzzard to the Heights of Bury Ditches

Enjoy magnificent views from a dramatic hill-fort

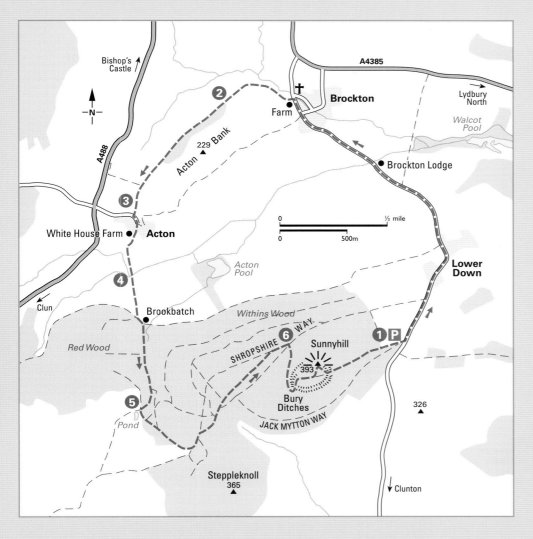

Distance 5.5 miles (8.8km)

Minimum Time 2hrs

Ascent/Gradient 804ft (245m) ▲▲▲

Level of Difficulty ●●●

Paths Field and woodland paths, one boggy and overgrown, fence and gates to climb at Acton Bank, 8 stiles

Landscape Hilltop woodland and plantation, mixed farmland in valley

Suggested Map OS Explorer 216 Welshpool & Montgomery

Start/Finish Grid reference: SO 334839

Dog Friendliness Off lead for much of way, but not round Acton

Parking Forestry Commission car park at Sunnyhill off minor road north from Clunton

Public Toilets None en route

1 From the car park at Sunnyhill, walk back to the lane and turn left. Descend through Lower Down to Brockton. Turn left on a track shortly before you come to a ford. Pass a collection of buses in a yard, then go through a gate on the left and walk along the right-hand edges of three fields, parallel with the track.

2 Climb over a fence into a wood then join the track just below, contouring round the base of Acton Bank. After leaving the wood the path continues through scrub, then through pasture below some old quarries, before it meets a lane at the hamlet of Acton.

3 Turn left, pass to the right of a triangular green and join a path past White House Farm. Frequent waymarkers guide you past the house, across a field, then left over a stile and along the right-hand edge of another field.

4 Cross a footbridge and continue straight across the field towards a building at the far side. Cross a stile in the hedge, turn left for a few paces then right on a track that passes by a house called Brookbatch on your left and into woodland. When the track bends to the left, go over a stile instead and then continue climbing.

5 Emerging on to a track, turn left past a pond on your right. Cross a defunct cattle grid into Forestry Commission property and leave the track, turning right on a footpath through beechwoods. At a crossroads of tracks turn left, then bear right on a forestry track by a Shropshire Way sign. Ignore all side turnings until the Shropshire Way goes left at a fork.

6 Climb gently for a while. Where the main track levels off and starts to descend, turn right. The path leads to Bury Ditches hill fort, then cuts through a gap in the ramparts and crosses the interior. At a colour-banded post (red, blue and green), a path branches left to allow a visit to the summit, with marvellous views. Bear right to return to the main path and turn left to follow it to the car park.

37 Gone to Earth on Lovely Lyth Hill

A gentle climb up Lyth Hill reveals the view that inspired Mary Webb, author of many novels of Shropshire life – including the celebrated *Gone to Earth*

Lyth Hill, which is included within a small country park, is of modest height, attaining only 557ft (169m). It's mainly grassland, with areas of scrub and woodland that support a variety of birds such as the great spotted woodpecker, the wood warbler and the tree pipit. The hill commands a superb view that includes the Clee Hills, Wenlock Edge, The Wrekin, the Stretton Hills, Long Mynd and Stiperstones.

This view inspired Mary Webb, or Mary Gladys Meredith as she was born in 1881 at Leighton, a small village south of Shrewsbury. In 1902 she moved with her family to Meole Brace, where she lived until her marriage to Henry Webb in 1912. Mary was a great walker and during the years at Meole Brace it was Lyth Hill that was her favourite

destination. She was enchanted not only by the view, but also by the small wood called Spring Coppice. In 1917, after the publication of her first novel, the Webbs bought a plot of land on the hill and Spring Cottage was built for them. This was Mary's home, apart from a short spell in London, until her untimely death in 1927. The cottage is there today, but much altered and extended.

Posthumous Fame

Mary adored Shropshire. She wrote several novels at Spring Cottage, each richly imbued with a sense of the local landscape – few writers have been so much in tune with their surroundings, or so able to convey their atmosphere. But she achieved little fame in her lifetime; it was only after her death that praise from the prime minister, Stanley Baldwin, sparked off public interest and acclaim.

Mary Webb's best novels are considered to be *Precious Bane* and *The Golden Arrow*, while *Gone to Earth* was made into a film, shot in Shropshire in 1950. Today, however, her novels are not generally fashionable – indeed, they're seen as being all too easy to make fun of and Stella Gibbons's classic *Cold Comfort Farm* was actually a parody of one of Mary's books (*The House in Dormer Forest*). But they are well worth reading if you love Shropshire.

Top right: Part of the walk follows the Shropshire Way

Right: Grassland near Lyth Hill

Below: Looking down over farmland and hills from Lyth Hill

37 Gone to Earth on Lovely Lyth Hill

Savour the panoramic views that gave inspiration to the novelist Mary Webb

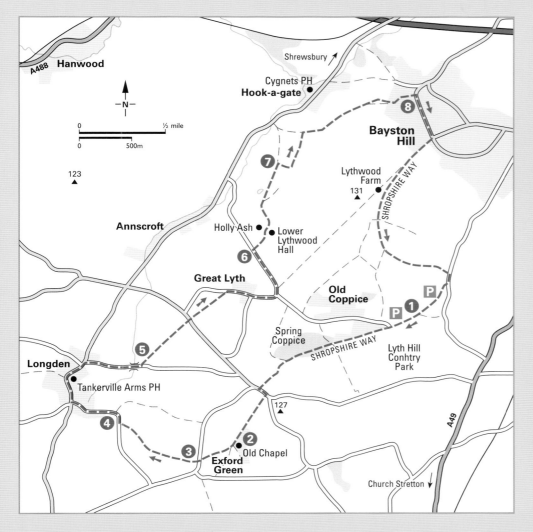

Distance 7.75 miles (12.5km)

Minimum Time 3hrs

Ascent/Gradient 500ft (152m) ▲▲▲

Level of Difficulty ●●●

Paths Cross-field paths, mostly well-maintained, about 30 stiles

Landscape Rolling farmland and views from Lyth Hill's grassy top

Suggested Map OS Explorer 241 Shrewsbury

Start/Finish Grid reference: SJ 473069

Dog Friendliness Must be on lead near livestock, also at Exford Green

Parking Car park in country park at top of Lyth Hill (signposted)

Public Toilets None en route

1 Head southwest on the Shropshire Way. Ignore a path branching right into Spring Coppice. The Way descends to a track. Follow this past The Yews to a lane, where you turn left, then first right, on a track to Exford Green.

2 Cross two stiles to skirt a former Primitive Methodist chapel. Leave the Shropshire Way, going diagonally across a field, heading for the far corner. Cross a stile close to the corner and go through a copse to reach a lane.

3 Cross to a path almost opposite, following the left-hand edge of a field until you come to a stile that gives access to another. Head diagonally across to a point close to the far right corner. Cross a stile and continue across another field, past two oak trees. A worn path goes obliquely right across the next two fields to meet a lane.

4 Turn right, then right again at the main road. Pass through Longden. Go right again on School Lane; this descends very slightly. Cross a brook, then go through a gate on the left and diagonally right across a field corner to a stile.

5 A yellow arrow directs you diagonally across the next field to a stile under an oak tree between two telegraph posts. Cross another field to reach a road. The path continues opposite, crossing two further fields until it meets a lane at Great Lyth. Turn right on the lane, keeping straight on at a junction, then turn left at the next.

6 Turn right on the access track to Lower Lythwood Hall and Holly Ash. At the end, turn left on a lush green lane. At its end turn right over a stile and cross a field. Pass a row

of three oak trees, then keep to the right of a pond to reach a stile at the far side. Follow the edge of the next field to a gate. Continue along a track for a few paces until you can cross a stile on the right.

7 Walk up the right edge of the field and turn left along the top. Follow a worn path across a field, go through a kissing gate, and along field-edges to a path behind houses.

8 Meeting a street, turn immediately right on a fenced path, then straight ahead on a street. Turn right then first left (Bredden Way). At the top turn right then left by a postbox through trees to a lane. Turn right to Lythwood Farm. Go straight through then fork left and follow the track across fields. Cross the last field aiming left of a small reservoir. Emerge to a lane and turn right, back to Lyth Hill.

38 Birth of a Revolution at Coalbrookdale

Nature has reclaimed sites once ruled by industry, making Coalbrookdale a lovely setting for a walk rich in natural beauty as well as historical interest

People have been smelting iron for many centuries, but production was originally small-scale because smelting was dependent on timber, which first had to be made into charcoal – a slow and laborious process. All that changed at Coalbrookdale in 1709 when Abraham Darby I perfected a method of smelting iron with coke instead of charcoal. It may sound like a small thing, but it sparked a revolution that changed the world. At long last, iron could be made cheaply in large quantities and it came to be increasingly used in many areas of engineering.

Centre of Industry

By 1785, the Coalbrookdale district had become the foremost industrial area in the world. It was particularly celebrated for its innovations: the first iron bridge, the first iron boat, the first iron rails and the first steam locomotive. Tourists came from far and wide to see the sights, and artists came to paint it all – furnaces lighting up the night sky was a favourite subject. Decline eventually set in due to competition from the Black Country and South Wales and the area fell into decay. Since

the 1960s, the surviving industrial relics have been transformed into a fascinating collection of museums and the gorge has been designated a UNESCO World Heritage Site. Perhaps even more remarkable than the industrial heritage is the way nature has made sites of industrial despoilation beautiful again. These regenerated woods and meadows are managed by the Severn Gorge Countryside Trust and are accessible to the public.

The ironmasters built housing for their workers and took an interest in their moral well-being. When you walk through Dale Coppice and Lincoln Hill Woods you will be using the Sabbath Walks, designed by Richard Reynolds to provide healthy Sunday recreation for his workers. A rotunda was erected at one viewpoint, but has since been demolished, though you can still enjoy the view. It's mostly woodland now, but you will see the remains of a great quarry that bit deep into Lincoln Hill. It extends so far underground that tours of its limestone caverns were popular with 19th-century day-trippers. Bands played in the illuminated caverns and thousands came on excursion trains from the Black Country and Birmingham.

Below: Dale House Museum of Iron

Bottom left: Ironworkers' cottages at Ironbridge

Below right: Iron Bridge – the world's first arch bridge made of cast iron

38 Birth of a Revolution at Coalbrookdale

Explore the wooded hills and valleys where the Industrial Revolution began

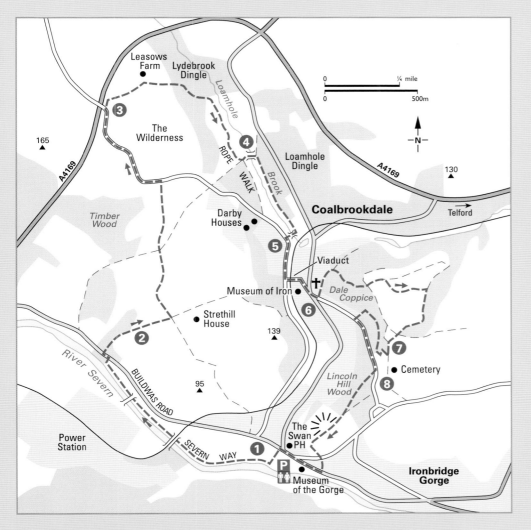

Distance 5 miles (8km)

Minimum Time 2hrs

Ascent/Gradient 770ft (235m) ▲▲▲

Level of Difficulty ●●●

Paths Woodland paths, lots of steps (mostly descending), may be fallen trees at Strethill, 2 stiles, some paths very overgrown

Landscape Wooded hills of Severn Gorge

Suggested Map OS Explorer 242 Telford, Ironbridge & The Wrekin

Start/Finish Grid reference: SJ 664037

Dog Friendliness Excellent, but keep under strict control at Strethill (sheep)

Parking Dale End Riverside Park, just west of Museum of the Gorge

Public Toilets In Museum of the Gorge car park

1 Follow the River Severn upstream under two bridges, then bear away from the river towards Buildwas Road. At the road, turn left for a few paces, then cross to a footpath that ascends through woodland. Keep close to the edge until a waymarker directs you to the right.

2 Cross a stile and continue over pasture. Go under a pylon, then join a track climbing to a gate. Turn right and follow the hawthorn hedge to a junction. Turn left and follow three field-edges, then go up through a meadow to a lane. Turn left and continue on the lane.

3 Leave the lane just before it bridges a road, going right on a farm track (Shropshire Way). Just before Leasows Farm, go through a gate on the right, then downfield to enter Lydebrook Dingle at a stile. Take a path through the wood then a path, Rope Walk.

4 Descend steps on the left into Loamhole Dingle. Cross Loamhole Brook at a footbridge and climb 41 steps on the other side. Turn right and follow the boardwalk to Upper Furnace Pool. Cross its far end on the first of two footbridges to meet the road.

5 The route is to the left, but a detour right leads to the Darby Houses and the Quaker Burial Ground. Resuming the walk, go down to Darby Road, go right beside the viaduct and the Museum of Iron, turn left under the viaduct, then follow the road past the museum and Coalbrookdale Works to a junction.

6 Cross into Church Road. After the Wesleyan chapel turn left, then go up steps to Dale Coppice. Follow signs for 'Church Road' at two junctions, then follow steps, left through the woods. Enter grassland and go

forward to a track. Turn left, then fork right, on the track. Bear left at another junction, then right at two. A cemetery is on the left.

7 Partway along the cemetery, a small wooden gate accesses Dale Coppice on the right. Turn right, then soon left, going downhill to a junction marked by a bench. Turn right, then left when a sign indicates 'Church Road', then left again down the road.

8 Turn right into Lincoln Hill Wood and follow signs to the 'Rotunda' to a viewpoint where the Rotunda formerly stood. Descend a steep flight of steps to a junction. Turn right, then left down more steps and left again, signposted 'Lincoln Hill Road'. Cross the road to a footpath that descends to the Wharfage. Turn right past Lincoln Hill lime kilns and The Swan to Dale End Riverside Park.

39 Crowds Flood to Peaceful Kingsbury Water Park

Historical associations, including links to Shakespeare and former prime minister Sir Robert Peel, add interest to a walk around Kingsbury and its fine water park

The water park around Kingsbury was once 620 acres (251ha) of old sand and gravel pits, but today it has become a major leisure facility with more than 30 beautiful lakes and pools attracting some 200,000 visitors each year. A path crosses the River Tame into the water park where you can stroll around a number of the larger pools to enjoy watching a wide variety of contemporary sporting activities taking place such as sailing, windsurfing, fishing and horse-riding. There are also several hides where you can do a spot of birding.

Shakespeare's Ancestors

The village of Kingsbury sits on a hill overlooking this wonderland of water. On this high ground is the Church of St Peter and St Paul with its 12th-century nave, 14th-century tower and 16th-century belfry. Kingsbury village has been associated with many famous families over the years. In the Middle Ages the Bracebridges and Ardens were involved in a Romeo-and-Juliet-type feud when Alice Bracebridge married John Arden against the wishes of both families. John's brother's granddaughter was Mary Arden, mother of William Shakespeare.

By the middle of the 19th century most of the land in the village was owned by Sir Robert Peel. The long-serving MP for Tamworth, one-time prime minister and founder of the modern police, lived at nearby Drayton Manor and was buried at Drayton Basset, a few miles up the Tame Valley.

The main business of the area had been agriculture, but coal mining took over. Later sand and gravel was extracted from the land on the other side of the River Tame.

You leave the water park over Hemlingford Bridge that crosses the River Tame. This bridge was first built by public subscription in 1783 and takes its name from the Hundred of Hemlingford in which Kingsbury stands (a hundred was an old Saxon local administrative area). There used to be a toll house at one end of the original bridge, but this was demolished in 1937. On New Year's Day in 1982 the original bridge was destroyed by catastrophic floods, which swept down the Tame Valley. Flooding has been a regular feature of the area, with the water frequently rising and spreading over the flood plain between Kingsbury village and the nearby hamlet of Bodymoor Heath. Most people now live on the east side of the River Tame.

Below left: Teasels growing in Kingsbury Water Park

Below right: Mallard ducks in the water park

Main picture: Twilight over Bodymoor Heath Water, one of the lakes on the walk

39 Crowds Flood to Peaceful Kingsbury Water Park

Take a relaxing stroll around a reclaimed area of sand and gravel pits

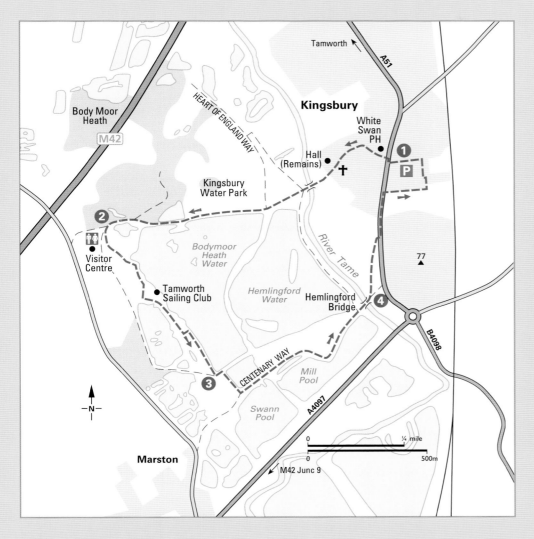

Distance 3 miles (4.8km)

Minimum Time 1hr 20min

Ascent/Gradient 33ft (10m) ▲▲▲

Level of Difficulty ●●●

Paths Reservoir paths and footpaths, 2 stiles

Landscape Reservoir parkland

Suggested Map OS Explorer 232 Nuneaton & Tamworth

Start/Finish Grid reference: SP 217962

Dog Friendliness Under control at all times

Parking Pear Tree Avenue car park (free)

Public Toilets Visitor centre in Kingsbury Water Park

---

1 From the car park, go left along Pear Tree Avenue to reach the A51 road. Go right along the pavement of the A51, then cross the road passing in front of the White Swan pub. About 35yds (32m) beyond the pub, cross the road and go left by the side of the churchyard. Follow the waymarkers for the Heart of England Way past the church and go down steps to a footbridge over the River Tame. Cross the bridge and follow a metalled track in to Kingsbury Water Park. With Hemlingford Water on your left, cross the footbridge and walk by the side of Bodymoor Heath Water, leaving the Heart of England Way behind and eventually bearing right by a miniature railway line over a footbridge to reach the visitor centre complex.

2 From the visitor centre, follow the signs to the watersports clubs along lanes and footpaths. Shortly the path returns to the side of Bodymoor Heath Water, then leaves it to pass by the entrance gate to Tamworth Sailing Club. Continue to the right-hand side of Bodymoor Heath Water, along a tarmac lane then back to the water's edge path.

3 At the end of the stretch of Body Heath Water bear left, then almost immediately right and follow the waymarkers for the Centenary Way. Turning left the waymarkers take you near to Swann Pool and then, across a small car park diagonally, between Mill Pool and Hemlingford Water as your route veers in a north-east direction. Continue on the path until it merges with a lane, then keep ahead to go over the Hemlingford Bridge.

4 Immediately across the bridge, go left over a stile and cross the edge of the field to a final stile on to the pavement of the A51, near the middle of the village of Kingsbury. Go left along the pavement until you reach an area of open land on the other side of the road. At the far end cross over the road and go right, through a kissing gate, to the right of No. 61, on to a clear footpath that goes along the back of some houses. In about 220yds (201m), turn left into Meadow Close, then left again into Pear Tree Avenue to return to the car park.

40 History at Hartshill Hayes

A Norman lord built a castle and a 16th-century poet was inspired by the landscape in a gentle corner of Warwickshire now gathered into a country park

Right: Part of the walk follows the Coventry Canal

Below: Look out for catkins in the Hartshill Hayes Country Park

Bottom: On a clear day you can see as far as the peaks of Derbyshire from the country park

In 1978, around 136 acres (55ha) of the hillside around Hartshill were made into the fine country park that forms the basis of this walk. It strays into Warwickshire proper and includes part of the Coventry Canal. Wildlife thrives in the country park: the spotted flycatcher is a frequent visitor and you may glimpse the low, swooping flight of a sparrow hawk. A sizeable area of woodland has developed at Hartshill, dominated by traditional broadleaved trees such as oak, beech, sycamore, hazel and alder. Elder and holly also thrive.

Hartshill History

Hartshill village is an old settlement, but there is little information to establish its full history. The Romans were here and may have built a military station; Hugh de Hardreshull built a motte-and-bailey castle on the hill in 1125. Robert de Hartshill, who became Lord of the Castle, was killed alongside Simon de Montfort at the battle of Evesham in 1265. Perhaps it fell into disuse then, for all traces of the fortification have disappeared.

The village's most famous resident was the poet Michael Drayton, a contemporary and friend of William Shakespeare. He was born at the long-demolished Chapel Cottage in Hartshill Green in 1563; there is a plaque in his memory. His poem 'A Fine Day' suggests he drew considerable inspiration from the local landscape:

> 'Clear had the day been from the dawn
> All chequered was the sky
> Thin clouds like scarfs of cobweb lawn
> Veiled heaven's most glorious eye.'

In 'Poly-Olbion' he described the River Anker, which weaves its way past his birthplace to join the River Tame, as 'trifling betwixt her banks so slow'.

Coventry Canal

The Coventry Canal came long after Drayton's day. It winds its way along the valley below the village linking Atherstone and the Fazeley Junction, where it joins the main canal system to connect with the Trent and Mersey. The canal reached Fazeley in 1790, happily coinciding with the completion date of the Oxford Canal and allowing it to improve a shaky financial position – under engineer James Brindley its construction had run massively over budget. It remained in a reasonably sound state until 1948 when nationalisation was followed by disuse and deterioration. In recent years, however, it has been restored for use by pleasure craft.

40 History at Hartshill Hayes

Walk in the Warwickshire ways that charmed Shakespeare's friend Michael Drayton

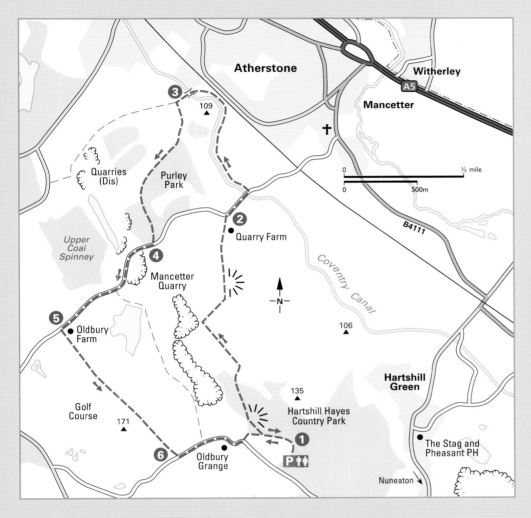

Distance 4.5 miles (7.2km)

Minimum Time 1hr 45min

Ascent/Gradient 295ft (90m) ▲▲▲

Level of Difficulty ●●●

Paths Lanes, field paths, woodland tracks and tow paths, no stiles

Landscape Country park and rolling countryside

Suggested Map OS Explorer 232 Nuneaton & Tamworth

Start/Finish Grid reference: SP 317943

Dog Friendliness Off lead in park and along tow path

Parking Hartshill Hayes Country Park, pay-and-display

Public Toilets Hartshill Hayes Country Park

1 From the car park enter the Hartshill Hayes Country Park at the back of the visitor centre. Pass the swings and take the path which arcs left (northwest) along the top of Hartshill, alongside a covered reservoir, and enjoy the superb view over the surrounding area. Continue ahead across the greensward on the path that then descends gently right into woodland. At the bottom of the woodland go over the two footbridges and then bear left to walk along a fine open path as you continue, initially to the left of the hedge, then to its right. In about 0.25 mile (400m) the path bends to the right and you will ascend northeast to the brow of the hill, from where you can overlook the Coventry Canal and get a great view. Bear left beside a kissing gate on to the path which becomes hedged as you progress northwards towards Quarry Farm. Go through the handgate to the left of the farm buildings on to Quarry Lane.

2 Turn right and stroll down the lane, bearing right at the junction until you come to bridge No. 36 over the Coventry Canal. Cross either bridge and descend right to the tow path, go right under the bridge to walk in a northwesterly direction and in 0.5 mile (800m) proceed beneath bridge No. 37.

3 Leave the tow path at bridge No. 38 and cross the canal on to a quiet lane. Walk up the lane for about 150yds (137m) then, just before a private house, go left through a tall kissing gate into meadowland and on into pastureland. Cross over the footbridge at the bottom of the field, then walk half right across the next field and on to a gate to a footbridge and a second tall kissing gate and enter the woodland of Purley Park. Follow the footpath up the right edge of the woodland. The path arcs left into the trees and you will exit on to Quarry Lane again.

4 Go right and head up the lane, past the entrance to Mancetter Quarry. Continue along the lane and in a further 600yds (549m), just past Oldbury Farm, go left.

5 Walk to the right of the farm buildings with market gardens on your right to reach a good bridlepath beside ponds going southeast. This lovely path crosses arable land, but soon you will be following yellow-topped marker posts across a golf course.

6 Exit on to a road, via a handgate, and then go left. The road passes by Oldbury Grange and Adbury Gardens. Where there is a sharp right-hand bend in the road, go left up towards the rear entrance to the gardens and enter Hartshill Hayes Country Park via two gates. Once you are in the park bear right and join the waymarked park path that takes you back to the visitor centre.

41 An Ancient Abbey and Manor at Polesworth

From the remains of an abbey founded by the Saxon king Egbert, a walk full of historical interest leads along a tranquil section of the Coventry Canal

Above: The Coventry Canal at Polesworth

Below: Ploughed summer fields in the gentle landscape near Polesworth

This trip to Polesworth allows you to experience a fragment of monastic England and to see a beautiful, ancient abbey church and vicarage. These buildings date back to AD 827 and form part of a nunnery built by Egbert, who is often claimed to have been the first Saxon king of all England. His daughter Editha was the abbess.

Tales of a Haunting

Polesworth vicarage used to be the manor house and displays some ornate chimneys. In the corner of the vicarage garden (sadly, not accessible to the public) is a fine sundial with a square cap displaying the Nethersole and Goodere coats of arms carved on its sides. The abbey's dovecote can be found tucked away behind the village library. The superb 14th-century nunnery gate now has two residential flats in its upper storey. The larger of the two is said to be haunted by a friendly ghost. Apparently this harmless apparition moves plant pots around the building.

The influence of the local squirearchy can be seen all around Polesworth. Nearby Pooley Hall was built by Sir Thomas Cockain in 1506, although there are records of an earlier Saxon hall on the site. The stones in the walls and the beams in the roof were taken from the ancient abbey, following its dissolution. Sir Henry Goodere became lord of the manor and, according to local stories, the poet Michael Drayton (1563–1631) and his regular companion William Shakespeare both served him as page-boys at Pooley Hall.

Although the population of Polesworth has expanded to more than 9,000 today, the place retains a village atmosphere with its old part largely untouched and its many public houses intact. The River Anker and the Coventry Canal offer a quick step into the countryside, although it has been many years since local people were able to skate along these gentle backwaters. This used to be a favourite wintertime activity for villagers.

This charming walk starts near the tourist information office and then takes you over the River Anker on to the tow path of the Coventry Canal. After reaching the canal's bridge No. 49, you'll leave the tow path, crossing fields and lanes to the village of Dordon, before returning along Common Lane back into Polesworth.

41 An Ancient Abbey and Manor at Polesworth

Step back more than a thousand years at historic Polesworth

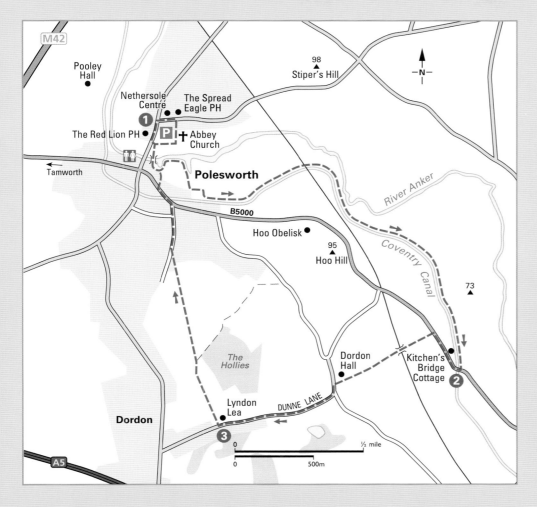

Distance 5 miles (8km)

Minimum Time 2hrs

Ascent/Gradient 115ft (35m) ▲▲▲

Level of Difficulty ●●●

Paths Canal tow paths, field paths and residential areas, 4 stiles

Landscape Gentle rolling farmland

Suggested Map OS Explorer 232 Nuneaton & Tamworth

Start/Finish Grid reference: SK 262024

Dog Friendliness Off lead along tow path, otherwise under control

Parking Hall Court car park (free)

Public Toilets Near Fire Station, Tamworth Road, Polesworth

1 From the car park at Hall Court, walk towards The Red Lion and left into Bridge Street, heading towards the bridge. After about 95 paces, turn left by the Spar shop into an alleyway that leads to a public footpath junction and turn right to take the path signed to the River Anker. Cross the footbridge over the river, then another and bear left through pleasant gardens, keeping by the river bank on a footpath. Leave the river and head for a sports pavilion. Beyond it turn left on a path beside the bowling green that arcs gently right towards bridge No. 51 over the Coventry Canal. Descend to the canal and turn left along its tow path, which you now follow for the next 1.5 miles (2.4km). You may see fishermen trying to catch some of the perch, roach and chub in the canal. Before walking beneath the railway line look up to your right and on the far bank you will see the obelisk on Hoo Hill. Stiper's Hill is visible to the left. Continue beneath the main electrified railway line.

2 Leave the Coventry Canal's tow path when you get to bridge No. 49 and ascend on to the road going left over the canal bridge and generally northwest past Kitchen's Bridge Cottage. Soon after passing the cottage, look out for a hedge gap on the left-hand side and go through this to cross the footbridge over the railway line via two stiles. Climb the hill passing through the farm gate to the left of the buildings of Dordon Hall farm and go up to the road. Over a stile go left along the road, then turn right when you reach a road junction, following the signpost to Dordon. This will take you along Dunne Lane into the village.

3 Immediately after passing a house called Lyndon Lea, at the crest of the hill, turn to the right down a track that leads to a gate on to a footpath over open farmland. Follow this footpath, heading generally northwards, towards the prominent trees of The Hollies. Continue left past the trees, crossing a stile

and, ignoring a kissing gate, continue ahead along a hedged path. Soon you will find yourself walking along a surfaced farm track that becomes Common Lane on the approach to Polesworth village. Take the pavement of the lane through a residential estate until you reach the B5000 Tamworth to Grendon road. Turn left and cross the road, with care as it can be busy, and stroll over the canal bridge. Turn right at Polesworth Garage down to the park area by the River Anker and cross back over the footbridge. The public footpath now leads up to a junction of paths where you go right, towards the abbey. Bear left and leave through the Old Nunnery Gateway on to the High Street. Now turn left and continue along the High Street, past the Nethersole Centre and turn left again into Bridge Street to return to Hall Court car park.

42 A Rutland Waterside Walk

A gentle and scenic walk near what was once the Gwash Valley provides a delightful introduction to the aquatic charms of Rutland Water

That England's smallest county contains its biggest stretch of inland water is impressive enough, but in fact Rutland Water's beautifully designed 3,100 acres (1,255ha) also make it one of the largest artificial lakes in the whole of Western Europe. Work began in 1973 with the flooding of the Gwash Valley and abandonment of the two villages of Nether and Middle Hambleton, leaving Upper Hambleton (now simply called Hambleton) virtually marooned on what was a ridge and is now a peninsula in the middle of the lake. Most of the village of Normanton survived, although its church was partially submerged. Although the reservoir was created in order to supply drinking water, Rutland Water has become a busy destination for outdoor pursuits. Sailing and windsurfing are very popular, while fishermen are to be found on the shores and out in boats in virtually all weathers. There are picnic sites along the northern edge, a museum at the preserved church at Normanton on the southern shore, and afternoon cruises on the *Rutland Belle* that plies the water daily between May and September. A 25-mile (40km) off-road cycling route runs around the whole of Rutland Water, and cycle hire is available at Whitwell and Normanton in the summer months.

Right: The former church of the village of Normanton – the lower storey is beneath water, but the upper part is a museum

Below: The walk tours the shore of the Hambleton Peninsula, with the waters of lake on three sides

Truly a Treat for Birdwatchers

The nature reserve at the far western end of Rutland Water is managed by Leicestershire and Rutland Wildlife Trust, and your first port of call should be the Anglian Water Bird Watching Centre at Egleton. From here you can obtain a permit to walk to the 20 different hides that are dotted around the secluded bays and artificially created lagoons, or go on to visit Lyndon Nature Reserve on the southern side of Manton Bay.

Rutland Water is one of the most important centres for wildfowl in Britain – as many as 23,500 ducks have been recorded on a single winter's day, and a total of 250 different species of birds have been seen since 1975. Ducks such as pochard, teal, gadwall and shoveler are a common sight around Rutland Water, while waders like redshank and sandpipers are frequent visitors. An hour or two in a hide and your list of birds spotted will probably include terns, lapwing, cormorants and grebes – plus, perhaps, a few more unusual sightings such as a merganser or a godwit.

However, there is one rare fish-eating bird that has had the birders fumbling at their binocular cases in excitement over the past few years. In 1996 a programme was initiated to translocate young osprey chicks from Scotland to Rutland Water, and since then several of these majestic birds of prey have returned from their hazardous African migration to set up home at Rutland – the first time ospreys have nested in England in more than 150 years. However, the long-term fate of the Rutland ospreys is far from secure, since the birds mate for life and have very few chicks, but with careful protection and gentle encouragement the outlook for the so-called 'fish eagles' is hopeful.

42 A Rutland Waterside Walk

Wander the shore of England's largest expanse of inland water

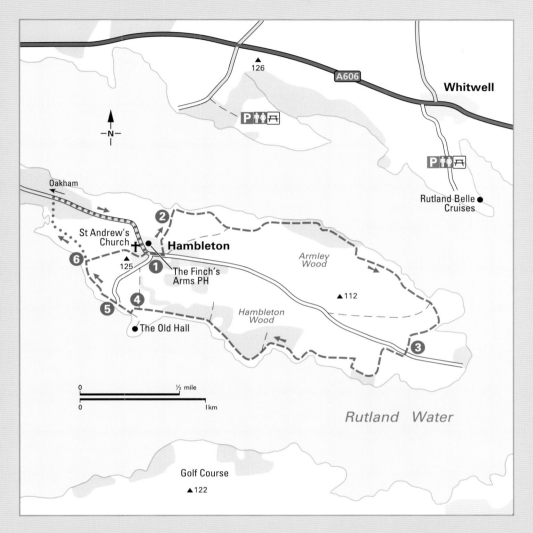

Distance 4.5 miles (7.2km)

Minimum Time 2hrs

Ascent/Gradient 311ft (95m) ▲▲▲

Level of Difficulty ●●●

Paths Wide and firm the whole distance, 3 stiles

Landscape Low-lying peninsula of dipping fields and woodland

Suggested Map OS Explorer 234 Rutland Water

Start/Finish Grid reference: SK 900075

Dog Friendliness On lead in fields of stock and around nesting birds

Parking Roadside parking in Hambleton

Public Toilets None en route (nearest in Oakham)

1 From St Andrew's Church in the centre of the village of Hambleton, walk eastwards on the long main street as far as the red pillar box. Turn left opposite the pillar box on a wide track indicated 'public footpath' that leads straight through a gate and down the middle of a sloping field.

2 Go through the gate at the bottom of the field and turn right on to the wide track that runs just above the shore. This popular and peaceful route around the Hambleton peninsula is shared with cyclists, so enjoy the walk, but be alert. Follow it from field to field, and through Armley Wood, with ever-changing views across Rutland Water. As you gradually swing around the tip of the Hambleton peninsula with views towards the dam at the eastern end, you can begin to appreciate the sheer size of the reservoir.

3 When you arrive at a tarmac lane – which is gated to traffic at this point, since it disappears into the water a little further on! – go straight across to continue on the same unmade track. It turns right and runs parallel with the road a short distance, before heading left and back towards the water's edge and a section of mixed woodland. Continue by the lakeside for just over 1 mile (1.6km).

4 Approaching The Old Hall, a handsome building perched just above the shore, turn left to reach its surfaced drive, then go right and walk along it for 160yds (146m) to reach a cattle grid.

5 At this point you can, if you wish, return directly to Hambleton by following the lane back uphill; otherwise veer left to continue along the open, waterside track, with

views across to Egleton Bay and the corner of Rutland Water specially reserved for wildlife – it's out of bounds to sailing boats.

6 After about 500yds (457m) look for the easily missed stile in the hedge on your right, and the public footpath that heads straight up the field. If you overshoot, or want to extend the walk by 0.5 mile (800m), simply carry on along the track to the very far end and return along the lane to the village. Aim for the apex of the field, where successive stiles lead to a narrow passageway between a hedge and a fence that eventually brings you out in the churchyard in the centre of the village.

43 Castle Ashby and its Estate

The grandiose Castle Ashby country house and its beautiful landscaped park and estate add glamour to a delightful walk in rural Northamptonshire

Castle Ashby is the ancestral home of the 7th Marquess of Northampton, and a fine pile he has too. Building work began in 1574 under the direction of the 1st Lord Compton, later Earl of Northampton, who originally had the house built in the shape of an 'E' before architect Inigo Jones filled in the openings. The house received visits from Queen Elizabeth I and later King James I.

Altogether the estate covers 10,000 acres (4,050ha) and is surrounded by landscaped parkland designed by Lancelot 'Capability' Brown. But aside from the neat lake and vast manicured lawns, the eye-catching feature has to be the stunning, mile-long avenue, first planted in 1695 after a visit by King William III.

Castle Ashby House is closed to the public, but the 200-acre (81ha) gardens are open daily – to get there, follow the signs through the village and across the avenue in front of the house. They include an arboretum and conservatory, and a more formal Victorian terrace and romantic Italianate designs. The latter reflected the 19th-century revival of interest in classical Italian gardens, based on the use of steps and balustrades, and on a structured transition that began with a geometrical layout through to more serpentine and irregular shapes. Parterres (formal floral beds) were created, using the family's crest as a motif.

Today, there are many varieties of trees and shrubs, including a giant horse chestnut described as one of the largest spreading trees in Britain, plus landscaped lawns and lakes complete with ornamental bridges and the so-called Triumphal Arch. Next to the gardens you can visit the 14th-century Church of St Mary Magdalene, which has various monuments to the Compton family.

Curious Floor Covering

The perimeter of the vast Castle Ashby estate is dotted, as you would imagine, with various lodges and gatehouses. But there's one that's rather different to the rest. Knucklebone Lodge (which sadly is private and cannot be visited) is so-called because of its knucklebone-patterned floor. But the thing is they are real animals' knucklebones, belonging to several thousand sheep, painstakingly arranged into a complete floor covering. Recycling it may be, but it really makes you want to reach for the carpet catalogue, doesn't it?

Right: St Peter's Church, Cogenhoe, dates to the 13th century

Below: Remains of Ashby Castle keep, Hastings Tower

Below right: The Orangery (1872) at Ashby Castle stands within Italianate gardens

43 Castle Ashby and its Estate

Take a turn around an estate once graced by royalty

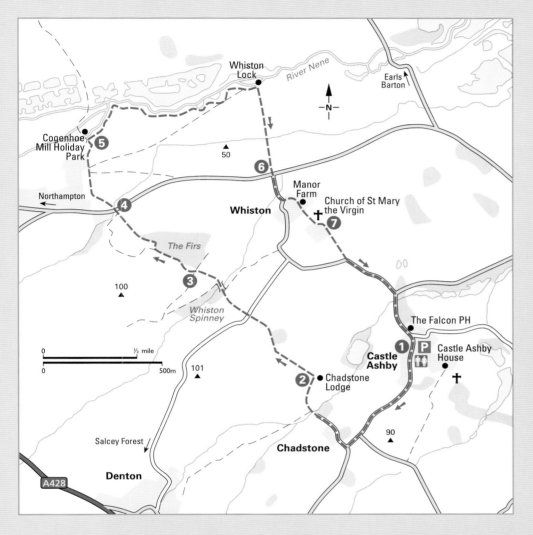

Distance 6.5 miles (10.4km)

Minimum Time 3hrs

Ascent/Gradient 557ft (170m) ▲▲▲

Level of Difficulty ●●●

Paths Field paths, farm tracks and river bank, some steps

Landscape Low rolling hills above gentle Nene Valley

Suggested Map OS Explorer 207 Newport Pagnell & Northampton South

Start/Finish Grid reference: SP 859594

Dog Friendliness Mostly arable fields, so generally good

Parking Roadside in Castle Ashby, or car park for visitors

Public Toilets Rural Shopping Yard, Castle Ashby

1 Walk out of Castle Ashby along the road heading southwestwards, with the house (and visitors' car park) over to your left. Where the pavement ends turn right for Chadstone. Drop down the lane past the cottages and expensive-looking converted barns and continue all the way out of the hamlet to the farm of Chadstone Lodge.

2 Turn left for the bridleway behind the hedge and, at the end of the bridleway, go on through the trees to continue the route alongside the next field and on down to a road. Cross over for a footpath opposite that leads down to Whiston Spinney, then continue via a footbridge through a lovely shady dell until you reach a junction of tracks on the far side. At this point continue straight on, and then climb directly up the sloping field ahead towards the trees on the far side.

3 Follow the path into the woods to climb some steps and head out along a field-edge with woodland on your right. Beyond a gate go down a sharp flight of steps to the right and across a field in order to turn left on the far side and drop down to the road below.

4 The route continues up through the field opposite. Head half left, then follow the bridleway waymarks to the right, through a long narrow field with the houses of Cogenhoe on your left. At the far side join a lane and descend to Cogenhoe Mill.

5 Just before the old mill buildings and sluice, with the holiday park beyond, turn right for a path alongside the River Nene (signposted 'Nene Way'). Follow this pleasant waterside walk for 1 mile (1.6km) as far as Whiston Lock, then turn right for a straight

farm track across the fields to the main road, heading towards Whiston church sitting astride the hilltop like a lighthouse.

6 Go across the junction and walk along the lane into Whiston, branching left at the small triangular village green. Take the gated passageway beside the outbuildings of Manor Farm and continue up towards the church. There are good views across the Nene Valley to Earls Barton and Wellingborough, and the eastern edge of Northampton.

7 Walk past the church to the far side of the churchyard, go over a metal rung in the wall and turn right on to an obvious field-edge path. This continues along a grassy strip between further fields and emerges on to the bend of a lane. Go straight on/left to walk this all the way back to Castle Ashby.

44 Woods and Heaths of Little Budworth

Across the distinctive heathland of Little Budworth country park, a walk through heather, gorse and bracken leads to a charming village

In the middle of rich, green farmland in lowland Cheshire is an island of something different – a little piece of an older landscape. To call it 'wild' would be misleading: there is probably no truly wild landscape anywhere in England. Usually it's peaceful, but a word of warning: it is very close to the Oulton Park motor-racing circuit. On race days not only is the traffic abominable, there's no escaping the noise, either.

Heathland Gorse and Heather

The area now called Little Budworth Country Park is a fragment of lowland heath. Britain has a substantial proportion of the world's lowland heath, but there is a great deal less than there used to be – only 18 per cent of what was recorded in 1800. Most of what remains is in Southern England, so Little Budworth is a bit special.

The essence of heath is an open landscape, with a mix of heather, gorse, bracken and grasses and with only scattered, if any, trees. Gorse is unmistakable and in summer the popping of its seed pods makes it one of those rare plants you can recognise with your ears. There are two characteristic species of heather: ling (which gardeners may know as *Calluna vulgaris*) and bell heather (*Erica cinerea*). They often grow together and look quite similar, but ling has slightly paler and more open flowers.

Heathland typically developed from areas cleared of trees from neolithic times onward: where poor soil made an area unsuitable for permanent cultivation, the land was used for grazing. Gorse was traditionally used as fuel and for animal fodder, while bracken provided animal bedding and was also a valuable source of potash. These activities, and the occasional natural fire, prevented the heath reverting to woodland. Much of today's country park is wooded, but you will also see large areas of heath, including some recently cleared.

The majority of the heathland at Little Budworth is dry, but there are some low-lying wetter areas. The pool you pass on the walk is a breeding ground for dragonflies and damselflies. By contrast the second half of the walk crosses farmland and then skirts the reedy margins of Budworth Mere. Finally the walk visits Little Budworth village. It is peaceful and attractive, but not so outrageously pretty that it has become a tourist magnet. You'll probably agree that this is to its benefit.

Above: Budworth Mere

Right: Little Budworth village

44 Woods and Heaths of Little Budworth

Take your chance to see the fascinating wildlife in a rare piece of lowland heath

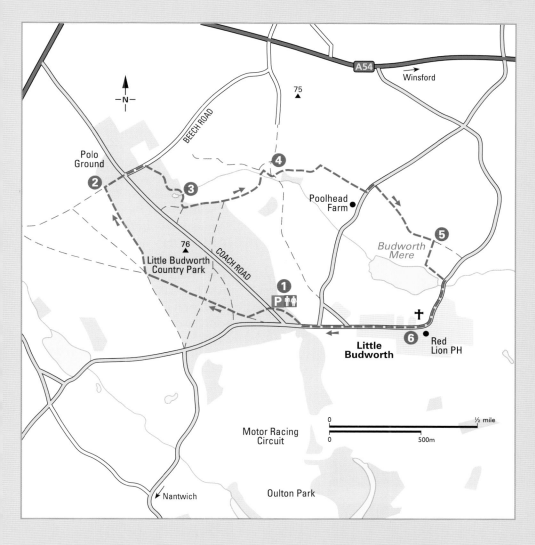

Distance 3.5 miles (5.7km)

Minimum Time 1hr 15min

Ascent/Gradient 98ft (30m) ▲▲▲

Level of Difficulty ●●●

Paths Easy tracks at first, field paths and some (usually quiet) road walking, 13 stiles

Landscape Mature woodland, open heath, farmland and mere

Suggested Map OS Explorer 267 Northwich & Delamere Forest

Start/Finish Grid reference: SJ 590654

Dog Friendliness Can run free in country park and fenced track

Parking Main car park for Little Budworth Country Park

Public Toilets At start

1 From the car park set off walking straight across the Coach Road to a path and then turn right on a wider path. Fork left and follow the main path, keeping straight on at a crossroads and carrying on again at the next crossing. When a field appears ahead, follow the path alongside to its right. This path veers away right, but you should go back left just before you reach a cleared area, by a Heathland Trail marker.

2 Go right on a wide track to the Coach Road and carry on straight across into Beech Road. After walking about 200yds (183m), turn right on a well-used path through open and very attractive woodland. Go through a gap in the fence, beyond which the path curves around a larger pool that is fringed with reeds and other vegetation – have a good look here, for this is a magnet for wildlife.

3 Cross a causeway/dam by the pool and gently climb a sunken track beyond. As it levels out, fork left by a Heathland Trail sign then turn left, with an open field not far away to the left. Bear left on a wider surfaced track, swinging down past houses to an ornamental pool in a dip. Immediately after this turn right on a sandy track.

4 Where another path crosses, most people evidently go through a gate ahead into the corner of the field. Strictly speaking, however, the right of way goes over a stile to its right then across the (very wet and smelly) corner of a wood to a second stile. From here bear right underneath a power line, carrying on as far as a stile in the far corner. Follow a narrow path (taking care to avoid nettles), then go over a stile on the right and straight across a large field. Aim just left of the farm to a gate and

stile. Go left on a lane for 60yds (55m) then right down a track. This becomes narrower, then descends slightly.

5 As the track levels out, there's a stile on the right, with a sign for Budworth Mere. Go down towards the water then left on a path skirting the mere. At the end go right up a road, swinging further right into the centre of Little Budworth.

6 Keep straight ahead along the road, going through the village then past open fields. Approaching the former entrance gates of Oulton Park, the pavement comes to an end. Here take a narrow woodland path on the right back to the car park.

45 The Dragon's Back

An invigorating walk in the Derbyshire White Peak delivers beautiful views from the Dragon's Back, the angular rocky protuberance better known as Chrome Hill

Right: Parkhouse Hill

Below: Looking from Hollinsclough at Chrome Hill and Parkhouse Hill

Bottom: Chrome Hill as seen from Tor Rock

When you stand on Axe Edge, you are standing on the Pennine watershed. Just to prove it, you can see five rivers – the Goyt, the Dane, the Dove, the Wye and the Manifold, each going their separate ways towards the Irish and North seas from near here. You are 1,660ft (506m) above sea level on one of the wildest gritstone moors of the Dark Peak, but when you look east you're looking across to the White Peak valley of the Dove. It is a fascinating view, with several rocky hills vying for your attention. One stands out from all the rest – Chrome Hill – and it is the high point of the day.

Derbyshire on the Equator

A pleasant, narrow lane takes the walk deep down into the valley, and soon you are following an old green road beneath Leap Edge. Chrome Hill hides behind Hollins Hill for a while, but once you've climbed round the limestone knoll of Tor Rock you see it again rearing up into the sky.

It's hard to believe, but Chrome Hill and its neighbours are the remains of coral reefs formed more than 320 million years ago, when Derbyshire lay under a tropical sea near the equator. Arches and caves, spires and fissures, have been carved out of the coral, creating this fascinating peak. You can see why it's sometimes known as the Dragon's Back.

There's a steep downhill section to do before the climb, then the footpath seems to take a timid line along the west side. Just as you think you've missed the summit path, the one you're on turns left and climbs for the sky. The path doesn't always keep to the crest, but avoids mild scrambles by plotting a devious course round the top rocks. Experienced walkers with a head for heights may well prefer to 'ride the dragon's back'.

Tea and Cakes in Hollinsclough

From the top, Parkhouse Hill captures your attention. Our route descends to the little road at its foot, then follows a pleasant farm track into Hollinsclough. On summer Sundays they serve tea and cakes in the village hall, a nice break before heading back across Hollinsclough Rake. The path comes to this shady corner between three hills and by the confluence of two brooks. There's an old packhorse bridge to cross, then the cobbled Leycote track takes you uphill. The paths around here are pretty ones, through woodland and across fields of wild flowers. Farm tracks and a narrow country lane make the last bit of this journey easy.

45 The Dragon's Back

Climb the remains of an ancient coral reef

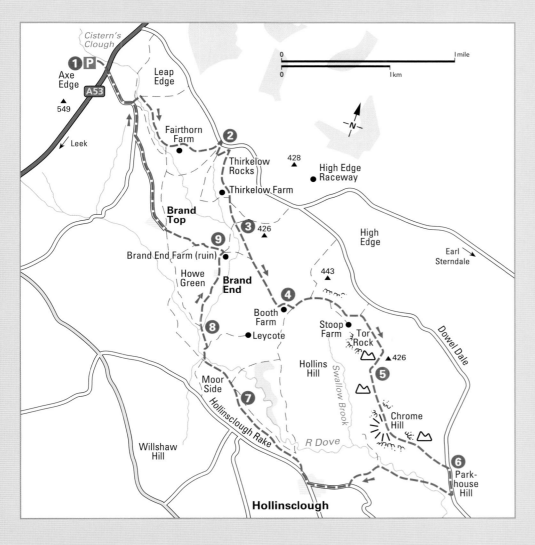

Distance 7.5 miles (12.1km)

Minimum Time 4hrs 30min

Ascent/Gradient 980ft (300m) ▲▲▲

Level of Difficulty ●●●

Paths Good paths except for ones between Hollinsclough and Brand End, can be slippery after rain, lots of stiles

Landscape Gritstone moors and cloughs with limestone hills

Suggested Map OS Explorer OL24 White Peak

Start/Finish Grid reference: SK 034697

Dog Friendliness Farmland, dogs should be kept under close control

Parking Axe Edge car park

Public Toilets None en route

1 From the car park cross the main road and descend the lane opposite. At the first right-hand bend turn left to take the left of two farm tracks, descending to cross the Cistern's Clough bridge heading for Fairthorn Farm. Past the house swing left on the drive up to the road at Thirkelow Rocks.

2 Turn right along the road for 200yds (183m), then take the farm track on the right, heading south past Thirkelow Farm. Take the right fork into the clough.

3 Where the track ends, veer slightly right to the waymarking posts highlighting a duckboard bridge and the route to Booth Farm.

4 Keep to the left of the farm and go over some steps in the wall ahead. After crossing a small field, turn left along the farm

road, then fork right for Stoop Farm. Turn left along a waymarked field path, bypassing the farmhouse and climbing to a footpath intersection at the top wall. Take the path signposted 'Glutton Bridge via Chrome Hill'.

5 Drop down to a stile and follow a wallside path that eventually climbs left to the crest before continuing over the summit, and descending to the lane beneath the conical shape of Parkhouse Hill.

6 Turn right to walk along the lane, then right again to follow a farm track. Along the track, take the left fork to reach a surfaced road, which is just short of Hollinsclough. Walk through the village, going right at the junction, then cross over a stile on the right-hand side. Take the higher left fork that traverses Hollinsclough Rake.

7 On reaching the green zig-zag track at Moor Side, descend right to pass a ruin and continue up a narrow valley. Cross the stream and go over the stile to reach an old packhorse bridge. Across the bridge take a stony track up towards the farm buildings at Leycote. On a right-hand bend go left through a gate and follow a narrow path heading north-west into a wooded clough.

8 Follow the path across the simple slab bridge and up towards Brand End. Go right at the fork at the top. The path becomes a track, passing Brand End Cottage and descending to the ruins of Brand End Farm.

9 Turn left up the bank by a wall here, passing to the left of another farm. Turn left along a farm track to Brand Top. Here the road leads you back to Axe Edge.

46 The Goyt Valley of the Manchester Grimshawes

In the remote upper valley of the River Goyt, a Manchester industrialist's princely country retreat gave way to Stockport's inexorable demand for more water

The River Goyt begins its journey on the wild heather moors of Axe Edge and Goyt Moss before flowing northwards to join the Mersey at Stockport. In times past its upper valley would have been filled with oakwoods. An old salters' and smugglers' road known as 'the Street' straddled it at Goyt Bridge before climbing over the Shining Tor ridge. In 1830, Manchester industrialist Samuel Grimshawe chose the valley to build Errwood Hall as a wedding present for his son.

The family lived here 'in the style of princes'. They imported 40,000 rhododendrons and azaleas for the ornate gardens, using their own ocean yacht, *Mariquita*. In its heyday the estate had a staff of 20, and included a coal mine, a watermill, housing for the servants and a private school.

Twin Reservoirs

Even the Grimshawes and their wealth couldn't resist Stockport's ever-growing need for water, however, and in 1938 the house was demolished for the newly built Fernilee Reservoir. The dark battalions of spruce and larch, planted for a quick and plentiful supply of timber, eventually engulfed the oakwoods, and 30 years later a second reservoir, the Errwood, was built, higher up the valley. Little Goyt Bridge was dismantled and rebuilt upstream;

and the valley was changed forever. For a while it was overrun with tourists and the valley's single road was choked by vehicles; then a pioneering traffic-management scheme was initiated by the National Park authority, including new car parks, a bus service and even road closures. The result was that this once peaceful beauty spot was restored to a state of relative tranquillity.

Remains of Errwood Hall

Part of the walk enter the grounds of Errwood Hall, where the order of the garden has been ruffled by nature, but the rhododendrons still bloom bright in the summer. The mossy foundations and floors of the house still exist, as do some of the lower walls, arched windows and doors.

Further on – uphill in a wild, partially wooded comb – lies the Spanish Shrine, built by the Grimshawes in memory of their beloved governess, Dolores de Bergrin. Inside the circular stone-built shrine there is a fine altar and mosaic.

On the return walk along the crest of Foxlow Edge, you can see most of the walk laid out as you survey the rolling moors, dappled with heather, bracken and pale moor grasses. Dinghies may be racing across Errwood Reservoir and even the spruce woods seem to fit into this exquisite jigsaw.

Below: The walk crosses a footbridge over a Goyt Valley stream

Bottom: Goyt Valley and reservoir

46 The Goyt Valley of the Manchester Grimshawes

Admire the ruins of Errwood Hall and see the reservoir that caused the house's demolition

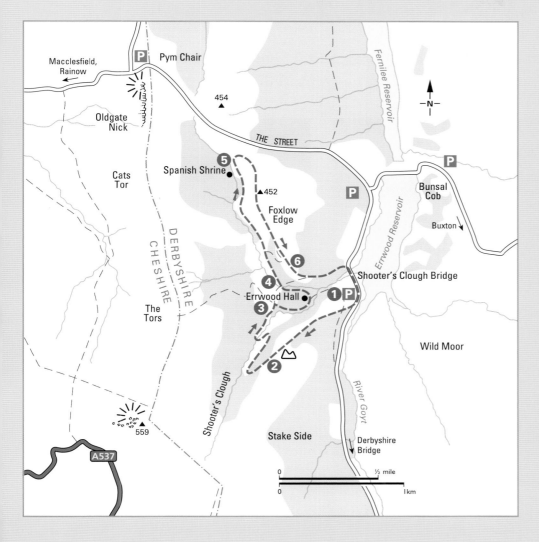

Distance 3.5 miles (5.7km)

Minimum Time 2hrs 30min

Ascent/Gradient 984ft (300m) ▲▲▲

Level of Difficulty ●●●

Paths Good paths and tracks, a few stiles

Landscape Park type woodland and moor

Suggested Map OS Explorer OL24 White Peak

Start/Finish Grid reference: SK 012748

Dog Friendliness Dogs should be kept under close control

Parking Errwood car park

Public Toilets 1 mile (1.6km) south at Derbyshire Bridge car park

1 The path, signposted 'Stakeside and the Cat and Fiddle', begins from the roadside south of the car park. Climb through a copse of trees, go straight across a cart track, then continue up the grassy spur that separates Shooter's Clough and the Goyt Valley.

2 Go through a gate in the wall (to the right) and follow a path that zig-zags through the woodland of Shooter's Clough before fording a stream. The path heads north (right), through rhododendron bushes before continuing across open grassland to a signposted junction of footpaths.

3 Turn right on a path skirting a wooded knoll, then ignore the first path through the gateposts and take the second left to Errwood Hall. Continue past the ruins, before descending steps to a footbridge.

4 Climb some steps on the right to reach another footpath signpost. Turn left along the path signposted 'Pym Chair'. This gradually swings north on hillslopes beneath Foxlow Edge. There's a short detour down and left to see the Spanish Shrine (which is visible from the main path).

5 About 100yds (91m) on from the Spanish Shrine, and before meeting the road at the very top, the path reaches open moorland. Take the narrow path forking right, which climbs to the top of Foxlow Edge. On reaching some old quarry workings near the top, the path is joined by a tumbledown dry-stone wall. Keep to the narrow corridor between the wall on the right and the fence on your left, ignoring little paths and tracks off to the right down into the valley. Continue the slow descent to the far end of the ridge.

6 At a fence corner, by the edge of woodland follow the path left, still downhill, around the edge of the trees and veer left again where it is joined by another path. With banks of rhododendrons on your right, follow the broad, gravelly track down through the woods to the roadside at Shooter's Clough Bridge. Turn right and cross the road bridge back to the car park.

47 Pennine Ways on Kinder Scout

One end of the celebrated long-distance trail from Derbyshire to Scotland ascends from the Edale Valley to the craggy outcrops of the Kinder plateau

Above: Up from the Edale Valley

Above right: The climb rewards walkers with views of the chequered valley floor

Edale sits peacefully in a paradise of pasture, riverside meadow and hedgerow, surrounded by high peaks. Its church spire towers above the cottages and farmhouses, but is in turn dwarfed by the castellated crags of Kinder Scout, and the rounded hills of the Mam Tor ridge.

In Depression-torn 1930s England, Tom Stephenson, then secretary of the Ramblers' Association, told the readers of the *Daily Herald* of his dream – to create a long, green trail across the roof of England. This dream would bring Edale to the world's attention. It was to take 30 years, a mass trespass and Acts of Parliament to achieve, but eventually, in 1965, the Pennine Way was opened. Spanning no less than 268 miles (431km) from Edale to Kirk Yetholm in Scotland, it was Britain's first official long-distance trail.

Go to Edale any Friday night and you'll see eager-eyed Pennine Wayfarers. They'll be in the campsite making their last minute preparations, or in the Old Nags Head poring over Ordnance Survey maps or looking though Alfred Wainwright's famous little blue guidebook.

Up Jacob's Ladder

Unfortunately the popularity of the Way has led to the main route through Grindsbrook being diverted along the foul-weather route up Jacob's Ladder. But as you leave Edale, or to be more strictly correct Grindsbrook Booth (Edale is the name of the valley), you can look across to the old route, which delves deep into the rocky ravine.

Your route climbs boldly to the top of Ringing Roger ('the echoing rocks'). From this magnificent viewpoint you can look down on the length of Edale and across to the great Lose Hill–Mam Tor ridge. What follows is an edge walk round the great chasm of Grindsbrook, taking you past Nether Tor to the place where the old Pennine Way track comes to meet you.

Down Beside Crowden Brook

Past weather-smoothed gritstone sculptures and the rocky peak of Grindslow Knoll you come to another ravine, Crowden Brook. This route descends by the brook, passing several waterfalls, proiding may opportunities for a paddle to cool hot feet. Beneath the open slopes the path seeks the shade of recently planted pine, larch, birch and oak. Wild flowers, including bluebells, daffodils and primroses, proliferate in this delightful spot, just above Upper Booth. Finally you're reacquainted with the Pennine Way, following the new route back across the fields of Edale.

47 Pennine Ways on Kinder Scout

Climb Jacob's Ladder to the viewpoint at Ringing Roger

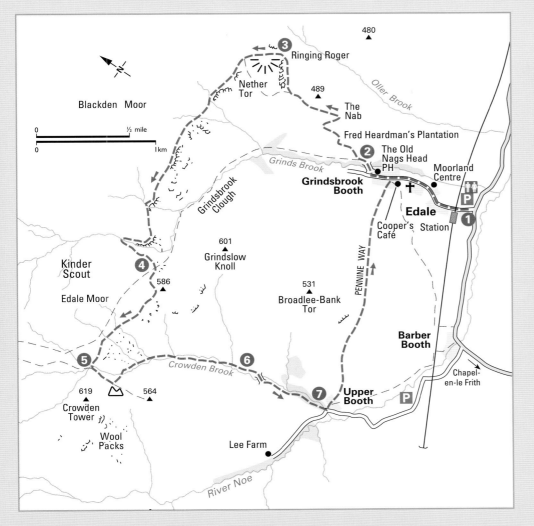

Distance 7 miles (11.3km)

Minimum Time 4hrs

Ascent/Gradient 1,650ft (500m) ▲▲▲

Level of Difficulty ●●●

Paths Rock and peat paths, some steep ascents and descents

Landscape Heather moor

Suggested Map OS Explorer OL1 Dark Peak

Start/Finish Grid reference: SK 125853

Dog Friendliness Walk is on farmland and access agreement land. Dogs should be kept on leads

Parking Edale pay car park

Public Toilets At car park

1 Turn right out of the car park and head north into Edale (the village), under the railway and past The Old Nags Head pub. By a gate at the far end turn right and then follow the path across the footbridge that leads over Grinds Brook.

2 Leave the main Grindsbrook Clough path by the side of a small barn, taking the right fork that climbs up the lower hill slope to reach a stile on the edge of open country. Beyond the stile the path zig-zags above Fred Heardman's Plantation then climbs up the nose of The Nab to the skyline rocks. Where the path divides, take the rather eroded right fork to the summit of Ringing Roger.

3 Pause to enjoy the views then follow the edge path left, rounding the cavernous hollow of Grindsbrook past Nether Tor. The walk meets the old Pennine Way route on the east side, at a place marked by a large cairn.

4 Ignoring the left fork to the outlier of Grindslow Knoll, follow the paved footpath westwards to the head of another deep hollow, the clough of Crowden Brook.

5 Cross Crowden Brook, then leave the edge to follow a narrow, level path traversing slopes on the left beneath the outcrop of Crowden Tower. Below the tower, turn left for a steep, bumpy track down the grassy hillside to the brook. Keep to the path that follows the brook, fording it on several occasions.

6 Go over a stile at the edge of open country, then cross a footbridge shaded by tall rowans to change to the west bank. From here the path threads through woodland before descending in steps to the road at Upper Booth. You now need to follow the Pennine Way path back to Edale.

7 Turn left along the road and left again into the farmyard of Upper Booth Farm before exiting at the top right corner. After following a track to a gateway, bear left uphill to a stile by an old barn. Here the Way traverses fields at the foot of Broadlee Bank before joining a tree-lined track into the village. Turn right along the road back to the car park.

48 Around Eastwood in the Steps of D. H. Lawrence

In the streets of Eastwood and the lanes and former Nottinghamshire mining sites around the town are the places D H Lawrence called 'the country of my heart'

David Herbert Lawrence was one of the most commanding English writers of the early 20th century, but his Nottinghamshire roots were distinctly humble. He came from the industrial town of Eastwood, north-west of Nottingham, and the terrace house he was born in has been preserved as a museum. The son of a miner, he won a scholarship to Nottingham High School and, after a short spell teaching in south London, he concentrated on writing full-time.

Lawrence's intense feeling for what he called 'the country of my heart' manifested itself in his writing, and many of the places you will see on this walk are represented in his books and short stories. Greasley Church is 'Minton' in *Sons and Lovers*, and Felley Mill is turned into 'Strelley Mill' in *The White Peacock*, his first novel. Some had dark associations, such as Moorgreen Reservoir, which as 'Willey Water' in *Women in Love* (and 'Nethermere' in *Sons and Lovers*) was the scene of a drowning tragedy – based, in fact, on a real incident. All the way around this walk, which forms part of a local heritage trail, there are well-designed boards relating the landscape to the stories.

But his depiction of Eastwood as a dour little mining town was often unflattering and caused so much local resentment that his name was hardly mentioned for some years. Mind you, his books often had troubled lives of their own. His novel *The Rainbow* was at first banned for alleged obscenity, and the full publication of his most notorious book, *Lady Chatterley's Lover*, was delayed for more than 30 years and led to a celebrated court case concerning its supposedly graphic sex scenes.

Colliery Reclaimed

The walk begins at the site of the former Moorgreen Colliery, renamed 'Minton Pit' by Lawrence in *Sons and Lovers*. Moorgreen was producing more than one million tons of coal a year as recently as the 1960s, but the seams were eventually exhausted and in 1985 the colliery closed. After landscaping the site was renamed Colliers Wood, and as part of Nottinghamshire's Greenwood Community Forest it has been planted with shrubs and trees, and ponds and wetland have been established to attract wildlife.

Left: Lawrence's birthplace in Eastwood – now a museum

Below: St Mary's Church, Greasley, near Eastwood

48 Around Eastwood in the Steps of D. H. Lawrence

Explore the countryside around the Nottinghamshire town that provided inspiration for much of the writer's work

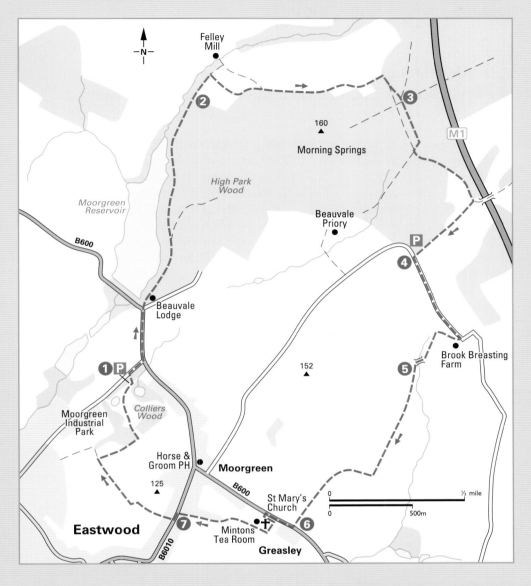

Distance 5.75 miles (9.2km)

Minimum Time 2hrs 30min

Ascent/Gradient 360ft (110m) ▲▲▲

Level of Difficulty ●●●

Paths Rough field and woodland tracks, 2 stiles

Landscape Farmland and woods, red-brick towns and villages

Suggested Map OS Explorer 260 Nottingham

Start/Finish Grid reference: SK 481481

Dog Friendliness On lead at start (poop scoop by-laws apply)

Parking Colliers Wood car park, Engine Lane, off B600

Public Toilets None en route (nearest in Eastwood)

1 Walk out of the entrance of Colliers Wood car park and turn right, then left along the pavement of the B600. At the bend turn right by Beauvale Lodge and take the track to its left (signposted 'Felley Mill'). Walk through High Park Wood, above Moorgreen Reservoir, branching left after 0.25 mile (400m) just before a gate. Carry on along the main track until an open field appears on your right.

2 Continue walking for 150yds (137m), then turn right at the stile and walk up the left-hand side of a line of trees separating two fields. At the far side turn left, follow the woodland edge, go around the corner and continue alongside the forest. After 0.5 mile (800m) turn right beyond the bench to locate a public footpath through the trees.

3 Where the public footpath emerges at a junction of three forest rides go straight ahead. With the growl of the nearby M1 motorway getting louder, turn left after the bend on to a clearly indicated footpath into the woods. This emerges to follow the edge of a field, swinging right on the far side and eventually reaching a lay-by.

4 Turn right if you want to view the remains of Beauvale Priory, otherwise go left and walk down the lane to the bend by the intriguingly named Brook Breasting Farm. Go sharply right, following along the left-hand edge of a field, then turn left and drop down through two more fields. Look for the gap in the undergrowth on the right-hand side, and go over a footbridge.

5 Turn left and follow the sign across the lower field. Continue along the top edge of successive fields, going right to skirt the final sloping field, then drop down to the road.

6 Cross over and turn right to enter the churchyard of St Mary's at Greasley. Walk around the church and exit the churchyard at the far side on a footpath signposted 'Moorgreen'. After crossing the cemetery, go across the field and continue to walk alongside paddocks to reach the road at the top.

7 Turn left and then right for a path between houses. Follow waymarks across and down through fields, and at the bottom go right for the path back into Colliers Wood. Turn first left to reach the ponds, and beyond is the car park.

49 A Merrie Tale of Sherwood Forest

A fascinating walk leads through the former royal hunting grounds where legendary outlaw Robin Hood is said to have ridden with his merrie men

Below: The majestic Major Oak

Below right: The walk leads past trees that have seen centuries roll by

Bottom: The ancient woodland is full of light and atmosphere

If Robin Hood or one of his merrie men were to return to Sherwood Forest today, he would no doubt be surprised at how dramatically this evocative woodland has shrunk. The modern Sherwood Forest Country Park covers 450 acres (182ha), whereas the original area was more like 100,000 acres (40,500ha). But there again this vast ancient forest, which at the time of the Norman Conquest covered most of Nottinghamshire north of the River Trent, was never in fact a blanket forest but always a mix of wood, heathland and scrub. It was the preserve of the nobility, where the King and his entourage hunted deer, and the commoners were subject to strict Forest Laws that could see a man's hand cut off for poaching.

Mighty Oaks from Little Acorns Grow

In England and Wales 'ancient woodland' generally refers to woods that have existed since 1600 (1750 in Scotland). Here at Sherwood the surviving woodland, although small, is a wonderful mixture of native broadleaved varieties, dominated by oak and birch. Both varieties of native British oak can be found in the forest – common or English oak (*Quercus robur*), and sessile or durmast oak (*Quercus petraea*) – while newer conifer plantations extend the tree cover east and west.

Walking is magical in this ancient woodland, which has survived the rise and fall of royal dynasties. The highlight is surely the gigantic old oak trees that pepper the forest. There are more than 900 trees that are more than 600 years old – sometimes these ancients are known as 'druids'; and while a few are simply gnarled and hollow old stumps, others still dominate the surroundings with their massive 'stag heads' of twisted limbs and spreading foliage.

The most famous of these druids is the Major Oak, visited on this walk, and one of the largest trees in England. Its exact age is somewhat uncertain, estimates having varied widely over the decades, from 500 to 1,500 years, but there's no doubting its sheer size. The hollow trunk is 33ft (10m) in circumference, and such is the spread of its colossal branches (92ft/28m) that they have to be propped up with artificial supports. But whether even the Major Oak's hollow trunk could have hidden Robin Hood and his entire band of merrie men, as legend has it, is rather more doubtful.

A Changing Landscape

Sherwood Forest changed from a royal hunting ground to a source of valuable raw material. The use of English oak by everyone from shipbuilders and furniture-makers to miners and charcoal burners meant that between 1609 and 1790 the number of oaks plummeted by 80 per cent. In 2005, Sherwood Forest was declared a National Nature Reserve, and there are plans to move the visitor centre to a new location outside the boundary of the reserve. It is expected to open in 2011 on the site of the former Thoresby Colliery, just east of the B6034 at Edwinstowe.

49 A Merrie Tale of Sherwood Forest

Walk where outlaw Robin Hood reputedly robbed the rich

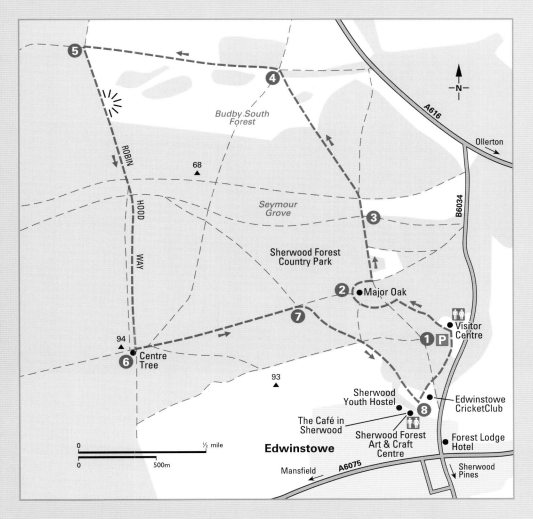

Distance 5.5 miles (8.8km)

Minimum Time 2hrs 30min

Ascent/Gradient 278ft (85m) ▲▲▲

Level of Difficulty ●●●

Paths Easy woodland tracks and wide forest rides

Landscape Beautiful mixed woodland, more open to north

Suggested Map OS Explorer 270 Sherwood Forest

Start/Finish Grid reference: SK 626676

Dog Friendliness On lead around Visitor Centre, otherwise excellent

Parking Sherwood Forest visitor centre (pay-and-display)

Public Toilets Sherwood Forest Visitor Centre

---

1 Facing the main entrance to Sherwood Forest visitor centre from the car park, turn left and follow the well-signposted route 'the Major Oak'.

2 Go along the curving path as it completes a semi-circle around the impressive old tree and continue as far as the junction with a public bridleway (signposted). Turn left here, then walk this straight and uncomplicated route for around 0.25 mile (400m), ignoring all paths that lead off.

3 At a green notice board, which gives warning of a nearby military training area, the main path bears left. Ignoring this, go straight ahead, past the metal bar gate, for a path that continues over a crossroads to become a wide, fenced track through pleasant open country of heather and bracken known as Budby South Forest.

4 At the very far side go through a gate and turn left on to an unmade lane, and walk this undulating route for 0.75 mile (1.2km).

5 At the major junction just before the plantation begins, turn left, indicated 'Centre Tree'. With the rows of conifers on your right, and good views across Budby South Forest on your left, keep to this straight track. Where the track divides into two parallel trails, the gravelly track on the right is the cycle route, while the more leafy and grassy ride to the left is the bridleway, but either can be used.

6 When you reach the Centre Tree – a huge spreading oak – the two routes converge to continue past a bench down a wide avenue among the trees. Don't go down this, but instead turn left and, ignoring paths off right and left, carry straight on along the main track back into the heart of the forest.

7 After almost 0.75 mile (1.2km) you pass a metal bar gate on the right and then meet a bridleway coming in from the left. Ignoring the inviting path straight ahead (which returns to the Major Oak) bear right on the main track, past some bare holes and dips hollowed out by children's bikes. At a large junction of criss-crossing routes go straight on (signposted 'Fairground') so that an open field and distant housing becomes visible to your right. This wide sandy track descends to a field by Edwinstowe cricket ground. The Art and Craft Centre and Sherwood Youth Hostel are on the far side, and the village centre beyond.

8 To return to the visitor centre and car park, follow the well-walked, signposted track back up past the cricket ground.

50 Churches of the Wolds

A gathering spot for ramblers, the hilltop 'Old Church' of All Saints commands grand views – while other fine churches are found in villages further down

Above top: Alone on the Walesby escarpment – the 'Old Church' of All Saints

Above middle: The Lady Chapel, with its stained-glass window showing ramblers and cyclists

Above bottom: The Viking Way passes through the churchyard

The villages of the Lincolnshire Wolds have many interesting and attractive old churches, and one of the most remarkable is the 'Old Church' of All Saints, situated on a remote hilltop above Walesby. It's 'old' in that it was replaced by a newer version in 1913, and in the succeeding years became dilapidated and rundown. But it was never deconsecrated and, in the early 1930s, a local rambling club began making an annual pilgrimage to the church. Twenty years later the Grimsby and District Wayfarers' Association dedicated the East Window of the Lady Chapel to 'lovers of the countryside', with a stained-glass depiction of walkers and cyclists. Local ramblers still hold an annual service on Trinity Sunday at what is now referred to as 'the Ramblers' Church', and most appropriately the Viking Way long-distance footpath passes through the churchyard.

Although repairs have been carried out over the last 20 years to protect All Saints from further weathering and decay, it retains its simple medieval character, a splendid example of what's known as the Norman-Transitional period. Several old, boxed pews remain, while another interesting feature is the old stairway behind the pulpit, which leads to the well-preserved rood loft – the name for the gallery above the rood screen that separates the nave (the main part of the church where the congregation sit) from the chancel (where the clergy and choir sit). From the church, the glorious views can include the towers of Lincoln Cathedral on a clear day. A Roman villa was unearthed to the east of the church, and a simple Saxon building almost certainly pre-dates the present church (built mainly between the 12th and 15th centuries). Its admirers include John Betjeman, who described All Saints as 'an exceptionally attractive church, worth bicycling 12 miles against the wind to see'.

Down the hill in the village of Walesby, St Mary's is a neat and simple affair by comparison, an example of the Arts and Crafts Movement. The then vicar campaigned for 30 years to get a new church built in the village, only to drop down dead on the very day that work finally started.

The Tennyson Connection

The charming village of Tealby is associated with Alfred, Lord Tennyson, Lincolnshire's very own Poet Laureate. His brother, Charles, was rector at the church for a while, and the impressive 1930s Tennyson D'Eyncourt Memorial Hall is named after another relation.

The parish church of All Saints in Tealby dates from around 1100. It was rebuilt for the Tennyson d'Eyncourts in the 1870s as a family shrine – notice the invented heraldry and imitation medieval tombs. The church also houses an impressive collection of more than 100 tapestry 'kneelers' embroidered by local women and depicting people and places from around the village.

50 Churches of the Wolds

Explore two beautiful Lincolnshire villages through their contrasting churches

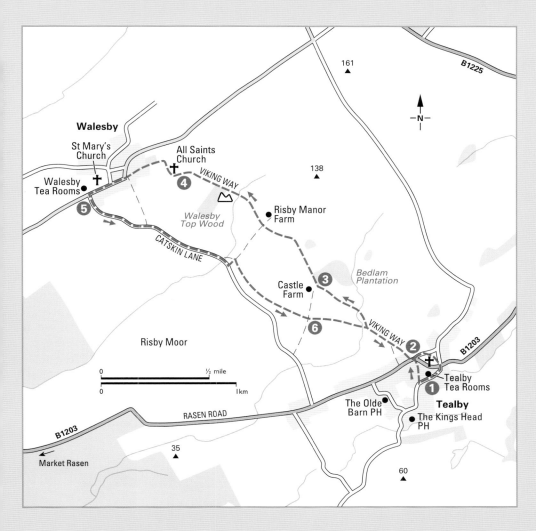

Distance 4.25 miles (6.8km)

Minimum Time 2hrs

Ascent/Gradient 721ft (220m) ▲▲▲

Level of Difficulty ●●●

Paths Field paths, some steep and others muddy

Landscape Undulating chalk hills, deep valleys and woodland

Suggested Map OS Explorer 282 Lincolnshire Wolds North

Start/Finish Grid reference: TF 157907

Dog Friendliness On lead near livestock, fine on hedged tracks and lanes

Parking Front Street, Tealby, near tea rooms

Public Toilets None en route (nearest in Market Rasen)

1 From the Tealby Tea Rooms walk down Front Street as far as B Leaning & Sons, a butcher and maker of traditional Lincolnshire sausages established in 1860. Turn right into Church Lane, which soon becomes a walkway. At the top, turn left and cross over Rasen Road to follow the public footpath that runs between houses on the opposite side. As far as Walesby you will be following the Norse helmet waymarks of the Viking Way.

2 Pass through a gate and cross open pasture, aiming for another gate in the far bottom corner. Go through this and along the path ahead, ignoring a footbridge to the left. Walk up the open hillside ahead to reach the corner of Bedlam Plantation which is above Castle Farm.

3 Turn right and go through a gate for a fenced path beside the woods. At the far end head diagonally left down a grassy field to pass below Risby Manor Farm. Cross the lane leading up to the farmhouse and continue ahead, crossing a deep valley and climbing steeply towards Walesby Top Wood. Pass through a gate and keep straight ahead across a field of crops to reach All Saints Church.

4 Walk through the churchyard and continue along the Viking Way as it drops down a wide track into the village. When you reach Rasen Road at the bottom go straight on, past the 'new' parish church of St Mary until you reach the junction with Catskin Lane.

5 If you need refreshment, cross the road to visit Walesby Tea Rooms. Otherwise turn left and walk along Catskin Lane for 0.75 mile (1.2km). Just past a right-hand curve,

turn left at the entrance of a farm drive and go over a cattle grid. This is in fact a public bridleway that leads back up to the hilltop, but you should turn right in a few paces and join a footpath across rough pasture, initially parallel with the road. Stay on this path as it runs along the left-hand side of a field to arrive at the drive to Castle Farm.

6 The public footpath now continues almost due east across the vast sloping field beyond. When you reach the far side of the field, pass through a gate and drop down to cross a wooden footbridge. Turn right on the far side of the bridge to rejoin the earlier route back into Tealby, this time turning left up Rasen Road to visit All Saints Church. Drop down through the churchyard and follow Beck Hill to the memorial hall, then turn right along Front Street to return to the start of the walk.

51 It All Comes Out in the Wilds of The Wash

A walk across part of England's largest national nature reserve provides many opportunities for birdwatching – or for admiring offshore RAF bombing practice

It has to be said that the Wash is a peculiar sort of place. On the Norfolk side is Hunstanton, England's only east coast resort where you can watch the sun setting across the water – since it faces west. The rivers Welland, Witham, Nene and Great Ouse all issue out into this vast, shallow lagoon covering 300 square miles (776sq km), which is sometimes covered by water but more often than not by endless tidal mudflats. These have built up over a long period as the four rivers have deposited huge quantities of clay and silt. The burrowing and surface invertebrates here have attracted a healthy bird population. In fact the Wash supports more birds than any other estuary in Britain, plus one of Europe's largest concentrations of common seals.

Much of the walking around the edge of the Wash is along high embankments, which mark more than 300 years of reclaiming farmland from the sea. This route around Gedney Drove End follows the old and the current sea bank, which as you will see has allowed the rich agricultural belt to be extended right up to the sea wall. Dykes and drainage channels, controlled by sluices and pumping stations continue to keep the salt water at bay and maintain this artificially fertile land.

RAF Manoeuvres
Military airfields dot the Lincolnshire coast, and planes from nearby RAF Holbeach in particular use a range off the Gedney coast for bombing practice: small but brightly coloured targets are scattered offshore across the salt marsh. Red flags fly all along the shore when bombing is taking place (weekdays between 9am and 5pm), but it is safe and legal to walk along the sea bank and watch the proceedings (as indeed many people do), as long as you obey official signs and don't venture beyond the sea wall or pick up any unusual-looking souvenirs.

Below: Peaceful setting and endless views in Lincolnshire

51 It All Comes Out in the Wilds of The Wash

Explore sea walls and tidal mudflats on the South Lincolnshire coast

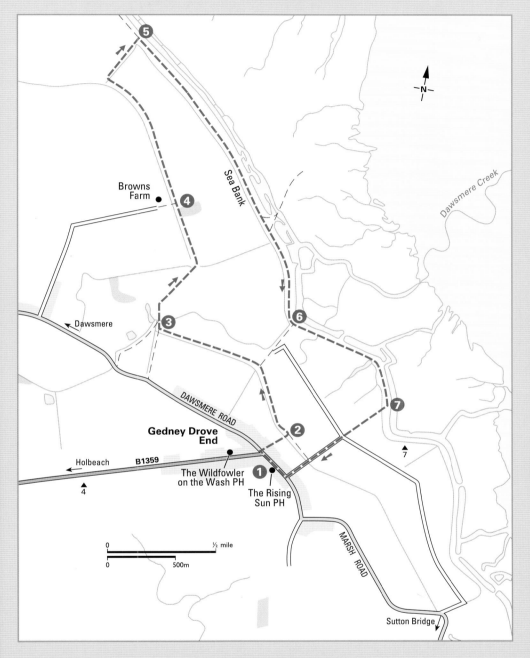

Distance 5.75 miles (9.2km)

Minimum Time 2hrs 30min

Ascent/Gradient Negligible ▲▲▲

Level of Difficulty ●●●

Paths Field, 1 stile

Landscape Open arable fields and bare marsh and mudflats

Suggested Map OS Explorer 249 Spalding & Holbeach

Start/Finish Grid reference: TF 463292

Dog Friendliness Overhead military planes on weekdays can be very loud

Parking Roadside parking in centre of Gedney Drove End (off A17 east of Holbeach)

Public Toilets None en route

1 With your back to The Rising Sun pub, turn left and walk along Dawsmere Road past the junction and take the signposted public footpath on the right, between bungalows. At the far side of the field go across a small footbridge and up some steps in order to turn left into a wide field.

2 For 1 mile (1.6km) walk along the edge of this field, which is in fact the line of the former sea wall, keeping more or less parallel with the present and much higher sea bank over to your right. As a sign indicates, continue straight ahead at the point where the old sea bank veers invitingly away to the right.

3 When the field ends turn right for 50yds (46m) then, faced with a small thicket, drop down to the farm track on your left. Turn right, and follow the main route (ignore the lower track) alongside a narrow shelter-belt of woodland. This wide, gravel track heads out towards the sea bank then bends left and continues past Browns Farm.

4 Stay on the main track for about 0.75 mile (1.2km) beyond the farm, then go right by an old wartime pill box for a short path over to the sea wall.

5 Turn right and follow either the grassy top of the sea bank (a public right of way) or the surfaced lane just below it past a succession of military observation towers. The bombing range is spread out before you, with the low Norfolk coast over to your right and the Lincolnshire seaboard towards Boston and Skegness leftwards.

6 After the third tower ignore the gated road that heads off inland (a short cut back to Gedney), but instead continue along the sea bank past one final watchtower until you reach a stile. Cross the stile and continue ahead for another 400yds (366m).

7 Turn right at a public footpath sign, down some steps, for a direct path along a field-edge to the junction of an open lane. Here continue straight ahead into Gedney, turning right at the end back on to Dawsmere Road.

Northern England

Northern England

Bounded east and west by the North Sea and the Irish Sea respectively, and along its northern frontier by the Anglo-Scottish border, Northern England possesses landscapes that are breathtakingly beautiful while often wild and desolate.

Here there are rugged heights, windswept moorlands, rivers and dales, lakes and forests, and invigorating coastal margins. There are towns and villages rich in history, intrigue and mystery and areas celebrated for their unusual or abundant wildlife. In the park surrounding Chillingham Castle, Northumberland you can see Britain's only wild cattle – a herd of white oxen protected by the Chillingham Wild Cattle Association (see Walk 67).

For many years the North was portrayed as a place of massive conurbations, coal mines, pollution, grime and grinding poverty. Although this imagery undoubtedly had its time and place, it only related to a small part, mostly confined to the industrial heartlands of Lancashire and Yorkshire. Beyond that lies, a dazzling display of rugged and beautiful scenery, geographically unique and historically rich – including some of the most varied and fascinating parts of Britain.

Above: Jorvik Viking Centre, York

Below: Berwick-upon-Tweed

Below right: Thirlmere reservoir in the Lake District

Far right: Looking down on Grasmere from Loughrigg Fell in the Lake District

Previous pages: Snow-capped peaks reflected in lake Buttermere

A Violent and Troubled Place

At the northern edge stands Hadrian's Wall, the greatest extant example of Roman determination in Britain. The main part was built between AD 122 and AD 126, during the reign of Roman emperor Hadrian (117–38), *qui barbaros Romanosque divideret* – 'to separate the Romans from the barbarians'. With a brief break to try out the more northerly Antonine Wall, built under Emperor Antoninus Pius (138–61), Hadrian's monument remained occupied until AD 383, by which time the Romans were withdrawing from Britain. Everywhere is at peace now but, long after the Romans had gone, the lands of the north were a violent place, where rustlers, outlaws and gangsters from both sides terrorised the Anglo-Scottish border, and spawned the building of fortified castles and strongholds called pele towers, many of which remain to this day. For centuries Scots and Englishmen competed violently for control of the prosperous port of Berwick (see Walk 68), and at enormous expense Queen Elizabeth I raised new fortifications, parts of which can still be seen in a remarkable state of preservation.

In the turbulent world of the 15th century the North of England was involved in the Wars of the Roses between, first, the royal houses of Lancaster and York and then those of York and Tudor. At Middleham (see Walk 59) you can visit the remains of the castle that was the boyhood home and later the favourite haunt of Richard III, whose defeat and death in the Battle of Bosworth Field brought the Wars of the Roses to an end in 1485.

Wild Pennines

Down the centre of the region, the Pennines form the geological 'backbone of England' – or, as the noted explorer and author of *Robinson Crusoe*, Daniel Defoe, wrote: 'the wildest, most barren and frightful' landscape he had ever seen. In *Britannia* (1586), English antiquarian and historian William Camden was less daunted: he wrote that the Pennines ran 'as the Appenines in Italy, though the middest of England, with a continued ridge, rising more with continued tops and cliffs one after another even as far as Scotland'.

Best of the Rest

Historic York
Founded by the Romans in AD 71 as Eboracum, the city was later, under the Angles, capital of the Kingdom of Northumbria as Eoforwic (see Walk 57). Conquering Vikings renamed it Jorvik, and it only became known as 'York' after the Norman Conquest of 1066. The 'Anglian tower' was built on part of the Roman city wall perhaps in the seventh century; St Olave's Church was founded by Earl Siward of Northumbria 11 years before the Norman invasion, in 1055. Other attractions in the city include York Minster, begun in its present form in 1220 on a site where a Christian church had stood since the 4th century. It is northern Europe's second largest Gothic cathedral (after Cologne in Germany). The Great East Window (1405–8) is among the world's biggest medieval stained-glass windows.

Norman hunting grounds
In the Lake District, between Eskdale and Miterdale are lands once set aside for hunting in Norman times by the king and his leading lords (see Walk 62). Locals lived under very strict rules and were forbidden to clear land or cut down trees without special permission.

Clougha Pike
Pick a clear day for your ascent of Clougha Pike in the Bowland Fells, Lancashire (see Walk 58), and you'll be able to see the peaks of Snowdonia in Wales, and the Isle of Man in the Irish Sea, as well as a fine view over Morecambe Bay and several peaks in Yorkshire and the fells of Lakeland. Look out for distinctive channels or cloughs cut through the ridge by water running off the melting ice sheet at the close of the last ice age. These give the peak its name.

Kielder Forest and Tarset Castle
England's largest forest, the expansive Kielder Forest plantation covers 250 square miles (about 650sq kilometres) in Northumbria. Surrounding the Kielder Water reservoir, it consists largely of conifers – especially the Sitka Spruce – and also contains the country's biggest population of red squirrels. Walk 65 takes you through a section of the forest, and also past the remains of Tarset Castle, near Lanehead. The castle was built by 'Red' John Comyn, Lord of Badenoch, who was stabbed to death by Robert the Bruce (afterwards King Robert I of Scotland) before the altar of Greyfriars Church, Dumfries, in 1306.

Birchen Clough and Dove Stones
An undemanding walk along the edge of the Dark Peak in the Peak District National Park (see Walk 53) commands great views of moorland, rocks and reservoirs – not least of the distinctive gritstone stack known as 'the Trinnacle'. Watch out for Canada geese on the upper part of Birchen Clough.

Martin Mere
On the West Lancashire Plain, Walk 52 provides views of the Martin Mere Wetland Centre, and is one particularly for birdwatchers. The centre occupies one of the few remaining areas of flat peat Lancashire mosslands – most of these once extensive areas were drained to create farmland. Martin Mere is one of a network of nine wetland visitor centres across the United Kingdom run by the Wildfowl and Wetlands Trust, a conservation organisation founded by artist and naturalist Sir Peter Scott in 1946 with the aim of protecting wetlands and the wildlife that depend upon them. The centre attracts flocks of ducks, geese and swans that feed on the wetlands, which are flooded in winter. There are ten lookout hides in the centre: a special attraction are the flocks of pink-footed geese. You can also see flamingoes, cranes, otters – and beavers in the newly opened beaver centre. The wetlands are designated a Site of Special Scientific Interest and a Special Protection Area.

Industrial Remains
The Pennines were a backbone in another sense, too, for they provided a source of employment for many northerners during, and for some time after, the Industrial Revolution. The highest summit, Cross Fell, was described by Defoe as 'a wall of brass'. He wasn't too far wide of the mark, as the Quaker-owned London Lead Mining Company demonstrated during their many years of operations in the Pennines.

The company also found lead to mine in the Yorkshire Dales, notably in Swaledale, where today the ancient trails of the miners enable walkers to explore vast tracts of uplands. Walkers with an interest in industrial archaeology will find themselves in seventh heaven in this region. Across northern England many former mines and industrial sites have been reclaimed as nature reserves or as museums of the industrial past. At Fairburn Ings in West Yorkshire (see Walk 55), a colliery has been transformed into a reserve now run by the Royal Society for the Protection of Birds (RSPB). In the Derwent Valley area of Gateshead (see Walk 66), once the centre of the British steel industry, the Derwentcote steelmaking furnace is maintained by English Heritage and open to visitors, while the former railway line forms a cycle and footpath in the Derwent Valley Country Park.

Rare and beautiful are the landscapes of Cumbria and the North York Moors, the coast and the quiet folds of Northumberland and Durham. At the edge of the North Yorks Moors stands an isolated hill with the curious name Roseberry Topping, thought to derive from words meaning 'fortress in the heath' (see Walk 61).

As elsewhere in the North, places, monuments and buildings of great historical interest are close to areas of great natural beauty. Close to the Roseberry Topping you can visit the Captain Cook Monument, 51ft (15.5m) tall, raised in honour of the British naval officer James Cook, born at nearby Marton, who led three expeditions to the Pacific Ocean and was among the first Europeans to land in Australia and Hawaii and the first recorded to sail around New Zealand.

In the Land of the Lakes

The beauties of the Lake District are well known, and attract vast crowds, but peace and solitude can be found within a short walk away from tourist centres such as Bowness-on-Windermere (see Walk 63). Up on Brant Fell, above the village, beautiful views can be had over Lake Windermere, England's largest natural lake – around 12 miles (19km) long and 1 mile (1.6km) wide – and as far as the Coniston Fells. In the idyllic setting of Buttermere

a very relaxing walk (Walk 64) leads around the lake and through the shoreline path tunnel – the only one of this kind in the Lake District – on part of the Hassness Estate. The visit to Buttermere may be enlivened by the village's associations with William Wordsworth and Thomas de Quincey; literary associations are woven through the fabric of the North. Walk in the footsteps of the Brontë sisters across the rugged moors above their home in Haworth in the Yorkshire Dales (see Walk 54), or in Thirsk (North Yorkshire) visit the veterinary surgery in which James Wight had the experiences he described under the pen name James Herriot in best-selling books such as *It Shouldn't Happen to a Vet* (1971). In Hurst Green, Lancashire (see Walk 56) visit a region familiar to and well loved by J. R. R. Tolkein that, according to some sources, was the model for 'the Shire' in *The Lord of the Rings*.

That this region is an important part of our national heritage is demonstrated by the designation in Northern England of four national parks, six Areas of Outstanding Natural Beauty, 41 national nature reserves and innumerable Sites of Special Scientific Interest. This is a place of dramatic distinctions and captivating harmonies, of ruggedness and vigour, of pastoral landscapes and relaxation, together producing a whole that is far more than the sum of its many parts.

Below: Looking across a wheat field at the curiously named Roseberry Topping, on the edge of the North York Moors

Below left: York Minster

52 Lancashire's 'Fens' and Birds at Martin Mere

Occupying an area that was once a lake, the Martin Mere Wetland Centre provides the setting for a fascinating walk under wide West Lancashire skies

Top: East African Crowned Crane at Martin Mere

Centre: Flamingoes at the centre

Bottom: A young visitor feeds Hawaiian Geese by hand

Bottom right: There are views into the heart of the reserve

The levels of south-west Lancashire seem to provide easy travelling: there are miles of canal with no locks and roads and railways with scarcely an incline – and there's easy walking too. However, for most of history these lowlands were an obstacle. Ancient roads and trackways follow the high ground because, until well into the 18th century, this gave easier and faster travelling.

The Industrial Revolution was closely paralleled by, and to some extent depended on, an agricultural revolution. In many cases the same engineers who built the great canals were responsible for drainage schemes. The flat peat Lancashire mosslands were largely transformed into farmland. They fed the growing towns elsewhere in the county with green vegetables, carrots and, above all, potatoes.

Only a few pockets of mossland survive in anything like their original state. The Martin Mere reserve is one – and now also a centre of importance for wildlife and birds. Martin Mere Wetland Centre is one of nine in the UK run by the Wildfowl and Wetlands Trust, founded by Sir Peter Scott. The reserve itself plays host to a wide variety of resident and migrant birds. Breeding species range from reed and sedge warblers and reed buntings to the graceful-looking avocet. However, it's the massive flocks of winter visitors that create the most spectacular displays.

Winter Geese

The reserve is a kind of nucleus and great numbers of geese and swans gather on the fields around, which are often partly flooded in the winter months. Look out for pink-footed geese – but don't assume that all geese with pink feet are necessarily pink-footed geese! They might be greylags, although these are larger and heavier, with longer bills, and may be seen all year round.

Please note that the Wildfowl and Wetlands Trust has waymarked a concessionary path around the south of the reserve from where you can enjoy the birds without disturbing them. This is particularly important when huge flocks of geese gather over winter. The reason is that if disturbed the birds may settle further away, on land owned by less sympathetic farmers, and risk being shot.

52 Lancashire's 'Fens' and Birds at Martin Mere

Admire pink-footed geese, swans and other birds in this beautiful reserve

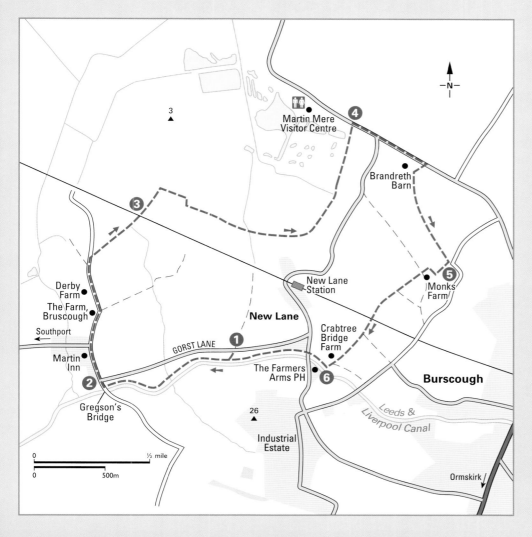

Distance 5 miles (8km)

Minimum Time 2hrs

Ascent/Gradient 50ft (15m) ▲▲▲

Level of Difficulty ●●●

Paths Canal tow paths, lanes, farm tracks and field paths, 4 stiles

Landscape Flat and open farmland with glimpses of wilder wetland

Suggested Map OS Explorer 285 Southport & Chorley

Start/Finish Grid reference: SD 423126

Dog Friendliness On lead across farmland, but can be let off on tow path

Parking Several small lay-bys near mid-point of Gorst Lane

Public Toilets None near by, unless using Martin Mere Visitor Centre

1 Near the mid-point of Gorst Lane there's a small timber yard. Follow a short track up through this to meet the canal by an old swing bridge. Go right along the tow path for about 0.75 mile (1.2km) to Gregson's Bridge. Go under the bridge, then continue up to a lane.

2 Go left and join a wider road (Martin Lane) and follow it away from the canal for about 350yds (320m). At a bend, by the Martin Inn, bear right down a narrow lane for about 700yds (640m), past the tea rooms at The Farm, Burscough, to an open section. Opposite some glasshouses there's a footpath sign on the right. Follow the track to the railway line.

3 Cross the line and continue down the track until you come to a green shed. Go right, alongside a drainage ditch, until another ditch appears ahead. From here go right and

then left on a waymarked concessionary route around the edge of Martin Mere Reserve. It's a clear track that at one point has a viewing position into the heart of the reserve. Keep to the outer edge of the embankment and eventually swing left. Beyond a gate follow the edge of a high fence to reach the road. (Turn left here to reach the main entrance to the reserve, about 400yds/366m further along.)

4 Turn right and follow the road for 500yds (457m). About 100yds (91m) past Brandreth Barn you will see a footpath sign on the right. Go along this as far as a large shed and turn left, past a pool, and on down an obvious track across wide open fields.

5 When you reach the end of the track, just before a lane, turn right on a concrete track. Then, turn right before a house and

follow the fence round to the left. Keep almost straight on, ignoring a signpost pointing right, and cross the field straight ahead – aiming towards a couple of trees. These act as direction posts down the field-edges to the railway line. Cross and keep straight on, following the slightly raised line of old field boundaries, then join a track to, and then through, Crabtree Bridge Farm.

6 Swing right on the tow path. It's about 200yds (183m) to the swing bridge by The Farmers Arms and another 500yds (457m) to the smaller one above the timber yard. Drop back down through this to Gorst Lane.

53 A 'Peak' Experience Around Dove Stones

On a magnificent ramble along the edge of the moors, your reward for making the steep climb up Birchen Clough is a series of breathtaking, wide-ranging views

Below: Dry-stone walls cut across the landscape

Main picture: The Peak District is arguably at its most beautiful beneath a coat of winter snow

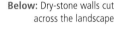

Cheshire's stake in the Peak District National Park is modest, but on this walk you can sample the vast moors so characteristic of the Dark Peak. These are notorious for tough walking over peat and heather, but this is an easy promenade along the edge of the moors; the only hard part is the steep ascent of Birchen Clough.

This route starts easily, by a series of reservoirs, allowing you to look up to the crags on the skyline. Dove Stones, directly above the start, has a natural edge as well as a large, long-abandoned quarry. Above the last of the reservoirs, you follow the Greenfield Brook, climbing gently. The forked tower dubbed the Trinnacle is eye-catching – and you'll get a closer look soon. Don't miss the water-sculpted rocks in the bed of the stream.

Up Birchen Clough

Now you make the transition from valley to moor, by the steep ascent of Birchen Clough. The steepest step is by a small waterfall and, if it looks uninviting, backtrack a short way to pick up a path (still steep) which traverses above the obstacle. The easier upper reaches of the Clough, and the flanking slopes leading out on to the moor, are

home to Canada geese. You reach the edge of the moor close to Raven Stones and soon find yourself looking down on the unmistakable Trinnacle. It's a great foreground for photographs and looks even better with someone standing on the top, but the ascent can only be recommended to experienced scramblers. You have to sidle along an exposed ledge below the lowest top; then it's easier climbing to the middle one but there's a long stride across a deep gap to the highest.

The edge is less defined for a time and you cross a vague shoulder past Ashway Cross before clarity is restored. Above Dove Stones the main path keeps back from the edge, but is exposed. Just beyond is the isolated tor of Fox Stone. Here a plaque commemorates two Dark Peak climbers who were killed in the Italian Dolomites.

In wild weather, the ruins of Bramley's Cot, once a shooters' hut, provide the best shelter if you need somewhere to take on food and drink. The end wall still stands and you can see the carved sockets where the roof timbers were once set. There's still a mile (1.6km) of moor-edge to go before you drop into the valley of the Chew Brook that gives easy walking back to the start.

53 A 'Peak' Experience Around Dove Stones

Climb from a series of reservoirs to drink in views of rugged moorland

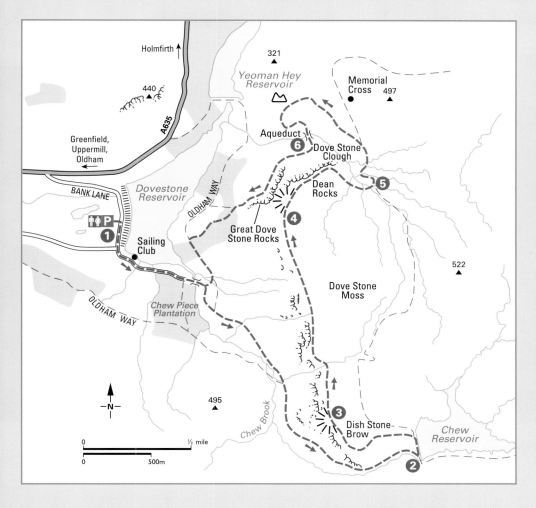

Distance 8 miles (12.9km)

Minimum Time 3hrs

Ascent/Gradient 1,296ft (395m) ▲▲▲

Level of Difficulty ●●●

Paths Mostly on good tracks but with some rocky sections, occasionally very steep, 2 stiles

Landscape Open and exposed moors, with sheltered valleys

Suggested Map OS Explorer OL1 Dark Peak

Start/Finish Grid reference: SE 013034

Dog Friendliness The condition of access to the moors is that dogs must be on leads

Parking Dovestone Reservoir, pay at weekends

Public Toilets At car park

1 From the car park walk up to the top of the Dovestone Reservoir dam and turn right, along the road past the sailing club. Where the Chew Piece Plantation ends go over a bridge and straight on to follow a private, vehicular track as it makes its way steadily up to eventually reach the very top of the Chew Valley.

2 When you reach Chew Reservoir turn left and walk along by the dam wall until just before it kinks right. Keeping your back to the reservoir (and near a sign warning of the dangers of deep water), drop down to the moorland and follow the wide, straight track opposite that heads back towards the edge of the hillside. The track bears left, then right, then becomes a thin path between the loose rocks around Dish Stone Brow.

3 With Dovestone Reservoir coming into view far below, continue along the high rim of the hillside past a series of rocky outcrops. If you occasionally lose sight of the path don't worry, just keep to the wide strip between the steep drop on your left and the banks of peaty bog on your right.

4 Nearing Great Dove Stone Rocks continue to follow the rocky edge as it swings back to the right. Beyond Dean Rocks is a clear path that winds its way around the head of a narrow valley known as Dove Stone Clough.

5 Cross over the stream as it flows over a rocky shelf and, as you continue across the slope on the far side, the narrow path slowly begins to drop down the grassy hillside. Fork left and ignore a higher path towards

a prominent stone memorial cross ahead. Soon the path curves steeply down to the left and there are numerous criss-crossing tracks through the long grass and bracken. If you are in any doubt then just aim for the unmistakable aqueduct below you, at the foot of Dove Stone Clough, and cross it by using the high footbridge.

6 Walk along the path below the rock face and the fence on your left and across an area of slumped hillside littered with rock debris. Eventually the path joins a wide, grassy strip that gently leads down between fenced-off plantations of young conifers. Go through the gate and drop down through the open field to reach the popular reservoir-side track. Turn left and then follow this track all the way back to the car park.

54 Haworth's Brontë Moors

This stirring walk across wild Pennine moors leads to a romantic ruin that may have inspired the manor in Emily Brontë's *Wuthering Heights*

Above: The walk leads past Brontë Waterfalls

Top: This way Wuthering Heights? Looking across Haworth Moor on the path towards Top Withins

Who could have imagined, when the Revd Patrick Brontë became curate of the Church of St Michael and All Angels in 1820, that the little gritstone town of Haworth would become a literary destination to rival Grasmere and Stratford-upon-Avon? Of the visitors who flock here in great numbers, some come to gain insight into the works of Charlotte, Emily and Anne Brontë, others simply to enjoy a day out on the Pennine moors.

If the shy sisters could see the Haworth of today, they would recognise the steep, cobbled main street. But they would no doubt be amazed to see the tourist industry that's built up to exploit their names and literary reputations. They would recognise the Georgian parsonage, too. Now a museum, it has been painstakingly restored to reflect the lives of the Brontës and the rooms are filled with their personal treasures.

That three such prodigious talents should be found within a single family is remarkable enough. To have created such towering works as *Jane Eyre* and *Wuthering Heights* while living in what was a bleakly inhospitable place is almost beyond belief. The public were unprepared for this trio of lady novelists, which is why all the books published during their lifetimes bore the androgynous pen-names of Currer, Ellis and Acton Bell.

Tracked by Tragedy

From the day that Patrick Brontë came to Haworth with his wife and six children, tragedy was never far away. His wife died the following year, in 1821, and two of his daughters did not live to adulthood. His only son, Branwell, succumbed to drink and drugs; Anne and Emily died aged 29 and 30 respectively. Charlotte, alone, lived long enough to marry. But after just one year of marriage – to her father's curate – she too fell ill and died in 1855, at the age of 38. Revd Brontë survived them all, living to the ripe old age of 84.

Tourism is no recent development; by the middle of the 19th century, the first literary pilgrims were finding their way to Haworth. No matter how crowded this little town becomes (and those who value their solitude should avoid visiting on a sunny summer weekend), it is always possible to escape to the moors that surround the town. You can follow, literally, in the footsteps of the three sisters as they sought freedom and inspiration, away from the stifling confines of the parsonage and the adjacent graveyard. As you explore these inhospitable moors, you'll get a far greater insight into the imaginative world of the Brontës than those who stray no further than the souvenir shops and tea rooms of Haworth.

54 Haworth's Brontë Moors

Gain an insight into the Brontës' imaginative world on a walk to Top Withins

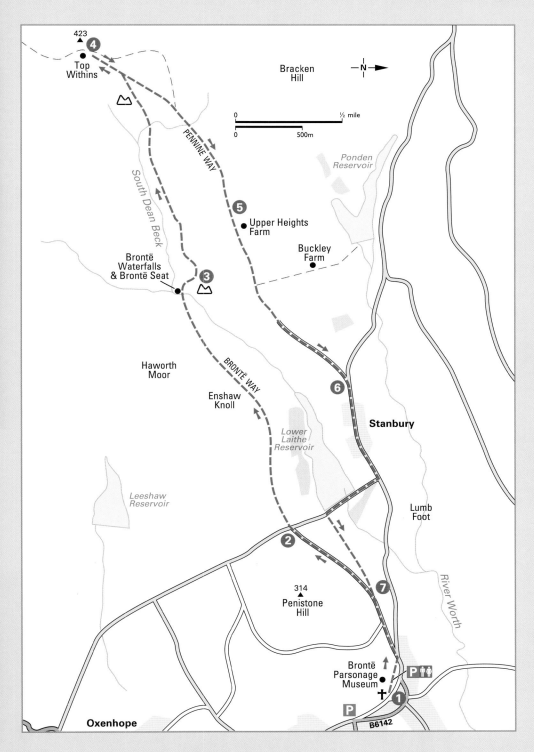

Distance 7.5 miles (12.1km)

Minimum Time 3hrs 30min

Ascent/Gradient 968ft (295m) ▲▲▲

Level of Difficulty ●●●

Paths Well-signed and easy to follow, 1 stile

Landscape Open moorland

Suggested Map OS Explorer OL21 South Pennines

Start/Finish Grid reference: SE 029372

Dog Friendliness Keep dogs under control near sheep on open moorland

Parking Pay-and-display car park, near Brontë Parsonage

Public Toilets Central Park, Haworth

3 Keep left, uphill, on a paved path signed 'Top Withins'. The path levels out beside a wall. Cross a beck on stepping stones, then climb uphill to a signpost by a ruined building. Walk left uphill to the ruin of Top Withins.

4 Retrace your steps to the signpost, then keep ahead on a paved path, downhill, signed 'Stanbury and Haworth and the Pennine Way'. Follow a clear track across the wide expanse of wild Pennine moorland.

5 Pass a white farmhouse – Upper Heights Farm – then bear left at a fork. Walk past Lower Heights Farm. After 500yds (457m), you come to a crossing path: continue on the track straight ahead to a road near Stanbury.

6 Bear right along the road through Stanbury, then take the first road on the right and cross the dam of Lower Laithe Reservoir. Immediately beyond the dam, turn left on a road that is soon reduced to a track uphill, to meet a road by Haworth Cemetery.

7 From here, retrace your outward route: go left along the road, take a gap stile on the right and follow the field path to Haworth.

1 Take the cobbled lane beside the King's Arms, signed 'Brontë Parsonage Museum'. The lane becomes a paved field path that leads to the Haworth–Stanbury road. Walk left along the road and, after just 75yds (69m), take a left fork signed 'Penistone Hill'. Continue along this quiet road to a T-junction.

2 Take the track straight ahead, soon signed 'Brontë Way and Top Withins', gradually descending to South Dean Beck where, within a few paces of the stone bridge, you'll find the Brontë Waterfalls and Brontë Seat (a stone that resembles a chair). Cross the bridge and climb steeply uphill to a three-way sign.

55 Fairburn Ings and Ledsham

A gritty industrial landscape has been transformed into West Yorkshire's very own 'Lake District', a network of water enclosures that rivals the Norfolk Broads

The coalfields of West Yorkshire were most concentrated in the borough of Wakefield. Towns and villages grew up around the mines, and came to represent the epitome of northern industrial life. Mining was always a dangerous and dirty occupation, and it changed the landscape dramatically. Opencast mines swallowed up huge tracts of land, and the extensive spoil heaps were all-too-visible evidence of industry.

For the men of these communities, mining was almost the only work available. When the industry went into decline, these communities were hit especially hard. Historians may well look back with amazement at the speed of the mining industry's decline: mines earmarked for expansion could be closed down a year or two later. To politicians of the left, the miners were sacrificial lambs; to those of the right, the miners exerted too much power. For good or ill, the mining industry was decimated – and thousands of miners lost their livelihoods.

The death of the industry was emphasised by the closing down of Caphouse Colliery and its subsequent conversion into the National Coal Mining Museum for England. The spoil heaps that scarred the landscape are going back to nature, a process hastened by tree planting and other reclamation schemes. Opencast workings have been transformed into lakes and wetlands – valuable havens for wildfowl and migrating birds.

Fairburn Ings Nature Reserve

Fairburn Ings, now under the stewardship of the Royal Society for the Protection of Birds (RSPB), was one of the earliest examples of colliery reclamation – being designated a Local Nature Reserve in 1957. The result is arguably the most important nature reserve in West Yorkshire. Superficially, the site might seem unpromising: it lies in proximity to the A1(M), the conurbation of Castleford, the River Aire, a railway and former spoil heaps. Nevertheless, the stark outlines of the spoil heaps are now softened by banks of silver birch, and mining subsidence has created a broad expanse of water near the village of Fairburn, as well as smaller pools and flashes.

There are plenty of birds to be seen at all times of the year, although the numbers of ducks, geese, swans and gulls are at their highest during the winter months. The 600 acres (243ha) of wetlands are also a magnet for birds during the spring and autumn migrations.

In summer there are many species of wildlife nesting on the scrapes and islands – including terns and a large, noisy colony of black-headed gulls. The best places from which to view all this activity are the public hides that overlook the lake.

'Dry' Sundays Guaranteed

Hidden away from the traffic hammering up and down the nearby motorway, the estate village of Ledsham is a tranquil little backwater, with an ancient church and a row of picturesque almshouses. The Chequers Inn is an old and characterful country pub with, unusually, a six-day licence. Some 170 years ago, so the story goes, the one-time lady of the manor was on her way to church when she saw some of her farm-hands in a drunken state. Horrified, she decreed that to prevent this happening again in the future, Sundays in Ledsham should be 'dry'.

Left: All Saints Church in Ledsham is mainly Anglo-Saxon and is one of the oldest in West Yorkshire

Below: Fairburn Ings offers peaceful walking through trees

55 Fairburn Ings and Ledsham

Cross a bird reserve of national importance and visit the picturesque village of Ledsham

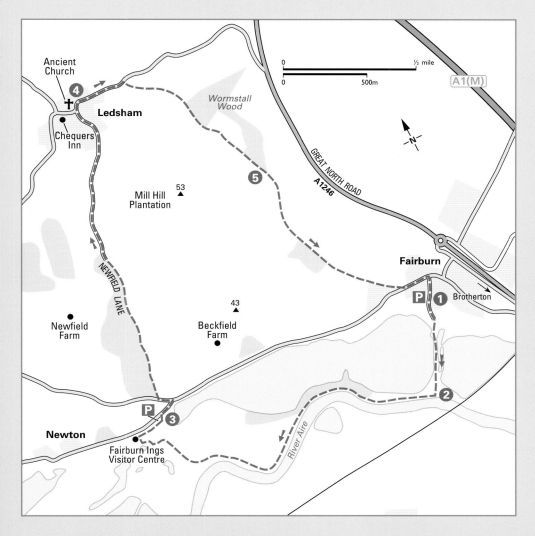

Distance 5 miles (8km)

Minimum Time 2hrs 30min

Ascent/Gradient 262ft (80m) ▲▲▲

Level of Difficulty ●●●

Paths Good paths and tracks, 2 stiles

Landscape Lakes, riverside and reclaimed colliery spoil heaps

Suggested Map OS Explorer 289 Leeds

Start/Finish Grid reference: SE 470278

Dog Friendliness Keep on lead around main lake, due to wildfowl

Parking Free parking in Cut Road, Fairburn, 100yds (91m) west of the Three Horseshoes pub, in the direction of Fairburn Ings

Public Toilets Fairburn Ings visitor centre

1 Walk down Cut Road as it narrows to a track. Soon you have the main lake to your right, and a smaller stretch of water to your left, overlooked by a hide, which is reached via a short detour. The ongoing route, however, follows the main path ahead and leads to a junction by the River Aire.

2 Go right through a kissing gate along the top of a wooded ridge (actually an old spoil heap), with the river to your left and the lake right. Look out for a couple of other bird hides, before you lose sight of the lake. The path crosses a broader expanse of spoil heap through open scrub, following the river before curving right above another small mere. At the bottom, swing left into more trees and then,

opposite a sculpted frog, go right on a wooden walkway across a marsh to the visitor centre. Leave through the car park to a lane.

3 Go right for 100yds (91m), then go left (signed 'Ledston and Kippax') for just 100yds (91m), and pick up a path on your right that hugs the right-hand fringe of a wood. Beyond the wood, take a path between fields; it broadens to a track as you approach the village of Ledsham. At an estate of houses, turn right, along Manor Garth.

4 You arrive in the village by the ancient church. Walk right, along the road (or, for refreshments, go left to Chequers Inn). Beyond the village, where the road bears left, leave

ahead through a gate on the bend on to an undulating track. Over a stile, walk towards woodland and continue within its periphery. Leave the wood by a stile and carry on along the foot of a rising pasture. Another stile at the far bottom corner takes the way through a narrow spur of woodland.

5 Head slightly left, uphill, across the next field, to follow a fence and hedgerow bounding the top. Keep ahead through kissing gates, remaining at the field-edge and passing barns that stand over to the left. Through a final gate, a developing track leads downhill. Go left, when you meet the road, and back into the village of Fairburn to get back to the start of the walk.

56 Beautiful Hurst Green and the Three Rivers

A ramble near Hurst Green in the Ribble Valley leads through countryside that may have been the model for 'the Shire' in J. R. R. Tolkien's *The Lord of the Rings* books

Above: Cromwell's Bridge over the River Hodder – so called because Cromwell is said to have vandalised it in the Civil War era

Main picture: A view fit for a hobbit – evening shadows lengthen as sheep graze Ribble Valley fields

You don't have to be a Tolkien fan to enjoy this walk, which has long been recognised as a logical and graceful outing. Recent research by Jonathan Hewat, a teacher at local preparatory school Stonyhurst St Mary's Hall, has uncovered the extent of the Tolkien connection. This much is certain: J. R. R. Tolkien, author of *The Lord of the Rings*, knew this area well. One of his sons studied for the priesthood at Stonyhurst, which is a local estate owned by the Jesuits, and which incorporates the public (fee-paying) school Stonyhurst College; Tolkien spent long periods here while he was writing his *The Lord of the Rings* trilogy. The rest, although fascinating, is largely conjecture. In the hobbits' Shire there's a River Shirebourn, and the Shireburn family once owned Stonyhurst. But does that mean that Hurst Green is Hobbiton?

Tolkien also drew great inspiration from the country of his boyhood in the West Midlands, deeply regretting its disappearance under roads and factories. Perhaps the Ribble Valley reminded him of that lost landscape. No doubt the Shire owes something to both. If the Tolkien angle intrigues you, a locally available leaflet gives more detail.

Water to Blackburn

Just after the Ribble, you pass the aqueduct, built in 1880 to supply water to Blackburn. An easy 0.75 mile (1.2km) brings you to Jumbles Rocks, outcrops of limestone that form natural weirs and a ford. In the fields near by are two mounds. The lower one was excavated in 1894 and dated to *c*1250 BC; the larger, although known to be artificial, has yet to be properly examined. As the Ribble swings round, the River Calder enters opposite, close to 17th-century Hacking Hall. Less than 0.75 mile (1.2km) further on is the confluence of the Ribble and the Hodder, which you follow briefly before leaving it near Winkley Hall.

You'll soon return to the river at Low Hodder Bridge, then follow the Hodder for almost another mile (1.6km) before climbing steeply away to Woodfields. Tolkien stayed in one of these houses. The track passes St Mary's Hall and then reaches Hall Barn Farm. Near by, on the edge of the college precincts is a small observatory. This was one of a network, observations from which helped the Norwegian physicist Kristian Birkeland confirm the magnetic origin of the Northern Lights.

56 Beautiful Hurst Green and the Three Rivers

Investigate Lancashire fields and river banks familiar to Tolkien, who often stayed locally

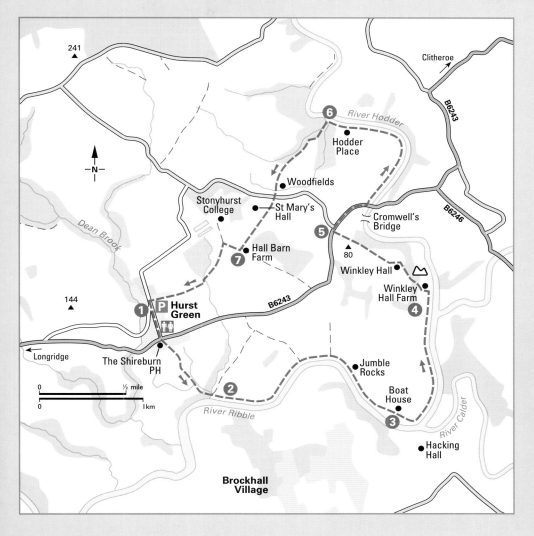

Distance 6.5 miles (10.4km)

Minimum Time 2hrs

Ascent/Gradient 459ft (140m) ▲▲▲

Level of Difficulty ●●○

Paths Grassy riverside paths, woodland and farm tracks, 11 stiles

Landscape Pastoral scenery, scattered woodlands, backdrop of moors

Suggested Map OS Explorer 287 West Pennine Moors

Start/Finish Grid reference: SD 684382

Dog Friendliness Can run free in woodland sections

Parking By Hurst Green village hall or on roadside adjacent

Public toilets Centre of Hurst Green

1 Walk down the road to reach the centre of Hurst Green village. Cross the main road and go down to the left of The Shireburn pub to a stile below the main car park. Go down the edge of a field and then follow a small stream to reach some duckboards and a footbridge. After a slight rise, descend via a stile and winding path to the River Ribble. Bear left just above the river.

2 Skirt the aqueduct and return to the river bank. Join a surfaced drive past Jumbles Rocks. Go over a large wooden stile beyond a small stone building to rejoin the river bank and follow it, towards the Boat House.

3 After rounding the big bend, go up slightly to a track. Follow this for about 0.5 mile (800m). Opposite the confluence of the Ribble and the Hodder, go over a stile by a bench.

4 The narrow path quickly rejoins the track. At Winkley Hall Farm go left to the houses, right between barns then left past a pond and out into a lane. This climbs steeply then levels out, swinging left past Winkley Hall. Go through a kissing gate on the right and across the field to another. Keep straight on across a large field, just left of a wood, then down via a stile and up to reach a road.

5 Turn right along a pavement to the river. Immediately before the bridge, turn left along a track. Follow the river round, then climb up past Hodder Place before descending again to a bridge over a stream.

6 Go up the track on the left, cross a footbridge and then climb a long flight of wooden steps. Follow the top edge of a plantation, then cross a stile into a field. Keep

to its edge and at the end cross a stile into a stony track. Keep left, past Woodfields and out to the road. Go down the track by the post-box to Hall Barn Farm and along the right side of the buildings.

7 Turn right and walk along a tarmac track for 200yds (183m). Go left through a gate by the end of a wall and along a narrow field. Drop down to the right on a track alongside a wood then up to a kissing gate. Follow the field-edge to another kissing gate. At the top of the final field, through a gate, a narrow path leads to a short lane. At its end turn left back to the start of the walk.

57 Hidden York

A walk through the historic streets and alleys of York leads from a 6th-century tower past medieval ecclesiastical palace buildings to York's first cinema

Top right: Clifford's Tower

Below left: The city walls date back to Roman times

Below centre: The Merchant Adventurers' Hall was built in 1357–61

Below right: The Shambles

Bottom left: The Cloister inside York Minster

Bottom right: Barley Hall museum

St Olave's Church, at the start of the walk, was founded in 1055 by Siward, Earl of Northumbria and heavily repaired after it was used as a gun platform in 1644 during the Civil War Siege of York. Further along, past the library, look right, as you ascend the steps, to the Anglian Tower. Built on the Roman ramparts during the time the Anglians ruled York (from the 6th century), this small building is now surrounded by the exposed layers of successive York defensive walls.

The King's Manor, on your left as you go towards Exhibition Square, was the house of the Abbot of St Mary's, and was appropriated by the king in 1539.

The residence of the President of the Council of the North from 1561 to 1641, it was apartments until 1833 and then a school. Since 1963 it has been leased to York University. The Minster Library, approached through Dean's Park, north of the Minster, is the only remaining substantial part of the palace of the Archbishops of York. Built about 1230 as the palace's chapel, it became the library in the 19th century.

Vicars Choral

Bedern, off Goodramgate, was where the Vicars Choral of the Minster lived. They sang the Minster services, and had their own Chapel and Hall (both of which you will pass) as well as a wooden walkway to the Minster precincts to avoid the undesirables who inhabited the area.

On St Saviourgate is the red-brick Unitarian Chapel. Designed in the shape of an equal-armed cross with a little tower, it was built for the Presbyterians in 1692. Lady Peckitt's Yard is beside the half-timbered Herbert House of about 1620. As you turn into Fossgate, notice Macdonald's furniture shop opposite. This was the Electric Theatre, York's first cinema, built in 1911. After passing Clifford's Tower and reaching Castlegate, visit Fairfax House, a fine town house of the 1740s.

On King's Staith, once the main wharf for the city, is the 17th-century King's Arms Inn, which has the distinction of being Britain's most flooded pub. Ouse Bridge was, for centuries, the only crossing place linking the two banks of the river. This 19th-century bridge replaced two earlier ones: the Elizabethan bridge had houses on it.

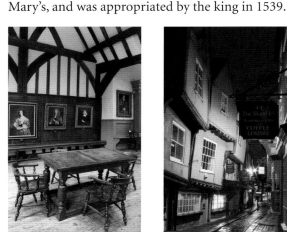

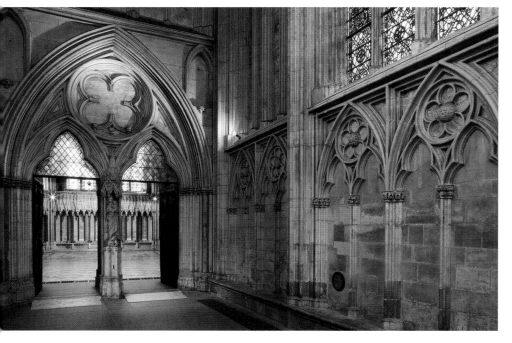

57 Hidden York

Make your way along the cobbled lanes and medieval thoroughfares of an ancient city

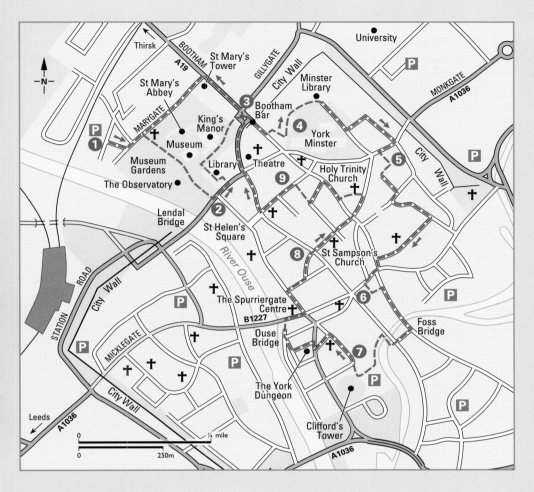

Distance 3.25 miles (5.3km)

Minimum Time 1hr 30min

Ascent/Gradient 82ft (25m) ▲▲▲

Level of Difficulty ●●●

Paths City pavements

Landscape Historic city

Suggested Map AA Street by Street York (page 2 C3)

Start/Finish Grid reference: SE 598523

Dog Friendliness City streets, so dogs should be kept on a lead

Parking Marygate Car Park, off Bootham

Public Toilets Museum Gardens and Bootham Bar

1 Walk back into Marygate, turn left, cross the road and enter Museum Gardens through the archway. Follow the path straight ahead, passing the Observatory, and leave the gardens by the lodge.

2 Turn left, then left again towards the library. Go left through a gate, and along the side of the library. Go up the steps, and through a gate in the wall. At the bottom of the slope, turn right and follow Abbey Wall into Exhibition Square.

3 Cross at the traffic-lights and go through Bootham Bar. A few paces on your left, take a passageway beside The Hole in the Wall pub and turn right down Precentor's Court. By the Minster, go left through the gate, signed 'York Minster Dean's Park'.

4 Follow the path left to the Minster Library building. Bend right through the gate and along the cobbled road. Turn left by the

postbox down Chapter House Street, bending right into Ogleforth. At the crossroads turn right, then go left through an archway opposite The National Trust Café.

5 Bear right into Bartle Garth, which bends left. At the T-junction turn right, and then go left down Spen Lane. Opposite Hilary House, go right along St Saviourgate. At the T-junction turn left, then right at the crossroads. Next to Jones's shoe shop on the left, take a passage, Lady Peckitt's Yard.

6 Go under the buildings, then turn left to Fossgate. Turn right, go over the bridge and then turn right along Merchantgate. At the T-junction, cross the road and take the glazed walkway beside the bridge, signed 'Castle Area', into the car park by Clifford's Tower.

7 Bend right and go to the right of the Hilton Hotel. Just after passing the church on the right, go left down Friargate, right

along Clifford Street, and then left by The York Dungeon. At the riverside turn right, ascend the steps by Ouse Bridge and turn right again. At the traffic-lights, turn left by The Spurriergate Centre. By the NatWest Bank go right, forking left into Feasegate.

8 Go ahead to cross Parliament Street and pass St Sampson's Church. Go straight on at the next crossroads into Goodramgate. After 50yds (46m), go left through a gateway into Holy Trinity churchyard, and leave by a passage to the left of the tower, to reach Low Petergate. Turn right, then take the next left into Grape Lane. Where it bends left, turn right down the narrow Coffee Yard into Stonegate.

9 Go left to St Helen's Square and turn right by Lloyds TSB. Go straight on at the next crossroads back to Exhibition Square. At the traffic-lights, turn left up Bootham. Turn left down Marygate by the circular tower to return to the car park.

58 Down to the Summit on Clougha Pike

This wild walk leads to a deceptive 'summit' that proves an unrivalled viewpoint looking over the Bowland Fells, and further – to Snowdonia and the Isle of Man

Clougha Pike is the finest viewpoint in the Bowland Fells, possibly in the whole of Lancashire. There is plenty to see at closer quarters, too, and the walk is always rewarding, but on a clear day it's nothing short of magnificent.

Although the ground is sometimes very rough, the ascent is rarely very steep and the views expand with every stride. The opening stages are almost level. After crossing the little aqueduct called Ottergear Bridge, the route swings round and climbs a little, then drops into a small, sharp-cut valley. This is the first of several curious channels, some of which cut right through the ridge of Clougha. These are relics from the end of the ice age. The edge of the ice sheet was stationary for a while in this area, dammed up behind the ridge. Torrents of meltwater pouring off the ice, and probably sometimes running underneath it, carved the network of channels. The most striking example is Windy Clough, near the end of the walk.

Across Heather Moorland

Now the walk begins its steady ascent across the broad flanks. Apart from a few wet patches marked by rushes and cotton grass, the dominant vegetation is heather and bilberry. Heather moorland is widespread in Britain but rare in most of the rest of Europe. Geology, climate and soils are partly responsible, but the management of the land is equally significant. Controlled burning of areas of moor encourages the heather to produce new shoots, the main food for the red grouse. Like it or not, grouse shooting for sport is part of the ecology of these moors.

Once the rocky crest of the ridge is reached, the climbing is over. The last stretch is generally level and when the summit of Clougha appears it definitely is slightly below you. This hardly detracts from the view, even though a sector is blocked by the higher ground of Grit Fell and beyond it Ward's Stone, the highest summit in Lancashire.

The Clwydian Hills in Wales are apparent much more often than the higher, but more distant, peaks of Snowdonia. The distinctive profile of the Isle of Man, more than 60 miles (97km) away in the Irish Sea, is also visible on a clear day. However, what grabs most of the attention is the sweep of the Lakeland skyline and the continuation of high ground eastwards, over the Howgill Fells and into Yorkshire, where the 'Three Peaks' of Whernside, Ingleborough and Pen-y-ghent are dominant.

As you descend, the nick of Little Windy Clough appears over your right shoulder, and then the much deeper Windy Clough appears. The stream draining Windy Clough runs underground where we cross it but surfaces again a little lower down.

Top: Sweeping moorland views in the Bowland Fells

Above: Bilberry leaves on Clougha Pike

Left: Towards the Trough of Bowland, the valley and pass at the heart of the Bowland Fells

58 Down to the Summit on Clougha Pike

Get a close look at several 'cloughs' or channels cut at the end of the last ice age

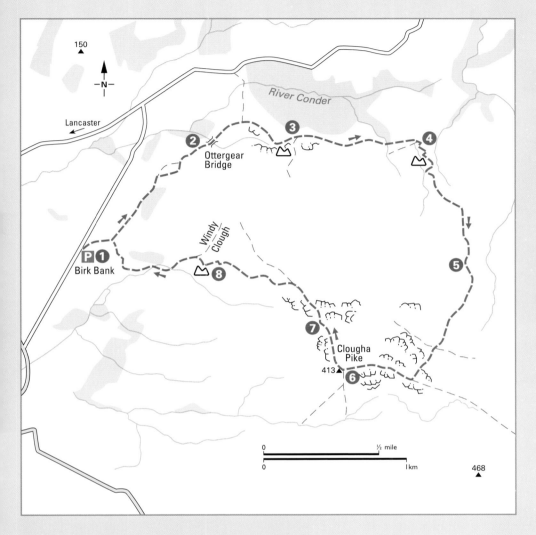

Distance 5.25 miles (8.4km)

Minimum Time 2hrs

Ascent/Gradient 1,050ft (320m) ▲▲▲

Level of Difficulty ●●●

Paths Mostly very rough moorland, often rocky, 4 stiles

Landscape Moorland with some rocky outcrops, above green valley

Suggested Map OS Explorer OL41 Forest of Bowland & Ribblesdale

Start/Finish Grid reference: SD 526604

Dog Friendliness Access Area – dogs not permitted

Parking Access Area car park at Birk Bank

Public Toilets Nearest at Crook O'Lune

1 Follow the track above the car park, then fork left. It becomes a green path, running generally level, to Ottergear Bridge.

2 Turn left and walk along a level track, then bear right at the next junction. The track climbs slightly, descends into a narrow valley, then climbs steeply up the far side before it finally eases and swings round to the right.

3 Go left on a narrow path, running almost level above a steeper slope. After 500yds (457m), it angles back down into the valley. Follow the base of the steep slope and cross a small stream. After 30yds (27m) a green track climbs to the right.

4 Wind up steeply to near-level moor. The path follows a slight groove, then skirts leftward around a boggy patch parallel to the

wall. The grassy path ahead is initially very faint. Keep just left of the continuous heather and it soon becomes clearer. There's another grooved section, then a clear stony path rises leftward across steeper ground.

5 As the slope eases the path remains clear, passing a few sketchy cairns. Follow a groove, past tumbledown shooting butts. As the ground levels, ease right past cairns and marker stakes to a new track. Cross and follow a thin grassy path with more marker stakes. Bear right up a slight rise and join a wider path at a cairn. Go right on a broad ridge, crossing a fence, to reach the summit trig point.

6 Descend a clear path on the right past a large cairn. There's a steep drop nearby on the left, with some small crags. A fence converges from the right, meeting a wall.

7 Scramble down rocks by the end of the wall. Continue down its left side for about 300yds (274m). Bear left at a levelling amid scattered boulders. Descend through a gap flanked by wrinkled rocks then across gentler slopes to a gate by the corner of a wall.

8 Head straight down until the ground steepens, then swing right and weave down towards Windy Clough. From a stile go left down a grooved path to an area of young trees. Fork left, closer to the stream, rejoining wetter alternative routes above larger oaks. Descend through gorse then follow duckboards skirting a bog. Turn right along a track then left over a slight rise to the car park.

59 A Kingdom for a Horse

From the ruins of Middleham Castle, favourite dwelling of Richard III, this walk leads to the galloping grounds of top racehorses on the nearby Low Moor

Top: The ruins of the square keep, built by Robert FitzRanulph in the 12th century

Above: A modern statue of Richard III in the castle grounds

Above right: The River Cover

Below right: There are fine views of the castle from Middleham Moor

When Richard III died at the Battle of Bosworth Field in 1485, Middleham lost one of its favourite residents. Richard had lived here, in the household of the Earl of Warwick ('the Kingmaker') when a boy, and set up home here with the earl's daughter, Anne, after their marriage. As Duke of Gloucester, it was his power base as effective ruler of the North under his brother Edward IV. Locals don't believe the propagandist depiction of Richard as a murderer found in Shakespeare's play – the Lord Mayor of York reported to his council after Bosworth that 'King Richard, late lawfully reigning over us, was through great treason piteously slain and murdered.' Middleham Castle today is a splendid and imposing ruin, with one of the biggest keeps in England, impressive curtain walls and a deep moat. It is in the care of English Heritage.

Hall and Hill-fort

From Middleham, the walk takes us to the River Cover and along its banks. After crossing Hullo Bridge the path passes near Braithwaite Hall. Owned by the National Trust and open by appointment only, this is a modest farmhouse of 1667, with three fine gables and unusual oval windows beneath them. Inside are stone-flagged floors, a fine oak staircase and wood panelling, all of the late 17th century. On the hillside behind are the earthworks of a hill-fort, thought to be Iron Age. After the Hall, the lane eventually crosses Coverham Bridge, probably built by the monks of nearby Coverham Abbey. There are a few remains of the abbey, founded in the 12th century, mostly incorporated into later buildings on the site. Miles Coverdale, who was the first man to complete a full English translation of the Bible, came from here.

At a Gallop

Middleham is known also as the home of famous racehorses, and you may see some in training as you walk over Middleham Low Moor. More than 500 horses train in Middleham, under the watchful eyes of 13 trainers. Both the Low Moor and the High Moor have been used for exercise for more than 300 years; one of the earliest recorded winners was Bay Bolton, born in 1705, which won Queen Anne's Gold Cup at York Races. Among early jockeys was 'Crying Jackie' Mangle, who won the St Leger five times in the 1770s and 80s.

To your left as you leave the Low Moor and make your way back to the castle is William's Hill, the remains of the original motte-and-bailey castle built here by the Normans after 1066 to guard the approaches to Wensleydale and Coverdale. The motte, 40ft (12m) high, is joined by a curved bailey surrounded by a ditch. It was abandoned in 1170 when the new castle was begun near by.

59 A Kingdom for a Horse

Take a walk fit for a king – and admire some thoroughbreds

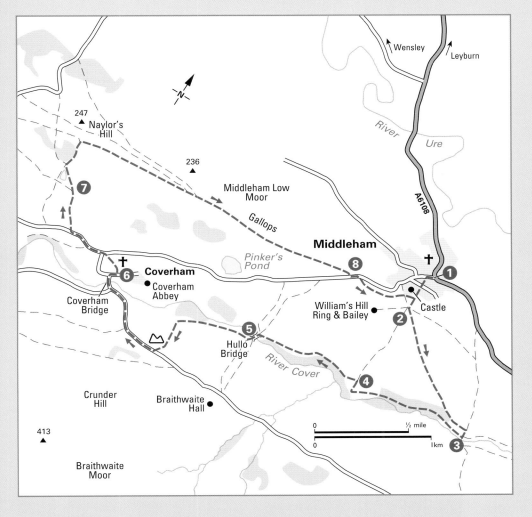

Distance 7 miles (11.3km)

Minimum Time 2hrs 30min

Ascent/Gradient 475ft (145m) ▲▲▲

Level of Difficulty ●●●

Paths Field paths and tracks, with some road walking, 14 stiles

Landscape Gentle farmland, riverside paths, views of Wensleydale

Suggested Map OS Explorer OL 30 Yorkshire Dales – Northern & Central

Start/Finish Grid reference: SE 127877

Dog Friendliness Livestock and horses in fields, so dogs on leads

Parking In square in centre of Middleham

Public Toilets Middleham

1 From the square, take the Coverham road then turn left up a passageway beside the Castle Keep Tea Rooms. Continue to the left of Middleham Castle, along a walled track towards a gate.

2 Bear left across the big field, following the sign for 'stepping stones'. Cross two more fields, clambering over waymarked stiles. After the third stile, follow the field-edge above a steep bank. When you reach a crossing wall turn right, going down to the River Cover by the stepping stones.

3 Turn right (do not cross the river) and follow the path along through woods and a field. A gate leads to some steps and an elevated section. After returning to the river bank, cross a stile into a field. After another stile at its end, turn immediately right. Climb steeply to a marker post.

4 Turn left and follow the edge of a wood. At the end of the field, go left through the trees, then straight ahead on an obvious descending path. Cross a stile and turn left to Hullo Bridge.

5 Cross the bridge and turn right on a permissive path, crossing three stiles. At a crossing wire fence turn left. Cross another stile. Where the fence bends right, go ahead up a steep bank to reach a gate on to a lane. Turn right and descend to Coverham Bridge. Cross the bridge and turn right on a track.

6 Before iron gates, turn left through a small gate, climbing beside a waterfall into the churchyard. Leave by the lychgate and bear left along the main road (signed 'Forbidden Corner'). After 0.25 mile (400m), go through a gate on the right opposite a disused factory. Bear slightly left, cross three stiles, then aim for a prominent gap between buildings and continue through a narrow strip of woodland.

7 Bear slightly left to a stile, to the right of a stone wall. Skirt ornamental ponds to meet a track. Turn right and then ascend, past a house, to a gateway on to a wider track. Turn right. Where the track bends right, keep straight ahead across the grassy moor; look for occasional blue-topped posts marking the line of a bridleway. When the long fenced gallops appear, keep them to your left and continue down to the road.

8 Turn left. Just before the Middleham sign, take a signposted path on the right. Cross the stile, turn left and follow the path parallel to the road. Go through a stile and a gate, then bear left down to another stile and go through a gate on to the lane. Turn left and make your way back to the square.

60 Herriot's Darrowby

A turn around Thirsk leads past the surgery that was the setting for James Herriot's tales of a vet's life in *If Only They Could Talk* and other bestsellers

The elegant Georgian village street of Sowerby – now joined on to the town of Thirsk – is lined with a handsome avenue of lime trees. Such a civilised aspect belies the origins of the village's name, for Sowerby means the 'township in the muddy place'. Once you begin the walk, the reason becomes evident, even in dry weather. Sowerby is on the edge of the flood plain of the Cod Beck. Sowerby Flatts, which you will see across the beck at the start of the walk, and cross at the finish, is a popular venue for impromptu games of soccer and other sports, but is still prone to flooding.

Once you've crossed the road by the end of New Bridge, you are walking between Old Thirsk and New Thirsk – though new in this context still means medieval. Old Thirsk is set to the east of the Cod Beck; like Sowerby, it too has a watery name, for Thirsk comes from an old Swedish word meaning a 'fen'. New Thirsk, to the west, is centred on the fine cobbled market place. The parish church, which you will pass twice, is the best Perpendicular church in North Yorkshire, with a particularly imposing tower.

South Kilvington, at the northern end of the walk, used to be a busy village on the main road north from Thirsk to Yarm. For much of the 19th century it was home to William Kingsley, who was vicar here until his death at the age of 101 in 1916. He entertained the painter Turner and the art critic John Ruskin here – as well as his cousin Charles Kingsley, author of *The Water Babies*. More than a little eccentric, the vicar erected signs in his garden saying 'Beware of Mantraps'. When asked where they were, he paraded his three housemaids.

Herriot Museum

For many visitors, the essential place to visit in Thirsk is Skeldale House in Kirkgate – on the right as you return from the church to the Market Square. This was the surgery of local vet James Wight, better known by his pen name: James Herriot. Now an award-winning museum, The World of James Herriot, this was where Wight worked for all his professional life. Thirsk itself is a major character in the books, appearing lightly disguised as Darrowby. The museum has reconstructions of what the surgery and the family rooms were like in the 1940s, and tells the history of veterinary science. Whether or not you're a fan of the Herriot tales, which began with *If Only They Could Talk* in 1970, you'll find it a nostalgic tour.

Left: James Herriot's fictional town gives its name to this Thirsk pub

Below: The medieval St Mary's Parish Church, Thirsk – sometimes called 'the Cathedral of North Yorkshire'

Bottom: The Dispensing Room in the World of James Herriot Museum

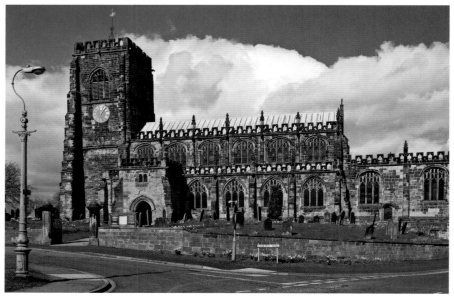

60 Herriot's Darrowby

Follow in the footsteps of James Herriot through town and country

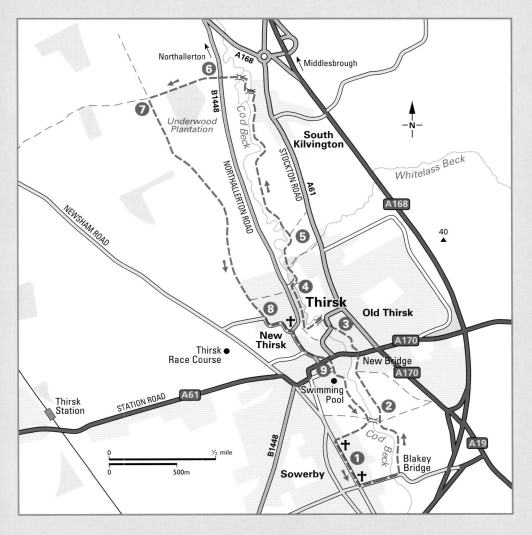

Distance 5 miles (8km)

Minimum Time 2hrs

Ascent/Gradient 66ft (20m) ▲▲▲

Level of Difficulty ●●●

Paths Town paths, field paths and tracks, 6 stiles

Landscape Streamside and undulating pastureland around town

Suggested Map OS Explorer 302 Northallerton & Thirsk

Start/Finish Grid reference: SE 430813

Dog Friendliness Keep dogs on leads

Parking Roadside parking in the main street of Sowerby village

Public Toilets Thirsk town centre

1 Walk down the village street, away from Thirsk. Just past the Methodist Church on the left, go left down Blakey Lane. Cross the bridge, turn left on a signed path and follow the stream, going through two kissing gates to a footbridge.

2 Continue beside the stream to a stile. Go through two gates to a car park and ahead to the road. Cross and take a path that curves left, then right by the bridge. At a paved area, turn right to go alongside a green to a road.

3 Cross the road and continue straight ahead, crossing a main road and going left at the top of the green. Cross the metal bridge and continue beside the beck by the church. Before reaching the road take the path heading to the right, beside a bench, to a footbridge on the right.

4 Cross the bridge and go straight ahead through two gates, curving left to follow the beck to a gate by a bridge. Go straight ahead (not over the bridge) and follow the path across the fields, veering diagonally right to a stile on your right.

5 Climb over the stile and then follow the stream, going over another two stiles as you pass beside houses. Continue left over a footbridge by some mill buildings. At this point the path winds right in order to cross a second footbridge. Follow the bridleway sign across the field and then through a gate to reach the main road.

6 Cross the road and go through a signed gate opposite, to another gate beside a wood. 150yds (137m) after the wood, turn left at a waymark.

7 Walk down the field with a hedge on your left. In the second field, go left over a stile and continue with the hedge on your right, bearing half left to another stile. Continue across the field, then down the next field-edge, bearing left, then right at the end to a path that becomes a grassy lane between hedges.

8 At a road go straight ahead, bearing left, then right past the church. Turn right into the town centre. In the Market Place, cross towards the Golden Fleece. Go down a signed passageway two premises to the pub's left, cross a lane and go down Villa Place.

9 Bear left to pass the swimming pool. Turn right round the pool building to a gate. Go ahead and parallel with the beck. At the bridge, turn right on a grassy track to a gate on to a lane, then straight to Sowerby.

61 Roseberry Topping and Captain Cook Country

A ramble at the edge of the North York Moors visits the distinctively shaped hill of Roseberry Topping and a monument to celebrated naval officer James Cook

Roseberry Topping, 1,051ft (320m) high, was once an integral part of the North York Moors plateau. Over the millennia, however, the forces of nature eroded the land around it, but the Topping itself was protected by a cap of harder sandstone. In time it became an isolated conical hill, stranded above the plain of the River Tees. Through the centuries it has been called many things, from Odinburgh (after the Norse god) to Rosemary Torp (by the notoriously inaccurate Daniel Defoe). Roseberry means 'fortress in the heath' and Topping, a 'point' – although there is no sign of a fortress there now.

Roseberry Topping retained its conical perfection until the night of 8th August 1912, when a huge chunk of land fell from its south-west slope and gave it the now characteristic jagged profile. The immediate cause of the fall was the ironstone mining operations that had been burrowing into the slopes of the hill since 1880, when the Roseberry Ironstone Company opened its first seam; like much of this part of the North York Moors, Roseberry Topping is rich in ironstone.

The company survived for only three years, but the seam was later re-opened, first by the Tees Furnace Company and then by its successor, Burton and Sons. Burton's were blamed for the 1912 collapse, and for another landslide ten years later, but the topping is geologically unstable and could have slipped at any time.

Monument on Great Ayton Moor

After the descent from Roseberry Topping, and the climb again to the woodland, the track descends over Great Ayton Moor. Ahead, the Captain Cook Monument, a stone obelisk 51ft (15.5m) high, dominates the view.

The great explorer was born in 1728 within sight of Roseberry Topping at Marton (then a village, but now a suburb of Middlesbrough) and went to school at nearby Great Ayton. The monument was erected in 1827, with an inscription that names James Cook as 'amongst the most celebrated and most admired benefactors of the human race'. From 1736 James's father worked at Aireyholme Farm (not open to the public), which is situated near Point 6 on the walk opposite.

Top left: The idyllic Newton Wood, just under Roseberry Topping's western peak

Left: An old shooting lodge, south of Roseberry Topping

Below: Looking north towards the Topping across fields of bluebells and rapeseed

61 Roseberry Topping and Captain Cook Country

Pay your respects to Captain James Cook and walk through beautiful flower-carpeted woodland

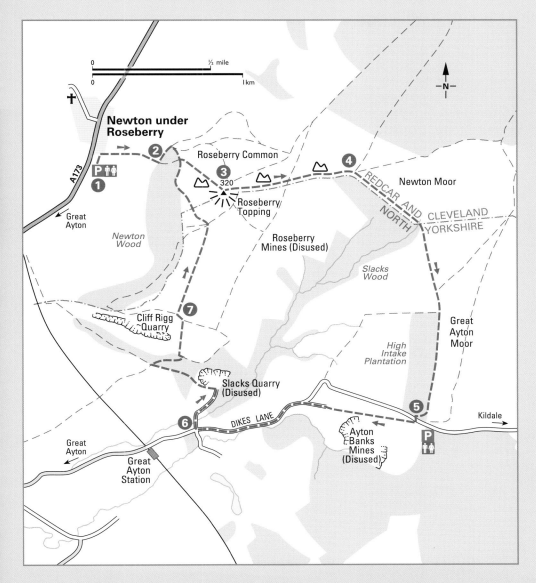

Distance 5.5 miles (8.8km)

Minimum Time 2hrs 30min

Ascent/Gradient 1,214ft (370m) ▲▲▲

Level of Difficulty ●●●

Paths Hillside climb, then tracks and field paths, 5 stiles

Landscape One of the best 360-degree views in Yorkshire

Suggested Map OS Explorer OL 26 North York Moors – Western

Start/Finish Grid reference: NZ 570128

Dog Friendliness Off lead, except in farmland

Parking Car park on A173 just south of Newton under Roseberry

Public Toilets In car park at foot of Roseberry Topping

1 Take the rough lane beside the car park towards Roseberry Topping. The path goes through a gateway then rises to a second gate at the beginning of the woodland.

2 Go through the gate into National Trust Land and then turn left. There is a well-worn, mostly paved path to the summit. It is a stiff climb to the trig point on the top of the hill.

3 From the summit, walk east from the trig point, past two iron poles set into rock, and straight on along the paved way. Go steeply downhill. At the bottom, bear right to go up a track that bends right around the corner of woodland to a gate.

4 Go through the gate and take the path alongside the wood, following yellow waymarkers. Continue on the path until it eventually follows a wall and descends the hillside to reach a road.

5 Turn right, cross the cattle grid and bear left between two benches, then go right, along the fence line, at first parallel with the road. Go down the field, through a gate and then over a stile and out into a lane. Walk past the cottages to reach a road, where you go straight ahead.

6 At a crossroads go right, down Aireyholme Lane. Follow the lane as it winds past houses, then take a signed footpath left over

a stile. Follow the fence to two gates into woodland. After 0.5 mile (800m), go right at a National Trust sign, up a path ascending through the woods to a signposted stile. Over it, turn left to another stile, then after it, go right along the edge of the woodland. Bend left to a gate near a house.

7 Walk across two fields to a stile, then continue uphill to the tower. Beyond it, take a grassy path left down a gully, to a gate into woodland. Follow the path downhill through the woods to return to the gate at the top of the lane leading back to the car park.

62 From Eskdale to Miterdale

Where Norman lords and monarchs rode to hunt, and peasants lived under harsh Forest Law, there is now a wide expanse of peaceful, if sometimes marshy, land

Below: Eskdale Farm

Bottom: Marshy land at Sineytarn Moss

Although William the Conqueror arrived in England in 1066, much of the North remained controlled by the Scots, and it was not until William II took Carlisle in 1092 that Norman influence spread through Lakeland. Some settlement was encouraged and land granted to found monastic houses, but much of the mountainous area remained undeveloped. The main reason for this lay in the Normans' almost fanatical devotion to the hunt, an activity, exclusively reserved for the king and a few favoured subjects. Vast tracts of this northern 'wasteland' were 'afforested', not in today's sense with the planting of trees, but set aside as wild game reserves and subject to special regulation, the Forest Law.

The area around Eskdale lay within the barony of Copeland, a name that derives from the Old Norse 'kaupaland' meaning 'bought land', and was granted to William de Briquessart in the early 12th century. His forest, together with the neighbouring Derwentfells Forest, extended all the way from the Esk to the Derwent and remained under Forest Law for more than a century. The forest was not devoid of settlement, but the few peasants who lived there were subject to many draconian laws that affected almost every aspect of their meagre existence.

The clearance of additional land for grazing or cultivation, known as 'assarting', was forbidden and it was illegal to allow cattle or sheep to stray into the forest. Even the collection of wood for fuel was strictly controlled.

Severe Penalties in Forest Courts

The estate was policed by foresters, who were keen to bring malefactors before the forest courts for punishment. The penalties were often severe, ranging from a complex system of fines for minor infringements to flogging, mutilation or even death for poaching. Often near to starvation themselves, the commoners were required to assist as beaters, butchers and carriers for the hunts, and watch their overlords kill, perhaps, more than 100 deer in a single day. Yet if game animals broke through the fences around their allotments and destroyed the paltry crop, they were powerless to do anything other than chase them away.

The hunting preserve gradually diminished during the 13th century, as larger areas were turned over to sheep farming The animals' constant nibbling prevented the regeneration of natural woodland and left the open landscape now so characteristic of the area.

62 From Eskdale to Miterdale

Discover gentle hills that were once a royal hunting forest

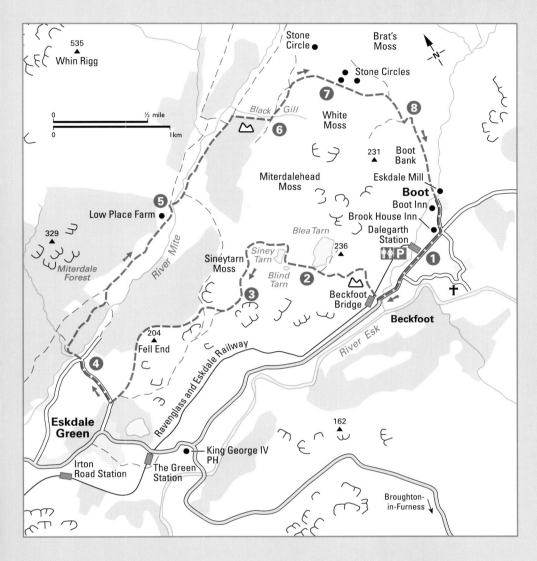

Distance 6.75 miles (10.9km)

Minimum Time 4hrs

Ascent/Gradient 1,312ft (400m) ▲▲▲

Level of Difficulty ●●●

Paths Good paths in valleys, but often indistinct on hills, 4 stiles

Landscape Heath and moor with views across surrounding valleys

Suggested Map OS Explorer OL6 The English Lakes (SW)

Start/Finish Grid reference: NY 173007

Dog Friendliness Keep on lead as sheep roam moors

Parking Car park beside Dalegarth Station (pay-and-display)

Public Toilets At Dalegarth Station

Note Walk not advised in poor visibility

1 Follow the lane down the valley towards Beckfoot Bridge. Before the railway halt, cross the line to a gate where a zig-zag path to Blea Tarn is signed up the hillside. Approaching the tarn, go left crossing a stream.

2 A vague path maintains the firm ground, right of Blind and Siney tarns, then, at a fork, bear left. Beyond a lone tree, go left again. The way is marshy around Sineytarn Moss but a dry route can be found. Eventually, the route joins a wall, dropping to level grass.

3 Bear right to a fence stile by a forest and continue along its edge below Fell End. Keep going near the wall, reaching its corner in about 0.75 mile (1.2km). A short track on the right descends to a junction, and another right turn takes you into Miterdale.

4 Emerge on to a tarmac lane at the bottom and go through a gate opposite into Miterdale Forest. Drop over the river and then bear right on an undulating, weaving path above its far bank. A lateral wall shortly forces you uphill on to a forest track. Turn right and follow the track out of the trees, joining another track from the right to continue up the valley to Low Place Farm.

5 Walk past the farmhouse and through a second yard, leaving by the right-hand gates, signed 'Wasdale'. Follow the river upstream before crossing a bridge to a track that continues along its opposite bank. Keep ahead for nearly 0.75 mile (1.2km) until you cross a stile at the far end of a plantation. Here, leave the track and climb the hill beside the trees to another stile at the top.

6 Bear left above Black Gill and then continue parallel to a wall towards the higher ground of Low Longrigg. After 400yds (366m) strike right on a barely visible path, making for the stone circles, which briefly break the horizon.

7 Bear right at the second circle and, after passing beneath a rocky outcrop, fork left. The way is still vague, but now drops towards stone huts, where a clear path descends by them to the right.

8 Follow it down Boot Bank and into Boot, and cross Whillan Beck by Eskdale Mill to continue through the village. At the end turn right to Dalegarth Station.

63 Brant Fell Above Bowness-on-Windermere

Climb Brant Fell to discover woods, open spaces and breathtaking views over lake Windermere – calm that contrasts markedly with the bustle in the resort below

Walking through Bowness-on-Windermere on a busy summer weekend, it is hard to imagine that just above the lakeside bustle there is a world of solitude and space. But there is – and this walk takes you there. With relatively little effort you can crest the heights of Brant Fell and enjoy a wonderful view out over Windermere to the Coniston fells and the central heights of the Lake District up to the mighty Fairfield.

Fed by the high rainfall of the Lake District fells, via the rivers Brathay, Rothay and Troutbeck, Windermere is England's largest natural lake. It is 12 miles (19km) in length, up to 1 mile (1.6km) wide in places, and reaches a depth of 220ft (67m). The Romans built their fort of Galava at Waterhead, on the northern tip of the lake.

Overlooked by this walk, the privately owned Belle Isle is said to have been used since Roman times. Today, this island is supplied by a little boat, which serves the 38-acre (15ha) estate. Belle Isle's interesting circular house, restored after extensive fire damage in 1996, was originally erected by Mr English in 1774. Apparently William Wordsworth accredited Mr English with the honour of being the first man to settle in the Lake District for the sake of the scenery. There have been many more since.

Once the Oxenholme and Kendal-to-Windermere railway line opened in 1847 the town of Bowness-on-Windermere developed rapidly. The town, which grew around the station from what was once a small village, is today the most popular holiday destination in the Lake District.

Retreat for Industrialists

In the late 19th century wealthy businessmen, principally from industrial towns in Lancashire, built luxurious residences overlooking the lake. Many of these houses are now hotels, such as the Langdale Chase, whilst Brockhole has been the National Park Visitor Centre since the late 1960s.

The Belsfield Hotel overlooking Bowness Bay was bought in 1860 by Henry Schneider, the chairman of the Barrow Steelworks and Shipworks. He reputedly breakfasted while crossing the lake to Lakeside on his steam yacht SL *Esperance*, then journeyed on by steam train, in his own private carriage to the works in Barrow.

Left: There are beautiful views of the lake from Brant Fell

Below: Solitude and peaceful walking on the hills

63 Brant Fell Above Bowness-on-Windermere

Escape the crowds to find peace and solitude on the hills above Bowness

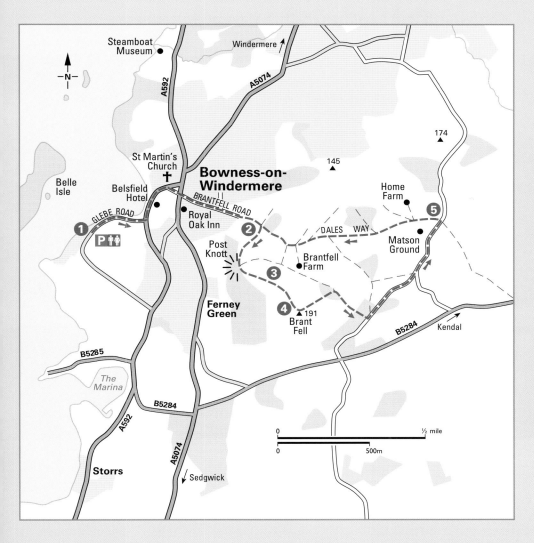

Distance 3.5 miles (5.7km)

Minimum Time 1hr 15min

Ascent/Gradient 525ft (160m) ▲▲▲

Level of Difficulty ●●●

Paths Pavement, road, stony tracks, grassy paths, 2 stiles

Landscape Town, mixed woodland, open fell, lake and fell views

Suggested Map OS Explorer OL7 The English Lakes (SE)

Start/Finish Grid reference: SD 398966

Dog Friendliness Popular route for dogs; busy roads and sheep grazing, so must be under control

Parking Fee car park on Glebe Road above Windermere lake

Public Toilets At car park and above information centre

1 Take Glebe Road into Bowness town. Swing left and, opposite the steamer pier, go right over the main Windermere road and then turn left. Opposite the impressive Church of St Martin turn right to ascend the little street of St Martins Hill. Cross the Kendal road to climb Brantfell Road directly above. At the head of the road a little iron gate leads on to the Dales Way, a grassy and stony path that climbs directly up the hillside. Continue to a kissing gate by the wood, leading on to a lane.

2 Pass through the kissing gate and turn right, signposted 'Post Knott', to follow the stony lane. Continue on the lane rising through the woods until it crests a height near the flat circular top of Post Knott. Bear left and make the short ascent to the summit. The view from here was once exceptional but is now obscured by trees. Retrace a few steps back to the track then bear right to find a kissing gate leading out of the wood on to the open hillside.

3 Beyond the kissing gate take the grassy path, rising to a rocky shoulder. Cross the shoulder and first descend, then ascend to a ladder stile in the top corner of the field by some fir trees. Cross the stile then bear right to ascend directly up the open, grassy flanks of Brant Fell to its rocky summit.

4 Go left (northeast) from the top of the fell, following a line of cairns down to a kissing gate. Descend through a young plantation to a second gate and a track. Turn right and follow the track to a stile and gate leading out to a road. Turn left along the road and continue left at the junction, to pass Matson Ground. Immediately beyond is a kissing gate on the left, waymarked for the Dales Way.

5 Go through the kissing gate and continue down the path to cross a track and pass through a kissing gate into another field. Keep along the track beneath the trees and beside a new pond, until the path swings left to emerge through a kissing gate on to a surfaced drive. Go right along the drive for 30yds (27m) until the path veers off left through the trees to follow the fence. An iron gate leads into a field. Follow the grassy path, first descending and then rising to an iron gate in the corner of the field. Continue to join a grassy track and go through the kissing gate. Cross the surfaced drive of Brantfell Farm and keep straight on to another kissing gate leading into a field. Follow the path, parallel to the wall, descending the hill to intercept a track, via a kissing gate, and regain Point 2. Retrace your steps back to Glebe Road and return back to the car park.

64 Around Lake Buttermere

A relaxing walk in one of Lakeland's most attractive valleys summons the spirits of de Quincey, Wordsworth and local beauty 'the Maid of Buttermere'

Above: Scots pines on the shore of lake Buttermere

Much has been written about Buttermere, the dale, the village and the lake. It remains, as it has been since Victorian times, a popular place displaying 'nature's art for art's sake', as W. G. Collingwood described it in *The Lake Counties* (1902). Nicholas Size's historical romance, *The Secret Valley* (1930), takes a rather different line, describing a tale of guerrilla warfare and bloody battles here with invading Norman forces.

The Daughter of the Fish Inn

Buttermere achieved considerable notoriety at the pen of Joseph Budworth, who stayed here in 1792 and encountered Mary, the daughter of the landlord of the Fish Inn. In his guidebook *A Fortnight's Ramble to the Lakes*, he describes Mary as 'the reigning Lily of the Valley' and began what must have been a reign of terror for Mary, who became a tourist attraction, a situation made worse in later editions of Budworth's book, in which he revelled in the discomfort all the unwanted attention heaped on Mary and her family.

More sinisterly, in 1802, the tale brought to Buttermere one John Hadfield, a man posing as the Honourable Anthony Augustus Hope MP. Hadfield wooed and won Mary, and they were married at Lorton Church on 2nd October 1802 (coincidentally just two days before William Wordsworth married Mary Hutchinson). With the honeymoon scarcely begun, Hadfield was exposed as an impostor, and arrested on a charge of forgery – a more serious offence than bigamy, of which he was also guilty – and later tried and hanged at Carlisle.

Accounts of the whole episode are given by Thomas de Quincey in *Recollections of the Lakes and the Lake Poets* and by Melvyn Bragg in his 1987 novel *The Maid of Buttermere*; this description was also used by Wordsworth in *The Prelude*. The whole saga found its way on to the stages of some London theatres. Happily for Mary, she later remarried, had a large family and by all accounts a happy life.

Seclusion and Silence

Against such a backdrop, it is intriguing that in a Victorian satire of 1851 by Henry Mayhew, entitled *The Adventures of Mr and Mrs Cursty Sandboys and Family, who came up to London to 'Enjoy Themselves' and to see the Great Exhibition*, Buttermere is described as the quietest and most secluded of Lakeland villages, where '…the knock of the dun never startles the hermit or the student – for (thrice blessed spot!) there are no knockers'.

64 Around Lake Buttermere

Experience the Lake District's only lakeside tunnel as you hug the shore of Buttermere

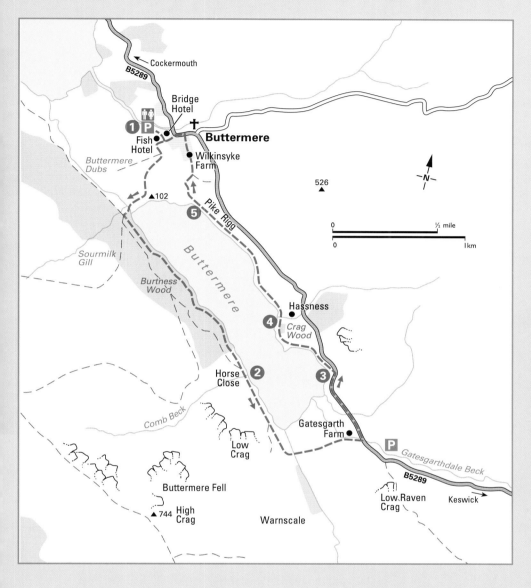

Distance 4.5 miles (7.2km)

Minimum Time 2hrs

Ascent/Gradient 35ft (11m) ▲▲▲

Level of Difficulty ●●●

Paths Good path, some road walking, 2 stiles

Landscape Lake, fells, woodland and farmland

Suggested Map OS Explorer OL4 The English Lakes (NW)

Start/Finish Grid reference: NY 173169

Dog Friendliness On leads near farms and open fells where sheep are grazing

Parking National Park car park beyond Fish Hotel (fee)

Public Toilets At start

1 Leave the car park and turn right, passing the Fish Hotel to follow a broad track through gates. Ignore the signposted route to Scale Force and continue along the track towards the edge of the lake. Then follow the line of a hedgerow to a bridge at Buttermere Dubs. Cross a small footbridge and go through a nearby gate in a wall at the foot of Burtness Wood and the cascade of Sourmilk Gill. Turn left on a track through the woodland that roughly parallels the lakeshore, finally emerging from the woodland near Horse Close, where a bridge spans Comb Beck.

2 Keep on along the path to reach a wall leading to a sheepfold and a gate. Go left through the gate, cross Warnscale Beck and walk out to Gatesgarth Farm. At the farm, follow signs to reach the valley road. A short stretch of road walking, left on the B5289, now follows, along which there are no pathways. Take care against approaching traffic.

3 As the road bends left, leave it for a lakeside footpath on the left. The path leads into a field, beyond which it never strays far from the shoreline and continues to a stand of Scots pine, near Crag Wood.

4 Beyond Hassnesshow Beck bridge, the path enters the grounds of Hassness, where a rocky path, enclosed by trees, leads to a gate. Here a path has been cut across a crag where it plunges into the lake below, and shortly disappears into a brief, low and damp tunnel, the only one of its kind in the Lake District. The tunnel was cut by employees of George Benson, a 19th-century mill owner who owned the Hassness Estate, so that he could walk around the lake without straying far from its shore. After you emerge from the tunnel a gate gives access to a gravel path across the wooded pasture of Pike Rigg. A path leads through a series of gates beyond the foot of the lake to a bridge of slate slabs.

5 A short way on, through another gate, the path leads on to Wilkinsyke Farm, and an easy walk out to the road, just a short way above the Bridge Hotel. Turn left to return to the car park.

65 Tarset, Thorneyburn and the Rievers Trail

From a village hall with no adjacent village, this delightful country walk leads through once lawless country to a section of the vast Kielder Forest

Above: Kielder pines

Below: A variety of trees and signed walks in Sidwood Forest

Bottom right: Purple heather in the Kielder Forest

The area around Lanehead is called Tarset. The name means 'the fold in the dry pine woods' and is first recorded in the early 13th century. Although the car parking area is beside Tarset Village Hall, there is in fact no Tarset village – only the burn in its valley, a parish name and the scant and confusing remains of Tarset Castle south of Lanehead. This was started in 1267 on the site of an earlier Scottish fortress by 'Red' John Comyn, a claimant to the throne of Scotland who was stabbed to death by the altar of the Greyfriars

Church in Dumfries by Robert the Bruce in 1306. The castle was burned by the Scots in 1525, and largely destroyed by a railway cutting in 1860. The walk takes you alongside the Tarset Burn before crossing it and heading across moorland to Thorneyburn. You'll find another fortified site here, on the open fell at Boughthill. This one is probably the remains of a 16th-century fortified farmhouse, or bastle, long-since abandoned to the sheep.

Greenwich Hospital and Thorneyburn

The tiny hamlet of Thorneyburn mainly consists of the church and the large former rectory. Both were constructed in 1818 for trustees of Greenwich Hospital. The hospital had been given the parish in 1735 after the former patron, the Catholic Earl of Derwentwater, had been disgraced for his part in the Old Pretender's rebellion of 1715. The charity, established by William III in 1694 to look after naval veterans, still maintains an estate in north Northumberland, as well as its valuable landholdings in the capital.

Like nearby Greystead, Wark and Humshaugh, Thorneyburn had a succession of naval chaplains as rector, and all four have very similar churches and rectories. The farmhouse at nearby Redhaugh also probably started life as a fortified bastle house; at the edge of the small field opposite is a pretty pyramid-roofed 18th-century dovecote.

Sidwood Picnic Area is the start of a number of waymarked trails though this part of the Kielder Forest, including the Rievers Trail. Over the ridge, you come to Slaty Ford – a peaceful place, but with a dark history. In September 1796 six workers in the nearby colliery shaft were killed, either by an influx of water from a disused shaft or from an explosion; the records are unclear.

65 Tarset, Thorneyburn and the Rievers Trail

Take a few hours' retreat on a woodland and moorland walk

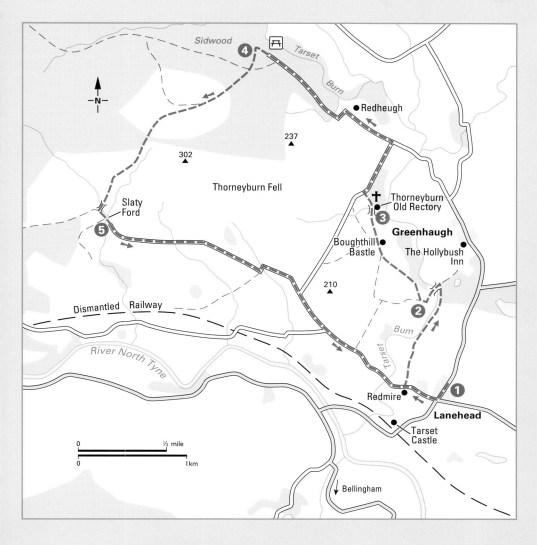

Distance 7.5 miles (12.1km)

Minimum Time 3hrs

Ascent/Gradient 1,083ft (330m) ▲▲▲

Level of Difficulty ●●●

Paths Burnside and moorland paths and tracks – some wet areas

Landscape Valleys with woodland and moorland

Suggested Map OS Explorer OL42 Kielder Water & Forest

Start/Finish Grid reference: NY 793858

Dog Friendliness Dogs on leads in farmland

Parking Beside Tarset Village Hall in Lanehead, on Greenhaugh road

Public Toilets None en route

1 Walk to the staggered crossroads in the middle of Lanehead and turn right, signed 'Donkleywood'. At the Redmire cottages turn right through a gate, and cross the yard to leave by two more gates. Cross the field, passing through a gap to reach a hand-gate. Bear left, descending to a kissing gate by the river. Follow the river bank right, through a series of gates before rising to a final gate and dropping to a bridge. Cross the Tarset Burn and follow the path down a ramp to join a farm track. Turn left along this to a farmyard.

2 Go though the farmyard and ascend the track on the far side. As it bears left, go ahead past a waymarker and downhill to cross the stream. Pass another waymarked post and go through a gateway. Bend right after it and go through a hand gate. Turn left along the fence, then, at a stile, bear half right across the open moor towards the woods and church. Keep left of the ruined wall, aiming for a dilapidated shed and a wall descending to a bridge over the burn.

3 Cross the stream. Veer left on the opposite bank to locate a gate at the side of a garden. Go through this and follow the track beside the churchyard to the road. Turn right and at the T-junction turn left. Follow the lane past Redheugh Farm and the 'Forestry Commission Sidwood' sign to Sidwood Picnic Area, near white-painted buildings.

4 Follow the path into the wood on the left, but after a short distance look for a right turn, crossing the burn and continuing up the hill. Cross a forest track and continue up the hill through an area of clear fell. Maintain your direction as the route levels out, now with a

ditch on your right. As you begin to descend, the forest gives way to moorland on your left and you reach a gate. Continue down through the enclosure, crossing a burn then rising to a crossing track. Turn left and follow this down to cross the burn with care at Slaty Ford.

5 Continue on this prominent enclosed track to a gate. Beyond this follow the minor road for a mile (1.6km) along the flank of the North Tyne valley passing through a gate after 0.5 mile (800m) to a junction. Keep ahead, over the cattle grid and down to the bridge over the Tarset Burn. Continue on this quiet lane as it ascends the bank back to the main road. Turn left to return to your car.

66 Derwent Valley's Past

Through what was once the heartland of the British steel industry, this fascinating walk leads back past 20th-century industrial remains as far as the Roman era

It was coal mining that created the village of Chopwell that we see today, with its red-brick buildings and no-nonsense atmosphere – and it was the miners who earned it the name 'Little Moscow' in the 1920s. The coal won from local mines was predominantly used for making coke to stoke the furnaces of the Consett Iron Company. When coal production declined after the First World War, many miners were made redundant or put on short-time working. These conditions allowed Communist sympathisers to assume the running of the village. A miners' strike from July 1925 to December 1926 led to accusations of a Communist takeover of the local Labour Party. A national newspaper declared that 'the village is known far and wide as the reddest in England'. Streets were renamed after Marx, Engels and Lenin, and it is said that there were Communist Sunday schools in the village, as well as *Das Kapital* on the lectern of the local church. For a time the hammer and sickle flag flew over the town hall.

Steelmaking at Derwentcote

The area between Blackhall Mill and Derwentcote Ironworks was once the centre of the steel industry in Britain. Steel was made here initially to supply the sword manufacturers of Shotley Bridge, eastwards along the river. Derwentcote, the earliest steel-making furnace to have survived, was built around 1720 and worked until the 1870s. Another furnace at Blackhall Mill lasted until 1834, when a flood washed away its mill dam; the mill was demolished in the early the 20th century. Derwentcote, now cared for by English Heritage is open to visitors on summer weekends.

Beyond Derwentcote the walk enters Byerside Wood and joins the old railway line that now forms the 12.5-mile (20.1km) footpath and cycle route of the Derwent Valley Country Park. This runs from Consett to Gateshead and connects with other former railway routes, including the Waskerley Way and the Consett and Sunderland Railway Path.

Roman Fort

In contrast to the industrial theme of much of the walk, the history of Ebchester stretches much further back in time. This was the site of the Roman fort of Vindomora, strategically placed where the road we know as Dere Street, which ran from York to the Firth of Forth, crossed the Derwent. Constructed around AD 80, the original timber buildings were later replaced by stone and the fort was finally abandoned in AD 410.

It is possible to see its ramparts north of the main road and in the village churchyard. There is a Roman altar in the church tower.

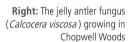

Right: The jelly antler fungus (*Calcocera viscosa*) growing in Chopwell Woods

Far right: Hamsterley Forest

Below: The early steel-making furnace at Derwentcote

66 Derwent Valley's Past

Step back to when the Romans fortified Ebchester

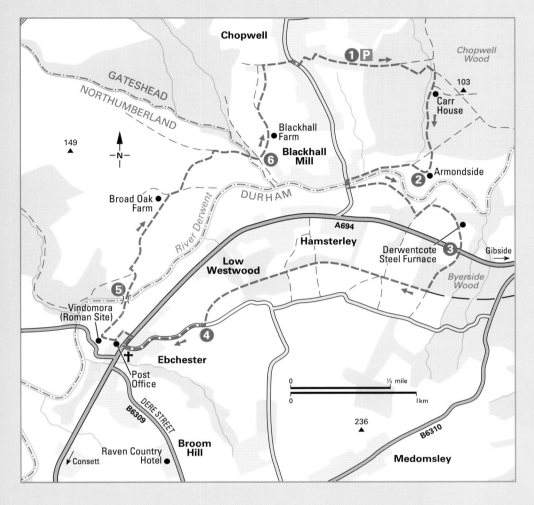

Distance 7 miles (11.3km)

Minimum Time 2hrs 30min

Ascent/Gradient 541ft (165m) ▲▲▲

Level of Difficulty ●●●

Paths Tracks, field paths and old railway line

Landscape Woodland and riverside, farm-land and industrial remains

Suggested Map OS Explorer 307 Consett & Derwent Reservoir

Start/Finish Grid reference: NZ122579

Dog Friendliness On lead, except on former railway line

Parking Roadside parking in Chopwell; follow signs 'Chopwell Park Car Park'. Car park opens irregularly

Public Toilets None en route

1 Walk up the entrance road to Chopwell Park. Turn right past a metal barrier and bear right, into the wood. Follow the woodland track to a junction in about 200yds (183m). Pick out a narrow path on the right, marked by a wooden post amongst broom and gorse. Follow this winding path, eventually over a little bridge and up to join a forest road. Turn right, on to the road marked Forestry Commission road and follow the track downhill, passing Carr House on the left. The path drops down to the right and continues downhill. As the forest track swings right, turn left through a gate and continue down between the fields to Armondside Farm.

2 Bear right and follow the track to the road in Blackhall Mill. Turn left, over the bridge. Just beyond it, turn left by a footpath sign and follow the field-edge path to the right of the hedge. Follow the fenced riverside path. You may find there are some diversions along here

where the floods of September 2008 caused landslides. At a crossing path, turn left, uphill. At the top go sharp left, following waymark signs. Go left of the buildings, over a stile and across the field. Go over two wooden stiles then right. Follow the track uphill, passing Derwentcote Steel Furnace, to the main road.

3 Cross and take a signed footpath almost opposite. Go over a stile and, at a crossing path, turn right to another stile. Follow the path through woodland to the former railway track. Turn right and follow the track, which crosses another track (barriers at each side) and eventually rises to another barrier on to a metalled lane.

4 Turn right and descend into Ebchester. Bend right by the community centre to the main road. Cross over and turn right in front of the post office. Turn left at the footpath sign beyond. Follow the fence on your left, bend left

at the end beside the wall, follow the footpath downhill to a metalled lane. Turn right and continue until you reach a footbridge.

5 Cross the bridge. The footpath bends right before going straight ahead across the field to a stile. Follow the green lane uphill, pass a farmhouse and follow the track through several gates. Where the main track bears left, go straight ahead. Go through a gate and along the field-edge. Go though two gates to a T-junction of tracks.

6 Turn left, up the track towards a farm. About 300yds (274m) after the farm go right, through a gate and walk across the field to a stile, hidden in a hedge. Continue up the field to another stile right of the houses, and along a narrow lane. At the end, turn right along the tarmac lane. At the main road turn right and then left, following the signs 'Chopwell Park Car Park'.

67 The Wild Cattle of Chillingham Castle

A circuit through beautiful Northumberland countryside offers views of Chillingham Castle and landscaped park, and the rare wild cattle that live there

The origins of the Chillingham wild cattle are not known. Their skull structure suggests similarities with the aurochs, so they may be descended from those ancient wild oxen that once roamed Britain. Recent DNA tests performed on dead animals show that they are unrelated to any other European cattle. Having remained uncontaminated by outside stock, they are probably the only genetically pure cattle in the world. They are always white; no coloured animals have ever been born. And they are definitely wild.

The Rule of the King

The Chillingham herd has roamed its 365-acre (148ha) park for almost 700 years, since Sir

Right: Calf at Chillingham

Below: The castle's Italianate garden was designed by Sir Jeffrey Wyatville in the 19th century

Thomas Percy was granted a royal licence to fortify Chillingham Castle and enclose the grounds. The captured cattle may have provided a food supply.

Over the years they have never been domesticated. The strongest bull leads the herd, he remains 'king', and sires all the calves born during his 'rule' until such time as another bull successfully challenges him. Even a birth is accompanied by a ritual, which must be observed before the new calf is accepted into the herd.

The number of cattle in the herd normally varies from 40 to 60, but during the severe winter of 1947 their numbers fell to 13. The animals' wild nature means that normal agricultural methods cannot be employed to help them. The Chillingham cattle never seek shelter other than in the surrounding trees and will eat only grass and hay and, even when starving, will not accept oats or prepared cattle food. Fortunately the cattle are rarely ill, but when disease does strike, they cannot be approached by a vet. The tragic outbreak of foot and mouth disease in 1967 and again in 2001 threatened the very survival of the herd: on the earlier occasion foot and mouth encroached within 2 miles (3.2km) of Chillingham.

Protected

The Chillingham Wild Cattle Association was formed in 1939 to look after the welfare of the herd. The 8th Earl of Tankerville bequeathed ownership of the herd to the association on his death in 1971. When the 9th earl died in 1980, the Chillingham estate was put up for sale. As a result of the intervention of the Duke of Northumberland, Chillingham Park was sold separately from the castle to the Sir James Knott Charitable Trust, which then granted the Wild Cattle Association grazing rights for 999 years.

Visitors can see the cattle in their natural surroundings, which look much as they did in medieval times. The cattle's behaviour, however, is unpredictable, so for safety reasons, you are permitted to enter the park only when accompanied by the warden. Binoculars are recommended for getting a closer view. The park is open daily, except Tuesday, and the entrance fee is relatively modest – it's well worth a visit.

67 The Wild Cattle of Chillingham Castle

Get close to the only wild cattle left in Britain

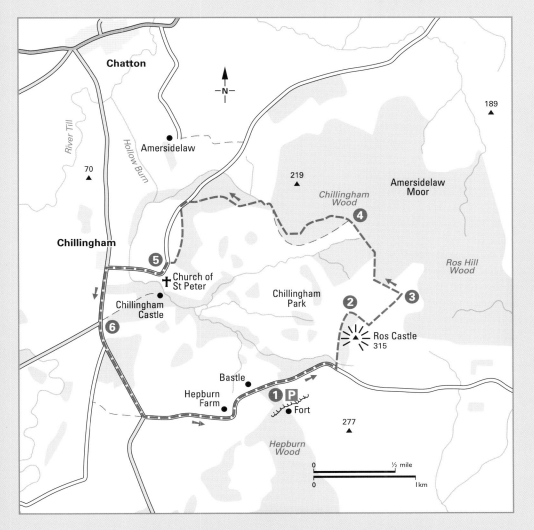

Distance 6 miles (9.7km)

Minimum Time 3hrs

Ascent/Gradient 754ft (230m) ▲▲▲

Level of Difficulty ●●○

Paths Hill track, surfaced road

Landscape Hill, arable and woodland

Suggested Map OS Explorer 340
Holy Island & Bamburgh

Start/Finish Grid reference: NU 071248

Dog Friendliness Dogs not allowed
in Chillingham Wood, even on leads

Parking Forest car park at Hepburn Wood

Public Toilets None en route

1 On leaving the car park, turn right on the road and go uphill for 0.5 mile (800m) and round a bend to a National Trust notice indicating 'Ros Castle'. Follow the track to a gate in the wall to your left and go through the gate into Chillingham Wood. Turning right, and then going to the left, aim to follow marker posts on to a broader track after a distance of about 100yds (91m). This track leads you uphill, then across a level stretch to a fence. On your left is a view over Chillingham Park, where you might, on occasion, be able to see the wild cattle grazing.

2 Turn right at the fence and walk uphill as indicated by the signpost 'Chillingham'. When you reach the wall, turn to the left and follow the track between the wall and the fence to a picnic table. Continue to the next stretch of forest, and walk between the wall and the forest for about 250yds (229m) to the next signpost 'Chillingham'.

3 Turn left and descend through the forest, following the marker posts about 50yds (46m) apart. When this small track reaches a junction with a track signed 'Forest Walk', turn right and continue to a signpost. Take the Chillingham direction, through two tall kissing gates to a picnic area with two tables.

4 Continue along the track to a forest road and turn right on to this, which becomes metalled lower down. A sign points you left over a small bridge, back into the woods, following the red markers. The track rises to a gate in the deer fence, then levels off to run parallel with a wall. Continue beyond some picnic tables to a gate and then turn right. Keep right at the next junction, down the hill. Keep right again to descend to the road in front of Garden Cottage.

5 Turn left and follow the road past the Church of St Peter, on your left, then past a gate leading to Chillingham Castle. Cross the Hollow Burn either by ford or footbridge and continue to a T-junction with the main road. Turn left and follow the road, passing the main castle gate after 550yds (500m).

6 At the next fork in the road, go left uphill to the crossroads. This road is not very busy with traffic and has good grass verges for walking on. Turn left on the road to Hepburn Farm. Follow this, past the farm buildings, and continue to Hepburn Wood car park.

68 Berwick Town Walls

The town walls, built at great cost by Queen Elizabeth I, are just one of many attractions in this historic Border town, much disputed by the Scots and English

Overlooking the Tweed Estuary, Berwick is a true Border town and, despite it standing on the river's northern bank, it is actually in England. Yet in the 12th century it was a Scottish royal burgh and the country's most prosperous port, busy with the export of grain from a richly fertile hinterland. The town first fell into English hands in 1174 but, for the next 300 years, was repeatedly attacked by one side or the other as each tried to wrest control. It changed ownership so many times that the long-suffering inhabitants must have wondered just whose side they were on.

When the political shuttlecock finally came to rest in 1482, Berwick found itself in England, although it retained the status of an independent state until 1836. However, the Scottish threat remained and, cut off from the surrounding countryside that had once made it rich, prosperity continued to be elusive until renewed threats of the 'Auld Alliance' prompted Elizabeth I to commission new fortifications in 1557. Wiping away much of the town's medieval walls, no longer effective against modern artillery, she spent £128,000 to enclose the town within thick ramparts and complex projecting bastions, from which defensive artillery could rake attacking forces. She probably wasted her money because the expected attack never came and the economic boost to the town was short-lived.

Below: Berwick Castle walls

Bottom: Royal Border Bridge (1847–50) designed by Robert Stevenson

Berwick Boom

It was not until the succession of James VI of Scotland to the English throne as James I in 1603 that the town embarked on its road to recovery. The graceful bridge was built and the harbour developed and, by the middle of the 18th century, there was a regular packet service to London carrying both passengers and cargo.

For the first time the salmon, for which the Tweed is still renowned, appeared in the capital's markets, kept fresh during the voyage by ice produced on the quayside. The boom continued into the 19th century, with a spate of elegant building catering for the civil, military, religious and domestic needs of the town.

After the Railway

The spanner that brought the economic wheel to a halt was the arrival of the railway – the very thing that one might have been expected to do just the opposite. Whilst it opened up new areas and industries by providing cheap, fast and convenient transport for freight and people, it did no good at all for the coastal seafaring trade.

The port, previously the key to the town's success, gradually dwindled. Yet Berwick continues to be an attractive market town, with much of interest to see as you wander around its Elizabethan defences, unique for their completeness.

68 Berwick Town Walls

Explore old Berwick, then take a longer ramble beside the Tweed

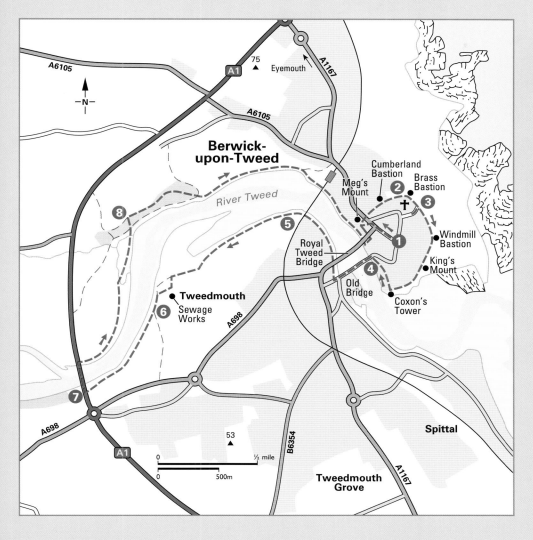

Distance 6.5 miles (10.4km)

Minimum Time 2hrs 15min

Ascent/Gradient 98ft (30m) ▲▲▲

Level of Difficulty ●●●

Paths Paved pathways and field paths; flood-meadows may be wet and muddy, particularly around high tide, 4 stiles

Landscape Town, riverside and woodland

Suggested Map OS Explorer 346 Berwick-upon-Tweed

Start/Finish Grid reference: NT 998529

Dog Friendliness On leads in town and near livestock

Parking Below ramparts outside Scots Gate

Public Toilets At car park, below ramparts

Note Sheer, unguarded drop from outer edge of town walls and bastions, keep to marked pathways

1 From the old Town Hall, walk west along Marygate to Scots Gate. Immediately before it, turn left to find a gateway on the right, where you can climb on to the walls by Meg's Mount. Follow the wall back over Scots Gate and on past the Cumberland Bastion.

2 The next battery, Brass Bastion, lies at the northern corner of the town. Some 100yds (91m) beyond, a path descends inside the wall to meet The Parade by the corner of the parish church graveyard. Turn right past the barracks to the church; both are worth visiting.

3 Return to the walls and go on, passing Windmill Bastion and the site of the earlier Edward VI fort. Beyond King's Mount, the walls rise above the Tweed Estuary before turning upriver at Coxon's Tower, past elegant Georgian terraces and on above the old quay.

4 Leave the walls at Bridge End and cross the Old Bridge. Turn right past the war memorial, go beneath the modern Royal Tweed Bridge and remain by the river beyond, shortly passing below Stephenson's railway viaduct.

5 The way continues upstream along a path. Where the bank widens to a rough meadow, pick up a track on the left, leading through a series of kissing gates to an open hide. A further gate leads out on to the next section of river bank. Beyond another gate, a contained path skirts a water treatment plant. Turn left through a second gate on to a tarmac track and turn right.

6 At a bend 40yds (37m) on, bear off right along a field-edge above the steep river bank. Continue in the next field but, towards its far end, look for a stepped path descending

the bank to a stream. Rising to a stile beyond, bear right to the main road.

7 Cross the Tweed and drop right on to a path, signed 'Berwick via Plantation', which crosses a couple of stiles to a riverside pasture. Walk away beside the left boundary for about 0.5 mile (800m). After crossing the head of a stream, move away from the hedge, aiming to meet the river below a wooded bank. Over a side bridge, bear right to a stile and continue through the trees beyond to a path at the top of the bank.

8 Go right, eventually dropping from the wood by a cottage, where a riverside promenade leads back to Berwick. Just beyond the Royal Tweed Bridge, turn sharp left, climbing back beneath it and continue beside the town walls to return to Meg's Mount.

Wales

Wales

A profoundly beautiful country with a fascinating history and culture, Wales has a character all its own – and is a land in which there is a strong desire to retain a local identity that is uninfluenced by external forces.

Wales is intrinsically rugged and wild. There are craggy heights, rock-strewn heather-clad hillsides, barren moors, bright green valleys, silver rivers and glassy mountain lakes, as well as rocky, storm-tossed coastlines with tumbling cliffs, picturesque coves and sublime golden beaches. And over it all lies a complex mantle of mystery and history. In his 1997 book *Visions of Snowdonia*, Jim Perrin notes '…whatever else Wales is, it is not England, it is other.' Ever since Mercian king Offa ordered the building of his now renowned dyke in AD 779 – for reasons that have never totally been clear, but probably have more to do with defining a national boundary than with a need for defence – the people of this wild country have been known as

wealas, the Anglo-Saxon word for foreigners: from this came the world Wales.

For walkers Wales has traditionally been a country of three parts – North, South and Mid-Wales. Each has its own distinctive character. In the late 12th century a native of South Wales, Giraldus (also know as Gerald of Wales) set out on a journey to North Wales in company with fellow churchmen. His arduous journey was full of intrigue and fascination and was connected with church politics and raising support for the Third Crusade. In the Wales of that era all the roads would have been green roads, and the only alternative to following them was to walk along the coastline – which usually meant no roads at all.

Right: Late light at Marloes Beach, Pembrokeshire

Below: A range of greens at Llyn Gwynant, Snowdonia

Previous pages: Double beauty – Craig Cau reflected in the lake of Llyn Cau on Cadair Idris in Snowdonia

Best of the Rest

Marloes Peninsula

At the westernmost point of the shore to the south of St Brides' Bay, the Marloes peninsula in Pembrokeshire, South Wales, offers gorgeous beaches, rugged cliffs, beautiful coves and breathtaking views of sea, coastline and the two offshore islands of Skomer and Skokholm (see Walk 69). Skomer is a National Nature Reserve and a haven for the Atlantic puffin, the Manx shearwater and many other species; it also contains Iron Age remains including a stone circle and standing stone. The swirling waters of Jack Sound, which separates Skomer from the mainland, are a fascinating sight in themselves, caused by a meeting of currents.

Vale of Ewyas Horseshoe

Beautiful views of the Wye valley and the Black Mountains can be had from Pen Rhos Dirion in the course of this walk around the head of the Ewyas Valley (see Walk 72). Near by is Hay-on-Wye, celebrated for its second-hand bookshops and its major literary festival, held in early summer each year.

Welshpool and Powis Castle

The highlight of any visit to the attractive town of Welshpool in central Wales is a visit to the originally medieval Powis Castle and its celebrated gardens with Italianate terraces, which were added in the 18th century (see Walk 77). The oldest part of the castle dates to about 1200; it was extensively rebuilt in 1587–95 by Sir Edward Herbert. The Long Gallery survives from this period. The castle was the scene of fighting in the Civil War and captured by the Parliamentarians in 1644, then rebuilt again after the Restoration of the Monarchy. Further rebuilding was carried out in 1772, 1815–18 and 1902 onwards. The castle came into the hands of the National Trust in 1952.

Barmouth

Originally a seaport, the town of Barmouth in Gwynedd, north-western Wales, is on the beautiful estuary of the river Mawddach and Cardigan Bay, and became a holiday resort in the mid-19th century (see Walk 78). Visitors included William Wordsworth, and Romantic landscape artist J. M. W. Turner, drawn by the beauty of the town's setting with mountains rising behind and the sea and estuary in front. There are excellent views across the estuary to the Cadair Idris ridge.

Cwm Bychan

From beautiful Cwm Bychan lake, in a remote corner of Snowdonia, the Roman Steps climb the Rhinogs mountains. The Steps may follow the route of a Roman original but in fact date from the medieval period. The walk (79) offers exhilarating climbing and beautiful views.

Llanystumdwy and Criccieth Castle

This village on the Llyn Peninsula in Gwynedd was where politician David Lloyd George, Liberal prime minister from 1916–22, was raised from infancy to the age of 16. Walk 80 passes one of his boyhood homes, Highgate, and takes in a Museum of Lloyd George memorabilia. Also in the village is the politician's grave, which was designed by Sir Clough William-Ellis. For those interested in more remote history the walk continues to visit nearby Criccieth Castle on a headland overlooking Tremadog Bay. The castle's twin-towered gatehouse was built by Welsh prince Llywelyn ap Iorwerth in c1230–40.

To make the same journey today would be less arduous but would likely prove just as fascinating. It would take you through the three regions of Wales in such a way that would leave you captivated by variety and enthralled by the beauty of the landscapes. The walks that follow pursue ancient footsteps and trackways from those of neolithic settlers on Anglesey (see Walk 85), to 1st-century tribes and their Roman conquerors in Snowdonia (see Walk 83) to Norman castle builders, right through to 20th-century miners and other labourers in industrial South Wales (see Walk 71).

'Place of Eagles'

Much of walkers' North Wales is contained within the Snowdonia National Park, from time immemorial known to its inhabitants as Eryri, the 'Place of Eagles'. Eagles did once haunt the cliffs and cwms (steep-sided hollows) of North Wales. The popularity of Snowdon, the Carneddau, the Glyderau, the Rhinogs and the other mountains of Eryri has scarcely abated since the first recorded ascent of Snowdon in 1639 by botanist Thomas Johnson. And although all the early ascents were made by scientists, by the time the English traveller George Borrow (author of the 1862 book *Wild*

Wales) appeared on the scene in the 1850s to quote Welsh poetry from Snowdon's summit, the ascent was a popular excursion. Yet it was not Snowdon alone that drew visitors. Black's *Picturesque Guide to North Wales*, published in 1857, comments that 'in savage grandeur the Glyder is not surpassed by any scene in Wales'.

Nor is the whole of North Wales Snowdonia. The eastern moorlands of Denbighshire flow westwards to the River Conwy below the eastern fringes of the Carneddau. On Walk 84 climb from Conwy for views of the estuary and town, and also of the Castell Caer Lleion fortress built by Iron Age settlers. North and west, the isle of Anglesey and the delectable Lleyn Peninsula boast renowned landscapes. On Anglesey admire the east coast of the island and visit the village of Moelfre (Walk 85). Further south, the Rhinogs are as rugged and rough as anything to be found in Britain.

Mid- and South Wales

One hundred years after the Domesday Book, Archbishop Baldwin of Canterbury began his mission to preach the Crusades in Wales in the quiet heartlands of Mid-Wales, at New Radnor, part of the great hunting Forest of Radnor.

However, for the next two and a half centuries it was an unhappy, oppressed place, where the lords Marcher held power of life and death over the inhabitants, ruling them by sword under the Jura Regalia, a severe form of martial law. In the south, the Black Mountains (Mynyddoedd Duon) are a paradise for walkers who revel in long, lofty ridges separated by valleys of quiet calm. To the west rise the flat-topped summits of the Brecon Beacons, another Black Mountain (Mynydd Du) and the Fforest Fawr, names that speak of wilderness and desolation, and all contained within the Brecon Beacons National Park. Clamber up the Blorenge in Monmouthshire (Walk 71) for views both of the mountains and of Abergavenny and the former industrial area around it.

The further west you go, the greater the feeling of isolation. On the Gower peninsula Walk 70 delivers stunning views of Rhossili Bay. In North Pembrokeshire, brave the steep climbs and descents of the coastal path near Strumble Head for the reward of likely views of Atlantic seals (Walk 74). Isolation is never over-powering, for the seclusion works as a panacea for workaday ills; the wild, ponied expanses are among the most refreshing of ingredients in the panoply of Wales.

Above: The beautiful Gower peninsula – Worms Head

Above left: Looking up the Roman Steps towards Rhinog Fawr in Snowdonia

Far left: Clouds reflected in water at Rhossili Beach – one of Wales's wildest beaches

69 Island Views from the Marloes Peninsula

A ramble around the edge of a windswept headland takes in wonderfully rugged coastline overlooking two offshore islands and a marine nature reserve

Top: Puffins' colourful beaks and clown-like markings make them a very distinctive birds

Above: Seaweed on Marloes Sands

Below: Cliffs, beach and sea views – the walk is captivating, even by Pembrokeshire standards

The Marloes Peninsula forms the westernmost tip of the southern shores of St Brides Bay. It is famous for its scenery, which includes two of the Pembrokeshire Coast National Park's finest and least-crowded beaches, as well as some secluded coves that are often inhabited by seals. There are also fine views over a narrow but turbulent sound to the small islands of Skomer and Skokholm – two significant seabird breeding grounds.

Many Attractions of Skomer

Skomer is the largest of the Pembrokeshire islands and is one of the most significant wildlife habitats in the British Isles. The island, separated from the mainland by the rushing waters of Jack Sound, measures approximately 1.5 miles (2.4km) from north to south and 2 miles (3.2km) from east to west. It was declared a National Nature Reserve in 1959 and, as well as the protection it receives as part of the National Park, it's also designated as a Site of Special Scientific Interest (SSSI), a Special Protection Area (SPA) and a Geological Conservation Review Site (GCR).

Much of the land is a Scheduled Ancient Monument, courtesy of a number of clearly visible Iron Age settlements and enclosures. Moreover, the sea surrounding the island is a Marine Nature Reserve, one of only two in the United Kingdom; the other is Lundy, off the North Devon coast.

Birds on Show

The two stars of the Skomer show are the diminutive puffin and the secretive Manx shearwater. There are around 6,000 nesting pairs of puffins on Skomer. They arrive in April and lay a single egg in a burrow. The chick hatches at the end of May and the adult birds spend two months ferrying back catches of sand eels for their flightless offspring. After around seven weeks, the chick leaves the nest, usually at night, and makes its way to the sea. Assuming that it learns to look after itself successfully, it will spend the next few years at sea, only returning when it reaches breeding maturity.

The shearwater is slightly larger than the puffin but it also lays its single egg in a burrow, overlooking the sea. It may not be as obviously endearing as its painted neighbour, especially as most visitors to the island never actually see one, but it's a beautiful and fascinating bird in its own right. There are around 150,000 pairs on Skomer, Skokholm and Middleholm – about 60 per cent of the world's total population. They are seldom seen because they are vulnerable to predators on land, so leave the nest at dawn and spend the whole day at sea, not returning to their burrow until it is almost dark. A careful seawatch at last light may reveal them gathering in huge rafts just offshore or even endless lines of flying birds returning to the island – against the sunset, it's quite a magical sight.

69 Island Views from the Marloes Peninsula

Tour a paddle-shaped peninsula that allows minimum inland walking for maximum time on the coast

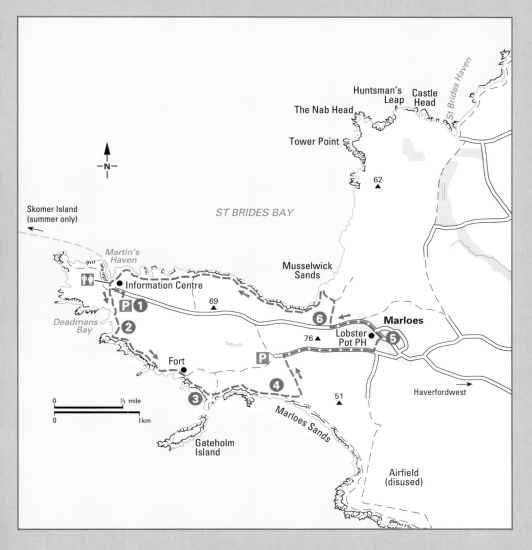

Distance 6 miles (9.7km)

Minimum Time 2hrs 30min

Ascent/Gradient 420ft (128m) ▲▲▲

Level of Difficulty ●●●

Paths Coast path and clear footpaths, short section on tarmac, 9 stiles

Landscape Rugged cliff tops and beautiful sandy beaches

Suggested Map OS Explorer OL36 South Pembrokeshire

Start/Finish Grid reference: SM 761089

Dog Friendliness Care near cliff tops and poop scoop on beaches

Parking National Trust car park above Martin's Haven, near Marloes village

Public Toilets Marloes village

1 From the bottom of the car park, walk down to the bottom of the hill. Bear around to the left, then go through the gate straight ahead into the Deer Park. Turn left and follow the path along to a gate and out on to the coast.

2 With the sea to your right, continue easily along over Deadmans Bay to a stile. The next section is easy walking, passing the earthworks of an Iron Age fort on the left and crossing another stile as you approach Gateholm Island.

3 It is possible to get across to the island at low tide, but care is needed to scramble over the slippery rocks. To continue the walk, follow the coast path above the western end of the beautiful Marloes Sands until you drop easily to the main beach access path.

4 Turn left and climb up to the road; turn right here. Follow the road along for around 0.75 mile (1.2km) to a hedged bridleway on the left. Follow this down and turn left into Marloes village.

5 Pass the Lobster Pot on the left and continue ahead to leave the village. Ignore tracks on the right, as the road bends to the left, and continue out into open countryside where you'll meet a footpath on the right.

6 Walk down the edge of the field and bear around to the left to descend to the coast path above Musselwick Sands. Turn left and follow the path west for 1.5 miles (2.4km) to Martin's Haven. Meet the road and climb past the information centre back to the car park.

70 The Highs and Lows of Rhossili Bay

A tramp over high ground on the Gower Peninsula offers views of beach, cliffs and sea and the chance to visit a sea-washed nature reserve once likened to a dragon

Of the many walks on the Gower Peninsula this is one of the very best – although rather oddly, for all the coastal views your feet won't leave a single footprint in the sand in the walk's short form. The lofty heights of Rhossili Down show the magnificent arc of sand in its best light and offer a feeling of spaciousness that's difficult to describe and almost impossible to equal in this part of the world. The ancient stones that define the ridge line only add to the captivating atmosphere.

The Gower Peninsula is a 15-mile (24km) finger of land that points westwards from Swansea. Its southern coast boasts dune-backed beaches of surf-swept, clean, yellow sand and magnificent limestone cliffs, chiselled in places into deep gullies and knife-edge ridges. The northern coast forms the southern fringes of the marshy Loughor Estuary. It's nothing like as dramatic as the southern coast, but it's an important habitat for wading birds and other marine life. Between the two coastlines, the land rises into a series of whaleback ridges, or downs, covered with gorse, heather and bracken and littered with prehistoric stones and remains. Scattered around the windswept landscape are a number of impressive castles. In 1957, the peninsula was designated Britain's first Area of Outstanding Natural Beauty.

On Rhossili Down

None of the Gower beaches are blessed with quite the untamed splendour of Rhossili Bay. It owes much of its wild nature to the steep-sided down that presides over its waves and provides a natural and impenetrable barrier to development. The down is a 633ft (193m) high, whaleback ridge that runs almost the full length of the beach. The path that traces the ridge is one the fairest places to walk in the whole of South Wales, especially in late summer when the heather tinges the hillsides pink. From The Beacon, at the southern end of the ridge, the views stretch a long way and it's often possible to see St Govan's Head in Pembrokeshire and even the North Devon coastline on a very clear day.

The string of islets that thrust into the Atlantic at the bay's southernmost tip are known as Worms Head. This is a derivative of the Old English *Orm*, 'dragon' or 'serpent'. The likeness can be seen. It is now a nature reserve, but can be reached at low tide by scrambling across a rocky causeway. Check the tide timetables before making such a sortie, as it's easy to be cut off by the rising tides.

Above: Looking down on Worms Head

Below: The golden sands of Rhossili Bay run for more than 4 miles (6.4km) from Worms Head to the outcrop of Burry Holmes

70 The Highs and Lows of Rhossili Bay

Wonder, as you walk, at the stunning views over one of Wales's finest and wildest beaches

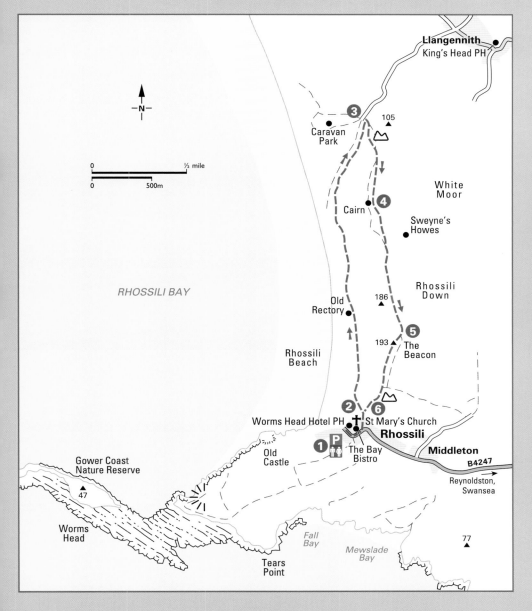

Distance 4 miles (6.4km)

Minimum Time 1hr 45min

Ascent/Gradient 590ft (180m) ▲▲▲

Level of Difficulty ●●●

Paths Easy-to-follow footpaths across grassy downs, 2 stiles

Landscape Rolling downland, rocky outcrops and views over gorgeous sandy beach

Suggested Map OS Explorer 164 Gower

Start/Finish Grid reference: SS 416880

Dog Friendliness Care needed near livestock

Parking Large car park at end of road in Rhossili

Public Toilets At start

1 From the car park, head out on to the road and continue uphill as if you were walking back out of the village. Immediately after passing St Mary's Church bear left down on a broad track to a gate at its end. Go through this and keep left to follow a grassy track that snakes along the steep hillside.

2 Follow this through the bracken, passing the Old Rectory on your left, and eventually you'll reach a sunken section with a wall on your left and a caravan park situated behind. Don't be tempted to break off right just yet; instead, keep going until you come to a gate on the left.

3 Don't go through the gate; turn sharp right and follow the grassy track steeply up on to the ridge. At the top of the steep section keep to the top track that follows the crest.

4 You'll pass some ancient cairns and drop slightly to pass a pair of megalithic cromlechs, or burial chambers. These are known as Sweyne's Howes and are more than 4,000 years old. Continue on a broad track up to the high point of The Beacon.

5 Keep straight ahead on a clear track that starts to drop easily then steepens to meet a dry-stone wall. Continue walking down the

side of the wall and you'll eventually come to the gate you passed through on the way out.

6 Follow the lane out to the road, turn right and pass St Mary's Church on your right to return to the car park.

71 Bird's-eye View from the Blorenge

With views of a Bronze Age burial site, a Norman castle and industrial spoil heaps, this walk examines evidence of centuries of human activity near Abergavenny

Top: The climb on to the Blorenge is rewarded with views of sweeping countryside

Middle: Forge Row, Cwmavon, part of the Blaenavon World Heritage Site,

Bottom: Looking up from Abergavenny at the Blorenge

There's no easier peak to climb in the Brecon Beacons National Park, but there are also few that occupy such a commanding position. The Blorenge – the English-sounding name probably derives from 'blue ridge'– towers menacingly above the cramped streets of Abergavenny, with the main sweep of the Black Mountains leading away to the north. The mountain actually dominates a small finger of the National Park that points southwards from Abergavenny to Pontypool. It's unique in being the only real peak south of the A465 Heads of the Valleys road. It also marks a watershed between the protected mountain scenery that makes up the bulk of the National Park and the ravaged industrial landscape that forms the southern boundary. Typically, its northern flanks boast a Bronze Age burial cairn and the ground above the escarpment is littered with grass-covered mounds, a remnant of past quarrying. The stone was then transported away on the canals and railways.

Abergavenny is a thriving market town that owes its success to weaving, tanning and farming. It feels a thousand miles away from the industrial valleys that nudge against its limits from the south. The name, which in Welsh means the confluence of the River Venny, refers to its position at the junction of the rivers Fenni and Usk, but oddly, in Welsh, it's known simply as Y Fenni – the name of the river.

The town sprang up around a Norman castle built to aid efforts by the invaders to rid the area of the Celts. The Welsh proved far more resilient than the Normans had expected and in the end, William de Braose, the lord of the town at the time, resorted to dirty tactics such as inviting Welsh leaders to dinner and then murdering them while they were unarmed. The castle is now a museum with display of local history. Another of Abergavenny's claims to fame is the fact that during the Second World War, Hitler's deputy, Rudolf Hess, was imprisoned here after his plane crashed in Scotland.

Industrial History at Blaenavon

Only 5 miles (8km) south of Abergavenny, Blaenavon tells the story of industrial expansion in South Wales. With iron ore, limestone, coal and water in local abundance, smelting began as early as the 1500s, but the town, and the iron works that came to dominate it, didn't really get going until the Industrial Revolution of the late 18th century.

The colliery, now known as the Big Pit Mining Museum, was founded a full century later than the iron works and closed as recently as 1980. It has been immaculately preserved and gives visitors a meaningful insight into the industry itself, the conditions that the people endured and the culture that grew up around them. As well as the engine houses, workshops and the miners' baths, a tour includes donning a miner's helmet to descend one of the shafts to the actual coal-faces. Blaenavon is considered such an exceptional example of industrial South Wales that it was declared a UNESCO World Heritage Site in 2000.

71 Bird's-eye View from the Blorenge

Enjoy a short sortie on to the hill that towers above the Beacons' eastern gateway

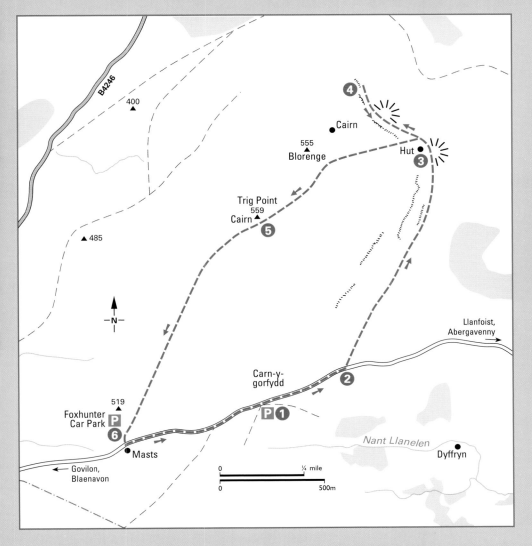

Distance 3 miles (4.8km)

Minimum Time 1hr 30min

Ascent/Gradient 530ft (161m) ▲▲▲

Level of Difficulty ●●●

Paths Clear tracks over open mountainside, quiet lane, no stiles

Landscape Rugged mountain scenery, huge views over Usk Valley

Suggested Map OS Explorer OL13 Brecon Beacons National Park Eastern area

Start/Finish Grid reference: SO 270109

Dog Friendliness Care needed near livestock and on road

Parking Small car park at Carn-y-gorfydd

Public Toilets None en route

1 From Carn-y-gorfydd Roadside Rest, walk downhill for 500yds (457m) and bear left, through a green barrier, on to a grassy track.

2 This leads easily uphill, through a tangle of bracken, eventually allowing great views over the Usk Valley towards the outlying peak of Ysgyryd Fawr.

3 As the path levels you'll pass a small hut. Continue along the escarpment edge, on one of a series of terraces above the steep escarpment, and enjoy the views over Abergavenny and the Black Mountains. The rough ground was formed by stone quarrying.

4 Return to the hut and bear right, on to a faint, grassy track that crosses flat ground and a small boggy patch before climbing slightly and becoming stony. Away to the right, you should be able to make out the pronounced hump of a Bronze Age burial cairn. The path now leads easily to the trig point and the huge cairn that mark the summit.

5 Continue in the same direction, drop down past an impressive limestone outcrop and towards the huge masts on the skyline. You should also be able to see the spoil heaps on the flanks of Gilwern Hill, directly ahead.

6 At the masts, you'll cross the Foxhunter Car Park to meet the road where you turn left and continue easily downhill, for 600yds (549m), back to the start.

72 Tackle the Vale of Ewyas Horseshoe

The climb may be tough, but the rewards make it worthwhile – and once you're up, you're staying up, as you trek around the head of the wonderful Ewyas Valley

Right: Countryside embraces town at Hay-on-Wye

Below right: Wonderful views in the Vale of Ewyas

Below: Shopping in Hay-on-Wye is all about browsing

Bottom: One of the many glories of Wales – winter sunset in the Black Mountains

The steep clamber up out of Capel-y-ffin will definitely have you searching for breath, but don't be put off. Once you've made the giant cairn at the top, the rest is child's play and the views, as you cruise comfortably along the giant whaleback that makes up the Ffawyddog ridge, are just superb.

Lord Hereford's Knob

At Pen Rhos Dirion, you nudge over 2,296ft (the 700m contour on OS maps) and reap the fruits of your labour with a sweeping panorama over the Wye Valley. East is Twmpa, often referred to as 'Lord Hereford's Knob', and beyond that, the Gospel Pass and Hay Bluff – the eastern end of the impressive Black Mountains escarpment.

The head of the Ewyas Valley is split in two by a rugged slither of upland known as Darren Llwyd. This offers an airy return route on this walk, with views to the east that match the earlier magnificent vista to the west. The spur drops away sharply at its southern tip and your eyes will be drawn straight ahead, where the Ewyas displays the classic U-shape of its ice-age roots.

Hay-on-Wye

This is the nearest walk in the book to the small town of Hay-on-Wye, which can be seen clearly from the northern escarpment. The town marks both the northernmost point of the National Park and also the Anglo-Welsh border, with Herefordshire to the east and Powys to the west.

Like many of the towns in the area, Hay-on-Wye grew up around its impressive Norman castle, which was built on the site of an earlier motte-and-bailey construction. This was burned by King John in 1216 and all but destroyed by Owain Glyndwr, the statesman-cum-warrior and self-declared Prince of Wales, during his crusades of 1400.

These days the town's deepest history is almost forgotten and the colourful municipality has reinvented itself as a bustling, cosmopolitan settlement with an upbeat feel that is totally different from the neighbouring farming communities. Known as the 'second-hand book capital of Wales', Hay contains around 30 major bookshops and hosts an internationally renowned literary festival each summer.

72 Tackle the Vale of Ewyas Horseshoe

Brave a steep climb to enjoy breathtaking views

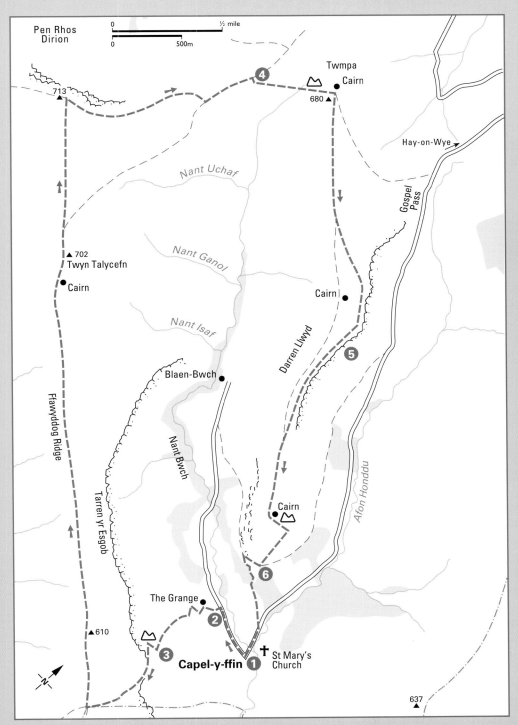

Distance 9 miles (14.5km)

Minimum Time 4hrs

Ascent/Gradient 1,560ft (475m) ▲▲▲

Level of Difficulty ●●●

Paths Easy-to-follow tracks, steep slopes, open moorland, 2 stiles

Landscape Classic U-shaped valleys, broad heather-strewn moorland

Suggested Map OS Explorer OL13 Brecon Beacons National Park Eastern area

Start/Finish Grid reference: SO 255314

Dog Friendliness Great for dogs but care required near livestock

Parking Narrow pull-in at southern edge of village, close to bridge

Public Toilets None en route

to a large one on the ridge. Turn right, then follow the track over Twyn Talycefn to the trig point on Pen Rhos Dirion. (To avoid the summit use the path that traverses left before the final climb.) Go right down into a broad saddle.

4 Keep straight ahead over the flat section, then climb steeply on to Twmpa. Turn right and then, for maximum effect, bear left on to a narrower track that follows the line of the east-facing escarpment. Stay with this track until the ridge narrows and drops steeply away.

5 Descend directly to a large square cairn, keep ahead down a steep spur and then zig-zag through the bracken to a junction with a broad bridleway. Keep straight ahead to cross this and drop down to pick up a narrow stony track that runs along the side of a wood.

6 Turn left to follow this down to a gate and keep straight ahead between houses. When you reach the drive, go straight ahead to cross a stile and continue in the same direction to cross another stile in the bottom corner. Turn right to follow the lane to return to your car.

1 Walk towards the bridge, but before you cross it bear left up a narrow lane, signposted 'The Grange Pony Trekking Centre'. Follow along the side of the stream to a drive on the left, again leading to the trekking centre, and follow this up to a cluster of barns.

2 Keep right and continue uphill to a large house on the right, with a gate blocking your progress. Bear left and climb a rocky track to another gate. Pass through and take a rough zig-zagging track up to easier ground. Cross the source of a small stream, and continue to the foot of a steep zig-zag track that climbs steeply up the escarpment.

3 Follow this, and as the gradient eases go ahead on a broad track past small cairns

73 The Escarpments of the Carmarthen Fan

Look down on the brooding waters of Llyn y Fan Fach, said to be home to the 'Lady in the Lake', on this exhilarating expedition into spectacular scenery

Above right: Healing waters? According to folklore the lady who arose from lyn y Fan Fach passed on rare medical skills

Above: Austere beauty on the Black Mountain

The view eastwards from the flanks of Bannau Sir Gaer across Llyn y Fan Fach to the steepest section of the Carmarthen Fan is particularly fine. There's something special about the shimmering black waters, their surface reflecting skywards a rippled mirror image of the shattered crags of the escarpment. Ravens, buzzards and red kites ride high on the updraughts and the picture becomes all the more sinister for the addition of a little light cloud, drifting in and out of the summits.

Shepherd Boy Bewitched

You won't be the first to become captivated by this scene. The lake was visited regularly long ago by a local shepherd boy known as Rhiwallon, who met a mystical lady, as beautiful as the reflection in the lake that she'd risen from. Her wisdom matched her beauty and she possessed the ability to make healing potions from herbs and flowers. Rhiwallon proposed marriage and the lady agreed, but only on the condition that he should never strike her with iron. Rhiwallon and his wife had a son before the inevitable happened, perhaps by accident, and the

lady returned to the dark waters, taking with her all of their worldly goods, including the animals they tended. Fortunately, before she left, she had passed on all of her healing knowledge to her son.

Far fetched? Maybe, but it's possible to see where the roots of the tale lie. The encroachment of the Iron Age would have certainly been treated with suspicion by the local population. The area was later renowned for its healers and there was a long line of practitioners known as the Physicians of Myddfai, after a small village north of the lake.

From the summit of Fan Foel, your grapple with gravity is rewarded by huge views across the bleak uplands of the Black Mountain (singular) – not to be confused with the Black Mountains (plural), which are 30 miles (48km) east of here and visible on a clear day. This is the westernmost mountain range of the National Park and, without doubt, the wildest and most remote. The majority of the land is made up of barren, windswept moorland that possesses an austere beauty with few equals. Unusually, a large percentage is actually owned by the National Park Authority.

73 The Escarpments of the Carmarthen Fan

Make a circuit above the bewitching lake that inspired a folk tale

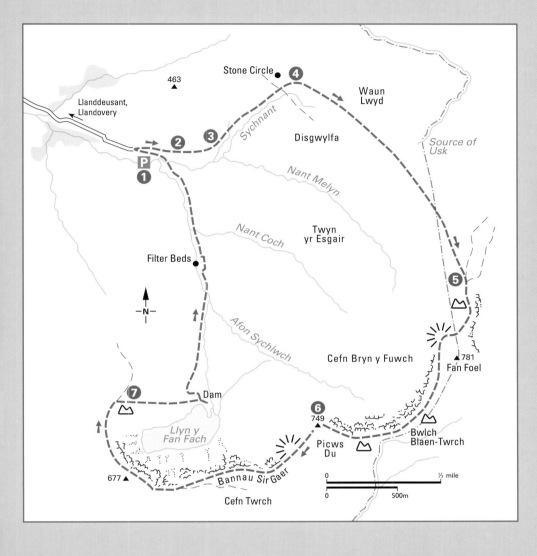

Distance 7.5 miles (12.1km)

Minimum Time 4hrs 30min

Ascent/Gradient 2,000ft (610m) ▲▲▲

Level of Difficulty ●●●

Paths Faint paths, trackless sections over open moorland, no stiles

Landscape Imposing mountains, hidden lakes, wild and remote moorland

Suggested Map OS Explorer OL12 Brecon Beacons National Park Western & Central areas

Start/Finish Grid reference: SN 798238

Dog Friendliness Care needed near livestock and steep drops

Parking At end of small unclassified road, south-east of Llanddeusant

Public Toilets None en route

Note Best not undertaken in poor visibility

1 From the car park at the end of the unclassified road, head back towards Llanddeusant and after about 100yds (91m) turn sharp right, almost doubling back on yourself, to continue on a faint track that contours eastwards around the hillside. Follow this track as it then veers northeast into the small valley carved out over the centuries by the Sychnant brook.

2 The track becomes clear for a short period, but don't be drawn uphill to the north, instead remain true to the course of the stream, keeping left at the confluence with another distinct valley, this one belonging to the Nant Melyn.

3 The track is faint but the going reasonably easy as you continue up the valley, crossing a small tributary and following the bank above the Sychnant. Numerous paths and sheep tracks cross your way in this section of the route, but continue unhindered upwards, aiming for the shallow saddle on the blunt ridge above. The stream eventually swings to the right and peters out. At this stage, bear right and head along the ridge.

4 You're now aiming for the steep and obvious spur of Fan Foel, which lies southeast of you, approximately 1.5 miles (2.4km) away. Follow whatever tracks you can find over Waun Lwyd and, as the ridge starts to narrow, keep to the crest where you'll meet a path coming up from the northeast.

5 Climb steeply up the narrow path on to the escarpment and keep right to follow the escarpment along. The path becomes clearer as it drops into Bwlch Blaen-Twrch.

From here, climb up on to Bannau Sir Gaer and continue to the summit cairn.

6 Stay with the main footpath and follow the edge of the escarpment above the precipitous cliffs into a small saddle or col and up again above Llyn y Fan Fach. Continue around the lake, with the steep drop to your right and you'll see a good path dropping down a grassy spur to the outflow of the lake.

7 Follow this obvious footpath and then, when you reach the dam, pick up the well-surfaced track that heads back downhill. This will lead you to the right of the waterworks filter beds and back to the car park.

74 On Towering Cliffs Around Strumble Head

This invigorating coastal walk visits some of the wildest countryside of the Pembrokeshire coast – with the added bonus of a chance to see seals in the waves

This is a magnificent stretch of Pembrokeshire coast, although at times it may feel like 'the coast path meets the Himalayas', as the narrow ribbon of trail climbs and drops at regular intervals throughout. The headland cliffs rise majestically above the pounding Atlantic surf, while the path cuts an airy, and at times precarious, line across their tops – and the sky is alive with the sound of seabirds. Garn Fawr, a formidable rocky tor that rises high above the peninsula, brings a touch of hill walking to the experience, and the shapely lighthouse flashes a repeating reminder of just how treacherous these spectacular waters can be.

Built in 1908 to help protect the ferries that run between Fishguard and Ireland, the Strumble Head Lighthouse guards a hazardous stretch of coast. The revolving lights, which flash four times every 15 seconds, were originally controlled by a massive clockwork system that needed rewinding every 12 hours; this was replaced in 1965 by an electrically powered system and the lighthouse was then converted to unstaffed operation in 1980. The waters off this strech of coast wrecked at least

Below: A bridge connects the Strumble Head Lighthouse, on St Michael's Island, to the mainland

60 ships in the 19th century alone. In 2003 a French shipwreck, possibly from an attempted invasion in 1797, was found in waters near by.

'Bottling' Seals

Atlantic grey seals, porpoises and even dolphins are regularly spotted in the turbulent waters along this stretch of the coast. Indeed, this is one of the best walks in Pembrokeshire to spot seals – you are most likely to see them in the bays of Pwll Bach and Pwlluog, near the start.

These lumbering marine giants reach more than 8ft (2.4m) in length and can weigh as much as 770lbs (350kg). They are usually seen bobbing up and down in the water with their head poking just above the waves – this is called 'bottling'. In autumn, when females give birth to a single pup, they often haul up on to beaches, where the young are suckled. The pups shed their white coat after around three weeks, when they are then weaned and taught to swim before being abandoned. The males are usually bigger than the females, with a darker coat and a more pronounced 'Roman' nose.

74 On Towering Cliffs Around Strumble Head

Take a turn up and down the often challengingly steep path – and marvel at the untamed beauties of the coastline

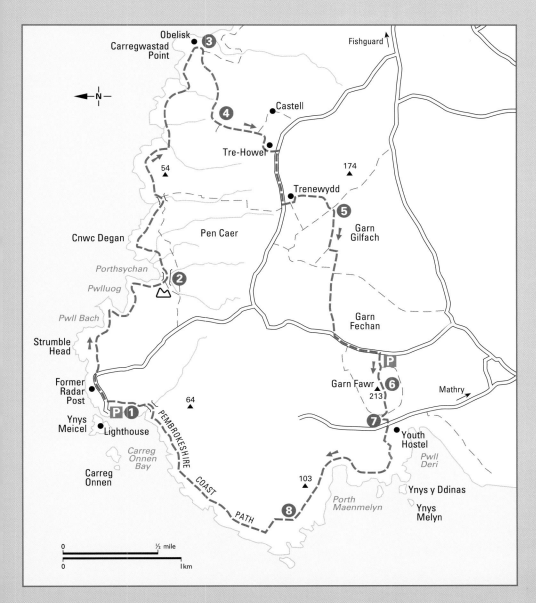

Distance 8 miles (12.9km)

Minimum Time 3hrs 30min

Ascent/Gradient 920ft (280m) ▲▲▲

Level of Difficulty ●●●

Paths Coast path, grassy, sometimes muddy tracks, rocky paths, 13 stiles

Landscape Rugged headland, secluded coves and rocky tor

Suggested Map OS Explorer OL35 North Pembrokeshire

Start/Finish Grid reference: SM 894411

Dog Friendliness Care needed near cliff tops and livestock

Parking Car park by Strumble Head Lighthouse

Public Toilets None en route

1 Walk back up the road and cross a gate on the left on to the coast path. Pass above the bays of Pwll Bach and Pwlluog, then drop steeply to a footbridge behind the pebble beach of Porthsychan.

2 Follow the coast path waymarkers around Cnwc Degan and down to another bridge, where a couple of footpaths lead away from the coast. Continue along the coast, passing a cottage on the right and climbing and dropping a couple of times, before you reach the obelisk at Carregwastad Point.

3 Follow the main path inland and cross a stile on to a farm track, where you turn right, away from the coast path. Continue with this path, which is vague in places, up through the gorse to a wall, then turn right on to a good track. Take this through a succession of gates and around a left-hand bend.

4 Ignore a track to the right and continue up the cattle track, eventually bearing right into the farmyard where you follow a walkway past livestock pens before swinging left, after the buildings, to the road. Turn right and then follow the road past a large house to a waymarked bridleway on the left. Pass Trenewydd and go through a gate on to a green lane. Follow this up to another gate and on to open ground.

5 Turn right here and follow the wall to yet another gate. This leads to a walled track that you follow to the road. Turn left and climb up to the car park beneath Garn Fawr. Turn right, on to a hedged track, and follow this up, through a gap in the wall, to the trig point.

6 Climb down and cross the saddle between this tor and the other, slightly lower, one to the south. From here, head west towards an even lower outcrop and pass it on the left. This becomes a clear path that leads down to a stile. Cross this and turn left, then right on to a drive that leads to the road.

7 Walk across on to the coast path. Bear right and cross a stile to drop down towards Ynys y Ddinas, the small island ahead. Navigation is easy as you follow the coast path north, over Porth Maenmelyn and up to a cairn.

8 Continue along the coast towards the lighthouse, until you drop to a footbridge above Carreg Onnen Bay. Cross a stile into a field, then another back on to the coast path and return to the car park.

75 Take a Walk on the Wild Side

A tough outing that explores the austere side of the Welsh uplands, this walk is a rare opportunity to see one of Britain's most beautiful birds – the red kite

Above: Majestic in flight – the red kite

Below: This excursion into the wilds starts from Llanwrtyd Wells

This is a foray into the wilder side of Wales, to a place that sees few footprints. If this may be considered a tough walk, the rewards, for those who are prepared to navigate their way carefully over one short stretch of trackless moorland, are rich almost beyond description. For less experienced walkers, this is one to tackle only after you've cut your teeth on the high ground of the Brecon Beacons, and then only in good visibility. Alternatively, if you're unsure about the navigation, or are in any doubt about the visibility, follow the outward leg on to Drygarn Fawr and return by simply retracing your steps.

The remote nature of the landscape links this area, more than any other, with one of Britain's most beautiful birds: the red kite. These uplands were the scene of this most majestic raptor's final stand. Free of persecution, pesticides and disturbance, a mere handful defiantly resisted extinction by scavenging these moors and nesting in the abundance of trees that line the valleys. Their decline was halted by conservation groups who, working closely with local landowners, began a release programme using birds imported from Scandinavia and Spain. Successful breeding in both England and Scotland began in 1992 and since then the population has increased so significantly they are almost common here today.

Silver Head, White Wing Patches

The birds are easily distinguished from the more common buzzard, which can also be seen in this area, as they are much slimmer with narrower, more angular wings and a distinct fork in the longer tail. The plumage is a mixture of russet red and chestnut brown with white wing patches and a silver head. Their flight is more agile, the tail constantly twisting as if trimming a sail.

75 Take a Walk on the Wild Side

Get away from the crowds on an excursion across remote moorland and beautiful Welsh valleys

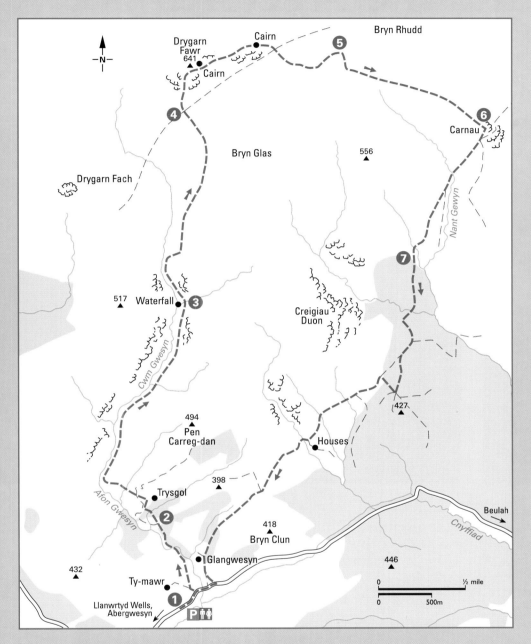

Distance 9.5 miles (15.3km)

Minimum Time 6hrs

Ascent/Gradient 2,000ft (610m) ▲▲▲

Level of difficulty ●●●

Paths Riverside path, faint or non-existent paths over moorland, some good tracks, some awkward stream crossings, no stiles

Landscape Stunning valley, remote moorland, some forestry

Suggested Map OS Explorer 200 Llandrindod Wells & Elan Valley

Start/Finish Grid reference: SN 860530

Dog Friendliness Care needed near livestock

Parking Car park north-east of Abergwesyn

Public Toilets At start

Notes Difficult navigation, avoid in poor visibility

5 Follow the track for 200yds (183m) until you see one stone offset to the right of the path. Turn right across wet ground to climb on to a ridge. Drop into a valley ahead and bear left on high ground with the valley to your right. Continue on sheep tracks until you reach a grassy hilltop. You should be able to see the cairn ahead. Take the clear path that leads to it.

6 Walk towards a gorge to the south-west. Pick up a track as you cross the river. Go downstream and bear right to cross hillsides before dropping into the bottom of the valley. Ford the stream to go through a gate.

7 Climb on a track, drop to cross a stream, then continue to a five-way junction. Turn right, go through a gate and then another on the left. Drop through the field and follow a track to a junction above houses. Keep right, cross a stream and then take the track across a field to a path junction. Go straight and down to the road. Turn right to return to your car.

1 Turn right on to the road and walk up to the bridge. Take a gravel track up left, then go right through a gate. Follow over fields and down to the Afon Gwesyn, which you ford, go on to a gate and up to where the track splits. Choose the top option and, as this bends left downhill, fork right, to a gap in the wood.

2 Follow the path down to a ford. Climb on to open ground and bear right to a farm track. Turn left through a gate, fork left beneath some crags. Continue to open ground. Follow the east side of the valley to a waterfall.

3 Pass this on the right, and go on until the path almost disappears. Follow the stream until a ridge comes from the right. Go uphill for 100yds (91m) then bear left until the cairned summit of Drygarn Fawr becomes visible.

4 Climb the grassy slope to the trig point, then go east past both cairns. Look for two grassy tops, 1.5 miles (2.4km) away, one with a large cairn – this is Carnau. A clear grassy track descends east from the cairn. Follow this until it levels and rounds a left-hand bend; look for a faint path forking right.

76 A Spectacular Stroll Around the Precipice

One of the finest short walks in Wales, the Precipice Walk follows a 'balcony route', with spectacular views of valley, mountain and Mawddach estuary

Above: First light on the waters of Llyn Cynwch and Craig Cau above, at Cadair Idris

Above right: Peaceful waters – Llyn Cynwch is a favourite spot for anglers casting for trout

There's been a house at Nannau since the 12th century, when the estate was owned by descendants of Cadwgan, Prince of Powys. That original building was burned down in 1404 after trouble between the owner, Hywel Sele, the 8th Lord of Nannau and his cousin Owain Glyndwr. Hywel attempted to kill Glyndwr while out hunting, and in reprisal Glyndwr burned down the house and killed his cousin, disposing of the body in a hollow tree. The skeleton wasn't found for 40 years and the house wasn't rebuilt until 1693.

The Nannau family, known called the Nanneys, still lived on the estate, but had financial problems. Hugh Nanney was heavily fined and imprisoned for trying to resolve his difficulties by felling 10,000 oaks. When the male line died out the female line, which had married into the powerful Vaughan family, took over. The Vaughans replanted many trees and, in 1796, built the mansion you see today.

As you start high there's very little ascent to do and the early part of the walk eases across woodland and farm pastures. As the path rounds Foel Cynwch and past the Sitka spruce of Coed Dôl-y-clochydd, spectacular views of the wooded Mawddach and Wen valleys open up. The high ridge seen on the other side of the Mawddach is Y Garn, one of the Rhinog outliers. It looks gentle enough from here, but Y Garn's other face is of thick heather and precipitous rock.

On the Terrace

Beyond another ladder stile the path itself gets spectacular, taking the form of an exciting terrace, high above the river. The precipice lasts an exquisite mile (1.6km), with little twists and turns to add a little spice to the walk. Before long you can trace the Mawddach past Dolgellau's plains, past the sandbars of its estuary, to the sea beyond.

It seems a shame to leave all this behind, but the little path veers left and descends to the shores of Llyn Cynwch. The lake also has an avenue of old oak trees, all that remains of what was quite a large forest until Hugh Nanney took to his axe. When you reach the far shores of the lake stop to take one last look south. Here you will see the cliffs of Cadair Idris reflected in the lake.

76 A Spectacular Stroll Around the Precipice

Take the high road around the Nannau Estate

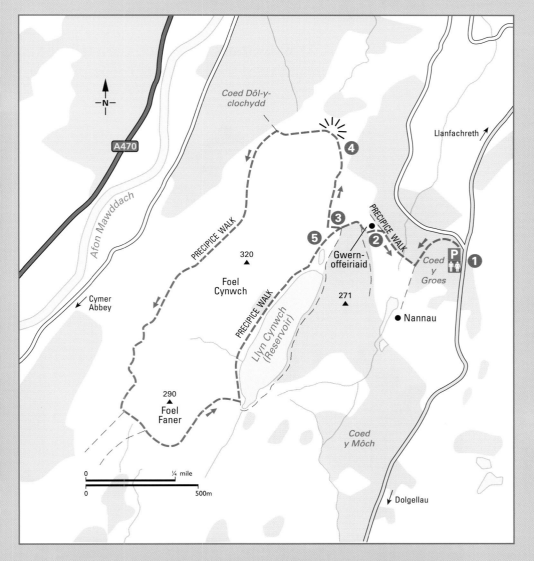

Distance 3 miles (4.8km)

Minimum Time 2hrs

Ascent/Gradient Negligible ▲▲▲

Level of Difficulty ●●●

Paths Stony tracks and good paths, occasionally rough, 4 stiles

Landscape Mountainside and pasture

Suggested Map OS Explorer OL18 Harlech, Porthmadog & Bala

Start/Finish Grid reference: SH 745211

Dog Friendliness Private land – dogs must always be on a lead

Parking Coed y Groes car park on Dolgellau–Llanfachreth road

Public Toilets At car park

Note Wear strong footwear as part of route follows narrow path with big drops down to Mawddach Valley. This is not a walk for vertigo sufferers

1 From the top end of the car park turn right on a level footpath that curves around to join another wide track. The Precipice Walk is a private path around the Nannau Estate, but its use has been authorised by the estate owners since 1890 on the understanding that all walkers will observe the country code. It has been one of Dolgellau's most famous attractions since those early days when Victorian tourists came for their constitutional perambulations. The track swings right at the edge of some fields.

2 Where the track comes to an estate cottage, Gwern-offeiriaid, turn left to follow a clear path to the hillside north of Llyn Cynwch. There you see the grand mansion of Nannau, built for the Vaughans in 1796.

3 At a footpath signpost fork right. The path climbs the hillside and turns northwards by the side of a dry-stone wall.

4 Beyond a stile the footpath curves around a crag-studded hill, with open slopes and fine views across to the village of Llanfachreth and the mountains of Rhobell Fawr and Dduallt behind. The path edges around Foel Cynwch and passes the woodlands of Coed Dôl-y-clochydd. Ignore a path signed 'Glasdir' and keep left, reaching the dramatic but even ledge path traversing the high hill slopes above the Mawddach Valley. Where the slopes ease, there's a promontory on the right, with a bench. The path arcs round to the southern side of Foel Faner, drops to the lake and turns sharp left to follow the western shore.

5 The path meets the outward route by the hill footpath sign. Retrace the outward route past the estate cottage of Gwern-offeiriaid and through the woods back to the car park and the start of the walk.

77 Powis Castle and the Montgomery Canal

A delightful walk leads through an impressive deerpark beneath the castellated mansion of Powis Castle before returning by way of the quiet Montgomery Canal

A prosperous market town set amid rolling green hills, Welshpool has always been synonymous with the River Severn, which flows through it. It was the Severn that brought trade to the town, for it was navigable by boat. The town was, until 1835, known as Pool and some of the old mileposts still refer to Pool. The 'Welsh' was added to distinguish the place from Poole in Dorset.

Architectural Treasures

When you walk up the busy High Street today you'll notice the fine architecture, much of it dating from Georgian times, like the Royal Oak Hotel, but also many older half-timbered buildings. Most tourists who visit Welshpool come to see the fine castle of Powis. On this route you turn off through the impressive wrought-iron gates before strolling along the long drive through the estate's parklands.

Today the castle is a grand red mansion, with castellated ramparts, tall chimneys and rows of leaded windows looking over manicured lawns and neatly clipped yews. But the scene would have been very different in 1200, when the castle was built for the warring Princes of Powys. The battlements would have been there, but there would have been no elegant windows or pretty gardens, for this place was designed to repel enemies, both English and Welsh: more often than not Powis sided with the English, even against the Glyndwr rebellion.

The fact that Powis has been continuously occupied has meant that it has made a successful transition from fortress to a comfortable grand mansion. In 1587 the powerful Herbert family, who became the Earls of Powis, took possession of the castle. They were to reside here until 1988, when the 6th Earl died, and were responsible for the castle's transformation. Only for a brief period, when they were attacked by Cromwellian forces and replaced by their bitter rivals, the Myddletons of Chirk, were the Royalist Herberts displaced.

On leaving the castle behind, you are in rural Wales and you descend to the tow path of the Montgomery Canal at the Belan Locks. Built by three different companies and opened in stages from 1796, the canal was designed for narrowboats. Today it is a quiet backwater and a pleasant return route to the wharf at Welshpool.

Far left: The Powis steam railway

Left: There are many historic town houses in Welshpool

Below: Today a grand mansion with celebrated gardens, Powis Castle was originally a fortress

77 Powis Castle and the Montgomery Canal

See how the earls of Powis lived on this pleasant and instructive visit to Welshpool

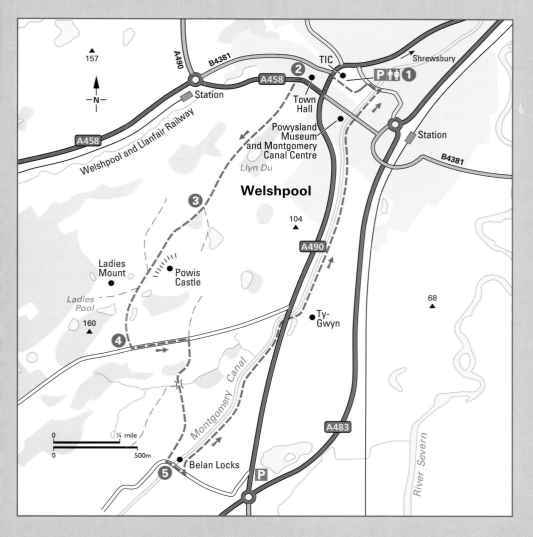

Distance 4 miles (6.4km)

Minimum Time 2hrs

Ascent/Gradient 328ft (100m) ▲▲▲

Level of Difficulty ●●●

Paths Tarmac drive, field path, canal tow path, 3 stiles

Landscape Country town, parkland and canal

Suggested Map OS Explorer 216 Welshpool & Montgomery

Start/Finish Grid reference: SJ 226075

Dog Friendliness Dogs not allowed on the Powis Castle Estate

Parking Large pay car park off Church Street, Welshpool

Public Toilets By information centre in car park

1 From the main car park go past the tourist information centre then go left along Church Street. At the crossroads in the centre of town turn right to head up Broad Street, which later becomes High Street.

2 When you get to a point just beyond the town hall, turn left past a small car parking area and pass through the impressive wrought iron gates of the Powis Castle Estate. Now follow the tarmac drive through the park grounds and past Llyn Du (which means 'the black lake' in English).

3 Take the right fork, the high road, which leads to the north side of the castle. You can detour from the walk here to visit the world-famous gardens and the castle with its fine paintings and furniture and collection of works of Indian art collected by Robert Clive.

Continue on the walk on the high road past two more pools on the left and the Ladies Pool on the right to reach a country lane.

4 Turn left along the country lane. Opposite the next estate entrance leave the lane over a stile beside a gate on the right, from which a grass track winds down to a bridge. Climb away beside the right-hand fence. Continue over another stile in the corner along an old way, which gently falls to a lane beside the Montgomery Canal. This canal, which runs for 33 miles (53km) from Welsh Frankton in Shropshire to Newtown in Powys, is gradually being restored. You may see a number of narrowboats cruising along this section.

5 Turn over the bridge at Belan Locks, immediately dropping left to the canal tow path. Head north along the canal, later passing beneath the main road. Entering Welshpool, remain on the tow path, passing the Powysland Museum and Montgomery Canal Centre (on the opposite bank), with its exhibits of local agriculture, crafts and the canal and railway systems. Beyond a short aqueduct and former railway bridge, climb out to the road and turn left back to the car park.

78 The 'Sublime' Mawddach

This walk treads in the footsteps of William Wordsworth, J. M. W. Turner and Charles Darwin, who all visited beautiful Barmouth to work and explore

Above: Sandbanks are visible in the estuary at low tide

Above right: Wild flowers on a hillside above the Mawddach estuary

Below: The beautiful waters of Llynnau Cregennen

Barmouth (once better known in Welsh as *Y Bermo*), used to be a seaport, trading the coarse woollen goods of Merionydd with the Americas. In those days the village cottages were strung out across terraces in the cliffs and there was one pub, the Corsygedol Arms, for the traveller. There wasn't enough room to squeeze the main road from Harlech between those rocks and the sea, so it bypassed the village and instead went inland, over the Rhinog mountain passes.

In the mid-19th century all this changed. Barmouth built a main street on the beach; visitors became more frequent and the resort's sea and sand attracted gentry from the Midlands. Barmouth also came to the notice of the famous: the poet Wordsworth said of the Mawddach Estuary that it was 'sublime' – and equal to any in Scotland. Artists like J. M. W. Turner and Richard Wilson came to capture the changing light and renowned beauty of estuary and mountainside. In 1867 the railway came, and a new bridge was engineered across the estuary sands. It was half a mile (800m) long and had a swing section across the main channel to allow shipping to pass.

Glorious Setting

Today you can see that Barmouth is not as smart as it was in its heyday. It's still in the most wonderful situation, though, and as you step on to the wooden boards of that half-mile foot and railway bridge you may feel exactly what Wordsworth felt. The view is best when the sun's shining and the tide's half out. That way the waters of the Mawddach will be meandering like a pale blue serpent amid pristine golden sandbars. Across the estuary your eyes cannot help but be drawn to mighty Cadair Idris. As you get to the other side and look back to Barmouth, you will see how this town has been built into the rocks of the lower Rhinogs. Across the bridge you're ready to explore those wooded foothills. Through Arthog the path climbs between oak trees and you find yourself looking across to waterfalls thundering into a wooded chasm. At the top you are presented with a view of all that you have seen so far: the estuary, the sandbars, the mountains and the yawning bridge. By the time you return to Barmouth you will have experienced that 'sublime' Mawddach.

78 The 'Sublime' Mawddach

Cross the Mawddach estuary by historic footbridge for grand views of mountains, sand and water

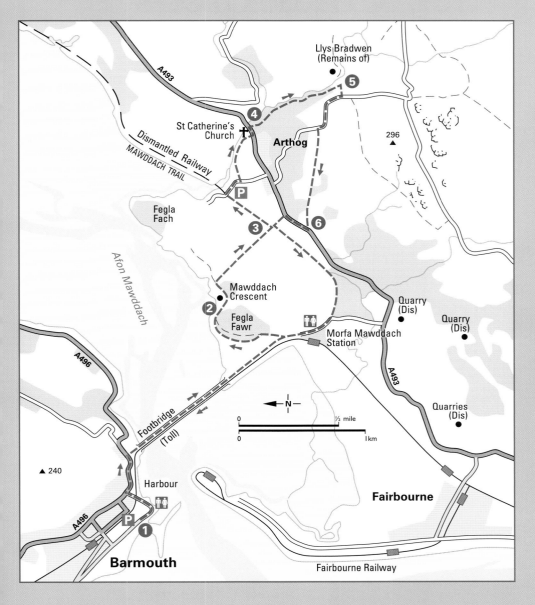

Distance 6 miles (9.7km)

Minimum Time 4hrs

Ascent/Gradient 656ft (200m) ▲▲▲

Level of Difficulty ●●●

Paths A bridge, good tracks and woodland paths, 6 stiles

Landscape Estuary and wooded hills

Suggested Map OS Explorer OL23 Cadair Idris & Llyn Tegid

Start/Finish Grid reference: SH 613155

Dog Friendliness Dogs should be on leads at all times

Parking Car park on seafront

Public Toilets At Barmouth's car park, or near Morfa Mawddach Station

1 Follow the promenade round the harbour, then go over the footbridge across the estuary (toll). On reaching the path along the south shore, turn left along the grassy embankment to a track rounding the wooded knoll of Fegla Fawr on its seaward side.

2 At the houses of Mawddach Crescent, take the track passing to their rear. Rejoin the track along the shoreline until you reach a gate on the right marking the start of a bridleway heading inland across the marshes of Arthog.

3 Turn left along the old railway track, then leave it just before the crossing of the little Arthog Estuary and turn right along a tarmac lane by a small car park. Bear left over a ladder stile and follow a raised embankment to a wall which now leads the path to the main Dolgellau road next to St Catherine's Church.

4 Opposite the church gate is a footpath beginning with steps into woodland. A waymarked path now climbs by the Arthog.

5 Beyond a stile at the top of the woods, turn right to a lane and right along the lane, then left along a track by the cottage of Merddyn. The track gets narrower and steeper as it descends into more woodland, beneath the boulders of an old quarry and down to the Dolgellau road by Arthog Village Hall.

6 Turn right along the road, then left along a path back to the railway track and the Mawddach Trail. Turn left along the trail and follow it past Morfa Mawddach Station and back across Barmouth's bridge.

79 Climbing with the Drovers Over the Roman Steps

A wonderful excursion takes you into the 'paradise' of Cwm Bychan – one of the treasures of Snowdonia – by way of a drovers' path called 'the Roman Steps'

Above: The way to paradise? Looking down the Roman Steps into Cwm Bychan

You've also seen it without the hardship of trudging through the knee-deep heather of the Rhinogs' rugged interior. Trudging through the Rhinogs has made many a day on the hills exhilarating for some, but it's certainly not for everybody. On this route we will stick to the paths.

In the Steps of Medieval Drovers

It seems a shame to lose the paradise that is Cwm Bychan, but we lose it for the shade of its oak woods. As the path climbs towards the Rhinog crags its surface becomes one of great rock slabs that form steps. These Roman Steps are in fact part of a medieval packhorse track, though the Romans, who had a fort in the Trawsfynydd area, might well have used their predecessors. Drovers would have passed this way too, on their way from Harlech to the markets in England, picking up local herds of Welsh Black cattle on the way.

The climb into the pass of Bwlch Tyddiad takes you into country that resembles the canyons of Utah or Arizona. Bwlch Tyddiad narrows and the walls of the surrounding hills close in. Suddenly you're at the top of the pass and looking across a huge rushy hollow surrounded by a million spruce trees, part of the Coed-y-Brenin forest. The trees provide cover for the next couple of miles as the route heads northwards along the ridge's east side.

The Lake That Steamed

From Moel y Gwartheg at the northern edge of the forest there's a good view of the knobbly northern Rhinog ridge and the huge Trawsfynydd reservoir. The Magnox nuclear power station on the far side is being decommissioned now, but the lake used to emit steam into the air as it was used by the station for cooling purposes. Controversy still rages, for they're considering turning the site into a nuclear waste plant. A slow and painstaking operation will restore the site to a greenfield status. It is hoped to be completed by 2098!

The last stretch of the walk climbs back over another wild heathery pass beneath the craggy mountains of Clip and Craig Wion. From here the path, a narrow ribbon of peat, winds through the heather to make a return to the greenery of Cwm Bychan, where paradise is regained.

The road from Llanbedr into Cwm Bychan is a joy in itself, passing through oak woods, by the banks of a babbling stream and beneath the small rocky castles of the Rhinog foothills. Llyn Cwm Bychan is stunning. If you see it on an August day, when the colourful heather contrasts with the vivid green of the sessile oaks, and the clouds' shadows play on the rocks of Carreg-y-saeth, then you've seen most of what is good about the Rhinogs.

79 Climbing With the Drovers Over the Roman Steps

Take one of Snowdonia's oldest pathways – but watch out for dangerous bogs if it has been raining

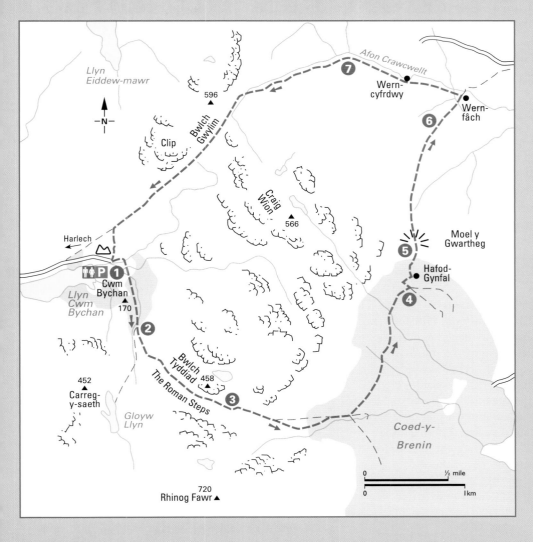

Distance 7 miles (11.3km)

Minimum Time 5hrs

Ascent/Gradient 1,575ft (480m) ▲▲▲

Level of Difficulty ●●●

Paths Rocky paths, tracks and boggy moorland, 9 stiles

Landscape Gnarled gritstone peaks with heather slopes

Suggested Map OS Explorer OL18 Harlech, Porthmadog & Bala

Start/Finish Grid reference: SH 646314

Dog Friendliness Can be off lead in upper heather-clad regions of walk

Parking Llyn Cwm Bychan

Public Toilets Portaloo at car par

Note The moorlands around the eastern end of the walk can be very wet and dangerous, with streams under the bogland. The walk is best tackled after a long dry spell

1 Go through the gate at the back of the car park at Llyn Cwm Bychan and over the paved causeway across the stream. Beyond a stile the path climbs up through woodland.

2 Over another stile you leave woodland behind and cross a stream on a small bridge. The path, always clear, climbs steadily to a gate. Now slabbed with 'the steps', it climbs through a heather-clad rocky ravine and on to the cairn marking the highest point along the rocky pass of Bwlch Tyddiad.

3 From the col, the path descends into a grassy moorland basin beneath Rhinog Fawr, then, beyond a stile, enters the conifers of the Coed-y-Brenin plantation. A well-defined footpath tucks away under the trees and eventually comes to a wide flinted forestry road, along which you turn left.

4 After about a mile (1.6 km), the road swings away to head east; watch out for a way-marked path on the left just beyond the turn. Waymarks guide the route left, then right, to pass the ruins of Hafod-Gynfal. Beyond this you head north to go over a ladder stile and out of the forest.

5 Go straight ahead from the stile, heading north across the grassy moor of Moel y Gwartheg. The ground gets wet as you descend, but it's wetter still further right. You're heading for the isolated cottage of Wern-fâch, which stands a little to the left of a small patch of conifers, but for now aim towards the green fields of Cefn Clawdd.

6 You meet a fence, which guides you down to Wern-fâch. Cross a stile, then just above the cottage turn left and go over two ladder stiles. Follow the main stream (Afon Crawcwellt) to Wern-cyfrdwy (house), pass behind it, then join the walls and fences that shadow the stream. These give the least wet line across the sodden moorland.

7 The going firms up as the ground steepens, climbing to the lonely col of Bwlch Gwylim, a narrow pass between Clip and Craig Wion. Descending the far side, Cwm Bychan and the start of the walk come back into view. The footpath now descends to the south-west, through heather and bracken. After a ladder stile, look for a small waymark where you turn left down steep slopes back to the car park.

80 In the Country of One of Wales's Most Famous Sons

From the birthplace of statesman David Lloyd George, a charmingly varied walk leads through idyllic woodland to Criccieth and a beautiful stretch along the coast

Above: The 18th-century Church of St John the Baptist beside the Afon Dwyfor in Llanystumdwy

Below: Criccieth Castle

David Lloyd George (1863–1945) came from modest beginnings in Llanystumdwy. This village on the banks of the Dwyfor is separated from the coast by half a mile (800m) of fields and coastal marshes. When you're barely out of the car park, you'll pass Highgate, his boyhood home, and the Lloyd George Museum. In the woods at the start of the walk you will come across the grave and a memorial to this last Liberal prime minister of Great Britain. It's a spot where he loved to sit.

'The Greatest Welshman'

Speaking in Parliament in 1945, Winston Churchill declared of Lloyd George that 'as a man of action, resource and creative energy he stood, when at his zenith, without rival… He was the greatest Welshman which that unconquerable race has produced since the age of the Tudors… and those who come after us will find the pillars of his life's toil upstanding, massive and indestructible.'

That Lloyd George was a great man is not in dispute, but his life was not without controversy. Although he was one of the early pioneers of the Welfare State and led Britain to eventual victory in the First World War, he was also linked with several dubious private moneymaking deals and gained a, perhaps unfair, reputation for allowing peerages to be awarded to wealthy political benefactors. A flamboyant, larger-than-life man Lloyd George just did not fit in with his rather stuffy Edwardian contemporaries. He is reputed to have been a womaniser, and at one time he had a wife in Criccieth and a mistress, his parliamentary secretary, whom he later married, in London.

Leaving things historical for a while, the walk through the woodland by the Dwyfor riverside is as good as woodland walking gets. The Dwyfor's crystal clear waters chatter to the rocks below and in spring the forest floor is carpeted with primroses, bluebells, garlic and wood anemones. So far we've been heading away from Criccieth and the coast, but soon the route takes us back across fields into Criccieth, a town with history in two episodes.

Criccieth and its Castle

Criccieth Castle stands on a huge volcanic crag that juts out into Tremadog Bay. The twin-towered gatehouse is believed to have been built by Llewelyn the Great, around 1240, but it was captured by Edward I in 1280. Despite its one-time strategic importance, Criccieth remained no more than a small fishing port until the Victorians' penchant for sun and sand saw it grow to today's proportions. You'll pass rows of Victorian terraces on the way to the rugged coastal path that takes you, by way of the sand and pebble beach, back to the Dwyfor and David Lloyd George's village.

80 In the Country of One of Wales's Most Famous Sons

Explore the coastal haunts of the last Liberal prime minister

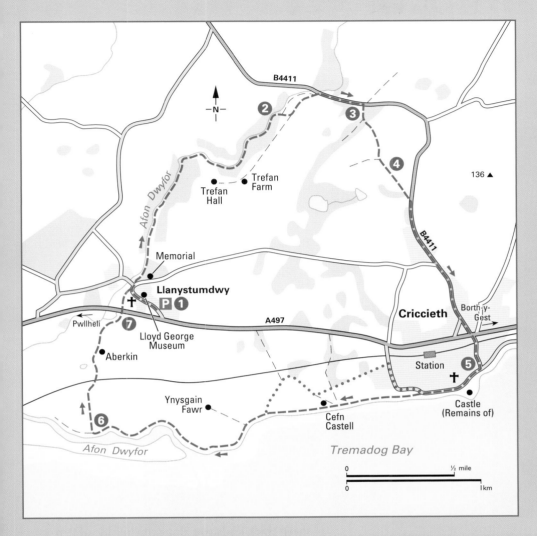

Distance 6 miles (9.7km)

Minimum Time 4hrs

Ascent/Gradient 300ft (91m) ▲▲▲

Level of Difficulty ●●●

Paths Generally well-defined paths and tracks, 4 stiles

Landscape Riverside woodland, fields, town streets, coastline

Suggested Map OS Explorer 254 Lleyn Peninsula East

Start/Finish Grid reference: SH 476383

Dog Friendliness Dogs can run free in riverside woods and on coast

Parking Large car park at east end of village

Public Toilets Near museum at Llanystumdwy and at Criccieth

Note Small section of coast path engulfed by highest tides. Make sure you know times of tides before setting off

1 Turn right out of the car park and go through Llanystumdwy village, past the museum to the bridge over the Afon Dwyfor. Turn right along the lane, then follow the footpath on the left past the memorial and down to the wooded river banks.

2 After 1.5 miles (2.4km) the path turns right, then goes under a stone archway to meet a tarred drive. Turn left along this, carry on to the B4411 and turn right.

3 After about 500yds (457m), turn right down an enclosed drive. As another drive merges from the left, turn half left along a path shaded by rhododendrons. After a few paces, go though the kissing gate, then cross the field guided by a fence on the left. Through another kissing gate the path veers half right, following a fence which is now on the right.

4 Beyond another gate the now sketchy route cuts diagonally (south-east) across two fields to rejoin the B4411 road, a mile (1.6km) or so north of Criccieth. Follow the B4411 into town. Keep straight on at the crossroads, and bear left after the level crossing to reach the promenade.

5 Follow the coast road past the castle and continue until it turns firmly inland. From here, tide permitting, simply follow the coast path or walk along the sands. Otherwise, follow the road to a bridleway on the left. Go past Muriau and then to the right of Ty Cerrig. Cross a track and a field then turn right on a green track, nearly to the railway. Head left, back to the coast east of Ynysgain Fawr. Follow the coast path west through coastal grasslands and gorse scrub to the estuary of the Dwyfor and some crumbled concrete sea defences.

6 At a metal kissing gate, waymarks point inland. Follow these, with the fence on your right. The route becomes a farm track that cuts under the railway and passes through the yard of Aberkin farm before reaching the main road.

7 Cross the main road with care and go through the gate on the opposite side. A short path leads to an unsurfaced lane, which in turn leads to the village centre. Turn right for the car park.

81 Past the Horseshoe Falls to Climb Velvet Hill

A delightful ramble beside the Horseshoe Falls then leads up the aptly named Velvet Hill to reveal glorious landscapes in a hundred shades of green

Right: Manmade waterfall – Thomas Telford's Horseshoe Falls

Below: A steam train enters Berwyn station on the restored Llangollen railway line

Bottom: Looking down from Velvet Hill on the River Dee

At the picnic site at Llantysilio Green, just outside Llangollen, there's an idyllic spot where the River Dee, enshrouded by trees, squeezes its way between Velvet Hill and the wooded hillside of Bryniau-mawr Bank. Yet the moment you leave the site and descend to the banks of the Dee you realise you're not quite in the countryside yet. Through the trees you can see the back of the Chain Bridge Hotel, the paraphernalia of the rejuvenated Llangollen Railway at Berwyn Station, and the Llangollen Canal. The canal ends after a short distance and you cross the meadows by the banks of the Dee. Just upstream are the Horseshoe Falls. Though they're a graceful piece of engineering, many visitors feel let down when they discover that the falls are a weir and not nature's own creation. Set on a natural curve of the river, the weir was Thomas Telford's solution to harnessing the waters of the Dee to feed and control the levels of the Llangollen and Ellesmere canals.

Beyond the falls the walk climbs to Llantysilio's little church, which has its origins in the 7th century, though much of the structure was added between the 18th and 19th centuries. A tractor track takes you above the tree tops and then a sheep track leads you along the hillside of Pen-y-bryn, with views of both the Dee and its tributary the Eglwyseg opening up before you.

Costly Disaster

A section of remade path beyond a quarry incline gives you a hint of a recent disaster. November 2000 saw violent storms all over Wales. This hillside was subjected to a massive landslide after days of torrential rain. Eyewitnesses reported that an 8ft (2.4m) high torrent of mud came down the hill. It carved up the main Horseshoe Pass road, causing a blockage that would last many months, and engulfed the Britannia Inn, leaving the landlord with a £200,000 repair bill. On Velvet Hill you can gaze down to where the Dee, now far below, meanders in crazy horseshoes. It's joined by the Afon Eglwyseg, which flows beneath the gleaming terraces of limestone that shares its name. In the valley bottom beneath the crags, the Cistercian abbey of Valle Crucis seems diminutive, as does the romantic castle-topped hill of Dinas Bran.

81 Past the Horseshoe Falls to Climb Velvet Hill

Take a camera if you have one – the views make this one of the prettiest walks in the book

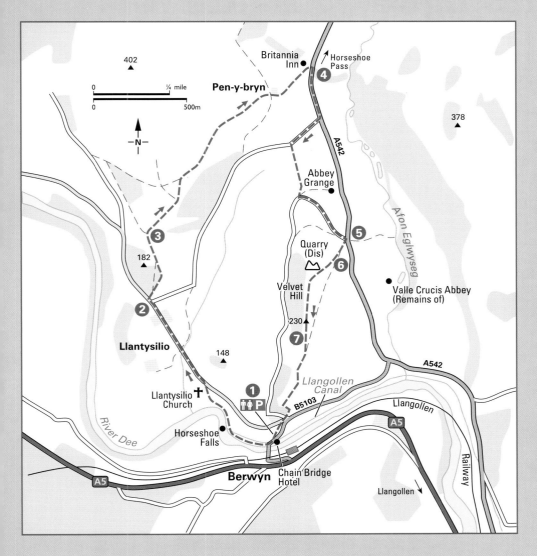

Distance 3.5 miles (5.7km)

Minimum Time 2hrs

Ascent/Gradient 902ft (275m) ▲▲▲

Level of Difficulty ●●●

Paths Field paths in valley and on hillside, 10 stiles

Landscape Rolling hillsides, woodland and riverside pastures

Suggested Map OS Explorer 255 Llangollen & Berwyn

Start/Finish Grid reference: SJ 198433

Dog Friendliness Farm pastures – dogs need to be on leads

Parking Picnic site and car park at Llantysilio Green on minor road north of Berwyn Station

Public Toilets At car park

1 From the car park walk down to the road, turn right for a few paces then descend steps to the back of the Chain Bridge Hotel. Turn right to follow the path between the river and the canal. Through a kissing gate at the end of the canal cross riverside fields past the Horseshoe Falls and climb to Llantysilio Church. On reaching the road, turn left through the hamlet of Llantysilio to reach a junction.

2 Continue a few paces further to find a stile on the right and then climb along a rutted track, which keeps a forest to the left, then climbs north on a high pastured hillside.

3 Over a stile at the top of the field the path swings right above a plantation. Keep right at a fork and later cross a stile before

eventually descending to cottages at Pen-y-bryn. An enclosed path drops to a stile, which leads out to the Horseshoe Pass road at Britannia Inn.

4 Turn right along the road, then right again when you get to the first junction. At a bend, mount a stile on the left to head south across the fields. Reaching a farm track briefly go right, leaving at a fork over a stile on the left on to a narrow lane. Go left here to meet the Horseshoe Pass road again.

5 Go over a stile on the right-hand side of the road, signposted to the Velvet Hill, and ascend by quarry workings.

6 Later, swing right along a wide grassy track climbing steeply through bracken to reach the ridge, and go left for the summit.

7 Descend south on a narrow footpath to reach a fence above some woods. Do not cross (as many have done), but follow the fence down left to a stile. After crossing the stile go right, along a path that leads back to the lane near the car park.

82 A Sight of Bala's Gem – 'The Lake of Beauty'

This pleasant walk climbs above Bala for wide views of Wales's largest natural lake, set amid lovely hills dotted with farmhouses and pastures

In his book *Wild Wales* (1862) English author George Borrow was full of praise for Llyn Tegid. He wrote: 'It was a beautiful evening… the wind was blowing from the south, and tiny waves were beating against the shore, which consisted of small brown pebbles. The lake has certainly not its name, which signifies Lake of Beauty, for nothing.' Borrow had been staying at the White Lion in Bala and had been highly impressed with both the place and its people. Bala stands close to the banks of two great rivers, the Tryweryn and the Dee, and the shore of the largest natural lake in Wales, Llyn Tegid.

Religion and Wool
To many Bala might seem an austere town. Its many chapels give a hint to its religious roots. You'll see the statue of Dr Lewis Edwards, founder of the Methodist College, and, opposite the White Lion, one of the Revd Thomas Charles, a founder of the British and Foreign Bible Society.

Bala's employment was based around the woollen industry, and the town was noted for its stockings. Thomas Pennant came here in 1786 and painted a fascinating picture of life in the town: 'Round the place, women and children are in full employ, knitting along the roads; and mixed with them Herculean figures appear, assisting their omphales in this effeminate employ.'

Recreational Activities
Llyn Tegid is every bit as beautiful as Borrow suggests and today it's very popular for watersports. When the south-westerlies blow, Bala has waves like an angry ocean. It's favoured by anglers, too: pike, perch, trout, salmon and roach are plentiful, but the fish Llyn Tegid is famous for is the Gwyniad, which is not unlike a freshwater herring. It is said these fish were trapped here after the last ice age.

You come to the old Norman motte-and-bailey castle of Tomen y Mur soon after turning your back on the lake. Some say that the mound goes back to Roman times, but it is known that the castle was captured from the Normans by Llewelyn ap Iowerth in 1202. One of those Welsh steam railways has its terminus right next to the old castle site and it's fascinating to see the old steam engines puffing along the lakeside. However, we are in search of

higher things, so climb through woods and upland fields until you get your view. From up high you can see Tegid's blue waters, seemingly perfect and still from this distance, and stretching 4.5 miles (7.2km) along its rift valley towards Dolgellau. White farmhouses are dotted on pleasant pastured hills. The Dee, so wide down river from Bala, has rather anonymous beginnings in the peat bogs beneath Dduallt, whose dark crags rise high on the north-west horizon. Then it is time to descend, through more oak woods, and further, beneath western hemlock and larch, finally to reach the lakeshores and the welcome comforts of the town.

Left: Fine views can also be had from the water's edge

Below: Beauty spot – as well as being a centre for watersports, the lake is celebrated for having particularly deep and clear waters

82 A Sight of Bala's Gem – 'The Lake of Beauty'

Get the big – and boldly beautiful – picture on Llyn Tegid

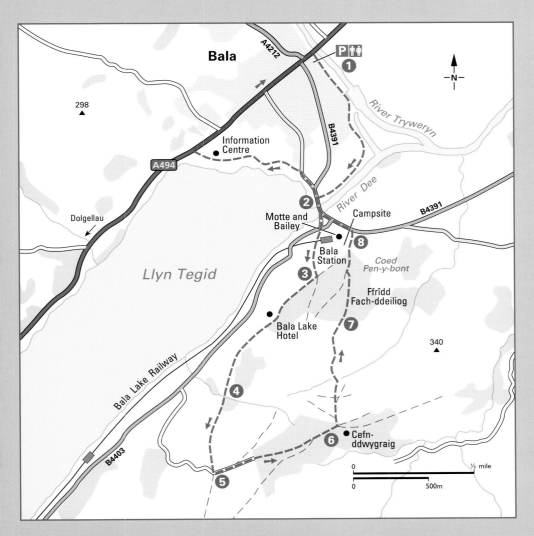

Distance 5 miles (8km)

Minimum time 3hrs

Ascent/Gradient 656ft (200m) ▲▲▲

Level of Difficulty ●●●

Paths Woodland and field paths, 7 stiles

Landscape Woods and upland pasture

Suggested Map OS Explorer OL23 Cadair Idris & Llyn Tegid, or OS Explorer OL18 Harlech, Porthmadog and Bala

Start/Finish Grid reference: SH 929361

Dog Friendliness Dogs should be on leads at all times

Parking Car park at entrance to Bala town from east

Public Toilets At car park

1 Go to the north corner of the car park in Bala to access the riverside path. Turn right to follow a raised embankment along the west bank of the Tryweryn. After a dog-leg to the right, passing through two kissing gates, the footpath continues, first by the banks of the Tryweryn, then by the north banks of the Dee.

2 On reaching the road, cross the bridge over the River Dee, then a smaller, older bridge. Go through a kissing gate to cross a small field to Bala Station on Bala Lake Railway. A footbridge allows you to cross the track before traversing two small fields.

3 Turn right along a cart track, and continue to pass behind the Bala Lake Hotel. A waymarker points the direction up a grassy bank on the left, and the path continues to a stile and then follows a fence on the right.

4 Descend slightly to cross a stream beside a small cottage, go up again then along a level fence to a stile. Bear left up through some bracken and wind up steeply at first, then continue more easily to a tarmac lane.

5 Turn left along the lane to a cattle grid from where you continue on a stony track, passing through felled plantations.

6 Just before the isolated house of Cefn-ddwygraig, turn left to a ladder stile. Follow a grass track across gorse-covered slopes. Keep left at a fork and drop down to a stile. The well-waymarked path continues north, with Bala town ahead.

7 Go over a partially hidden step stile into the commercial forestry plantations of Coed Pen-y-bont. A narrow footpath descends

to the bottom edge of the woods (ignore the forestry track you meet on the way down).

8 At the bottom of the woods turn right along a track that reaches the road by the Pen-y-Bont Campsite. Turn left along the road, cross the Dee again, bear left and then follow the lakeside footpath past the information centre. When you reach the main road, turn right to explore the fascinating town centre.

83 Ancient Stones and Settlements on Tal y Fan

On a road trodden since the Bronze Age, and later paved by the Romans, this fascinating walk takes you through the 'Pass of Two Stones' to Tal y Fan plateau

When you're driving along the A55 past Colwyn Bay, the first close-up views of Snowdonia reveal themselves across the Conwy estuary. The peak that captures the eye here rises up behind Conwy Mountain and has just enough crags on top to ruffle its otherwise smooth whaleback outline. The mountain is Tal y Fan, an outlier of the Carneddau range, and the most northerly 2,000-footer (610m) in Wales.

Now you can be a hero and climb Tal y Fan from sea level, but there's a peak-baggers' route that begins from Bwlch y Ddeufaen, 1,400ft (427m) up in the hills above the Conwy Valley. The road you walk is centuries old: Bronze and Iron Age tribesmen would have used it regularly, for they had large settlements all over the northern Carneddau. Monoliths either side of the road give the pass, Bwlch y Ddeufaen ('Pass of the Two Stones') its name. When you climb to the top of Tal y Fan you can see their settlements in plan, for here on a great high plateau the Ordovices tribesmen could farm and watch out for enemies from over the seas. The Roman invasion under Gnaeus Julius Agricola must have come as a shock to these farmers. Between AD 75 and AD 77 the invaders set up forts at Segontium (Caernarfon) and Canovium (at Caerhun in the Conwy Valley). When the Roman cohorts marched into the hills they made the Bwlch y Ddeufaen road their own, surfacing it and adding mileposts. The Ordovices were defeated. Great forts like Caer Bach, on the southern slopes of Tal y Fan, were abandoned. Today, Caer Bach lies beneath turf and gorse, but its earth ramparts and a circle of stones are still visible.

After the Romans

As the Roman Empire declined, native tribes returned to Tal y Fan, tending sheep on the high plateau and growing crops on the southern flanks. Looking down to the castle at Conwy you are reminded that although Edward I of England came to conquer, it took the land clearance and enclosure acts of the early 19th century to force the Welsh hill people away from their settlements.

Above: Derelict farm buildings on the southern flanks of the Tal y Fan plateau

Right: Impassive observers of your climb – the ancient way up to Tal y Fan was part of a drovers' road headed for Anglesey

83 Ancient Stones and Settlements on Tal y Fan

See how Bronze and Iron Age settlers lived on the most northerly 2,000ft (610m) hill in Wales

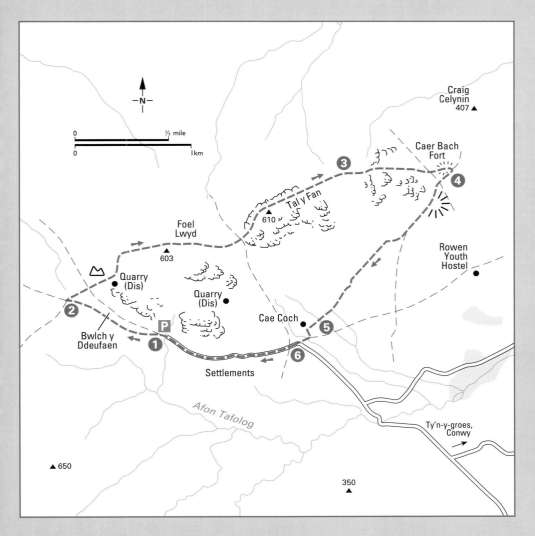

Distance 5 miles (8km)

Minimum Time 3hrs

Ascent/Gradient 984ft (300m) ▲▲▲

Level of Difficulty ●●●

Paths Cart tracks and narrow mountain paths, 7 stiles

Landscape Moor and mountain

Suggested Map OS Explorer OL17 Snowdon

Start/Finish Grid reference: SH 720715

Dog Friendliness Can be off lead on high ridges, but should be kept under tight control in farmland

Parking Car park at end of Bwlch y Ddeufaen road, off B5106 Conwy–Llanwrst road

Public Toilets None en route

1 From the car park at the top of the metalled section of the road to Bwlch y Ddeufaen, continue along the road, which is now unsurfaced, and follow it past the ancient standing stones to the high pass itself, where you go through a gate in a crossing wall.

2 Turn right and follow the course of the wall, across the pass under three lines of pylons, and then up the steep slopes of Foel Lwyd. A narrow footpath continues, first descending to a little saddle, or col, then climbing to the rockier summit of Tal y Fan.

3 The descending footpath follows the line of the dry-stone wall: when the wall turns right, go straight ahead, towards the hill of Craig Celynin. Thread between outcrops to reach a green valley running down to the right; look for the mound of Caer Bach Fort.

4 When you reach the remains of the fort turn right to follow a tumbledown wall heading south-west across high pastureland overlooking the Conwy Valley. Except for a short stretch this wall now acts as your guide, as do the frequent ladder stiles and locked gates sited in all the intervening cross-walls.

5 The footpath becomes a cart track, which passes beneath the whitewashed cottage of Cae Coch before turning left to join the stony vehicle track that has come from Rowen Youth Hostel.

6 Turn right along the track, which soon joins the Bwlch y Ddeufaen road at a sharp corner. Go straight ahead along the road and follow it back to the car park.

84 Conwy: Castle High and Castle Low

Conwy's magnificent castle lies at the foot of the Carneddau, but up in the foothills this walk also visits the Iron Age or Roman remains of Castell Caer

Above: The imposing Conwy Castle has eight drum towers and a high curtain wall

Below: Heather-covered slopes looking from Conwy Mountain towards Penmaen-bach

Conwy is special. Approaching from Llandudno Junction, three fine bridges (including Thomas Telford's magnificent suspension bridge of 1822) cross the estuary beneath the mighty castle, allowing the road and the railway into this medieval World Heritage Site. The fortress dates back to 1283–88, when King Edward I of England built it as part of his 'iron ring' to repress the rebellious troops of Llewelyn the Great. Great town walls with gates and towers still encircle old Conwy. You should walk these walls – for they offer fine views of the castle, the Conwy Estuary and the rocky knolls of Deganwy.

From the Quayside

The walk description begins at the quayside, not the car park, as you will probably want to take a good look around this medieval town. The route starts on a shoreline path under the boughs of Bodlondeb Wood. Not long after passing through Conwy's suburbs you're walking the hillside, on a path threading through gorse and small wind-twisted hawthorns. If you liked the views from the

castle walls, you'll love the view from the Conwy Mountain ridge. Looking back you can see the castle, towering over the town's roof tops; but now added to the scene are the Carneddau, the limestone isthmus of the Great Orme and, across the great sands of Lafan, Anglesey.

There is quite a network of paths criss-crossing the ridge and usually the best course is the highest: you'll need to be on the crest path to see the remains of Castell Caer. This 10-acre (4ha) fort has been linked to both Roman and Iron Age settlers – it has formidable defences, with clearly visible artificial ramparts that overlook spectacular sea cliffs on one side, and a wide view of the land to the south. Beyond the fort, the path misses out the peaks of Penmaen-bach and Alltwen. Instead you should descend to the Sychnant Pass, a splendid, twisting gorge that separates Conwy Mountain from the higher Carneddau peaks.

It's all downhill from here, but the scenery becomes more varied and still maintains interest. As you descend you can see the tidal River Conwy, twisting amongst an expanse of chequered green fields. Little hills present themselves to you, on your way back north. One last one has pleasant woods with primroses and bluebells, and it gives you another fine view of Conwy Castle to add to your collection before returning to base.

84 Conwy: Castle High and Castle Low

Take a tour from historic Conwy up to an outpost of the Celtic era

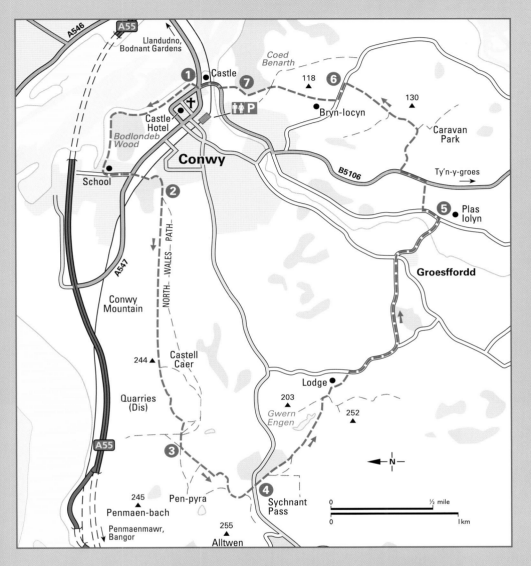

Distance 6.75 miles (10.9km)

Minimum Time 4hrs

Ascent/Gradient 1,493ft (455m) ▲▲▲

Level of Difficulty ●●●

Paths Good paths and easy-to-follow moorland tracks, 5 stiles

Landscape Town, coastline high ridge, farmland and copse

Suggested Map OS Explorer OL17 Snowdon

Start/Finish Grid reference: SH 783775

Dog Friendliness Can run free on high ridges, but keep on lead elsewhere

Parking Large car park on Llanrwst Road behind Conwy Castle

Public Toilets At car park

1 From Conwy Quay head north-west along the waterfront, going past the Smallest House and under the town walls. Next fork right along a tarmac waterside footpath that rounds Bodlondeb Wood. Turn left along the road, past the school and on to the A547. Cross the road, then go over the railway line by a footbridge. The track beyond the railway skirts a wood in order to reach a lane, and at this point you should turn right.

2 At a fork bear right past a house to a waymarked stile, from which a footpath makes its way up the wooded hillsides on to Mynydd y Dref (Conwy Mountain). Follow the undulating crest of Conwy Mountain and continue past the remains of the 10-acre (4ha) Castell Caer fortress.

3 Several tracks converge in the high fields of Pen-Pyra. Here, follow signposts for the 'North Wales Path' along the track heading to the south-west over the left shoulder of Alltwen and down to the metalled road traversing the Sychnant Pass.

4 Follow the footpath from the other side of the road, skirting the woods on your left. Climb over a stile, then carry on past Gwern Engen to meet a track. Go right on the track and then bear left, dropping above the Lodge to reach a lane. Turn right along the lane, then turn left, when you reach the next junction, into Groesffordd village. Cross the road, then take the road ahead that swings to the right past a telephone box, then left (south-east) towards Plas Iolyn.

5 Turn left at the end then opposite a white house take a path up to a cottage. Cross a track and go upfield to the B5106, then left to Conwy Touring Park. Follow the drive to a hairpin, take a waymarked path through trees, recrossing the drive. Through a kissing gate, go up the field-edge, then left along a ridge above successive pastures, finally meeting a lane.

6 Turn left, then right along a track past a communications mast to Bryn-locyn. Continue to a stile by Coed Benarth, from which a path drops beside the wood.

7 Go over a ladder stile on your left-hand side and across a field to a roadside gate. Turn right on to the B5106 to quayside, or turn left to get back to the main car park.

85 Moelfre and the Ancient Village

Along Anglesey's beautiful east coast, this walk leads from charming Moelfre past a sobering reminder of a disaster at sea to provide a glimpse of a 4th-century Celtic village

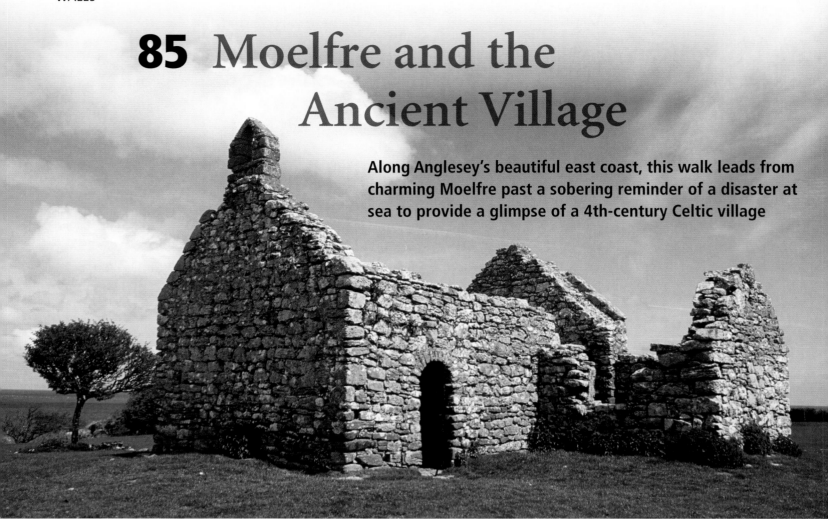

Being in Moelfre is like being in Cornwall: the pebble beach, the whitewashed cottages, small boats in a tiny harbour, and bracing air. As you stroll along the rocky coastline above the low cliffs, past the two lifeboat stations and the Seawatch Centre, all thoughts are on ships and the ocean. If it's sunny and the breeze is only slight, everything appears so picturesque and peaceful, but as you read the inscriptions on the Royal Charter memorial, you get a different story…

The monument recalls the night of 26 October 1859. A proud British cutter, the *Royal Charter* was on its homeward journey from Melbourne to Liverpool. Caught in a savage storm, Captain Taylor signalled for a pilot, but none would come on such a night. In deep trouble, he set anchor, but at 1:30am the chain parted. At daybreak two locals saw the wreck being pounded against the rocks. To their horror they saw a man shimmy down a rope from the decks and into the furious sea. He was Joseph Rogers, an able seaman from Malta, who had volunteered to try to swim with a hawser for shore, the only means to secure the ship and save the lives of the crew and passengers. Twice he failed, but finally made it and lashed the ship to a rock. The gallant seaman and the men of Moelfre made a human chain into the breakers. They managed to rescue 18 passengers, 5 riggers and 18 crew, but on

that day 452 people, including all the officers and 28 men from Moelfre, lost their lives.

Ancient Anglesey

On the way back to Moelfre you leave the sea and follow country lanes. Through the hedges you'll spot a roofless 12th-century chapel, which you pass en route to Din Lligwy, an ancient village hidden in the woods. This is a wonderfully preserved Celtic settlement dating back to the last years of the Roman Empire in the 4th century AD. In a field further down the lane are the remains of a neolithic burial chamber. The Lligwy tomb has a massive capstone weighing 25 tons. The excavation in 1909 revealed the remains of 15 to 30 people and Beaker and grooved ware pottery.

Above: Anglesey past – remains of a 12th-century house at Capel Lligwy

Left: Several centuries further back – some dwellings in the 4th-century village of Din Lligwy are still partially standing

85 Moelfre and the Ancient Village

Enjoy bracing sea air and stirring coastal views before visiting Celtic remains on Anglesey

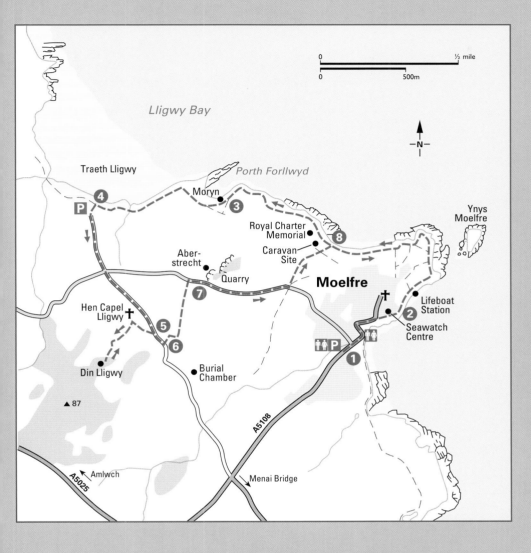

Distance 5 miles (8km)

Minimum Time 3hrs

Ascent/Gradient 541ft (165m) ▲▲▲

Level of Difficulty ●●●

Paths Well-defined coastal and field paths, 5 stiles

Landscape Sea cliffs and coastal pasture

Suggested Map OS Explorer 263 Anglesey East

Start/Finish Grid reference: SH 511862

Dog Friendliness Can be off lead on coastal path

Parking Car park at entrance to village

Public Toilets In car park and by harbour

1 From the car park, follow the main road (A5108) down to the shore. The road winds behind the bay before swinging left. Leave the road at that point for a shoreline path on the right.

2 Pass the Seawatch Centre and the lifeboat station and ignore the footpath signs pointing inland. Instead follow a clear coast path that provides fine views across to the island of Ynys Moelfre. After passing to the right of some terraced cottages and going through a couple of kissing gates, the path crosses a small caravan site. It then goes through another kissing gate and climbs past the Royal Charter memorial.

3 Swinging left into Porth Forllwyd, the path ends beside a cottage, Moryn. Follow a track to a gate, turning before it along a fenced path into a field. Keep ahead to rejoin the coast, which turns in above the large bay of Traeth Lligwy.

4 On reaching the beach car park, turn left along the narrow lane before going straight ahead at the next crossroads.

5 Take the next path on the right, signposted to Din Lligwy ancient village. First, turn half right across the field to see the old chapel. Then bear left across two fields and into a wood concealing Din Lligwy. Return to the lane and turn right along it.

6 Leave after 50yds (46m) over a ladder stile on the left. Follow the dog-legging boundary right to a stile, over which turn left, walking downfield to emerge by a roadside quarry at Aber-strecht.

7 Follow the lane right to the edge of the village and go left on a waymarked track. Around the first bend, swing left through a gate, keeping right at a fork to walk through the caravan site again.

8 Follow the shoreline path retracing the outward route back to the car park at the start.

Scotland

Scotland

A tour of Scotland offers the chance to see Britain's landscape on a grand scale – all the island's highest mountains lie north of the English-Scottish border, along with a rugged, thrillingly beautiful coastline and vast tracts of wilderness.

Scotland displays many faces, even on first acquaintance: the rolling hills of the Southern Uplands, the industrial urban belt between the Clyde and the Forth, then the Highlands in all their splendour, breaking up west and north into a succession of headlands and sea lochs, islands and stacks. There is a greater degree of freedom to roam than elsewhere, and a distinct culture and tradition evident wherever you travel. For this is a country with a history, law and culture all its own, but one whose affairs have been inextricably linked over

centuries with those of Ireland and England – to say nothing of a profound Nordic influence.

Waves of invaders from Europe were slow to penetrate the last rugged recesses of Scotland, but once in place would turn and defend hills and glens with great ferocity. We know little of the origins of the ancient British tribe of the Picts, but we do know that they had a well-established social structure and capital at Kilmartin in Argyll on the west coast, and left evidence of military success at Abelemno in Angus on the east coast, where carved

Right: Standing stones at Kilmartin in Argyll

Below: Looking west from close to the summit of Cairn Gorm mountain towards Cairn Toul

Previous pages: Reflective waters at Loch Long

stones are believed to celebrate victories of the 6th-century Pictish king Bridei (see Walk 97).

Irish Influence – and Centuries of War

Two men, both from Donegal in Ireland, helped to shape Scotland's early culture: St Colomba, who in the 6th century settled on Iona and sent his followers to preach Christianity on the mainland, and Somerled, the 12th-century ruler of the Hebrides and Isle of Man, who was known as 'King of the Isles' and was the progenitor of the great clan MacDonald. Many others made their mark – including St Ninian, who in the 4th century brought Christianity into Scotland by way of Whithorn in the southwest of the country, and the successive English kings who waged war against the Scots, from the time of Edward I (reigned 1272–1307) right through to the 18th century.

Almost wherever you look, you can find evidence of strife. Largs (1263), Bannockburn (1314), Stirling Bridge (1297) and Culloden (1746)

Above: The National Monument on Calton Hill, Edinburgh

Below: Salisbury Crags, seen from the foot of Arthur's Seat just outside Edinburgh

these centuries of conflict there were many shameful episodes, some of which are painfully seared into folk memory. These include the Massacre of Glen Coe (see Walk 96), and the brutal Highland Clearances of the 19th century, in which thousands were evicted from the land and forced into migration, either to the industrial south or further afield, to the USA and Canada.

Highland Adventures

Yet there were also many great and stirring adventures. Legends developed around the exploits of cattle rustlers in the Highland clans, tales of bravery and recklessness that are written in the landscape. At the 'Corrie of Booty' (see Walk 96) the MacDonalds hid their stolen cattle, while at the Devil's Beef Tub (see Walk 89) the Johnstone Clan concealed their purloined animals. The Devil's Beef Tub, also known as the Corrie of Annan, also served to hide Covenanters in the 17th century.

Around Balquhidder you can investigate the tale of notorious Highland outlaw Rob Roy MacGregor, hero of Sir Walter Scott's 1817 novel *Rob Roy*, and even track down his burial place (see Walk 95). On the Rothiemurcus Estate near Aviemore in the Highlands, the island castle of Loch an Eilein stood close to a cattle-rustling route – known as 'Robbers' Way' – through the Rothiemurcius Forest used by Rob Roy and others (see Walk 100). The castle was the scene of brutal conflict between clans.

Birds and Beauty

The walk at Loch an Eilein is of great interest to birdwatchers as well to those with a taste for Highland history. In the Rothiemurcus Forest, an ancient Caledonian pine forest that is a mere remnant of a much more widespread wildwood, you may see birds such as the crested tit and the Scottish crossbill, unique to Scotland. Many of the walks in this section take you close to or though places where unusual species cling to a precarious

were all great and decisive battles. Conflict arose with the English again and again over the border between the countries, or as English kings sought to impose their sovereignty – and also repeatedly over religion. In the 17th century the Covenanters defied the authority of King Charles II to appoint bishops and ministers in the Scottish kirk and affirmed in a covenant initially signed in Greyfriars churchyard, Edinburgh, in 1638 their right to maintain their own forms of church government.

There are many sobering but fascinating reminders of these conflicts. At Wigtown (see Walk 86) you can walk in the footsteps of two women Covenanters martyred by government troops. On the Pentland Hills near Edinburgh (see Walk 91) you will be near the site on which a Covenanter army was defeated by Scottish royalist general General Tam Dalyell of the Binns in the Battle of Rullion Cross in 1666.

Dalyell won himself the nickname 'Bloody Tam' for the ferocity of his reprisals, and throughout

existence in safe havens. At Portree Bay (see Walk 101), you have a wonderful opportunity to see the white-tailed eagle, reintroduced to western Scotland and the Highlands in the 1970s and 1980s after becoming extinct in Scotland in the early 20th century. If you visit Rogie Falls (see Walk 102) between July and September, you may see a wild salmon defy the force of the river as it leaps upstream to return to the place of its birth. On salt marshes near the extraordinary triangular castle of Caerlaverock (see Walk 87), you have the chance to visit a splendid nature reserve where you can see whooper swans and barnacle geese in winter.

Wherever you go it pays to treat the landscape with respect: the weather can be extreme on the high ground, so use due caution. You can wander into the wilderness near Loch Kernsary in the Highland region (see Walk 103), but you need to know when it's time to turn back. If the really high mountains look daunting, there are plenty of smaller hills you can climb. It is worth asking the question 'What is wilderness, anyway?' because even in the apparent wilds of Scotland most the landscape is man-managed. Sheep are grazed in many places, continually nipping back any tree seedlings that take root, leaving hills looking quite bare. Deer roam huge upland estates and are subject to annual shoots and culls. Even extensive heather moorland may be strictly managed for grouse shooting with 'vermin' being controlled and strip burning taking place in rotation to create an environment that favours the needs of the birds.

There are many old tracks you can follow. The first rough highways through the glens and high passes were trodden by drovers, and the first attempt to establish a real road network came under the auspices of General Wade after the 1745 Jacobite Rebellion. Scotland soon developed a thriving tourism: no doubt its appeal was developed by the enthusiastic writings of native Scotsmen and visitors alike.

Literary Greats

This is a country with a great literary tradition, from ancient bards through Robert Burns and Sir Walter Scott (Walk 95) to Alasdair Gray or Alan Warner in the contemporary era. In Edinburgh a delightful walk in the New Town (Walk 93) celebrates the memory of writers with connections to that city, authors as diverse as the poet Shelley and Sherlock Holmes creator Sir Arthur Conan Doyle, or First World War poet Wilfred Owen.

Scotland is a land of conflicts and contrasts, of lovely scenery and loveless battlefields. Romantic-looking castles sit uneasily with a history of appalling bloodshed. Craggy peaks look welcoming one moment, then threatening when the weather takes a turn for the worse. This endless variation is an essential part of Scotland's fascination.

Best of the Rest

Rosslyn Chapel
This 15th-century chapel near the village of Roslin in Midlothian will be well known to fans of Dan Brown's best-selling novel *The Da Vinci Code* and was a location in the 2006 movie starring Tom Hanks and Audrey Tautou. The chapel, founded by Sir William St Clair 1st Earl of Caithness in 1456 as a private place of worship, has many remarkable features including the ornately carved Apprentice Pillar, reputedly created by an apprentice while his master was away and so beautiful that upon his return the master killed the young man in a moment of jealous rage, and more than 100 intriguing carvings of the Green Man, a pagan symbol associated with rebirth and fertility. Various traditions suggest that the chapel's sealed vault contains treasure belonging to the medieval military order of the Knights Templar, perhaps the mummified head of Jesus Christ or even the mysterious Holy Grail (the cup used by Christ in the Last Supper with his disciples before the crucifixion; see Walk 92).

Ailsa Craig
Known in Gaelic as *Creag Ealasaid*, this island in the Firth of Clyde was a haven for Roman Catholics during the years of religious violence in the Reformation. In 1597 one Catholic even hoped to use it as a staging point for a Spanish invasion of Scotland intending to re-establish the Catholic faith there. Today it hosts a bird sanctuary where you will find puffins and gannets; it also is the premier source of the granite used in curling stones. Fine views of the crag are had throughout Walk 88.

Alexander Thomson and Victorian Glasgow
Born in Stirlingshire, Alexander 'Greek' Thomson designed and built a series of elegant classical buildings and terraces in Glasgow during the second half of the 20th century. Those to be seen on Walk 90 include his terrace at Moray Place (1858), St Vincent Greek Terrace (1859), the Great Western Terrace (1869) and the Egyptian Halls (1871–3). He was an influence both on Charles Rennie Mackintosh and the American architect Frank Lloyd Wright and has been recognised as a pioneer in theories of sustainable architecture.

Old Aberdeen
Aberdeen on Scotland's North Sea coast was the country's top fishing port in 1933, based on the success of local steam-powered trawlers. A fascinating ramble around the old port (see Walk 99) takes in the beach, harbour area and Maritime Museum and gives an insight into life as it was lived there before North Sea oil financed a major boom and transformed the city, attracting upwards of 200 companies and thousands of new residents.

Pass of Ryvoan
Running between Glen More and Nethybridge, the Pass of Ryvoan offers wonderful views of the ancient pine woods of Abernethy Forest and the Cairngorm Mountains. The route (Walk 98) has added interest because it was part of the Thieves' Road used by the cattle rustlers of the Highland clans, and also passes Lochan Uaine ('Green Loch') which, according to tradition, acquired this colour because the Highland fairies used its waters to wash their clothes, which were green.

Kilmartin Glen
Kilmartin Glen in Argyll is in a region frequented by some of Scotland's earliest peoples. There is evidence here of activity by hunter-gatherers as early as 5000 BC, and within 6 miles (9.7km) of the village of Kilmartin there are no fewer than 350 ancient monuments. The site (Walk 94) is best known for its Bronze Age cemetery, an alignment of five burial cairns. There is also a henge monument and an arrangement of standing stones. In the village of Kilmartin is a fine church, with remarkable carved medieval gravestones in its cemetery and two justly celebrated stone crosses.

86 On the Trail of the Wigtown Martyrs

In the Machars peninsula of Galloway, south-western Scotland, this instructive walk visits the memorial to two women drowned at the stake for their religion

On 11 May, 1685, two Wigtown women were dragged out on to the salt marshes near the town and tied to stakes. Eighteen-year-old Margaret Wilson and her companion, Margaret McLaughlan, aged 63, had been sentenced to death for their religious beliefs.

This was during that period in Scots history known as the 'Killing Times' when the Covenanters were persecuted for their beliefs. They were called Covenanters after a petition signed in Greyfriars churchyard in Edinburgh, in 1638, and thereafter in churches throughout the country. The Covenant reaffirmed the belief of Scottish Presbyterians that there was a special relationship between God, as head of the Church, and the people. This ran contrary to the belief of the Stuart monarchy in the divine right of kings. Charles II sought to control the Church by appointing Episcopalian bishops and ministers. Presbyterian ministers were ousted from their churches, but simply took to the hills with their congregations and held open-air services called conventicles. Troops patrolled the hills and moors and, if they came across these illegal meetings, broke them up by taking some people prisoner and killing others on the spot.

Margaret Wilson and Margaret McLaughlan were two Wigtownshire Covenanters who were tried in the tollbooth at Wigtown for rebellion and taking part in several battles against the Crown.

Found guilty, they were sentenced to death by drowning and taken to the tidal Bladnoch River.

Fearless in the Face of Death

When they reached the execution site, the soldiers placed the older woman's stake further out in the estuary so that she would die first and thus terrify her younger companion into swearing an oath to the king. But this was to no avail.

While Margaret McLaughlan drowned the younger woman sang the 25th Psalm and then began to pray aloud. The water covered her but the soldiers pulled her up, revived her and asked her if she would pray for the king. A friend urged her to say 'God save the king', but all she said was 'God save him if he will, for it is his salvation I desire.' On hearing this, her relatives begged the commanding officer to release her. He asked her to swear the oath or be returned to the water. She refused saying 'I will not, I am one of Christ's children, let me go.' But they would not let her go and she was again thrust under the water until she died.

Below: Wigtown Bay

Bottom left: Looking over Wigtown from Windyhill

Bottom right: The Martyrs' Stake

86 On the Trail of the Wigtown Martyrs

Stand where two Scottish women lost their lives for defying an English king

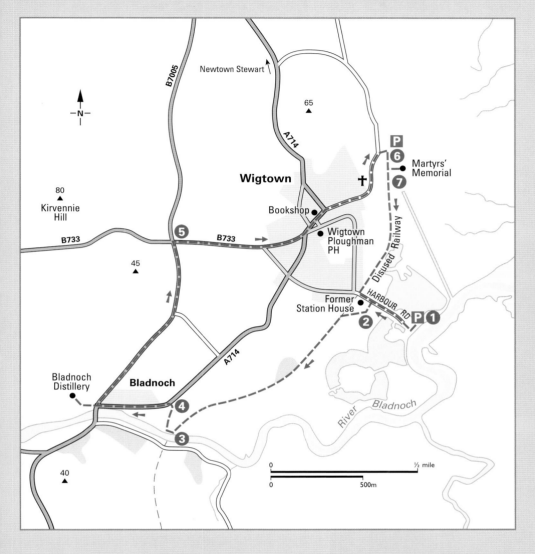

Distance 4 miles (6.4km)

Minimum Time 3hrs

Ascent/Gradient 98ft (30m) ▲▲▲

Level of Difficulty ●●●

Paths Roads, old railway tracks and pavements

Landscape River estuary, pasture and woodland

Suggested Map OS Explorer 311 Wigtown, Whithorn & The Machars

Start/Finish Grid reference: NX 439547

Dog Friendliness Keep on lead near livestock

Parking At Wigtown harbour

Public Toilets None on walk

1 Leave the car park, turn right and then head uphill on a narrow country lane called Harbour Road. The house situated on the left near the top of the road was the former station house for Wigtown. Just before it you will see a farm gate on the left. Go through the gate and on to a farm track.

2 Follow the track to the point where it goes through another gate then veer right and climb up the old railway embankment. This has a good grassy surface along its entire length. Proceed along the length of the embankment.

3 A wall across the track will stop you at the point where the former railway bridge carried the track across the River Bladnoch. Turn right and go down the side of the embankment and cross a gate into a field. Veer right and head across the field to the far corner then go through a gate on to the main road.

4 Turn left and walk through the hamlet of Bladnoch. At the junction by a roundabout, cross the road to enter the Bladnoch Distillery car park. After visiting the distillery head back out of the car park and turn left at the roundabout. Continue along this road (the B7005) for approximately 1 mile (1.6km) until you get to a crossroads.

5 Turn right on to the B733 road and walk along it to reach Wigtown. When you reach the centre of the town bear left around the square and head towards the large and impressive former county buildings. Pass them on your right, then carry on past the church and war memorial on your left and continue

downhill. Eventually turn right into the car park for the Martyrs' Memorial.

6 Walk through the car park and then turn right and head along the path leading to the Martyrs' Memorial. Turn left and walk out over the sands on a specially constructed wooden causeway to reach the poignant memorial erected on the spot where the two women were drowned.

7 Return to the path and turn left. Go through a kissing gate then another gate, slightly below the level you are walking on and to the left. At the end of the path go through another gate in front of the station house, turn left on to Harbour Road to the car park.

87 Caerlaverock Castle and the Solway Merses

An invigorating tramp across the wide flatlands of the Solway merse, or salt marsh, leads to the curious triangular fortress known as 'the Castle of the Lark'

Against the impressive backdrop of Criffel, guarded by the wide waters of the Solway Firth, the salt marshes and the impressive medieval castle of Caerlaverock, this out-of-the-way corner of Scotland is a haven for wildlife and a treasure trove of history. Caerlaverock, the Castle of the Lark, was once the main gatekeeper to south-

Right: Barnacle geese over the Caerlaverock Wildlife and Wetlands Trust Reserve

Below: Caerlaverock Castle is surrounded by a moat as well as by salt marshes

west Scotland. Protected by mudflats and the shifting channels of the sea, it was vulnerable only from the landward side. From the siege of Caerlaverock by Edward I in 1300 through to the 17th century it was continually beseiged, levelled and rebuilt. Its garrison last surrendered in 1640. Partially demolished, it crumbled to an ivy-covered ruin until restoration began in the mid-20th century. Within its ruined walls today, conservators continue their work on one of the finest Renaissance residences in Scotland.

In Reserve

Conservation work of a different kind takes place on the merse (salt marsh) that bounds the Solway coast. Here Scottish Natural Heritage (SNH), the Wildfowl and Wetlands Trust (WWT) and the Caerlaverock Estate work at preserving the delicate balance that allows farming and wild fowling to exist alongside a National Nature Reserve.

The desolate open spaces echo in winter to the cry of wild geese, in summer to that of oystercatchers or herons and in spring to the mating chorus of the natterjack toad. But it wasn't always so. Wildfowling had reduced the goose population to a few hundred by 1957, when local landowner the Duke of Norfolk agreed to divide the merse into an area for controlled shooting and a wildlife sanctuary, now the National Nature Reserve. In 1970 the duke offered the naturalist Sir Peter Scott a lease of Eastpark Farm for the WWT.

Here, every October, the Spitsbergen population of barnacle geese fly in from Norway to their winter quarters along the merse. The birds can be seen from hides along roads shielded with high hedges to minimise disturbance to wildlife. Whooper swans overwinter here too, along with the pink-footed goose, pintail, scaup, oystercatcher, knot, bar-tailed godwit, curlew and redshank.

Staff at Eastpark organise a variety of events to help visitors appreciate the reserve, including birding, natterjack toad and bat spotting, and pond dipping. As part of the conservation process, wildfowling is permitted in winter. Barnacle geese are protected but other species are fair game. The wildfowlers are experts at recognition and SNH wardens ensure fair play.

87 Caerlaverock Castle and the Solway Merses

See seasonal birds in the reserve – and bring a picnic to eat at the castle

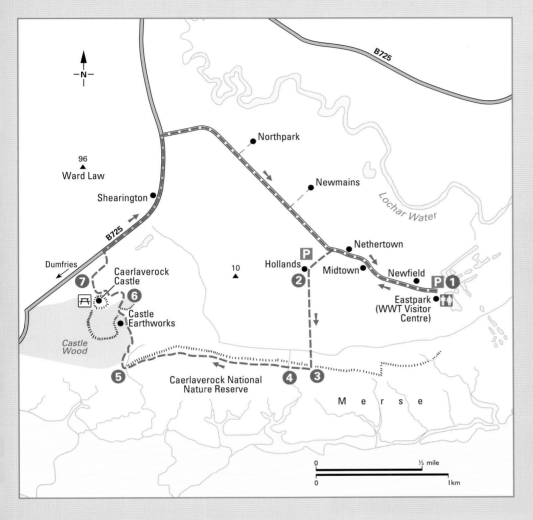

Distance 5.25 miles (8.4km)

Minimum Time 2hrs 30min

Ascent/Gradient 82ft (25m) ▲▲▲

Level of Difficulty ●●●

Paths Country lanes, farm tracks and salt marsh, 1 stile

Landscape Pastures, salt marsh, riverside and hills

Suggested Map OS Explorer 314 Solway Firth

Start/Finish Grid reference: NY 051656

Dog Friendliness Keep on lead while on reserve

Parking Car park at Wildfowl and Wetlands Trust Reserve

Public Toilets At Wildfowl and Wetlands Trust Reserve

1 Exit the car park and turn right on to a farm road. Follow this past the farms of Newfield and Midtown, then turn left and go past a bungalow and some houses. Just before the farm of Hollands there is a waymarker pointing to a car park on the right, and straight ahead for walks. Go straight ahead and continue to the farm steading, then turn left.

2 Go through a gate and on to a farm track. This stretches away into the distance and has high hedges on both sides. Continue along this track between the hedges and on, over an overgrown section, until you reach the end, then turn right when you reach the signpost indicating 'Caerlaverock'.

3 A sign here informs visitors that regulated wildfowling (shooting) takes place between 1 September to 20 February. Follow the rough track through the grass along the edge of the merse in the direction of the arrow on the footpath waymarker post. The path can be very boggy at all times and the grass will be high in the summer.

4 The path through the nature reserve varies from faint to non-existent; Wellington boots are recommended for all. It splits at several points and then meanders back and forth, but all the lines of the path rejoin and you'll end up at the same place whichever one you decide to take.

5 Eventually some cottages can be seen in the field to the right. Bear right, going through a gate and into the field. Walk to the left around the field perimeter, past some cottages, then take a left turn through a gate to emerge on to a farm track, passing a sign for 'Caerlaverock Castle' and going into the castle grounds.

6 Follow the road past the old castle, which has been excavated and has information boards to explain the ruins, and go through a wood with nature trail information boards to Caerlaverock Castle. There is a children's playground, a siege machine and picnic tables around the ramparts of the castle.

7 At the far end go through an arch and continue to the T-junction with a country lane. Turn right and continue for about a mile (1.6km), then turn right on to another lane signposted 'Wildfowl and Wetlands Reserve'. Continue on this road past the farms of Northpark, Newmains and Nethertown and then return to the car park at Eastpark.

88 Byne Hill and the Island of Ailsa Craig

As you walk up and around Byne Hill, enjoy views across the Firth of Clyde and to Aisla Craig, the island source of the granite used in the world's curling stones

Above: The island is uninhabited by humans – but home to gannets and puffins

Above right: Ailsa Craig is roughly 10 miles (16km) out to sea from the South Ayrshire coast

The lone sentinel of Ailsa Craig in the Firth of Clyde, which dominates the seaward views on this walk, is the plug of a volcano, extinct since prehistoric times. First mentioned in the charters of the Abbey of Crossraguel in 1404 as the Insula de Ailsay, the island was part of that estate until the Reformation in 1560. Since then it has belonged to the Cassillis family, and has given its name to the senior family member, the Marquis of Ailsa. To generations of immigrant Irish it was known simply as 'Paddy's Milestone' because it is located approximately half-way between Belfast and Glasgow. But Ailsa Craig's main claim to fame is as the source of granite used in the world's supply of curling stones: the fine micro-granite from Ailsa Craig has been used to make curling stones since the beginning of the 19th century.

On the island there are several kinds of granite, Common Ailsa, Blue Hone and Red Hone. All three have been used in curling stone manufacture but the Blue Hone, a finer grained variety, produced the best running surface. Quarrying stopped in 1971 and Welsh granite was substituted. But each stone still had an 'Ailsert' – a small coaster of Ailsa Craig Blue Hone granite, inserted in the base.

Summer Quarrying

Originally quarrying on the island was carried out by the Girvan family, who had a lease from the Marquis of Ailsa. They lived in a cottage on the island during the summer months, blasting and extracting the rock for transport back to Girvan harbour and onwards to the curling stone factory in Mauchline. A small railway line was built to carry the rocks to the island pier for loading on to small fishing boats. During the summer Ailsa Craig was a busy place. As well as the resident lighthouse keepers, the Girvan family and their workforce, there was a constant stream of day-trippers on cruises from Girvan harbour who could climb to the small ruined castle, take a tour of the lighthouse and wander around the island. Mrs Girvan supplied afternoon teas in a small café. By the 1950s the Girvans had given up quarrying, shut the café and removed their sheep and goats.

Kays of Mauchline, the world's only manufacturer of curling stones, started using Welsh Trevor granite to produce their stones with the Ailsert to preserve the smooth running surface. However, in the summer of 2002, Kays removed some 1,500 tons of granite boulders from the old quarries on the island. No blasting or quarrying took place. They simply collected what was already there to avoid disturbing the island's population of seabirds. Now they will be able to make curling stones entirely from Ailsa Craig granite again.

88 Byne Hill and the Island of Ailsa Craig

Climb Byne Hill for one of the finest views over the Firth of Clyde to be had anywhere

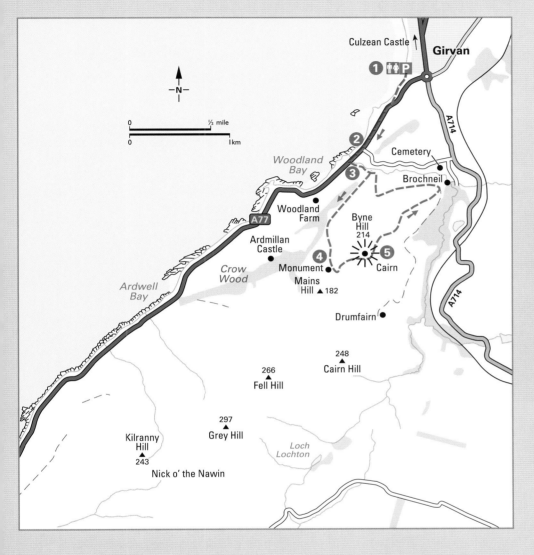

Distance 3.75 miles (6km)

Minimum Time 3hrs

Ascent/Gradient 571ft (174m) ▲▲▲

Level of Difficulty ●●●

Paths Farm roads, dirt tracks and open hillside, 1 stile

Landscape Hill, pasture, woodland and seaside

Suggested Map OS Explorer 317 Ballantrae, Barr & Barrhill

Startf/Finish Grid reference: NX 187955

Dog Friendliness Keep on lead, this is sheep country

Parking Ainslie Park car park

Public Toilets At the car park

1 From the car park head south along a pavement alongside the A77. Pass a nursing home on the right, then come to a lane on the left past former Shalloch mill.

2 The pavement disappears so continue along the verge for 200yds (183m). Just before it reappears cross a bridge, then turn left and cross the road.

3 Go on to a farm track that runs alongside a burn. Go over a metal gate and turn right. Follow this newly created road, which runs behind Woodland Farm and Ardmillan Castle Holiday Park. There are several metal gates to go through along the way. Please take careful notice of these – ensure that you always close them behind you while leaving open any that are not closed.

4 Continue on to the saddle between Mains Hill on your right-hand side and Byne Hill on your left, passing the remains of a monument that was erected to the memory of Archibald C B Craufurd of Ardmillan Estate. As the monument is in poor repair keep a safe distance from it. There used to be a plaque on the front, but some years ago this was removed and dumped in the woods below. Turn left through a gap in the wall and head up the side of Byne Hill to reach a prominent commemorative cairn at the summit. From this vantage point there is one of the finest views available of the Firth of Clyde. On a clear day you can see the Antrim coast of Northern Ireland, the island of Arran and the Mull of Kintyre to the north and west, and, about 8 miles (12.9km) out in the sea, the distinctive outline of Ailsa Craig.

5 With the cairn at your back, walk straight ahead. Cross a saddle between the summit and the lower part of the hill, keeping at first to the higher ground then towards the north side of the hill. Descend very carefully and at the bottom, turn left and follow the wall. Continue until you pass a gate then turn right over a stile and cross the field to then go over the gate on to the farm road at Point 3. From here retrace your steps to the start.

89 A 'Beefy' Devil of a Walk in Moffat

There are many points of historical interest on this hearty walk around the intriguingly named valley of the Devil's Beef Tub near the small town of Moffat

Above: Turbulent in the past, perhaps, but serene in the present – the Devil's Beef Tub

Below right: Memorial to John Hunter, a Covenanter shot dead at the Tub by Colonel Douglas's Dragoons in 1685

Dark, forbidding and dramatic (Sir Walter Scott once described it as a 'black, blackguard-looking abyss of a hole'), the hollow known as the Devil's Beef Tub has a history as turbulent as its name suggests. Over the years this deep, natural bowl has been used as a hiding place by thieves, formed a refuge for the persecuted and witnessed feats of daring – and even murder. Once known as the Corrie of Annan, it gained the name 'the Devil's Beef Tub' in the 16th century when it was frequently used by the Johnstone clan, a local reiving (rustling) family, to hide stolen cattle after a raid. In reference to this it was also sometimes sardonically referred to as 'the Marquis of Annandale's Beef Stand'.

In the Killing Times

The Tub was not only useful for sheltering stolen animals, however – it was also used as a hideout by persecuted Covenanters during Charles II's so-called 'Killing Times'. The origins of the covenanting movement went back to the time when bishops were imposed on the Church of Scotland by James VI; years later his son, Charles I tried to interfere further in Scottish ecclesiastical affairs. This provoked a riot in Edinburgh, resulting in the signing in 1638 of the National Covenant, a document affirming the authority of the Church

of Scotland over the king in all spiritual matters. Throughout the 17th century, religious fanaticism grew and Covenanters became a powerful force in Scotland. When Charles II, who had Roman Catholic sympathies, was restored to the throne he tried to suppress the movement. There were many battles, and prisoners were often brutally treated. Finding themselves outlawed, some ministers of the Church began holding illegal services, known as 'conventicles', in the open air. Persecution only fuelled resistance and during 1684–87 hundreds of people were slaughtered by officers of the Crown. The most notorious of these was Graham of Claverhouse, later Viscount Dundee. There's a reminder of these violent times near the car park at the Devil's Beef Tub, where you can see a stone dedicated to John Hunter, a Covenanter who was shot on the hills here in 1685.

This violent period in history came to an end when James II's son-in-law, William of Orange, came to the throne in 1689 – but was soon replaced in the following century by the violence of the Jacobite Rebellion. In 1746 a prisoner from the Battle of Culloden, which had brought the rebellion to an end the previous year, was being marched through this countryside to Carlisle for trial. He escaped his guards by leaping into the Devil's Beef Tub and disappearing in the swirling mist.

89 A 'Beefy' Devil of a Walk in Moffat

Tour a cattle-rustlers' hideout that was later a natural sanctuary for religious dissenters

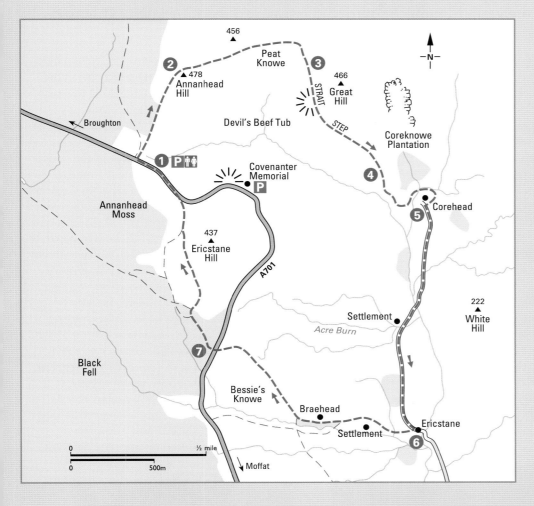

Distance 4.5 miles (7.2km)

Minimum Time 2hrs

Ascent/Gradient 1,076ft (328m) ▲▲▲

Level of Difficulty ●●●

Paths Farm tracks, small paths; narrow path across steep Beef Tub slope

Landscape Dramatic Beef Tub hollow and views of the Borderlands

Suggested Map OS Explorer 330 Moffat & St Mary's Loch

Start/Finish Grid reference: NT 057128

Dog Friendliness Keep on lead when passing sheep and cattle

Parking Lay-by just south of forest gateway

Public Toilets Lay-by just south of forest gateway

Warning Bull with cows occasionally at Point 4

1 Walk up the A701 to the forest gateway on the right. Don't take the wide gravel track, but a wooden gate on the right-hand side, to a small path to the left of a fence. Climb rails at a fence end, and head up the grassy slope of Annanhead Hill, keeping to the right of the plantation area to the trig point on the summit.

2 The small path continues around the flank of Peat Knowe, keeping the wall and fence to your left. Follow the path down the grassy slope of Annanhead Hill, keeping to the head of a gully, where your path meets the wall. Walk to the other side of the gully.

3 Past the gully head, turn right on a small path that runs just above, and to the left of, the grassy gully. As the slope drops away steeply, the path, called Strait Step, bends left and contours on a level line across the steep slope, below some small craggy outcrops. As

the slope eases, the path slants down through bracken, heading towards the Coreknowe plantation at the valley end. Just before the plantation, you'll reach a metal gate leading into a field.

4 A bull occasionally grazes in this field, so if you need to avoid him, pass along above the field and climb an awkward fence into the plantation. Slant down to the right, under the trees, as far as a gate into the field with the tiny footbridge mentioned below. Otherwise, go through the grey gate and down along beside a grassy bank. Turn left on a rough track that leads to the bottom corner of the plantation. The track reaches a gate above a red-brick house. Through the gate, following signs for 'Moffat', head out into the field to a tiny footbridge, then bear right to pass to the left of the white buildings of Corehead farm. A fence on the right leads to a gate on to the farm's access track.

5 Follow the farm road along the bottom of the valley. The small area of undulating land visible on the right is the remains of an ancient settlement.

6 After a cattle grid, at the start of the buildings, turn up right through a gate signed 'footpath'. A stony track leads past a house and through a gate. Turn right, following the track as it runs above a stone wall. Eventually you'll reach the main A701. Cross over – taking care, because the road is often busy – on to a rough track opposite.

7 The route passes over Ericstane Hill. Bear right and follow the track as it runs north round the far side of the hill. On open hill, the track is indistinct, deep ruts half-hidden under rushes. Pass through a slight col to the left of the hill summit, to rejoin the A701. Turn right here to visit the Covenanter memorial, or turn left to return to the start of the walk.

90 Alexander 'Greek' Thomson

An instructive cultural tour concentrates on highlights of Victorian Glasgow, particularly the work of highly regarded classical architect Alexander Thomson

More than any other architect Alexander Thomson was responsible for the shaping of Glasgow with his innovative use and interpretation of classical Greek designs. Born in 1817, in the Stirlingshire village of Balfron, he moved to Glasgow to live with an older brother. He was apprenticed to an architect and began studying the plans, drawings and engravings of classical architecture. This influence dominated his later style and earned him the nickname 'Greek' Thomson although he never travelled abroad.

Villas to Tenements

The range of his buildings was extraordinary, from churches to villas, warehouses, tenements and even a set of steps. Much of his work was destroyed by German bombing during the Second World War and even more disappeared in the relentless modernisation of Glasgow during the 1960s and 1970s. However, those buildings that have survived provide a fine cross-section of his work. His one remaining church (1857–9) on St Vincent Street is a remarkable building with Grecian columns and an imposing tower, built on the side of Blythswood Hill. Near by, in Union Street, the curiously named Egyptian Halls (1871–3) started life as an early shopping centre or bazaar. In the West End, near the Botanic Gardens, Thomson created the Great Western Terrace (1869), the 'grandest terrace in Glasgow'. Another example of his terraces, Moray Place (1858), is where Thomson took up permanent residence. Most of the houses he designed are in private ownership, but one exception is Holmwood House (1858) in Cathcart, 4.5 miles (7.2km) from the city centre, now owned by the National Trust for Scotland. Built for a wealthy paper manufacturer, it is an asymmetrical villa with a bay window, which looks like a Greek temple attached to the front of the building.

Although he gained prominence during his lifetime and had a major influence on later architects such as Charles Rennie Mackintosh and Frank Lloyd Wright, Thomson is little known today. Records of his work are limited to a few drawings held in Glasgow's Mitchell Library. The Alexander Thomson Society, established with its headquarters in his former home in Moray Place, has campaigned to preserve his remaining 24 buildings within the city and Thomson is beginning to regain the recognition he deserves.

Right: The walk passes Glasgow School of Art, designed by Charles Rennie Mackintosh, who was influenced by Thomson

Far right above: Holmwood House is hailed by many as 'Greek' Thomson's masterpiece

Far right below: Classical Greek motifs in Thomson's St Vincent Street Church

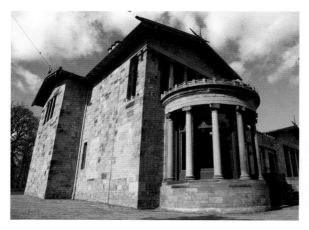

90 Alexander 'Greek' Thomson

Discover the beauties of a Victorian city and the architect who shaped it

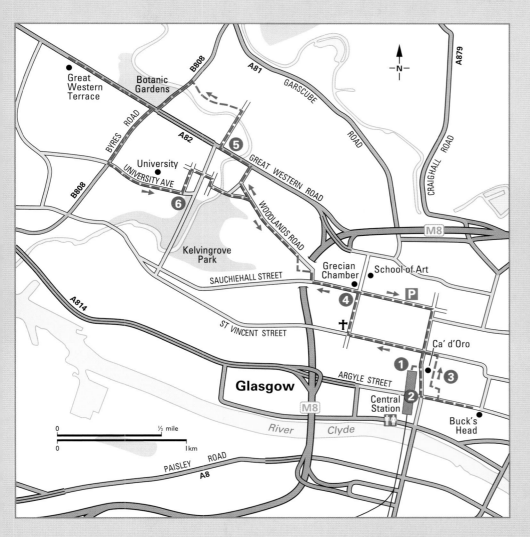

Distance 6.5 miles (10.4km)

Minimum Time 3hrs 30min

Ascent/Gradient 98ft (30m) ▲▲▲

Level of Difficulty ●●●

Paths Pavements

Landscape City streets

Suggested Map OS Explorer 342 Glasgow; AA Street by Street Glasgow

Start/Finish Grid reference: NS 587653

Dog Friendliness Not great walk for dogs

Parking Sauchiehall Street multi-storey or on-street parking

Public Toilets At Central Station

1 Exit Central Station and turn right. At the junction with Union Street turn right. The building on the opposite corner is the Ca' d'Oro building, a late 19th-century Italianate warehouse by John Honeyman, based on the Golden House in Venice. The upper storeys are made of cast iron. A little way down Union Street from here on the same side as the Ca' d'Oro is Thomson's Egyptian Halls, sadly in need of some renovation.

2 Cross over then head down Union Street turning left into Argyle Street at the next junction. Cross Argyle Street, then walk to the junction with Dunlop Street, where you will find the Buck's Head building named after an inn that once stood on this spot. Cross Argyle Street again, retrace your steps, turning right into Buchanan Street. Turn left into Mitchell Lane, pass the Lighthouse, then turn right.

3 Walk up Mitchell Street, continue along West Nile Street then turn left into St Vincent Street. Continue on this for just under 0.5 mile (800m), going uphill to the junction with Pitt Street. You are now standing in front of Alexander 'Greek' Thomson's St Vincent Street Church, one of his greatest achievements. Cross St Vincent Street here then head up Pitt Street to Sauchiehall Street.

4 On the opposite corner is Thomson's Grecian Chamber (1865) and to the right along Scott Street is Rennie Mackintosh's Glasgow School of Art. From the front of the Grecian Chamber turn left, head down Sauchiehall Street to Charing Cross, then take the pedestrian bridge over the motorway to Woodlands Road. Go along this until it ends at Park Road, then turn right before turning left again into Great Western Road.

5 Go right on Belmont Street, left at Doune Gardens, continue along Doune Quadrant, then left again at Queen Margaret Drive. Cross the road and head down past the Botanic Gardens to turn right, back into Great Western Road. Cross the road and continue to Great Western Terrace, another Thomson masterpiece. Retrace your steps back from here to the top of Byres Road and turn right then, near the bottom, turn left into University Avenue.

6 Go left into Oakfield Avenue, pass Eton Terrace on the corner with Great George Street. Turn right into Great George Street, right at Otago Street, left into Gibson Street and keep going when it becomes Eldon Street. Turn right into Woodlands Road and return to Sauchiehall Street. Follow this to the junction with Renfield Street, turn right and head downhill to Central Station.

91 Soldiers and Saints on the Pentlands

A bracing walk in the Pentland Hills near Scotland's capital leads past the city's reservoirs through a landscape rich in stories of saints and of battles won and lost

Above: Silence and light – winter dawn over the craggy Pentlands

Right: Glencorse Reservoir, overlooked by Castlelaw Hill

Although this walk starts just beyond Edinburgh's busy city bypass, you'll soon think that you're miles from the city. The Pentlands are an uncompromising range of hills: their peaks rise 1,500ft (457m) above the sea and offer many great walks on which you can escape the crowds.

This walk takes you past several reservoirs that keep Scotland's capital supplied with water. The first you pass is Torduff Reservoir, built in 1851 and 72ft (22m) deep. Later on you come down to Glencorse Reservoir: beneath its waters are concealed the remains of the Chapel of St Katherine's (or Catherine's) in the Hopes. This dates back to the 13th century and the reign of Robert the Bruce. In the unlikely event that it's been extremely dry and the waters are shallow, you might even see it peering out above the surface. By coincidence (or perhaps not), in Mortonhall,

on the other side of the bypass, is the site of St Catherine's Balm Well, or Oily Well. Tradition has it that St Catherine travelled through here carrying holy oil from Mount Sinai. She dropped a little and the well appeared in answer to her prayers.

The oily water was said to heal skin diseases and attracted many pilgrims. The nearby suburb of Liberton is a corruption of 'leper town'. A modern explanation for the oily water was deposits of paraffin shale. James VI visited the spot in 1617 and ordered that the well be protected by a building. This was destroyed by Cromwell's troops when they camped on the hills in 1650. Cromwell, who had been helped to victory in England by the Scottish Covenanters, had fallen out with them after they decided to recognise Charles II as king.

The Pentlands are full of similar memories. The Camus Stone near Farmilehead commemorates a battle fought against the Danes. And in 1666, General Dalyell of The Binns beat a Covenanting force at Rullion Green on these hills, crushing the so-called Pentland rising.

In Praise of the Peerless Pentlands
At the start of the walk you'll pass Bonaly Tower, once the home of Lord Cockburn (1779–1854). A writer and judge, he was inspired by the glories of his surroundings to pen the words: 'Pentlands high hills raise their heather-crowned crest, Peerless Edina expands her white breast, Beauty and grandeur are blent in the scene, Bonnie Bonally lies smiling between.'

91 Soldiers and Saints on the Pentlands

Get away from it all in peaceful countryside just beyond the Edinburgh city bypass

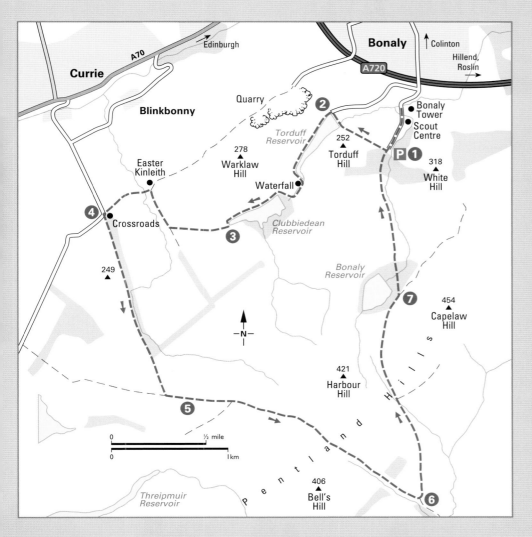

Distance 7 miles (11.3km)

Minimum Time 3hrs

Ascent/Gradient 837ft (255m) ▲▲▲

Level of Difficulty ●●●

Paths Wide firm tracks, short stretches can be muddy, 3 stiles

Landscape Reservoirs, fields and hills

Suggested Map OS Explorer 344 Pentland Hills

Start/Finish Grid reference: NT 212679

Dog Friendliness Good, but beware of ground-nesting birds

Parking Car park at end of Bonaly Road, beyond Bonaly Tower

Public Toilets None en route

1 From the car park, go through the gate and take the right-hand path, signposted 'Tordruff Reservoir'. Beyond a wooden gate, the path crosses over the reservoir dam to intersect with a tarmac lane.

2 Turn left along the lane, keeping Tordruff Reservoir on your left-hand side. When you reach the top of the reservoir, walk over the little bridge and follow the metalled track as it bends round to the right beside a waterfall. Walk under a line of electricity pylons, and go over a small bridge, passing a water chute on your left-hand side, and continue past Clubbiedean Reservoir.

3 Your path now bears right, with fields on either side. Pass under another line of pylons and walk to Easter Kinleith farm. Now follow the lane as it bends back to the left,

signposted 'Harlaw'. Pass a sign for 'Poets' Glen' and continue ahead, walking over a bridge and on to a large white house on the left-hand side called Crossroads.

4 Turn left. Follow the track past a conifer plantation situated on your left-hand side, then go through a small gate. Continue walking ahead until you reach an intersection of ways. Turn left through a gate, which is signposted 'Glencorse'.

5 Follow the path across the moorland and on up into the hills, carrying on until you come to a stone stile. Cross the stile and then continue in the same direction until you come to a copse of conifers standing on the right-hand side, with Glencorse Reservoir visible ahead. Turn left at this point, following the sign 'Colinton by Bonaly'.

6 Walk uphill and maintain direction to go through a metal gate. The track now narrows and takes you through the hills, until it eventually opens out. Continue in the same direction to reach a fence encircling conifers. Keep the fence on your left and walk down to a gate on the left-hand side.

7 Turn left through the gate. Walk past Bonaly Reservoir, then through a kissing gate and walk downhill, getting good views over Edinburgh as you descend. When you reach a wooden gate, go through and continue ahead, walking downhill, with trees on either side. Go through another kissing gate and follow the tarmac path ahead to return to the car park and the start of the walk.

92 The Romance of Roslin Glen

Tree-lined paths take you beside the river to a very special chapel, key location in *The Da Vinci Code* and thought by some to conceal ancient riches and secrets

Despite the splendour of its lush woodland, gurgling waters and delicate wild flowers, the most striking feature of romantic Roslin Glen is artificial rather than natural. It's Rosslyn Chapel, the exquisite little church that you meet right at the end of this walk. Founded in 1446 by Sir William St Clair, it took 40 years to build and was originally intended to be a much larger structure.

The interior of the chapel is full of intricate stone carvings, created by foreign masons commissioned by Sir William, who supervised much of the work himself. The carvings are not just rich in biblical imagery, as you might expect, but also depict masonic and pagan symbols. For instance, there are over one hundred images of the 'green man', the pagan figure that once symbolised goodness and fertility – as well as evil. There is also a depiction of a *danse macabre*, an allegorical representation of death's supremacy over mankind.

Perhaps the most stunning carving in the chapel is the Apprentice Pillar, an extraordinarily ornate piece of work. It is said that the pillar was carved by a talented apprentice while his master was away. When the master mason returned he was so jealous of the beauty and craftmanship of the work that he killed the boy in a fit of jealousy.

Rosslyn's greatest mysteries come from its associations with the Knights Templar, the medieval order of warrior monks. They were originally formed to protect pilgrims travelling to the Holy Land – and one of their founders was married to a relative of Sir William. The Templars became immensely wealthy and powerful and were eventually persecuted, being accused of immorality and even pagan idolatry. Many fled to Scotland, with help from the freemasons, taking their treasures with them.

Templar Treasures – and the Holy Grail?
The St Clairs have strong masonic links and Rosslyn Chapel is said to have been built as a memorial to the Templars. Some archaeologists think it hides many of their treasures, such as ancient scrolls from Jerusalem, jewels, perhaps the Holy Grail. Some have even speculated that under the Apprentice Pillar is buried the skull of Christ. This little chapel played an important role in Dan Brown's novel *The Da Vinci Code* (2003) and in the movie of the same name (2006), which starred Tom Hanks.

Below: Stained-glass windows in the chapel were added by the 4th Earl of Rosslyn in the 1860s

Below: The chapel may have been intended to form part of a larger design, but building stopped in 1484, when founder William St Clair died

92 The Romance of Roslin Glen

See the Scottish chapel that has become a movie star

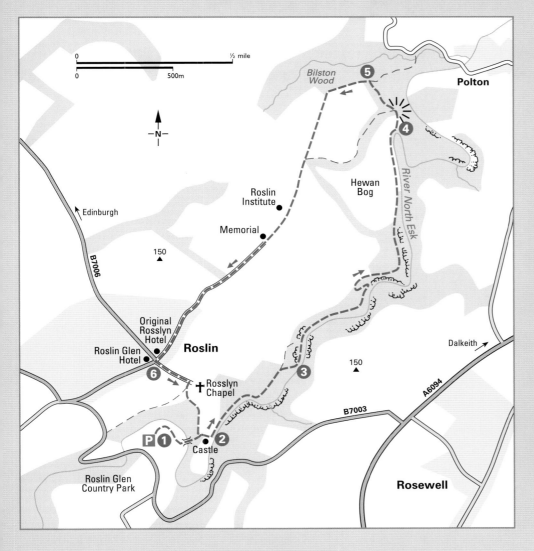

Distance 5 miles (8km)

Minimum Time 2hrs 30min

Ascent/Gradient 279ft (85m) ▲▲▲

Level of Difficulty ●●●

Paths Generally good, but can be muddy and slippery

Landscape Woodland and fields, short sections of road

Suggested Map OS Explorer 344 Pentland Hills

Start/Finish Grid reference: NT 272627

Dog Friendliness Can mostly run free, steps and climbs might not suit some

Parking Roslin Glen Country Park car park

Public Toilets None en route; nearest at Rosslyn Chapel Visitor Centre

1 From the country park car park, walk north-east with the sound of the river through the trees to your left. Go up the metal stairs, cross the footbridge, then walk ahead, following the path uphill. In summer, the smell of wild garlic will soon waft over you. At the bottom of a flight of steps, turn right, walk under the old castle arch, down some stone steps, then turn to your left.

2 Follow the path through scrub and up some steps, going ahead into dense woodland. When you reach a muddy burn, bear left, keeping to the main path with the gorge to your right. Beyond a line of yew trees growing from an old stone wall, take a right turn and follow the path that winds steeply downhill until you reach the water's edge.

3 Walk to your left, then follow the path as it climbs again. At a crossing of paths turn right, following the direction of the river. Your way now takes you high above the river, and you continue ahead to cross a stile. After you cross another stile the view opens out to fields on your left, then takes you closer to the river again, until you reach a kissing gate.

4 Turn left and follow the path up steps with fields to your left. When you reach the top of the ridge there are good views to your right. Continue until you go through a kissing gate

5 Turn left and follow the wide path. You eventually walk past buildings of the Roslin Institute, where Dolly the sheep was cloned, then pass a memorial to the Battle of

Rosslyn on your right-hand side. Keep walking straight ahead, through the outskirts of Roslin and up to the crossroads at the village centre.

6 Turn left here and walk ahead. After a short distance you see Rosslyn Chapel on the right-hand side. The chapel is well worth closer inspection. If you don't intend to visit the chapel, take the path that bears downhill to the right, just in front of it. When you reach the cemetery turn left, following the signpost for Polton, and walk between the cemeteries to the metal gate for Rosslyn Castle. Go down the steps on the right-hand side, over the bridge again and return to the car park at the start.

93 Edinburgh's Elegant and Airy New Town

Through the beautiful streets and crescents of Edinburgh's New Town, this fascinating walk visits the haunts of a wide range of Victorian and modern writers

Above top: An elegant house on Queen Street in the New Town

Above middle: Beautiful proportions in Glenfinlas Street, next to Charlotte Square

Above right: Busy Princes Street

Below right: Looking down on the New Town from Argyll Battery

Edinburgh's New Town was built in the 18th century and is an elegant development of wide and airy streets, punctuated with sweeping crescents and lined with soft grey Georgian buildings. It was a planned development, designed to move the focus of the city away from the filthy, overcrowded streets of the medieval Old Town.

James Craig and Robert Adam

The New Town was laid out in the mid-18th century by James Craig, a young architect who won a competition for the design. It is separated from the Old Town by Princes Street, the main

thoroughfare and once the smartest shopping street in Scotland. In later years Robert Adam contributed to the development, notably designing Charlotte Square in 1791. Houses in the New Town were soon the most coveted in the city and became the haunt of the Scottish literati.

Literary associations abound. Kenneth Grahame, author of *The Wind in the Willows* (1908) was born at 30 Castle Street in 1859; Robert Louis Stevenson grew up at 17 Heriot Row; Percy Bysshe Shelley stayed at 60 George Street with his runaway teenage bride in 1811; and Sir Walter Scott once lived at 39 Castle Street. The city seems to hold a fascination for writers and many historic meetings have taken place here, including that between Walter Scott and Robert Burns. The war poet Wilfred Owen often came into Edinburgh while he was recuperating from 'shell shock' at nearby Craiglockhart War Hospital. One of his early poems was entitled *Six O'clock in Princes Street*. It was at Craiglockhart that Owen met Siegfried Sassoon, already an acclaimed poet, who encouraged him in his writing and made amendments to early drafts of some of his greatest works. Owen left Edinburgh in 1917 and returned to the Front, where he was killed in action at the Sambre-Oise canal on 4 November, 1918.

Another New Town location, Milne's Bar on Hanover Street, was a favourite haunt of several of Scotland's most influential modern poets. Hugh MacDiarmid and his friends, fellow poets and drinking partners Norman MacCaig and Sorley MacLean are just some of the figures who used to meet here in the last century, and the pub walls are still covered with their memorabilia.

In the latter stages of this walk you will pass a statue of Sherlock Holmes, a tribute to his Edinburgh-born creator Sir Arthur Conan Doyle, who lived near by at 11 Picardy Place, which has now been demolished. Conan Doyle studied medicine at Edinburgh University and modelled his fictional detective Holmes on one of his former lecturers – Dr Joseph Bell. Bell was an extremely observant individual and combined his instincts with science to help the police in solving several murders in the city. Many believe that Conan Doyle assisted Bell with his work in this capacity – acting as Dr Watson to his Holmes.

93 Edinburgh's Elegant and Airy New Town

Take a walk in the footsteps of literary giants

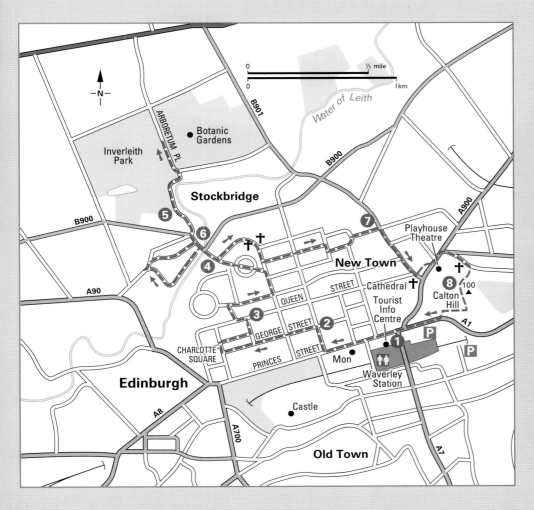

Distance 3 miles (4.8km)

Minimum time 1hr 30min

Ascent/Gradient 164ft (50m) ▲▲▲

Level of Difficulty ●●●

Paths Busy city streets

Landscape Elegant Georgian townscape

Suggested Map AA Street by Street Edinburgh

Start/Finish Grid reference: NT 257739

Dog Friendliness Keep on lead, not allowed in Botanic Gardens

Parking Several large car parks in central Edinburgh

Public Toilets At Waverley Station

1 From the tourist information centre, turn left and walk along Princes Street. Just after you pass the Scott Monument on your left, cross the road to reach Jenners department store, Scotland's answer to Harrods. Continue along Princes Street, then take a right turn up Hanover Street.

2 Take the second turning on your left and walk along George Street to reach elegant Charlotte Square. Then turn right and right again to go along Young Street. At the end, turn left and walk down North Castle Street to reach Queen Street.

3 Cross the road, turn left, then right down Wemyss Place and right into Heriot Row. When you reach Howe Street turn left and, before you reach the church in the middle of the street, turn left and walk along South East Circus Place. Walk past the sweep of Royal Circus and then down into Stockbridge.

4 Cross the bridge, then turn left along Dean Terrace. At the end, turn right into Ann Street. When you reach Dean Park Crescent turn right and follow the road round into Leslie Place and into Stockbridge again. Cross the main road, turn left and then right at the traffic lights down St Bernard's Row. Follow this, then bear left into Arboretum Avenue.

5 Follow this road past the Water of Leith down to Inverleith Terrace. Cross and walk up Arboretum Place to reach the entrance to the Botanic Gardens on the right. Turn left after exploring the gardens and retrace your steps to Stockbridge again.

6 Turn left at Hectors bar and walk uphill, then turn left along St Stephen Street. When you reach the church follow the road, cross over Cumberland Street then turn left and continue along Great King Street. At the end, turn right, then immediately left to walk

along Drummond Place, past Dublin Street and continue ahead into London Street.

7 At the roundabout turn right and walk up Broughton Street to reach Picardy Place. Turn left, walk past the statue of Sherlock Holmes, then bear left towards the Playhouse Theatre. Cross over, continue left, then turn right into Leopold Place and right again into Blenheim Place. When you reach the church turn right, walk up the steps and turn left at the meeting of paths.

8 Go up the steps on the right, walk over Calton Hill, then turn right to pass the canon. Go downhill, take the steps on your left and walk down into Regent Road. Turn right and walk back into Princes Street and the start.

94 The Stones of Kilmartin Church and Glen

This profoundly interesting ramble leads back many centuries to see neolithic circles and burial sites as well as carved medieval stones in Kilmartin Church

Kilmartin Glen with its lush alluvial plains, easy landfalls on the coast near Crinan and abundant supply of water has attracted human settlers since the earliest times. In around 5000 BC, nomadic hunter gatherers frequented this area but left little evidence of their presence other than piles of bones and shells in caves.

The arrival of small groups of neolithic people from around 3000 BC provided the first lasting signs of habitation. These early settlers – farmers, skilled weavers and potters – cleared the ground for grazing and erected the first stone shrines and circles, probably an early form of astronomical calendar for determining when to plant and harvest crops or to move cattle and perhaps also used in religious rituals. Around Kilmartin Glen, 25 different sites of standing stones have been found: some are simple arrangements, others single stones, while in Temple Wood there are two stone circles.

Later Bronze Age people were responsible for the monuments that can still be seen in the prehistoric linear cemetery, built over the course of 1,000 years, that runs for a mile (1.6km) down the glen. Each of the huge stone-lined burial chambers is slightly

different in design and construction. The Glebe Cairn, which looks like a pile of boulders with a cap stone, is situated near the church and is typical of the burial cairns of 1700–1500 BC: at its centre are two stone cists for burials that also contain pottery and a jet-bead necklace. The North Tomb contains a large slab carved with pictures of axe heads and cupmarks. The last cairn in this direction, the South Cairn is the earliest, and was originally a chambered tomb dating from 4000 BC.

In the Iron Age, warring tribes ringed the glen with hill-forts and it was on one of these, at Dunadd, that the Scotti tribe from Ireland founded their capital in the 6th century AD. St Columba came to Kilmartin in the 6th century AD and established the first Christian church here.

Kilmartin Church and Stones

Within Kilmartin parish church can be found relics from a later age. The ornately carved Kilmartin Cross is one of the most moving images of Christ to have survived from the early Scottish Christian Church and the churchyard has one of the finest collections of medieval gravestones in Scotland.

Above top: The sheep have seen it all before – Temple Wood stone circle

Above left: Aerial view looking north over the Kilmartin Valley

Above centre: The walk passes Nether Largie chamber tomb

Above right: Nether Largie standing stones

94 The Stones of Kilmartin Church and Glen

See ancient stones and burial sites in the grandeur of their natural setting

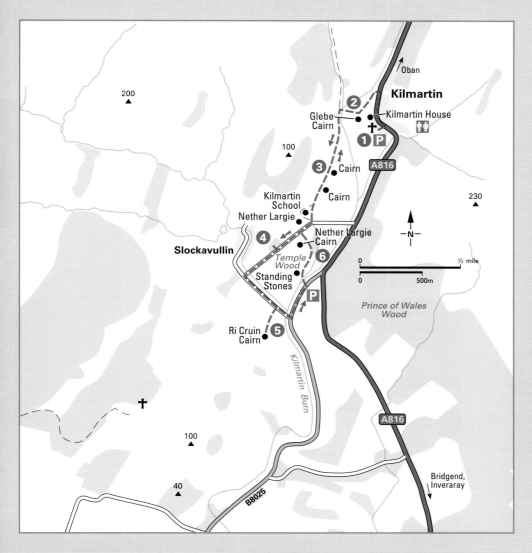

Distance 3.5 miles (5.7km)

Minimum Time 3hrs

Ascent/Gradient Negligible ▲▲▲

Level of Difficulty ●●●

Paths Boggy fields, old coach road and country lanes, 3 stiles

Landscape Pasture, hills, woodland

Suggested Map OS Explorer 358 Lochgilphead & Knapdale North

Start/Finish Grid reference: NR 835988

Dog Friendliness Dogs fine on route

Parking Car park outside Kilmartin Church

Public Toilets Kilmartin House

1 From the car park visit Kilmartin Church to spend a little time inspecting the medieval gravestones and to see the exquisite Kilmartin Cross. When you have finished and are leaving the church, turn left and walk along the road past Kilmartin House, walk out of the village and begin to head downhill towards a garage on the left. Just before the garage turn left, go through a kissing gate and head across the field to the Glebe Cairn.

2 From the cairn head half right across the field to climb over a stile. In wet weather this area can be very boggy, so stout footwear is advisable. Cross the stream by a bridge, then go on through a gate and take a left turn on to the old coach road. Follow this coach road to the next cairn. Go left over a stile and follow the path to visit the cairn.

3 Return to the road and turn left, continuing to the next cairn. After exploring this cairn, follow the coach road to Kilmartin School, where the route becomes a metalled road. Go over a crossroads, then walk on past Nether Largie Farm and, ignoring the cairn on the left, continue for a short distance towards Temple Wood, which is clearly visible ahead on the right.

4 Go through a gate on the right into Temple Wood, and when you have finished return by the same route. Turn right on to the road and continue until you reach a T-junction. Turn left at the junction and walk along this road until you come to a sign on the right for 'Ri Cruin Cairn'. Cross the wall by way of a stile and then proceed along the well-defined path to visit the ancient monument.

5 Return by the same route and turn right on to the road. Follow it to a T-junction then turn left and keep straight ahead until you reach the car park at Lady Glassary Wood. Opposite this take a path to the left signposted 'Temple Wood'. Cross a bridge, go through a gate and head towards the standing stones.

6 Turn right and walk across the field away from the stones towards a wood. Go through a gate and follow the fenced path to Nether Largie Cairn. From here continue along the fenced path, go through another gate and turn right on to the road. Continue past Nether Largie Farm and Kilmartin School and then retrace your steps back to reach Kilmartin Church and the car park.

95 From Balquhidder to Creag an Tuirc

This walk picks up the trail of Highland outlaw Rob Roy, whose motto 'MacGregor despite them' defied a ban on the clan, and leads to his final resting place

The romantic myth of the life of Rob Roy MacGregor was immortalised by Sir Walter Scott in his novel *Rob Roy* (1817). Born in 1671, the third son of Lieutenant Colonel Donald MacGregor of Glengyle, Rob Roy was exceedingly strong, with long arms; 'Roy' – from the Gaelic *rhuadh*, meaning 'red' – denoted the colour of his hair. After his marriage to Mary Campbell, he acquired land on the east shore of Loch Lomond and rented grazing at Balquhidder; soon he was a prosperous cattle dealer. But an arrangement with the Marquis of Montrose led to his downfall. In 1711 the Marquis gave Rob Roy £1,000 to buy cattle, one of his men absconded with the money and Rob Roy was charged with embezzlement. Failure to answer the court summons led to his being outlawed and a warrant being issued for his arrest. Meanwhile Montrose's factor (his agent handling his business affairs), Graham of Killearn, evicted Rob Roy's wife and family from their home at Craigroyston.

The Earl of Breadalbane gave Rob Roy land in Glen Dochart, but as an outlaw he was unable to trade in cattle. Undeterred, he turned to sheep and cattle rustling and offering protection. His most vicious attacks were reserved for the Marquis of Montrose, stealing his cattle and lifting his rents. Twice Rob Roy was captured but both times he managed to escape.

'MacGregor Despite Them'

In Rob Roy's lifetime clan MacGregor was banned by the Crown because of an earlier clash with the authorities. For some time Rob Roy used the name of his mother's clan, Campbell, but once an outlaw he used MacGregor a defiance of authority – and his motto, now visible on his grave, became 'MacGregor despite them'.

In 1715 he raised Clan Gregor for the Jacobite rising of the Old Pretender. When it failed, Rob Roy was charged with high treason but again he managed to give his pursuers the slip and retain his freedom. Government forces burned his house in Glen Dochart, but in 1716 the Duke of Argyll let him build another in Glen Shira. After years of being a wanted man he finally turned himself in to General Wade in 1725 and was pardoned by the King. His remaining years were spent in his house at Inverlochlarig at the head of Balquhidder Glen. He died there, peacefully, on the 28th December, 1734. His funeral procession came down the 15-mile (24km) glen on New Year's Day 1735, led by the MacGregor piper. His grave is beside the ruined church in front of the present Balquhidder parish church.

Left: The graves of Rob Roy, his wife and his two sons at Balquhidder parish church

Below: Braes of Balquhidder and Loch Voil

95 From Balquhidder to Creag an Tuirc

Pay your respects at the grave of the Highlands' most famous outlaw

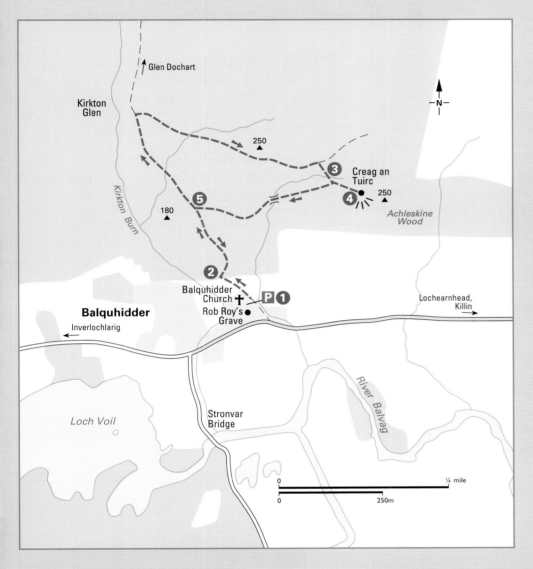

Distance 2.5 miles (4km)

Minimum Time 2hrs

Ascent/gradient 328ft (100m) ▲▲▲

Level of Difficulty ●●●

Paths Forest roads and hillside, 2 stiles

Landscape Hills, loch and woodlands

Suggested Map OS Explorer 365 The Trossachs

Start/Finish Grid reference: NN 536209

Dog Friendliness Dogs ok on this route

Parking At Balquhidder Church

Public Toilets None en route

1 The walk starts at the car park at Balquhidder Church. From here, walk along a dirt track, go past a shed and turn on to a path on the right-hand side that gives access into the forest. Follow the direction arrows on the green signposts pointing to 'Creag an Tuirc', along a forest track and heading up the hill.

2 Continue on this obvious trail for about 0.5 mile (800m) and then turn right, alongside a green building, again following the clearly signposted and waymarked route along a forest road. After walking for another 0.5 mile (800m), go through a gate on the right-hand side, then carry on walking slightly downhill over some stone steps and then go across a small stream.

3 The path now heads uphill on some stone steps, through old pine trees and on towards the summit of a knoll. Here is a cairn erected by the Clan MacLaren Society in 1987 to commemorate their 25th anniversary. The plaque proclaims that this place is the ancient rallying point of their clan.

4 A seat below the cairn is a grand place to rest after the climb up here. Sit for a while and enjoy the magnificent views over the meandering line of the River Balvag and the length of Loch Voil with the Braes of Balquhidder rising steeply above it. You can see the route that Rob Roy's funeral procession would have taken from Inverlochlarig down to the village itself, and the churchyard where his body lies. From here, retrace your steps back

down the hill but before reaching the top of the stone steps on which you came up, take the path to the left signposted 'Forest Walk'. This continues downhill following waymarked poles, down some steps and across a small bridge. The path goes through some bracken, over a small stream and then across a stile. Eventually it will pass through a small wood of young native trees before emerging on to the forest road.

5 Turn left here and retrace your steps back downhill over the stile and then turn left to return to reach the car park at the start of the walk. From here enter the churchyard and turn left. Rob Roy's grave is on the left in front of the ruins of a pre-Reformation church.

96 Into the Lost Valley

A rugged ramble takes you past waterfalls and into a 'lost valley' also known as the 'Corrie of Booty' – the place in which the MacDonalds hid their stolen cattle

Below: Scene from the MacDonalds' era? A Highland cow 'hidden' in Glen Coe

Bottom left: The Three Sisters from the Glencoe Pass road

Bottom right upper: In the Pass of Glencoe

Bottom right lower: Looking down Glen Coe with the Three Sisters to the left

The romantically named Lost Valley is *Coire Gabhail* in Gaelic, the 'Corrie of Booty'. Here, during the centuries leading up to the famous massacre of 1692, the MacDonalds hid their stolen cattle when the owners came storming in over the Moor of Rannoch with torch and claymore. It seems incredible that even the sure-footed black cattle of the clans could have been persuaded up the slope to Coire Gabhail. The corrie entrance is blocked by two old landslides from the face of Gearr Aonach, the middle hill of Glen Coe's Three Sisters. The economic system of Highland Scotland, until 1745, was based on the keeping and the stealing of cattle. It was an unsettled and dangerous lifestyle, and its artform was the verse of the bard who celebrated the most ingenious or violent acts of thievery and kept track of blood feuds.

The clan, gathered under its chieftain, was an organisation for protecting its own glen and for stealing from its neighbours. The MacDonalds of Glen Coe were particularly good at this. They raided right across the country, passing the fringes of the Cairngorms to steal from Aberdeenshire and Moray. In 1689, when Campbell of Glen Lyon was a guest in the house of MacIan, chief of Glen Coe, his eyes may have dwelt on a particular cooking pot. Twice in the previous ten years, MacIan had come raiding into Glen Lyon, dishonoured the women by cutting off their hair; on the second occasion, he had also stolen that pot from Campbell's mother.

Glen Coe Massacre

By the late 1600s, the clan and the claymore were being replaced by a legal system backed by the central government and its army. But because they were so good at cattle thieving, the MacDonalds of Glen Coe continued the practice long after everyone else had reluctantly started to move into the modern world of cash. As a result, the government decided to make an example of them.

On a February day, a squad of soldiers arrived in the valley. Traditional hospitality meant that its leader from Glen Lyon, a Campbell and an enemy, was welcomed into the house of MacDonald. Five nights later, at a given signal, the soldiers rose and murdered their hosts. The Glen Coe Massacre was either incompetent or mercifully half-hearted. Of the valley's population of 300, just 40 were killed, with the remainder escaping through the snow to the Lost Valley and other high corries.

96 Into the Lost Valley

Visit the valley that was the scene of an infamous massacre

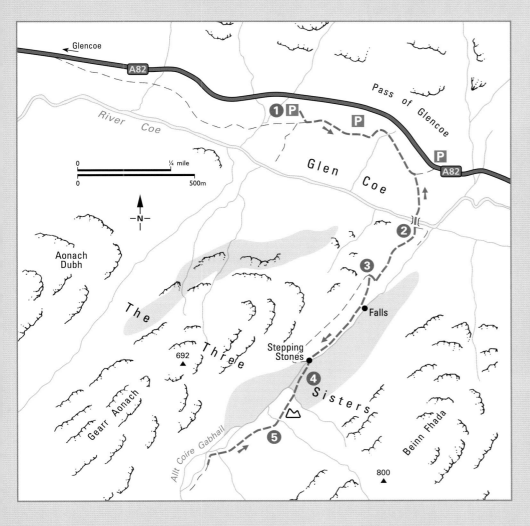

Distance 2.75 miles (4.4km)

Minimum Time 2hrs 15min

Ascent/Gradient 1,050ft (320m) ▲▲▲

Level of Difficulty ●●●

Paths Rugged and stony, stream to wade through

Landscape Crags and mountains

Suggested Map OS Explorer 384 Glen Coe & Glen Etive

Start/Finish Grid reference: NN 168569

Dog Friendliness Dogs must be reasonably fit and agile

Parking Lower of two roadside parking places opposite Gearr Aonach (middle one of Three Sisters)

Public Toilets Glencoe village

1 From the uphill corner of the car park, a faint path slants down to the old road, which is now a well-used wide path. Head up the valley for about 650yds (594m). With the old road continuing as a green track ahead, your path now bends down to the right. It has been rebuilt, with the bog problem solved by scraping down to the bedrock. The path reaches the gorge where the River Coe runs in a geological dyke of softer rock. Descend here on a steep wooden step ladder, to cross a spectacular footbridge.

2 The ascent out of the gorge is on a bare rock staircase. Above, the path runs through regenerating birch wood, which can be very wet on the legs; sheep and deer have been excluded from the wood with a temporary fence. Emerge from this through a high gate. The path, rebuilt in places, runs uphill for 60yds (55m). Here it bends left;

an inconspicuous alternative path continues uphill, which can be used to bypass the narrow path of the main route.

3 The main route contours into the gorge of the Allt Coire Gabhail. It is narrow, with steep drops below. Where there is an alternative of rock slabs and a narrow path just below, the slabs are more secure. You will hear waterfalls, then two fine ones come into view ahead. After passing these, continue between boulders to where the main path bends left to cross the stream below a boulder the size of a small house. (A small path runs on up to right of the stream, but leads nowhere useful.) The river here is wide and fairly shallow. Five or six stepping stones usually allow dry crossing. If the water is above the stones, then it's safer to wade alongside them; however, if the water is more than knee-deep then you should not attempt to make the crossing.

4 A well-built path continues uphill, now with the stream on its right. After 100yds (91m) a lump of rock blocks the way. The path follows a slanting ramp up its right-hand side. It continues uphill, still rebuilt in places, passing above the boulder pile that blocks the valley, the result of two large rockfalls from under Gearr Aonach opposite. At the top of the rockpile the path levels, giving a good view into the Lost Valley.

5 Drop gently to the valley's gravel floor. The stream vanishes into the gravel, to reappear below the boulder pile on the other side. Note where the path arrives at the gravel, as it becomes invisible at that point. Wander up the valley to where the stream vanishes, 0.25 mile (400m) ahead. Anywhere beyond this point is more serious hillwalking than you have done up to now on this walk. Return to the path and follow it back to the start of the walk.

97 The Mysterious Stones of Aberlemno

At Aberlemno in eastern Scotland, this walk leads through agricultural land once inhabited by the Picts – with a chance to look at their intriguing carved stones

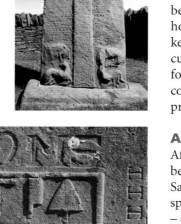

Top left: Aberlemno Church and churchyard, which contains one of the village's Pictish stones

Top right: Pictish stone carved with Christian cross in Aberlemno village – this is the stone called Aberlemno III

Above left: Known as the Serpent stone, this bears Pictish symbols including a serpent (top)

Above right: One of the stones in Aberlemno churchyard

Had history turned out differently, you would have been doing this walk in Pictland, not Scotland. The Picts probably inhabited this northern part of Britain for thousands of years, yet today we know very little about them. Neither their language nor manuscripts have survived and much of their culture remains a mystery.

The best reminders we have of them are the intriguing carved stones that dot the landscape of eastern Scotland – the greatest concentration being in Angus and around the Moray Firth. You can see several of these beautiful pieces of ancient art on this walk, which takes you through the heart of the land of the Picts.

Mystery surrounds the origins of the Picts. The only thing that seems to be certain is that they were the occupants of what we now call Scotland when the Romans arrived; it is possible that they could have been there for more than 1,000 years before that. The Romans imposed their military might further south and the Roman Empire soon stretched from southern England to the central belt of Scotland; the culture and language of the tribes living under the occupation gradually began to alter under their influence.

The Romans never spread north of a line between the estuaries of the rivers Forth and Clyde, however, and so the tribes beyond that boundary kept their distinct language and particular customs. The Romans called them the *Picti*, Latin for 'painted ones' – a reference to their warriors' continued habit of daubing themselves in woad prior to fighting a battle.

Advent of the Scots

After the fall of the Roman Empire, new tribes began to invade Britain, with the Angles and Saxons gradually conquering the south, and Gaelic speakers from Ireland, who called themselves Scotti – or Scots – moving into the far north-west.

The Picts were pagans, but they had been exposed to Christian ideas from AD 400 onwards, brought into the country by the great Celtic missionaries Ninian, and later Columba. In AD 565 Columba travelled to Inverness to meet a powerful Pictish king, Bridei. The two men had a competition to see whether Columba's Christian miracles could beat the wiles of Pictish magic. It isn't clear who won, but gradually the Picts converted to Christianity.

Of course there were wars between the various tribes, the Picts fighting the Gaels and Angles, as well as battling among themselves. The carved stone that you pass in Aberlemno churchyard is thought to commemorate one of Bridei's major victories. Stone carving became more and more important in their culture, with increasingly intricate patterns being created, often combined with a Christian cross. However, in AD 794 the Vikings began to raid northern and western Scotland, weakening the Pictish kingdom. The Gaelic-speaking Scots saw their opportunity – in AD 843 a Scot called Kenneth MacAlpin seized their throne, and the Pictish nation died.

97 The Mysterious Stones of Aberlemno

Inspect Pictish stones and climb to an Iron Age hill-fort

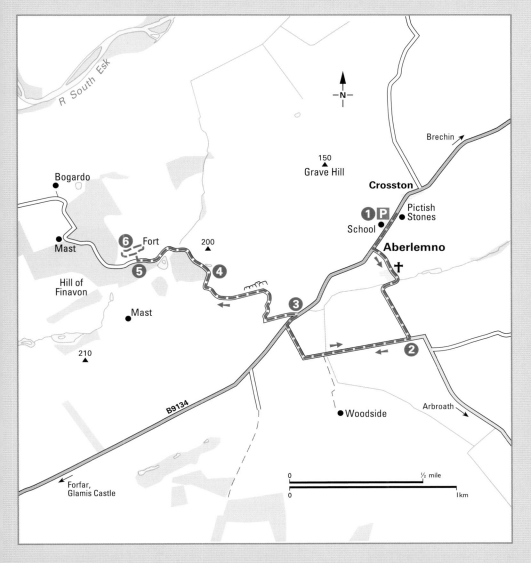

Distance 5 miles (8km)

Minimum Time 1hr 45min

Ascent/Gradient 394ft (120m) ▲▲▲

Level of Difficulty ●●●

Paths Mainly quiet roads but one extremely overgrown area

Landscape Quiet agricultural land and ancient carved stones

Suggested Map OS Explorer 389 Forfar, Brechin & Edzell

Start/Finish Grid reference: TQ 522558

Dog friendliness Overgrown area makes this unsuitable for dogs

Parking Car park by school in Aberlemno

Public Toilets None en route; nearest in Forfar

1 From the car park opposite the Pictish stones turn right along the road, then go first left, signed 'Aberlemno Church and Stone'. Walk past the church – another Pictish stone is found in the churchyard – and follow the road as it bends round to the right and then to the left. Continue until you reach a T-junction.

2 Turn right and follow this road, passing the entrance to Woodside on the left. At the corner, follow the road right. Walk down to join the B9134, turn right and follow this a short distance until you reach a turning on the left.

3 Turn left along this road, signed 'Finavon Hill'. The road winds uphill, past several outcrops, then under a line of pylons. Continue on this road as it skirts a hill.

4 Continue following the road uphill, passing a small loch half-hidden in woodland to the left. Pass an old stone wall on your right, then just beyond a rusty gate in the corner of a field, hop over a section of collapsed wall, taking care to avoid the strand of wire.

5 Head uphill now to explore the turf-covered ramparts of Finavon vitrified fort. Dating from the Iron Age (1000 BC), the hilltop stronghold had walls built of stones that were fused together by tremendous heat. As you walk around the summit, keep a sharp eye out for vitrified material found in the bank.

6 From the hilltop, return to the road and turn left to retrace your steps back to the start of the walk in Aberlemno.

98 The Pass of Ryvoan and the Thieves' Road

Take the high road used by cattle thieves and drovers, and visit the lochan said to have been turned green by the Highland fairies washing their laundry in its waters

The Pass of Ryvoan is a scaled-down version of the fearsome Lairig Ghru that cuts through the Cairngorms from Aviemore. You pass from the shelter of the forest to a green lochan, trapped between two high and stony mountainsides. Once through the narrow gap, you'll find wide moors and a ring of peaks around the horizon.

Ryvoan marked the exit of the Thieves' Road out of Rannoch and Lochaber by secret ways through the Rothiemurchus Forest. The MacDonalds of Glen Coe used to come raiding here in the 17th century, as did Clan Cameron from Loch Eil near Fort William. Once through the pass, they could take their pick from the rich lands of Moray and Aberdeenshire. In more settled times, raiding chieftains became landlords, and rents were paid in the small black cattle of the glens. Every autumn, the drove herds assembled for a long walk to the markets of Falkirk, Perth and northern England.

The drovers used the same road as their thieving grandfathers, but once through the pass turned sharp right across the flank of the mountain. The Lairig an Lui, 'the Pass of the Calves', crosses the ford of the Avon and runs down Glen Derry to Braemar. It's 30 miles (48km) to the next grazing and shelter – two full days for the drove. Overnight the cattle would snatch some grazing from the rough grasses, while the drovers cooked their oatmeal and potatoes, before rolling themselves in

their woollen plaids on a bed of heather. As late as 1859, Queen Victoria found the Lairig path torn up by hooves and scented with fresh cow pats.

The Green Loch

Lochan Uaine means 'Green Loch'. Some say the green colour is caused by flecks of mica; others claim that it's where the fairies wash their green garments. The Highland fairies or Sithe (pronounced 'Shee') don't dance around with wands and grant you wishes. They are touchy and vengeful, and if you meet one it is best to address him politely in good Gaelic. Precautions you can take are to avoid wearing green, which is known to annoy them, and never to address your friends by name while under the trees.

Above right: A winter's day by mountain waters

Below: The final stretch of the walk leads along the shore of beautiful Loch Morlich

98 The Pass of Ryvoan and the Thieves' Road

Follow a scenic tour in drovers' footsteps near Glenmore village

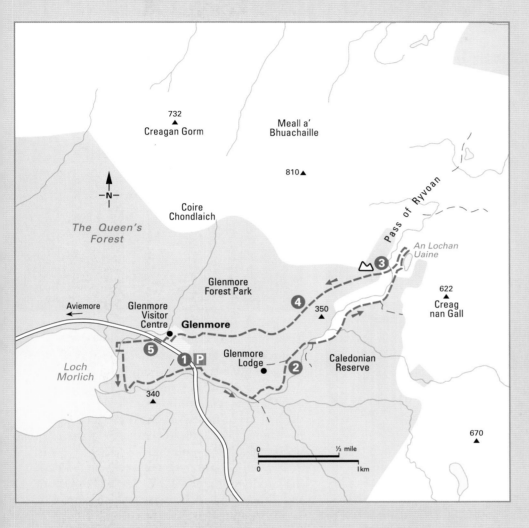

Distance 5 miles (8km)

Minimum Time 2hrs 15min

Ascent/Gradient 400ft (122m) ▲▲▲

Level of Difficulty ●●●

Paths Smooth tracks, one steep ascent, no stile

Landscape Views over Rothiemurchus Forest to Cairngorm

Suggested Map OS Explorer 403 Cairn Gorm & Aviemor

Start/Finish Grid reference: NH 980095

Dog Friendliness Off lead but under close control

Parking Bridge just south of Glenmore village

Public Toilets Glenmore village

1 Head upstream on a sandy track to the left of the river. Interpretation signs explain the flowers of the forest you may come across, many of which are ferns and mosses. After 550yds (503m), turn left on a wide smooth path with blue/yellow waymarkers. Ahead is a gate into Glenmore Lodge rifle range; here the path bends right, to a wide gravel track.

2 Turn right, away from Glenmore Lodge, to cross a concrete bridge into the Caledonian Reserve. Immediately keep ahead on a smaller track (marked by a blue waymarker) as the main one bends right. The track narrows as it heads into the Pass of Ryvoan between steep wooded slopes of pine, birch and scree. At this, the most scenic part of the route, a path turns left, with a blue waymarker, which you take in a moment. Just beyond this, steps on the right lead down to Lochan Uaine. Walk round to the left of the

water on the beach. At the head of the loch a small path leads back up to the track. Turn sharp left, back to the junction already visited; now turn off to the right on to the narrower path with the blue waymarker.

3 This small path crosses some duckboard and heads back down the valley. Very soon it starts to climb steeply to the right, up rough stone steps. When it levels off, the going is easier, although it's still narrow with tree roots. The path reaches a forest road at a bench and a waymarker.

4 Continue to the left along the track. After a clear-felled area with views, the track re-enters trees and slopes downhill into Glenmore village. When you reach the point just above the main road, turn right through a green barrier to reach Glenmore Visitor Centre. Pass through its car park to the main road.

5 Cross to Glenmore shop. Behind a post-box, steps lead down to the campsite. Pass along its right-hand edge to a path into woods. Head left across a footbridge to the shore of Loch Morlich and follow the beaches until another river blocks the way. Turn left along the river bank. Ignore a footbridge, but continue on the wide path with the river on your right. Where the path divides, the smaller branch continues beside the river through bushes to the car park.

Extending the Walk
In good weather you can continue through the Pass of Ryvoan. Return to Glenmore by taking a hill path from the bothy, over the summit of Meall a' Bhuachaille and then down through the Coire Chondlaich.

99 Around the Elegant 'Old Town' of Aberdeen

This delightful walk leads around the old fishing port of Aberdeen, revealing the wealth of what was a major maritime centre before North Sea Oil was discovered

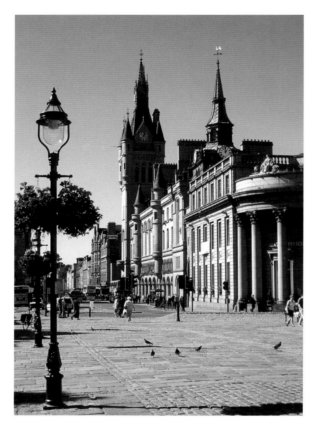

Top left: Town House clock tower

Above: Lion guardian at Schoolhill War Memorial

Above right: Elegant Aberdeen – by the Tollbooth and Town House

Above far right: The 16th-century Provost Skene's House

Aberdeen was a major maritime centre throughout the 19th century, starting when a group of local entrepreneurs purchased an ageing paddle tug and launched it as the first steam-powered trawler. From small beginnings the steam trawling industry expanded and by 1933 Aberdeen was Scotland's top fishing port, employing nearly 3,000 men with 300 vessels sailing from its harbour.

By the time North Sea oil was coming on stream in Aberdeen, much of the massive trawling fleet had relocated to Peterhead. An early morning visit to the fish market will verify that Aberdeen still brings in substantial catches, but the tugs, safety vessels and supply ships for the offshore rigs packed into the harbour far outnumber the trawlers.

North Sea Riches

Geologists had speculated about the existence of oil and gas in the North Sea since the middle of the 20th century, but tapping its deep and inhospitable waters was another story. However, with the Middle Eastern oil sheiks becoming more aware of the political and economic power of their oil reserves and government threats of rationing, the industry began to consider the North Sea as a viable source of oil. Exploration commenced in the 1960s and the first major find in the British sector was in November 1970 in the Forties field, 110 miles (177km) east of Aberdeen.

By late 1975, after years of intense construction, the hundreds of miles of pipes, massive oilshore rigs, supply ships, helicopters and an army of oil workers were finally in place. In Aberdeen, at British Petroleum's headquarters, the queen pressed the button that would set the whole thing moving. Oil flowed from the rig directly to the refinery at far-away Grangemouth. While many ports have suffered decline, Aberdeen remains busy due to the oil trade, as the influx of people connected with the industry and a subsequent rise in property prices have brought prosperity.

However, there was a terrible human cost to pay for oil wealth. On the night of 6 July 1988 the Piper Alpha oil platform exploded 120 miles (193km) offshore – and helicopters flew all night bringing dead and injured to Aberdeen. In all, 167 died; and many of the survivors live with the scars of that night and horrific memories of escaping the rig. A memorial to the dead stands in Hazlehead Park. The subsequent inquiry revealed that safety regulations had been ignored: the industry learned a bitter lesson, and the rigs are now safer places to work. The oil industry still supports about 47,000 jobs locally and known reserves are such that oil will continue to flow well into the 21st century.

99 Around the Elegant 'Old Town' of Aberdeen

Explore the sights of old Aberdeen

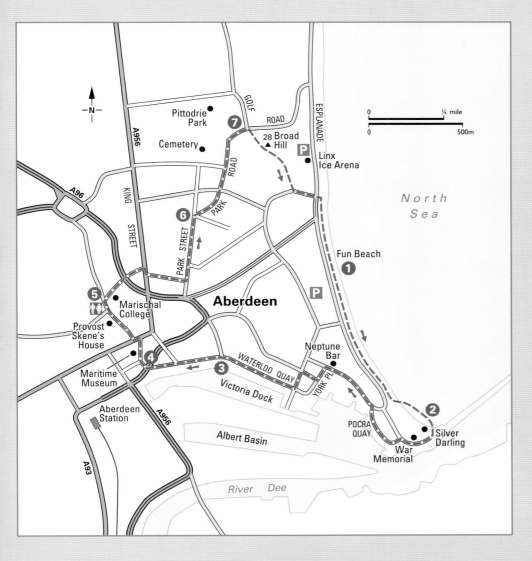

Distance 3.75 miles (6km)

Minimum Time 2hrs

Ascent/Gradient Negligible ▲▲▲

Level of Difficulty ●●●

Paths Mainly pavements; along beach (underwater at high tide)

Landscape Old fishing port

Suggested Map OS Explorer 406 Aberdeen & Banchory

Start/Finish Grid reference: NJ 954067

Dog Friendliness Keep on lead

Parking Esplanade at Fun Beach or Linx Ice Arena

Public Toilets Upperkirkgate, opposite Marischal College

1 From your parking place, head southwards on the promenade, walking beside the shore with the sea on your left. Go down the slipway on to the beach for a short distance to wooden steps on the right and leave the beach to enter a children's play area. (But if the tide is high at the slipway clamber over the sea wall on your right, and pass along a row of fishermen's cottages.)

2 Walk past the Silver Darling restaurant and on into the harbour area. Continue past the war memorial, making sure you keep the blue storage tanks to your left, and go along Pocra Quay as it bends to the right. Turn left into York Street and then when you reach the Neptune bar turn left into York Place. Take the first right, the first left and the second right to emerge on Waterloo Quay.

3 Where Waterloo Quay becomes Commerce Street, turn left into Regent Quay and then at the T-junction cross the dual carriageway at pedestrian lights. Turn left and then first right to reach Aberdeen Maritime Museum and John Ross's House. (Ross was Lord Provost of Aberdeen in 1710–11.) If you have time, visit the Maritime Museum.

4 From here head along Exchequer Row, to turn left into Union Street. At once turn right into Broad Street, where you will find Provost Skene's House on the left, reached by passing underneath an office block.

5 Continue ahead past Marischal College (which houses the Marischal Museum), turn right into Littlejohn Street, and then cross North Street. At the end of Meal Market Street,

turn right into King Street and then left into Frederick Street. At the junction with Park Street turn left and keep walking ahead until the road crosses a railway.

6 Shortly after the crossing is a roundabout. Head slightly right along Park Road. Follow the road through the Trinity Cemetery and towards Pittodrie Park, which is the home of Aberdeen Football Club, to the junction with Golf Road.

7 At the junction with Golf Road, turn up right, on the well-made path over Broad Hill. There are wide views of the sea and Aberdeen. At the path end, turn left to a roundabout with subtropical plants on the Esplanade. The shoreline promenade leads back to your car.

100 Loch an Eilein's Castle and Ord Ban

A walk around Loch an Eilein provides wonderful views of ancient pines and a 13th-century island castle built to guard the cattle-rustling route used by the clans

Above: Ancient forest on the shore

Below: The island castle is said to be connected to the mainland by a zig-zag underwater causeway

An island castle, surrounded by ancient pines, and the mountains rising behind – Loch an Eilein has it all. Loch an Eilein Castle was built by John Comyn II, known as the Red Comyn, in the 13th century. It guards the strategic cattle-stealing route which runs along the shore of the loch. Locals used to keep a cow tied to a tree in the hope that the raiders would take that and leave the rest alone. The three murderers of a Macintosh chieftain were imprisoned in chains here for seven years, before being executed in 1531. The castle was most recently fought over in 1690, when Grizzel Mhor (Big Grizelda), the chieftain's wife, held it for Clan Grant against the king.

Walk quietly with binoculars and you may see some of the unique birdlife of the forest. The crested tit resembles the more familiar coal tit, with brown body and striped head, but its crest has a Mohican hair-style effect. It nests in holes in old, rotten trees, so will only be found in wild forest. The Scottish crossbill, found only in Scotland, has a parrot-like beak, adapted for cracking open pine cones. The capercaillie is the large grouse of the forest and its name means 'horse of the woods'. The male challenges and intimidates other males with a noise like the clip-clop of hooves, or like a wine-bottle being opened.

Ospreys used to nest in the castle ruins. An egg collector once swam across wearing nothing but his cap, which he used to bring back his plunder. Ospreys are back in the Cairngorms, and though they won't return to this over-public island, you might see them elsewhere, plunging feet-first as they strike for a trout. Try the trout farm at Inverdruie, on the edge of Aviemore. Sadly, the egg-collectors are back as well. In 2000, a man in Leicester was caught with three stolen osprey eggs.

Island Romance

In the romantic novel *The Key above the Door* by Maurice Walsh (1926), the hero and heroine spend many hours gazing at each other from cottages on opposite sides of Loch an Eilein before being shipwrecked on the island. More recently, Archie and Katrina from TV series *Monarch of the Glen* had their own romantic encounter on the island.

100 Loch an Eilein's Castle and Ord Ban

Take a tour through ancient pines around a picturesque loch

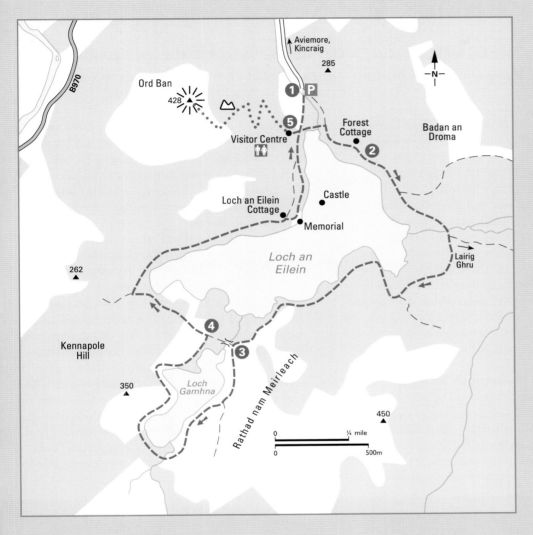

Distance 4.25 miles (6.8km)

Minimum Time 1hr 45min

Ascent/Gradient 100ft (30m) ▲▲▲

Level of Difficulty ●●●

Paths Wide smooth paths, optional steep hill with high ladder stile

Landscape Ancient pine forest around loch

Suggested Map OS Explorer 403 Cairn Gorm & Aviemore

Start/Finish Grid reference: NH 897084

Dog Friendliness Keep on lead on Rothiemurchus Estate

Parking Estate car park near Loch an Eilein, charges apply

Public Toilets Visitor centre

1 From the end of the car park at the beginning of the walk, a made-up path leads to the visitor centre. Turn left to cross the end of Loch an Eilein, then turn right on a smooth, sandy track. The loch shore is near by on the right; there are paths leading down to it if you wish to visit. Just past a red-roofed house, a deer fence runs across, with a gate.

2 The track now becomes a wide, smooth path, which runs close to the loch side. After a bridge, the main track forks right to pass a bench backed by a flat boulder. The smaller path on the left leads high into the hills and through the famous pass of the Lairig Ghru, eventually to Braemar. After crossing a stream at a low concrete footbridge, the path bends right for 120yds (110m) to a junction. Just beyond the junction you'll find a footbridge with wooden handrails.

3 To shorten the walk, cross this footbridge and go along the main track, passing Point 4 in 170yds (155m). For a longer walk, turn left before the footbridge on to a narrower path that will pass around Loch Gamhna. This loch soon appears on your right-hand side. Where the path forks, keep right to pass along the loch side, across its head (rather boggy) and back along its far side, to rejoin the wider path around Loch an Eilein. Turn left here.

4 Continue around Loch an Eilein, with the water on your right, to a reedy corner of the loch. About 55yds (50m) further, the path turns right, signposted 'footpath'. After a gate, turn right to the loch side and a memorial to Major General Brook Rice who drowned here while skating. Follow the shore until opposite the castle, then go back to the track above. A deer fence (left) leads to the visitor centre.

5 From here, a stiff climb (500ft/152m) can be made on to the rocky little hill of Ord Ban, a superb viewpoint. Cross a ladder stile immediately to the right of the toilet block and follow the deer fence to the right for 150yds (137m), to a point behind the car park. Just behind one of the lowest birches on the slope, a small indistinct path zig-zags up the slope. It slants to the left to avoid crags, then crosses a small rock slab (take care if wet) and continues on to the summit. Descend by the same path.

101 Seeing Sea Eagles at Portree Bay

An engaging coastal walk around Portree Bay leads to a pasture called the Bile, then returns by way of Ben Chracaig – with a great chance of seeing sea eagles

While walking beside Portree Bay, keep at least one eye looking out to sea. You may spot what has been described as Britain's greatest conservation story. The last sea eagle in Scotland died on Skye in the early 1900s. Like all large raptors, it was shot at by shepherds and gamekeepers. An attempt to reintroduce them in 1959 failed. In 1975, a secret RAF mission flew four young birds from Norway to the island of Rum. Over the next ten years, they were joined by 80 more. Today, about a dozen pairs are nesting here, with a total population of around 100 spread up along the western coast and the Hebrides.

More than a Twinkle in its Eye

In Gaelic it is called *iolaire suil na greine* – 'the eagle with the sunlit eye' – as its eye is a golden colour. In English it's also called the white-tailed eagle, the white-tailed fish eagle and the European sea eagle; it hasn't been back here long enough to finalise its name. It is not a heavy bird: even with its 8ft (2.4m) wingspan, it weighs in at just 7lb (3kg). The sea eagle nests in cliffs. One nest, with an RSPB hide, is at Loch Frisa on Mull, another here at Portree. The Aros Experience visitor centre has a closed-circuit TV camera trained on the nest, and the Portree fishermen have taken to throwing seafood to the birds outside the bay.

The first few eagles you think you see are almost certainly buzzards. When you see a real eagle, and even though you can't tell how far away it is, you'll know it for what it is: it's four times the size of a buzzard and its wingbeats are so slow and powerful. That's when it isn't gliding from one horizon to the other apparently without moving a feather. The sea eagle is even bigger than the golden one, and has a white tail – but so does a young golden eagle. But if the eagle is flying over the sea, then it's a sea eagle. Naturalists believed that the bird's main problem would be the golden eagle, which during the years of extinction had taken over the nest sites. But sadly, the real enemy is still humans and their greed. In 2000, and despite a 24-hour guard, thieves took the two eggs from the Mull pair.

Above: The sea eagle's nickname is 'the flying barn door' because it is so big

Right: Portree harbour

101 Seeing Sea Eagles at Portree Bay

Celebrate the success of a determined conservation effort

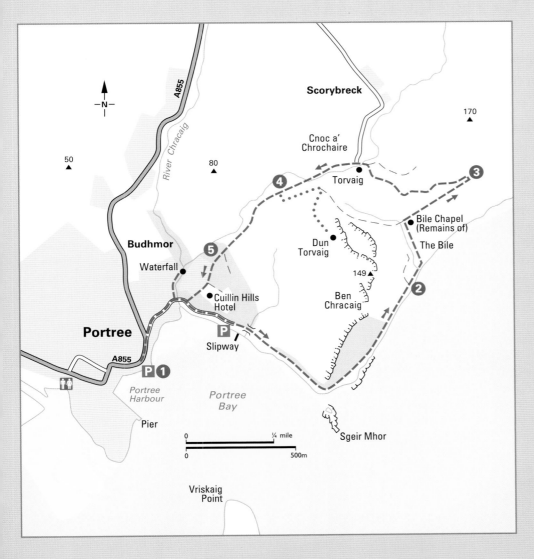

Distance 3.5 miles (5.7km)

Minimum Time 1hr 15min

Ascent/Gradient 459ft (140m) ▲▲▲

Level of Difficulty ●●●

Paths Smooth, well-made paths, farm track, 3 stiles

Landscape Views across Minch from wooded coast and hill above

Suggested Map OS Explorer 409 Raasay, Rona & Scalpay or 410 Skye – Portree & Bracadale

Start Grid reference: NG 485436

Dog Friendliness Dogs on leads through farmland, scoop poop on shore path

Parking On A855 (Staffin Road) above Portree Bay. Another small parking area near slipway

Public Toilets Town centre, just off main square

1 Turn off the main A855 on to a lane signed 'Budh Mor', to walk down to the shoreline and then continue to a small parking area. A tarred path continues along the shore past a slipway. After a footbridge, it passes under hazels that show the typical ground-branching habit of bushes formerly coppiced, cut back every seven years for firewood. The path passes below a viewpoint with flagpoles and then rounds the headland to reach the edge of a level green field called The Bile.

2 A wall runs up the edge of The Bile. A sign points up left for 'Scorybreck'; ignore it and go through a small gate ahead. A path leads into the corner of The Bile field. Go up its left edge and across the top, to a stile. Cross the top of the next field on an old path to a stile at its corner. You will see a track beyond.

3 Turn sharp left, up the track. At the top it passes through two gates to reach a stony road just to the right of Torvaig. Turn left past the house and cross the foot of a tarred road into a gently descending track. It runs down between two large corrugated sheds and then through to a gate with a stile.

4 The grassy path ahead leads down into Portree, but you can take a short, rather rough, diversion to Dun Torvaig (an ancient fortified hilltop) above. For the dun, turn left along the fence, and left again on a well-made path above. It leads to a kissing gate above the two sheds. Turn sharp right along the fence for a few steps, then bear left around the base of a small outcrop and head straight up on a tiny path to the dun. Remnants of dry-stone walling can be seen around the summit. Return to the

well-made path, passing above Point 4 to join the wall on the right. The path leads down under goat willows into a wood where it splits; stay close to the wall.

5 At the first houses (The Parks Bungalow 5), keep downhill on a tarred street. On the left is the entrance to the Cuillin Hills Hotel. A few steps later, fork right on to a stony path. At the shore road, turn right across a stream and right again on a path that runs up for 60yds (55m) to a craggy little waterfall. Return to the shore road and turn right to the walk start.

102 Strathpeffer and the Rogie Falls

From a 19th-century spa town, whose waters were said in 1819 to be the healthiest in Britain, this charming walk climbs to the beautiful Rogie Falls

Stand on the bridge at Rogie Falls near Strathpeffer between July and September, when the river's fairly full, and you might catch a glimpse of a leaping salmon. It's a thrilling sight to see a 3ft (1m) long fish attempting to swim up against the force of the water. Eventually it'll make it, or else discover the easy way round – the fish ladder carved out of the rock on the right-hand side. But if you'd been here 200 years ago, that single salmon would have been a dozen, even a hundred.

Salmon was once food for the taking. You went down to the river and took as many as you could eat. Smoked above a peat fire, it was a staple winter food. Farm workers even used their industrial muscle to demand that they shouldn't have to eat salmon more than three times a week. Today, however, wild salmon are heading for extinction. Numbers in Scotland's rivers are falling fast due to netting in the estuaries, and in their feeding grounds around the Arctic pack ice. Angling clubs have bought up and discontinued estuary netting rights but the international community squabbles on about the Arctic drift nets and now parasites and disease from fish farms pose a new danger.

From Fresh to Salt Water and Back

Egg, fry, alevin, parr, smolt, salmon, kelt – these are the seven ages of the salmon's life. For one or two years it behaves like a trout, hanging in the still water behind a boulder, waiting for food to float by. But then its scales become silver and it turns downstream, totally altering its body chemistry to enable it to live in salt water.

Four or five years later, now called a salmon, it returns. We don't know how it navigates from Greenland back to the Cromarty Firth. Once there, it identifies the outflow of the Conon by the taste of the water and works its way upstream to return to the patch of gravel where its life began.

Below: The walk leads through beautiful landscape above Strathpeffer

102 Strathpeffer and the Rogie Falls

Look for a leaping salmon at a wild forest waterfall

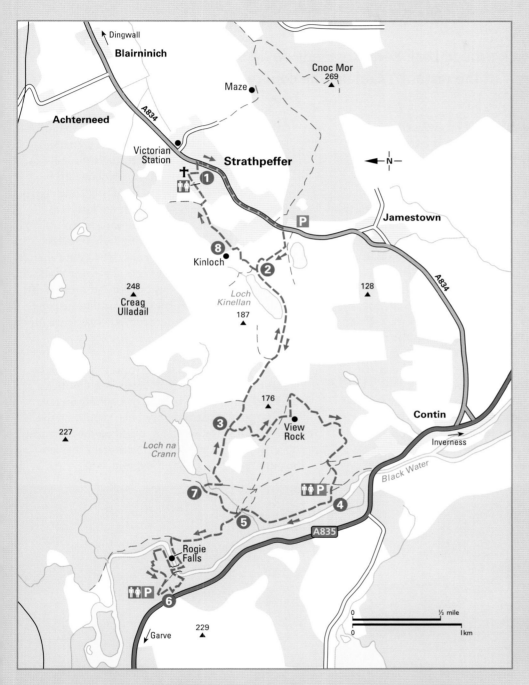

Distance 10 miles (16.1km)

Minimum Time 5hrs

Ascent/Gradient 1,200ft (366m) ▲▲▲

Level of Difficulty ●●●

Paths Waymarked paths and tracks, no stiles

Landscape Plantation, wild forest and riverside

Suggested Map OS Explorer 437 Ben Wyvis & Strathpeffer

Start/Finish Grid reference: NH 483582

Dog Friendliness Keep on lead for section past Loch Kinellan

Parking Main square, Strathpeffer

Public Toilets At start, Contin (Point 4) and Rogie Falls car parks

1 Go along the main road to Contin. At the edge of town, turn right signed 'Garve' then, at a bend, turn left at another signpost.

2 Follow a track left of Loch Kinellan. As it bends right, go up to a plantation, then into forest for 0.5 mile (800m) to a signpost.

3 Turn left for View Rock on a good path with green waymarkers. At View Rock, a side-path diverts to the right for the viewpoint, then rejoins. After a long descent, follow green waymarkers downhill. At a forest road go straight over, and across two further forest roads to Contin Forest car park.

4 At the end of the car park, pick up a wide path. Where red waymarkers turn right, follow deer-head markers to a forest road. Turn left and in 80yds (73m) bear left, downhill.

5 After 600yds (549m) take a track left signed 'Rogie Falls Bridge'. Cross a footbridge below the falls and turn right; after 0.25 mile (400m) bend left. Cross rocky ground to a junction. Turn right, to Rogie Falls car park.

6 Leave through a wooden arch and follow green waymarkers to the bridge. Retrace the outward route to Point 5 and turn left up a forest road to where a fainter track crosses.

7 Turn right down the smaller track to a signpost, then left, signed 'Strathpeffer'. After 600yds (549m), at the signpost of Point 3, go ahead and retrace the outward route to Point 2. Turn left. At Kinloch house go right, then left through kissing gates into a plantation with a signpost for Strathpeffer.

8 Follow the main path until you see Strathpeffer. At the next junction bear right then right into town. Go left past a church with a square steeple, then right to the main square.

103 Looking into Scotland's Great Wilderness

A pleasant walk around Loch Kernsary leads down Scotland's shortest river, and opens up views of the distant 'Maiden', the county's most remote mountain

When you walk inland from Poolewe, you're entering one of the largest empty areas in Britain. If you turn left instead of right at Kernsary Farm, you can walk for two full days before you reach any road. On the slight rise before Loch Kernsary, you get a view right into the heart of this mountain wonderland.

At the back of the view is A'Mhaighdean, 'the Maiden', Scotland's most remote mountain. It takes a full half a day's walk to get to this hill from anywhere – and that walk will be along the edges of long, dark lochs and under large crags. Beinn Lair has a quartzite cliff with an evil north-face gleam that's 3 miles (4.8km) wide, as big as the north face of Ben Nevis, but a whole lot less visited. Behind A'Mhaighdean is An Teallach, called 'the Forge' because of the cloudy vapours that stream across its semicircular ridge. The ridge has great lumpy towers to scramble round, 3ft-wide (1m) ridges to walk along and an edge so high that if you fall off it will take about four seconds in freefall before you land on anything at all.

All this belongs to a gentleman from Holland called Paul van Vlissingen. In 1993 he signed an agreement with the Mountaineering Council of Scotland that first set out the principle of responsible access for all. Deer stalking restrictions would be only on days when deer stalking was actually taking place – a step forward when walkers were sometimes threatened with high-velocity rifle fire from August to February; the estate also undertook not to build any new landrover tracks. As a result, business here is carried out on foot, by boat and by pony. This Letterewe Accord became the foundation of a new century's access legislation.

Members' Paths

The paths used on this walk are, as it happens, on established rights of way. Even so, you'll notice a sudden change near the head of Loch Kernsary. The first part of the path has been rebuilt by the National Trust for Scotland, using members' annual subscriptions. At the edge of National Trust land the path repairs stop abruptly, mid-bog.

Below: Evening mist around the shoulders of the remote A'Mhaighdean

Bottom left: Loch Kernsary

Bottom right: River Kernsary with the loch beyond

103 Looking Into Scotland's Great Wilderness

Take a gentle ramble while gazing with wonder far into the wilds

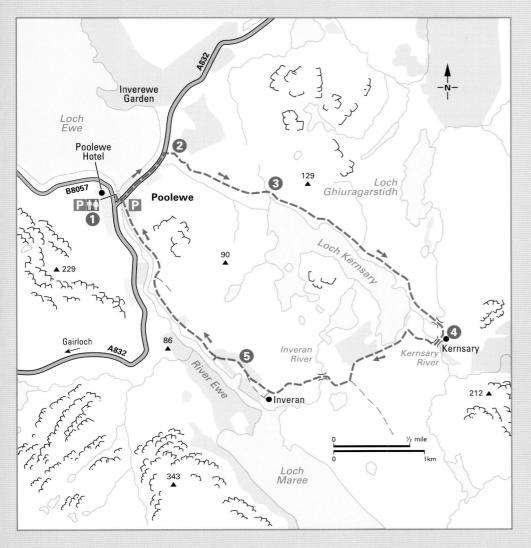

Distance 6.5 miles (10.4km)

Minimum Time 2hrs 45min

Ascent/Gradient 250ft (76m) ▲▲▲

Level of Difficulty ●●●

Paths Mostly good, but one short rough, wet section, 3 stiles

Landscape Moorland and loch side

Suggested Map OS Explorer 434 Gairloch & Loch Ewe

Start/Finish Grid reference: NG 857808

Dog Friendliness Close control on moorland and tracks carrying estate traffic

Parking In Poolewe, just up B8057 side street

Public Toilets At start

1 A kissing gate beside the public toilets leads to a path that crosses the Marie Curie Field of Hope to the main road. Turn left to cross the bridge over the River Ewe and then head all the way through the village. At the 40mph derestriction sign, there's a white cottage on the right. Beside it, a tarred trackway has a Scottish Rights of Way Society signpost for Kernsary.

2 Follow the track over a cattle grid as far as a new track that forks off to the left. After 50yds (46m), keep ahead on a path with a wall on its left. It passes through a kissing gate into Cnoc na Lise, the Garden Hill. This has been replanted as a community wood with oak and birch trees. Another kissing gate leads out of the young wood. The good, reconstructed path runs through gorse and then under a

low-voltage power line. It crosses a low spur to a fine view of Loch Kernsary and the remote, steep-sided hills of the Great Wilderness, then goes over a stream to the loch side.

3 The path follows the left-hand shore of the loch, passing through patches of birch scrub. After a stile, near the loch head, it suddenly deteriorates, becoming a braided trod of boulder and bog. Once past the loch head, slant to the left down a meadow to find a footbridge beneath the branches of an oak tree. Head up, with a fence on your right, to join a track beside Kernsary farm.

4 Turn right, through a gate. Follow the track past the farm, to a culvert crossing of the Kernsary River. This becomes a ford only after heavy rain. If needed, you will find a footbridge

70yds (64m) upstream. After crossing, turn right on a smooth track. The new track bears left, away from Loch Kernsary towards the hollow containing Loch Maree. After the bridge over the Inveran River is a gate with a ladder stile. Signs welcoming responsible walkers and cyclists reflect the principles of the Letterewe Accord. Soon come the first views of Loch Maree. The driveway of Inveran house joins from the left and the track becomes tarred.

5 At a sign, 'Blind Corners', a green track on the left leads down to the point where the narrow loch imperceptibly becomes a wide river. Return to the main track and follow it above and then beside the River Ewe. It reaches Poolewe just beside the bridge.

Index

Acknowledgements

The Automobile Association would like to thank the following photographers, companies and picture libraries for their assistance in the preparation of this book. Abbreviations for the picture credits are as follows – (t) top; (b) bottom; (c) centre; (l) left; (r) right; (AA) AA World Travel Library.

3 AA/M Kipling; 6 AA/M Kipling; 8/9 AA/T Mackie; 10/11 AA/G Edwardes; 12/13 AA/A Burton; 12t AA/M Moody; 12b ©Malcolm McHugh/Alamy; 13 AA/J A Tims; 14 AA/D Hall; 15bl AA/A Burton; 15br AA/R Newton; 16t AA/R Ireland; 16bl AA/R Ireland; 16br AA/P Baker; 18t ©Dom Greves/Alamy; 18c AA/W Voysey; 18b AA/A Burton; 20tl AA/D Hancock; 20cl AA/C Jones; 20cr ©David Noton Photography/Alamy; 22t ©Theo Moye/Alamy; 22b ©Trevor Smithers ARPS/Alamy; 24cl ©Norman Walstow/Alamy; 24cr ©The National Trust Photolibrary/Alamy; 24b ©Martin Beddall/Alamy; 26t ©Agripicture Images/Alamy; 26b ©Rex Hughes/Alamy; 28t AA/N Hicks; 28b AA/A Lawson; 30tl AA; 30cl AA/R Moss; 30cr ©David Chapman/Alamy; 32cl AA/J Wood; 32c AA/C Jones; 32b AA/J Wood; 34t AA/D Hancock; 34c AA/J Wood; 34b ©Dave Porter/Alamy; 36c AA/J Wood; 36bl AA/J Wood; 36brc AA/S Viccars; 36br AA/J Wood; 38bl ©Steve Taylor ARPS/Alamy; 38br ©Lynne Evans/Alamy; 40l ©Graham McPherson/Alamy; 40r AA/R Ireland; 42t ©Stephen Spraggon/Alamy; 42b ©Lee Pengelly/Alamy; 44t AA/J A Tims; 44cl AA/J A Tims; 44c AA/J A Tims; 46tl AA; 46tc AA/M Moody; 46b AA; 48t ©Manor Photography/Alamy; 48c ©Sean Bolton/Alamy; 48b ©Anna Stowe/Alamy; 50/51 AA/T Mackie; 52/53 AA/S & O Mathews; 53tl AA/T Souter; 53tr AA/A Burton; 54 AA/T Mackie; 55t AA/A Baker; 55c AA/T Mackie; 56c AA/A Burton; 56bl AA/A Burton; 56br AA/A Burton; 58tl ©Gerry Walden/Alamy; 58c AA/D Forss; 58b AA/A Burton; 60c AA/J Miller; 60bl AA/R Ireland; 60br AA/J Miller; 62c AA/D Croucher; 62b AA/J Miller; 64cl AA/J Miller; 64c ©Robert Bird/Alamy; 64b AA/J Miller; 66t AA/N Setchfield; 66c AA/N Setchfield; 66b AA/N Setchfield; 68t ©Malcolm Fairman/Alamy; 68b ©CountryCollection – Homer Sykes/Alamy; 70t AA/J A Tims; 70l AA/J A Tims; 70r AA/J A Tims; 72blt AA/M Moody; 72blb AA/M Moody; 72br AA/M Moody; 74l AA/S & O Mathews; 74r AA/J A Tims; 76l ©Bildarchiv Monheim GmbH/Alamy; 76c ©Dave Pattison/Alamy; 76b ©placenames ©ian sanders/Alamy; 78tr ©Quentin Bargate/Alamy; 78b AA/T Mackie; 80t AA/T Mackie; 80bl AA/T Mackie; 80br AA/T Mackie; 82c AA/P Davies; 82b AA/T Mackie; 84t AA/T Mackie; 84c ©Clive Tully/Alamy; 84b AA/T Mackie; 86t ©Angelo Hornak/Alamy; 86c ©Holmes Garden Photos/Alamy; 86b ©CountrySideCollection – Homer Skyes/Alamy; 88t AA/T Mackie; 88c AA/T Mackie; 88b AA/M Hayward; 90/91 AA/M Hayward; 92/93 ©David Mawer/Alamy; 92 AA/T Mackie; 93 AA/T Mackie; 94tl AA/M Morris; 94tr ©Robert Estall photo agency / Alamy; 95 AA/T Mackie; 96blt ©Denny Ellis/Alamy; 96blb ©Denny Ellis/Alamy; 96br ©Denny Ellis/Alamy; 98l ©mark sadlier/Alamy; 98r ©Mike Hayward/Alamy; 100c ©Peter Barritt/Alamy; 100b ©Simon Evans/Alamy; 102blt AA/M Hayward; 102blb AA/M Hayward; 102br AA/M Hayward; 104cl AA/C Jones; 104cr AA/C Jones; 104b AA/C Jones; 106cl AA/C Jones; 106c AA/C Jones; 106b AA/C Jones; 108t ©david martyn hughes/Alamy; 108b ©Geoff Poulton; 110c ©Peter Packer/Alamy; 110b ©Richard Drewe/Alamy; 112c ©Cath Evans/Alamy; 112bl ©Ronnie McMillan/Alamy; 112bc ©ImagesEurope/Alamy; 114l ©Alan Novelli/Alamy; 114r ©Alan Novelli/Alamy; 116l ©Robin Weaver/Alamy; 116c ©Chris Herring/Alamy; 116b ©Stephen Butler/Alamy; 118c AA/T Mackie; 118b AA/T Mackie; 120l AA/T Mackie; 120r AA/T Mackie; 122t ©DAVID NOBLE PHOTOGRAPHY/Alamy; 122b ©JASON BATTERHAM/Alamy; 124cl ©Edward Parker/Alamy; 124c ©eye35.com/Alamy; 124b ©David Mark/Alamy; 126t ©John Leslie/Alamy; 126c Photolibrary Group; 126b Photolibrary Group; 128 AA/D Forss; 130/131 AA/T Mackie; 132t AA/D Clapp; 132b Photolibrary Group; 132/133 AA/S Day; 133 AA/T Mackie; 134 AA/D Clapp; 135 AA/M Kipling; 136ctl AA/C Jones; 136cl AA/C Jones; 136bl AA/C Jones; 136br AA/C Jones; 138c ©Alan Novelli/Alamy; 138b ©Derek Stone/Alamy; 140t AA/J A Tims; 140c AA/J A Tims; 142c ©Andy Marshall/Alamy; 142b AA/J Morrison; 144c ©Nigel Ollis/Alamy; 144b ©Lancashire Images/Alamy; 146t AA/D Clapp; 146cl AA/D Clapp; 146c AA/D Clapp; 146r AA/D Clapp; 146bl AA/D Clapp; 146br AA/D Clapp; 148t ©Katharine Eastham/Alamy; 148c ©Jon Sparks/Alamy; 148b ©Jon Sparks/Alamy; 150t AA/D Tarn; 150cl ©Holmes Garden Photos/Alamy; 150cr AA/S & O Mathews; 150b ©Mike Kipling Photography/Alamy; 152t ©International Photobank/Alamy; 152c ©Mike Kipling Photography/Alamy; 152b ©Mike Kipling Photography/Alamy; 154t AA/M Kipling; 154c AA/M Kipling; 154b AA/M Kipling; 156t ©The National Trust Photolibrary/Alamy; 156b AA/J Sparks; 158t ©John Morrison/Alamy; 158b ©Barry Wakelin/Alamy; 160 AA/T Mackie; 162t AA/R Coulam; 162c ©Trinity Mirror/Mirrorpix/Alamy; 162b AA/R Coulam; 164cl ©Roger Coulam/Alamy; 164cr ©Graeme Peacock/Alamy; 164b ©Leslie Garland Picture Library/Alamy; 166c AA/R Coulam; 166b AA/R Coulam; 168c AA/J Beazley; 168b AA/J Beazley; 170/171 AA/S Lewis; 172 AA/A Grierley; 173 AA/C Warren; 174 AA/N Jenkins; 175l AA/S Lewis; 175r AA/N Jenkins; 176t AA/R Coulam; 176c AA/C Warren; 176b AA/C Warren; 178t AA/H Williams; 178b AA/M Moody; 180t ©DAVID NOBLE PHOTOGRAPHY/Alamy; 180c ©Garntec Images; 180b ©Chris Howes/Wild Places Photography/Alamy; 182t AA/D Santillo; 182cl AA/N Jenkins; 182c ©The Photolibrary Wales/Alamy; 182b ©The Photolibrary Wales/Alamy; 184t Photolibrary Group; 184b Roy Rainford/Robert Harding; 186 AA/N Jenkins; 188tl ©Graham Eaton/naturepl.com; 188b Photolibrary Group; 190l AA/S Lewis; 190r AA/S Lewis; 192tl AA/R Newton; 192tl AA; 192b AA; 194t AA/W Voysey; 194c ©David Noton Photography/Alamy; 194b ©Tim Mossford/Alamy; 196 AA/S Lewis; 198t AA/R Eames; 198b AA/P Aithie; 200tl ©Keith Morris/Alamy; 200tr ©Adam Burton/Alamy; 200b ©The Photolibrary Wales/Alamy; 202c AA/N Jenkins; 202b AA/N Jenkins; 204l ©Terry Walton/Alamy; 204r ©Matthew Dogget/Alamy; 206t ©Jon Arnold Images Ltd/Alamy; 206b AA/S Lewis; 208t AA/I Burgum; 208b ©Simon Evans/Alamy; 210 AA/D W Robertson; 212/213 AA/M Hamblin; 213 AA/S Anderson; 214t AA/K Blackwell; 214b AA/J Smith; 216c ©Philip Dunn/Alamy; 216bl ©britpik/Alamy; 216br AA; 218t ©Ann and Steve Toon/Alamy; 218b AA/M Alexander; 220l ©Skyscan Photolibrary/Alamy; 220r ©Paul Bock/Alamy; 222t ©Dave Porter/Alamy; 222b ©Mark Pink/Alamy; 224l AA/M Alexander; 224cr ©tom Kidd/Alamy; 224br ©Peter Marshall/Alamy; 226t ©Jason Baxter – Panoramic Imagery/Alamy; 226c ©Phil Seale/Alamy; 228c AA/K Blackwell; 228b AA/M Alexander; 230t AA/J Smith; 230cl AA/J Smith; 230c AA/K Blackwell; 230b AA/J Smith; 232t AA/S Anderson; 232cl ©David Lyons/Alamy; 232c ©Robert Estall photo agency/Alamy; 232cr ©Anne Gilbert/Alamy; 234t AA/D W Robertson; 234b ©Robert Harding Picture Library Ltd/Alamy; 236t AA/S Day; 236bl AA/S Anderson; 237brc AA/P Sharpe; 237br AA/J Henderson; 238tl ©M.Brodie/Alamy; 238tc ©David Lyons/Alamy; 238cl ©Alex Ramsay/Alamy; 238c ©David Robertson/Alamy; 240t AA/S Anderson; 240b AA/M Hamblin; 242tl ©imagebroker/Alamy; 242c AA/S Whitehorne; 242tr ©Holmes Garden Photos/Alamy; 242c ©UK City Images/Alamy; 244t AA/J Smith; 244b AA/J Smith; 246c ©Chris Gomersall/naturepl.com; 246b AA/K Paterson; 248 AA/J Smith; 250c ©Angus Mackie/Alamy; 250bl ©Lynne Evans/Alamy; 250br ©D.G.Farquhar/Alamy

Every effort has been made to trace the copyright holders, and we apologise in advance for any accidental errors. We would be happy to apply any corrections in the following edition of this publication.